Political Economy from Pufendorf to Marx

Culture, Needs and Property Rights

István Hont

Edited by
Lasse S. Andersen
University of St Andrews

with

Béla Kapossy
University of Lausanne

Richard Whatmore
University of St Andrews

Shaftesbury Road, Cambridge CB2 8EA, United Kingdom

One Liberty Plaza, 20th Floor, New York, NY 10006, USA

477 Williamstown Road, Port Melbourne, VIC 3207, Australia

314–321, 3rd Floor, Plot 3, Splendor Forum, Jasola District Centre, New Delhi – 110025, India

103 Penang Road, #05–06/07, Visioncrest Commercial, Singapore 238467

Cambridge University Press is part of Cambridge University Press & Assessment, a department of the University of Cambridge.

We share the University's mission to contribute to society through the pursuit of education, learning and research at the highest international levels of excellence.

www.cambridge.org
Information on this title: www.cambridge.org/9781009597555

DOI: 10.1017/9781009597562

© István Hont, Lasse S. Andersen, Béla Kapossy and Richard Whatmore 2026

This publication is in copyright. Subject to statutory exception and to the provisions of relevant collective licensing agreements, no reproduction of any part may take place without the written permission of Cambridge University Press & Assessment.

When citing this work, please include a reference to the DOI 10.1017/9781009597562

First published 2026

A catalogue record for this publication is available from the British Library

A Cataloging-in-Publication data record for this book is available from the Library of Congress

ISBN 978-1-009-59758-6 Hardback
ISBN 978-1-009-59755-5 Paperback

Cambridge University Press & Assessment has no responsibility for the persistence or accuracy of URLs for external or third-party internet websites referred to in this publication and does not guarantee that any content on such websites is, or will remain, accurate or appropriate.

For EU product safety concerns, contact us at Calle de José Abascal, 56, 1°, 28003 Madrid, Spain, or email eugpsr@cambridge.org

Political Economy from Pufendorf to Marx

István Hont (1947–2013) defected from Communist Hungary in the 1970s and became renowned globally as a scholarly visionary in European political ideas. Following his death, a wealth of unpublished material from an early project rewriting the history of liberty, politics and political economy from Samuel Pufendorf to Karl Marx was discovered. This book brings together seven of Hont's previously unpublished papers, providing a revolutionary intellectual history of the Marxian notion of communism and revealing its origin in seventeenth-century natural jurisprudence. Hont aspired to integrate the history and theory of politics and economics, to infuse present-day concerns with a knowledge of past events and theoretical responses. The essays selected for this volume realise Hont's historical imagination, range and intellectual ambition, exploring his belief that Marxism ought to be abandoned and explaining how to do it.

István Hont was born in Hungary, before defecting from the communist regime and moving to the United Kingdom in 1975. He became a Fellow at King's College, Cambridge in 1978 and University Reader in the History of Political Thought. Hont was renowned globally as a leading intellectual historian of political economy, although much of his writing remained unpublished during his lifetime. His co-edited volume with Michael Ignatieff, *Wealth and Virtue: The Shaping of Political Economy in the Scottish Enlightenment* (1983), and his collected essays, *Jealousy of Trade: International Competition and the Nation-State in Historical Perspective* (2005), combine political theory with intellectual history and seek to illuminate contemporary debates.

Lasse S. Andersen is Associate Director of the Institute of Intellectual History at the University of St Andrews. He has published articles on the history of political thought and political economy in the *Journal of the Philosophy of History* and *Intellectual History Review*.

Béla Kapossy is Professor of Early Modern History at the University of Lausanne. He is the author of many works concerned with Enlightenment politics and political economy, including *Iselin contra Rousseau: Sociable Patriotism and the History of Mankind* (2006), and a number of edited works and editions, including *Commerce and Peace in the Enlightenment* (2016) and *Edward Gibbon et Lausanne* (2022).

Richard Whatmore is Professor of Modern History at the University of St Andrews and Co-director of the Institute of Intellectual History. His most recent books are *The End of Enlightenment* (2023) and *The History of Political Thought: A Very Short Introduction* (2021).

István Hont (1947–2013)

The learned indeed well know how little novelty or variety is to be found in scientific disputes. The same truths and the same errors have been repeated from age to age, with little variation but in the language; and novelty of expression is often mistaken by the ignorant for substantial discovery ... [However], every age must be taught in its own language. If a man were now to begin a discourse on ethics with an account of the 'moral entities' of Puffendorff [*sic*], he would speak an unknown tongue.

Sir James Mackintosh,
A Discourse on the Study of the Law of Nature and Nations, 1799

Contents

Acknowledgements		*page* viii
Editors' Note		ix
Editorial Practice		x
List of Abbreviations		xi
	Introduction	1
1	Theoretical History and Natural Law in the Scottish Enlightenment	43
2	Samuel Pufendorf's Jurisprudential Theory of History	56
3	Natural Jurisprudence, Political Economy and the Concept of Civilisation: Samuel Pufendorf's Theory of *Cultura*	124
4	Negative Community and Communism: The Natural Law Heritage from Pufendorf to Marx	159
5	The Antinomies of the Concept of 'Use-Value' in Marx's *Capital*: Economy and Polity after the Market	198
6	Socialist Natural Law, Commercial Society and Political Economy: A Contribution to the Understanding of the Idea of Social Science	227
7	Unsocial Sociability: Eighteenth-Century Perspectives	252
Select Bibliography		273
Index		275

Acknowledgements

The editors would like to thank István Hont's many friends for their contribution to this edition, especially Gregory Claeys, John Robertson, Michael Sonenscher and Keith Tribe. Since establishing the Intellectual History Archive, far broader debts have been incurred concerning Hont's papers, including archivists and librarians at the University of St Andrews, especially Maia Sheridan and Helen Faulds, and also the broader community of intellectual historians interested in Hont, including John Dunn, Raymond Geuss and Knud Haakonssen. Elizabeth Friend-Smith was outstandingly supportive as always, and we would like to thank the anonymous referees for their comments. The book could not have been completed without the advice and guidance of Anna Hont. In gratitude, the book is dedicated to her.

Editors' Note

This volume is a product of a long-standing collaboration between scholars convinced of the continued relevance of István Hont's work and an ongoing cooperation between the University of Lausanne, the Swiss Federal Technology Institute of Lausanne (EPFL) and the University of St Andrews. At the same time, it is necessary to make clear that the task of putting together this volume, as well as the drafting of the Introduction and the textual notes, was largely undertaken by Lasse S. Andersen. Béla Kapossy and Richard Whatmore were very much in the back seat.

Editorial Practice

All the papers included in this volume have been faithfully reproduced in the way that they were left by István Hont and subsequently donated to the Institute of Intellectual History at the University of St Andrews in 2014. While all papers were completed to the point that they could have been submitted for publication, several of the papers had yet to be provided with the proper references. Therefore, where these have been found missing or incomplete, they have been added or corrected to the best of our ability, using as far as possible the editions and translations known to have been used by Hont. Where an editorial note has been deemed helpful, it has been provided in square brackets. Throughout, the editors have attempted to retain as much as possible of Hont's characteristic style of writing and have therefore restricted interventions to a minimum. However, the preparation of these papers for publication has unavoidably entailed correcting obvious errors and certain infelicities of composition, as well as occasionally substituting a word or rephrasing a whole sentence for the purpose of clarity. The occasional reproduction of a sentence or a paragraph has been retained, and no systematic correction of gendered language has been imposed by the editors. Unless otherwise stated, all emphases in quotations are in the original sources.

The papers of István Hont are located at the University of St Andrews Library, Special Collections, where they are being catalogued. A selection of these papers has been made available online in the Hont Collection of the Intellectual History Archive, a digital repository of papers from eminent intellectual historians curated by the Institute of Intellectual History at the University of St Andrews.

Abbreviations

Archival Material

IHA — Intellectual History Archive: https://arts.st-andrews.ac.uk/intellectualhistory

SC — Special Collections, University of St Andrews, United Kingdom

Immanuel Kant

KPW — *Kant: Political Writings*, ed. H. S. Reiss, trans. H. B. Nisbet (Cambridge: Cambridge University Press, 1970; 2nd enlarged ed., 1991)

On History — *Kant: On History*, ed. Lewis W. Beck, trans. Robert E. Anchor, Emil L. Fackenheim and Lewis W. Beck (New York: Bobbs-Merrill, 1963)

Karl Marx

Capital I — *Capital: A Critique of Political Economy*, Vol. I, trans. Ben Fowkes (London: Penguin, in association with New Left Review, 1976)

Capital III — *Capital: A Critique of Political Economy*, Vol. III, trans. David Fernbach (London: Penguin, in association with New Left Review, 1981)

CCPE — *A Contribution to the Critique of Political Economy*, ed. M. Dobb, trans. S. W. Ryazanskaya (London: Lawrence & Wishart, 1971)

Foundations — *Pre-Capitalist Economic Foundations*, ed. E. Hobsbawm, trans. Jack Cohen (London: Lawrence & Wishart, 1964)

Grundrisse	*Grundrisse: Foundations of the Critique of Political Economy (Rough Draft)*, trans. Martin Nicholas (London: Penguin, in association with New Left Review, 1973)
MECW	*The Collected Works of Karl Marx and Frederick Engels*, 50 vols. (London: Lawrence & Wishart, 1975–2004)
MEGA^2	*Die Marx-Engels-Gesamtausgabe*, prosp. 120 vols. (Berlin: Dietz Verlag, 1975–1998; then Berlin: Akademie Verlag, 1998–)
Paris Manuscripts	*Economic and Philosophic Manuscripts of 1844* (*'Paris Manuscripts'*) [1932], in *Karl Marx: Early Writings*, trans. Rodney Livingstone and Gregor Benton (London: Penguin, in association with New Left Review, 1975)
TSV I	*Theories of Surplus Value*, 3 vols. ('Capital IV'), Vol. I, ed. S. W. Ryazanskaya, trans. Emile Burns (London: Lawrence & Wishart)
TSV III	*Theories of Surplus Value*, 3 vols. ('Capital IV'), Vol. III, ed. S. W. Ryazanskaya and Richard Dixon, trans. Jack Cohen and S. W. Ryazanskaya (London: Lawrence & Wishart)

Natural Jurisprudence

De Legibus	Francisco Suárez, *Tractatus de legibus, ac Deo legislatore* [1612], in English *A Treatise on Laws and God the Lawgiver*, trans. Gwladys L. Williams, Ammi Brown and John Waldron (Oxford: Clarendon Press, 1944); republished in Francisco Suárez, *Selections from Three Works*, ed. Thomas Pink and Knud Haakonssen (Indianapolis, IN: Liberty Fund, 2015)
De Officio	Samuel Pufendorf, *De officio hominis et civis* [1673], in English *The Whole Duty of Man According to the Law of Nature*, trans. Andrew Tooke [1691] (London: R. Gosling, J. Pemberton, and B. Motte, 5th revised ed., 1735)
De Officio^M	*On the Duty of Man and Citizen According to the Natural Law*, trans. Frank Gardner Moore (Oxford: Oxford University Press, 1927)

DJBP	Hugo Grotius, *De jure belli ac pacis libri tres* [1625], in English *Of the Laws of War and Peace, in Three Books*, trans. Francis W. Kelsey (Oxford: Clarendon Press, 1925)
DJNG	Samuel von Pufendorf, *De jure naturae et gentium libri octo* [1672, 2nd ed., Amsterdam, 1688], in English *On the Law of Nature and Nations*, trans. C. H. Oldfather and W. A. Oldfather (Oxford: Clarendon Press, 1934)
DJNG^K	*Of the Law of Nature and Nations*, trans. Basil Kennett (London: J. Walthoe, R. Wilkin, J. and J. Bonwicke, S. Birt, T. Ward, and T. Osborne, 4th revised ed., 1729)
Prædæ	Hugo Grotius, *De jure prædæ commentarius* (or perhaps correctly *De indiis*) [c. 1604], in English *Of the Law of Prize and Booty*, trans. Gwladys L. Williams and Walter H. Zeydel (Oxford: Clarendon Press, 1950)
ST	Thomas Aquinas, *Summa theologiae*, vol. 38., ed. Marcus Lefèbure and Thomas Gilby (London: Blackfriars, 1975)

Adam Smith

Account of Smith	Dugald Stewart, 'Account of the Work and Life of Adam Smith, LL.D.' [1793], in *Essays on Philosophical Subjects*, ed. W. P. D. Wightman (Oxford: Oxford University Press, 1980)
ED	'Early Draft of Part of *The Wealth of Nations*', in *Lectures on Jurisprudence*, ed. R. L. Meek, D. D. Raphael and P. G. Stein (Oxford: Oxford University Press, 1978)
ER	'Letter to the *Edinburgh Review*' [1756], in *Essays on Philosophical Subjects*, ed. W. P. D. Wightman (Oxford: Oxford University Press, 1980)
LJ(A)	'Lectures on Jurisprudence, Report of 1762–3', in *Lecture on Jurisprudence*, ed. R. L. Meek, D. D. Raphael and P. G. Stein (Oxford: Oxford University Press, 1978)
LJ(B)	'Jurisprudence, or Notes from the Lectures on Justice, Police, Revenue, and Arms Delivered in the University of Glasgow by Adam Smith,

	Professor of Moral Philosophy. Report dated 1766' [1763–4], in *Lectures on Jurisprudence*, ed. R. L. Meek, D. D. Raphael and P. G. Stein (Oxford: Oxford University Press, 1978)
TMS	*The Theory of Moral Sentiments* [1759], ed. D. D. Raphael and A. L. Macfie (Oxford: Oxford University Press, 1976)
WN	*An Inquiry into the Nature and Causes of the Wealth of Nations* [1776], ed. R. H. Campbell, A. S. Skinner and W. B. Todd, 2 vols. (Oxford: Oxford University Press, 1975)

These volumes are part of the *Glasgow Edition of the Works and Correspondence of Adam Smith*. References to Smith's works follow the adopted practice of citing the relevant section of the work with the paragraph number(s) as they are printed in the *Glasgow Edition* (e.g. *TMS*, VI.ii.3.2 = *The Theory of Moral Sentiments*, part 6, section 2, chapter 3, §2).

Introduction

Lasse Andersen

An Unfinished Project

The intellectual historian István Hont (1947–2013) is today remembered as one of the most insightful interpreters of modern European political thought, his name being associated with some of the most groundbreaking studies of eighteenth-century political economy. Hont's scholarly influence now reaches far beyond the walls of King's College, Cambridge, his home for most of his academic career, and his work remains as relevant as ever, providing an indispensable historical guide to the political thought of modern commercial society. Furthermore, his work presents a persistent challenge for political theory to overcome, through historical study, the impasse he believed had come to characterise the intellectual landscape of the West by the closing decades of the twentieth century.

In the aftermath of the collapse of communism in the USSR, Hont called for a return to the Scottish Enlightenment in general and the political economy of Adam Smith in particular. 'Marx will not be truly buried', Hont wrote in 1994, 'until we understand better the politics of "classical" political economy'.[1] Such a return to the intellectual world of the eighteenth century was necessary, he believed, not only because Soviet communism had shown itself to be a political and ideological dead end, unable to improve upon, let alone transcend, the politics of commercial society, but also because the political problem of transitioning from a managed economy to a free market system, a problem for which Marxism had no real answers, resembled the transitional problem faced by Adam Smith in his efforts to imagine a reform-path from the mercantile system to a system of natural liberty. For Hont, the presumed novelty of the late twentieth-century situation demonstrated that intellectual history had something important to offer to contemporary political debate, and the increased focus on the 'problem of transition' also held out the

---

[1] István Hont, 'Ricardian Politics', *Political Theory* 22/2 (1994): 343.

possibility that the dramatic events of the 1990s could help illuminate the problems of the 1770s. 'Nowadays', he commented, also in 1994,

> many argue that our generation, at the end of the twentieth century, is the first to face the problem of transition from 'socialism to the free market'. We will not understand Smith properly until we see that, to a significant degree, the transition from the mercantile state (where the economy was made subservient to the state's political aims and ambitions) to free trade posed a very similar problem. What was Smith's council for this period of transition?[2]

The political and theoretical crisis which European Marxism increasingly faced in the latter half of the twentieth century, exacerbated by the eventual fall of the Berlin Wall and the proliferation of new democracies in Eastern Europe, precipitated a general reassessment of Marxism on the left, often taking the form of a retreat to earlier theoretical developments which Marx and orthodox Marxism believed had long been surpassed. Hont was critical of many such retreats, especially those that explicitly or implicitly divorced the 'political' from the 'economic'. This was most evidently the case with the surge of interest in the revolutionary or utopian thinking of the late eighteenth and nineteenth century, about which Marx himself had been so scathing. Commenting on the state of political theory in 1996, Hont delivered the following remark:

> Karl Marx once prophesised that the intellectual and theoretical development of the Left will have to repeat the entire development of Western thought (and of society itself), exploring every *cul-de-sac* and blind alleyway which have been previously explored in grand political culture. Little he suspected that after the predictable demise of the vulgarised and bastardised version of his own avant-garde insights this very process will also be repeated in the reverse. Nowadays it is fashionable to praise the so-called utopian socialists over Marx ... Retreating from Marxism, post-Marxism for some now means reading Tom Paine and the anti-federalists. Political theory at the end of the twentieth century, for a not at all insignificant group, is the rehash of the political thought of the eighteenth century.[3]

Much like the recourse to utopian politics devoid of substantial economic thinking, a retreat to English political economy was also not an option for Hont. Ricardian economics, the bourgeois bedrock on which the Marxian theory of exploitation had been built, lacked a theory of history, and regarding a theory of politics it was no improvement on Marx either. As Hont put it in his dismissive review of the book *Ricardian Politics* (1991) by Milgate and Stimson, most 'post-Marxists realize that Marx's

---

[2] Hont, 'Commercial Society and Political Theory in the Eighteenth Century: The Problem of Authority in David Hume and Adam Smith', in Willem Melching and Wyger Velema (eds.), *Main Trends in Cultural History* (Amsterdam: Rodopi, 1994), pp. 81–82.
[3] See Chapter 7, this volume.

Introduction 3

greatest weakness was the elimination of politics from his model of post-capitalism', but to derive a theory of politics from David Ricardo was to 'collect a rent from the most marginal land in the Ricardian landscape'.[4]

Only a complete return to eighteenth-century Scotland could avoid making the retreat from Marx a retrograde journey, because the Scottish 'ancestors' of historical materialism could provide – in light of the failure of communism – the hitherto best and fullest understanding of those aspects of modern commercial society that Marx had believed it possible to transcend, namely a theory of individual property rights based on the analysis of human needs; a theory of political authority based on human psychology rather than a social contract; and a theory of the modern (representative) nation state that took seriously the 'economic' limitations to politics as defined by relative scarcity, limited generosity and international market competition.

Such a retreat, however, should not be understood as either a dismissal or a denigration of Marx, nor indeed as an embrace of liberalism, because moving backwards from Marx to Smith did not constitute a transition from one tradition of thought to another in Hont's mind. In contrast to the rhetoric of the Cold War, both Marx and Smith were in fact best understood as belonging to the same discourse on civilisation and sociability whose origin could be traced to seventeenth-century natural jurisprudence. Thus, if Marx by the end of the twentieth century had to be 'buried', he also needed to be resurrected as an essentially eighteenth-century thinker. 'Somewhat frivolously', Hont stated on a visit to West Germany in the mid 1980s, 'but nonetheless not without some truth, one can fruitfully see Marx as the major eighteenth-century type thinker of the nineteenth century'.[5]

By 1989, Hont had already carried out this combined burial and resurrection to his own personal satisfaction. But the outcome of this project remained largely hidden from view, disseminated only through conference papers and conversations with fellow historians. In fact, aside from a few suggestive remarks scattered across his essays, Hont's entire published oeuvre reveals remarkably little of his continued struggle to come to terms with Marx and Marxism, despite its evident centrality to his intellectual development. Fortunately, his unpublished papers tell a different story. From the late 1970s and throughout the 1980s, Hont was writing and gathering material for an ambitious book project, which he envisioned as a study of the development of Western political thought from Pufendorf to Marx, uncovering the hidden linkages between what

[4] Hont, 'Ricardian Politics', p. 341.
[5] See Chapter 1, this volume.

he then considered the three major idioms of modern political thought: natural law, political economy and Marxism. Hont named the project *Culture, Needs and Property Rights*, a title signalling his aim to subordinate the discussion of rights to the underlying philosophical anthropology – or theory of sociability – embedded in all three of these modern discourses.

Aside from exploring internal theoretical connections, there were also obvious institutional parallels between these successive discourses, a topic which Hont explored during the 1980s in his role as leading organiser of a pioneering, international project of comparative historical research entitled 'The Institutionalisation of Political Economy'.[6] The formative period of modern natural law thinking was the seventeenth century, with Hugo Grotius, Thomas Hobbes and Samuel Pufendorf as the main contributors, but the foundation of natural jurisprudence as an academic discipline, and its dissemination into social discourse, was the achievement of the eighteenth century. Similarly, political economy emerged in the eighteenth century largely as an embedded discourse within natural jurisprudence, and only during the nineteenth century did it receive widespread institutional recognition as an independent field of study at universities. An analogous life cycle had unfolded with Marxism, Hont believed. Emerging in the nineteenth century as an outgrowth and critique of political economy, Marxism 'became a dominant idiom of thinking about society only in the 20th century'.[7] Hont's point was that this progressive emergence and institutionalisation of new

---

[6] This project, which took shape through planning meetings in Cambridge and Paris in 1983 and 1984, was intended to provide the historical groundwork for understanding late eighteenth- and nineteenth-century political economy by conducting research into the political and institutional context surrounding the establishment of political economy as a taught subject in British, European, and North American universities (subsequently Japan was included as well). While recruiting and liaising with collaborators in multiple countries, organising them into sections doing research on their respective national institutions, Hont himself contributed to the British research group, which convened in March 1985 at Keele University for a workshop on Britain and Ireland. The focus here was on the gradual transformation of England's two 'ancient' universities, the four universities of Scotland and Trinity College, Dublin, including also the establishment of a chair in political economy at East India College (Haileybury) and the eventual creation of the London School of Economics. Out of a projected four, Hont completed two long papers for this project, one on Lord Townshend's failed attempt to introduce of a 'theory of trade' into the Cambridge curriculum in 1755–1756, and one updated version of an unpublished article on Dugald Stewart's evening classes on political economy at the University of Edinburgh, 1800–1809. The planned result of this workshop – a collaborative volume provisionally entitled *Trade, Politics and Letters: The Art of Political Economy and British University Culture*, co-edited with Keith Tribe – was ultimately abandoned, however, and Hont's work was left unpublished.

[7] István Hont and Hans Erich Bödeker, 'Unsocial Sociability and the 18th-Century Discourse of Politics and Society', Unpublished manuscript [1989], SC, The Papers of István Hont, p. 7.

Introduction 5

discourses entailed a cost that showed itself in the obfuscation of inherited concepts and shared concerns that in fact ran as a continuous thread from one idiom to the next. Reconstructing this continuity thus required occasional acts of 'translation' in order to overcome those inevitable variations of language that served only to impart an air of novelty to old ideas. For good reason, the sentiment about the elusiveness of language expressed by Sir James Mackintosh in the epigraph to this volume was one that Hont found congenial to his own approach, as evidenced by the fact that it served as the epigraph to no less than three of the papers collected in this volume.[8]

Unlike several of his Cambridge peers, Hont never wrote specifically or at length about methodological issues. Nonetheless, in an unpublished manuscript from c. 1986 he indicated very clearly what he thought was amiss in most forms of discourse analysis, including the linguistic contextualism of the 'Cambridge school'.[9] In its pure form, discourse analysis was static, able to identify a break but unable to explain why it had come about or why it was significant. While it was undoubtedly effective in exposing and opposing various forms of material or sociological reductionism, it often proceeded under the assumption that the boundaries of human experience were narrowly circumscribed by the inherited vocabularies of historical actors, and thus that it was the linguistic context that defined the problems which historical actors sought to explain or confront. What this assumption ignored was the degree to which language itself became an *experienced* reality in certain situations. Although most people could agree that language was an imperfect representation of the world, the implicit assumption behind much discourse analysis was that 'language is always felt to be adequate by its users to the tasks which they set for it'.[10] In reality, writers often struggled to convey accurately the testimony of their senses and the precise meaning of their ideas, especially when faced with novel and confusing phenomena. 'At such a moment', Hont argued, 'discourse and the world of appearance no longer complement each other but break apart into a sort of mutually accusing division'.[11] The relationship between words and things, in other words, becomes palpably unstable, and words themselves appear as 'things' in the world to be contended with. One implication of this was that contemporaries were often no better at understanding each other than the present-day historian was at interpreting utterances of the past.

[8] Chapters 3, 4, and 6.
[9] Hont, 'Conjectural History, Development Theory, and the Context of Scottish Backwardness', Unpublished manuscript [c. 1986], SC, The Papers of István Hont, p. 1.
[10] Ibid.
[11] Ibid.

Hont had received an early lesson in this, having cut his teeth as a historian on the 'Hume–Tucker debate', which was replete with misunderstandings and, in the case of Hume, marked by his inability to properly convey a novel idea in the language available to him and his interlocutors. Hont's reinterpretation of this debate, which relied on a meticulous and imaginative study of Hume's economic thought and, importantly, of the larger real-world problem that he sought to address, caused Hont to reflect that 'real debates between historical actors often were and are "comedies of error"'.[12]

In fact, Scotland in the eighteenth century was an ideal place to observe the way in which a rapid and unevenly developing society forced observers to stretch or reject inherited categories of thought. Moreover, the main protagonists of the Scottish Enlightenment had been highly aware of the novelty of their situation and even took it upon themselves to theorise the inadequacy of their own inherited vocabularies:

> When the Scottish political economists themselves asked the question of where their economic reasoning came from, they all agreed that market theory *was* sociologically dependent on the emergence of market society in England. The relation was a loose one – most of them dated the emergence of English commercial society to the late 16th century, especially to James I's reign [1603–1625], while theoretical discourse on the market was a lagged phenomenon, following only a century later. France and the Low Countries were also understood as commercial societies. No matter how delayed the response, the Scots did see their own work as an attempt to interpret a reality which could no longer be grasped by classical oeconomics or Renaissance treatises on statecraft. This sense of the radical discontinuity of their own present comes through clearly in their own essays on the historical sociology of culture. Smith's and Rousseau's dissertations on language and Hugh Blair's introduction to *Ossian* argued that modern commercial peoples could appreciate but could no longer equal the lyric and rhapsodic achievements of the poets of pastoral ages. Similarly, modern erotic sensuality, John Millar argued, could no longer express itself in the courtly love tradition, since this was rooted in the political and economic weakness of feudalism. In historicizing their own cultural heritage, the Scots highlighted their distance from the available languages of understanding and pointed up [*sic*] the radical challenge facing linguistic attempts to encompass and understand the new.[13]

Although he often described himself as a sceptic, Hont nevertheless knew that a sceptical attitude alone was not enough to constitute a genuine revisionist project. Famously, he characterised the 'Cambridge

---

[12] Hont, 'The "Rich Country–Poor Country" Debate in Scottish Classical Political Economy', in István Hont and Michael Ignatieff (eds.), *Wealth and Virtue: The Shaping of Political Economy in the Scottish Enlightenment* (Cambridge: Cambridge University Press, 1983), p. 276.
[13] Hont, 'Conjectural History', p. 4.

school' of intellectual history as an 'anti-school', agreeing only on the negative task of purging the history of political thought of its inherent Whiggishness – in all its various shapes and ideological guises.[14] In other words, it lacked that shared vision of history that alone would render it into a school, properly speaking. By failing to consider the social or economic context that created the impetus for linguistic innovation, scepticism about proleptic signposts in history, as necessary as it was, ran the risk of narrowing the sight of the historian to the point where isolated reconstructions of political discourses were substituted for the actual historical landscape, which never quite conformed to the tunnels dug by the historian. If the history of modern political thought was to be given some sort of structure or shape, the task of the intellectual historian inevitably had to be that of a 'translator' of past discourses, examining the ways in which political languages collide and converge, especially in response to new political challenges and crises. 'Scepticism concerning meta-historical or teleological organising principles of explanation is an integral part of pursuing this strategy', Hont wrote in 1993, adding that 'it is not a disguised effort (or should not be) to substitute a new metahistory for an old one'. But such a new meta-history had to emerge from the concerns of the historical actors themselves. 'By examining the intersections of political languages', Hont continued, 'our understanding of their particular internal architectures may change and a larger historical pattern emerge, one which lays bare concerns common to several of them'.[15]

Hont's intellectual ambition was breathtaking. His vision of intellectual history as both scrupulously contextual and conceptually soaring high above the particular set a standard that was both admirable and inspiring yet also daunting and perhaps too demanding. In the words of his friend John Dunn: 'His was not a modest vision; but he paid a high price for the condescension it sometimes conveyed in the still greater ferocity with which he turned his critical powers on his own efforts to take in this immense vista.'[16] Consequently, several papers and projects that Hont worked on inevitably fell short of what he was hoping to achieve. In fact, the work that he published throughout his academic

---

[14] Hont, 'The Cambridge Moment: Commerce and Politics in 18th Century Political Thought', Unpublished manuscript [2005], IHA/Hont/548.
[15] Hont, 'The Politics of Necessity and the Language of "Reason of State"', Unpublished manuscript [1993], IHA/Hont/558, p. 4.
[16] John Dunn, 'Why We Need a Global History of Political Thought', in Béla Kapossy, Isaac Nakhimovsky, Sophus A. Reinert and Richard Whatmore (eds.), *Markets, Morals, Politics: Jealousy of Trade and the History of Political Thought* (Cambridge, MA: Harvard University Press, 2018), pp. 285–309.

career represents only the visible part of a substantial scholarly iceberg, composed of articles, lectures and conference papers that for all sorts of reasons – reasons often only known to Hont – were put aside and thus never shared with a wider public. With the posthumous publication of *Politics in Commercial Society: Jean-Jacques Rousseau and Adam Smith* (2015), one late addition to this Hontian iceberg has already surfaced, bringing into clear view Hont's interpretation of Rousseau's political economy such as he expounded this, while contrasting it with that of Adam Smith, in his Carlyle Lectures at Oxford in 2009. But while these lectures display Hont's thinking as it had evolved and matured over a long career, many of Hont's hitherto unpublished papers shed some important light on the development of his thinking in the formative and extraordinarily prolific years in Budapest, Oxford and Cambridge in the 1970s and 1980s. These were the years in which Hont became the historian that he was, an act of self-creation that was deeply marked by his complicated relationship with Marx, involving both acts of exorcism and emulation as he made Britain his home and found a new intellectual homeland in eighteenth-century Scotland.

The present volume recovers Hont's early project on the history of political economy spanning from Pufendorf to Marx, the project he entitled *Culture, Needs and Property Rights*. The selection of papers to be included has been guided by Hont's explicit designation of certain works as part of this project as well as by his own brief prospectus of the book, delivered in a report written in 1983. As he then envisioned it, it was to be a study of

> the theory of needs, rights and the stages of history in the major texts of those 17th-century natural law jurists who provided the theoretical framework to 18th-century British, French and Italian political economy, culture and civilisation, and political economy as the science articulating the 'logic' of modern civilisation in the discussion. The book also connects the reconstruction of this discourse to Hegel's Philosophy of Right and to Karl Marx's Economic and Philosophical Manuscripts.[17]

Although this project never came to fruition in the sense of being completed as a book, it is clear from Hont's papers that its central ideas and arguments were fully worked out. Moreover, at least one of Hont's published papers can be categorised as falling squarely within the confines of this project, namely his 1987 article on 'Samuel Pufendorf and the Theoretical Foundations of the "Four-Stages Theory"', which presented

---

[17] István Hont and Biancamaria Fontana, 'Political Economy and Society: Dr Hont's and Dr Fontana's Report' [1983], IHA/Hont/535, p. 5.

Introduction 9

an abbreviated version of the first half of the story.[18] The final twenty pages or so of Hont and Ignatieff's introduction to *Wealth and Virtue*, entitled 'Needs and Justice in the *Wealth of Nation*: An Introductory Essay' (1983), also clearly relied on research that Hont intended to expand upon and include in this book, as can be seen from the manuscript published as Chapter 2 in this volume. The genesis of the entire project, however, undoubtedly lies in Hungary. Hont's lifelong desire to integrate the history and theory of politics and economics – to infuse present-day concerns with a knowledge of past events and theoretical responses – was an ambition that was born out of his Marxist beginnings. In fact, it was this essentially Marxian ambition that animated his frustration with the orthodox academic environment that he encountered as a young student in Budapest, and which drove him towards the Scottish Enlightenment.

Budapest, Oxford, Cambridge

István Hont was born in Budapest in 1947 into a privileged family committed to the socialist cause and well-connected with the communist regime. His mother, Klára Kemény (1923–1973), was an agricultural engineer and later a professor of engineering. His father, János Hont (1914–1982), was deputy president of the National Planning Office and subsequently deputy in the Ministry of Agriculture. In this latter capacity, he worked to reverse the trend of collectivisation by implementing reforms that allowed peasant proprietors to keep possession of their smallholdings. By the standards of the time, he was remarkably un-corrupt and even refused to exempt his son from the dreaded mandatory enlistment in the People's Army, from which Sgt István Hont was officially discharged with honour on 3 August 1966 after a year's service in the Air Defence Corps.

Hont's intellectual formation was naturally dominated by the heavy hand of Marxist officialdom, permeating the nation's political and educational institutions.[19] After completing his studies at the Eötvös Loránd University (ELTE) in Budapest, gaining a master's degree in 1973 and defending his PhD in June 1974 (summa cum laude), he was promoted to Research Officer at the Institute of History at the Hungarian Academy

---

[18] Hont, 'The Language of Sociability and Commerce: Samuel Pufendorf and the Theoretical Foundations of the "Four Stages Theory"', in Anthony Pagden (ed.), *Languages of Political Theory in Early Modern Europe* (Cambridge: Cambridge University Press, 1987), pp. 253–276.

[19] For more on Hont's intellectual formation, see 'Introduction', in Kapossy, Nakhimovsky, Reinert and Whatmore (eds.), *Markets, Morals, Politics*, p. 7; see also Keith Tribe, 'Revision, Reorganisation, and Reform', in Kapossy, Nakhimovsky, Reinert and Whatmore (eds.), *Markets, Morals, Politics*, p. 137.

of Sciences (MTA), a purely research-oriented institution, which had given him a junior fellowship during his studies, and which required his membership of the Hungarian Socialist Workers' Party (MSZMP). Partly out of obligation to his family, however, Hont had already joined the party by 1970.

Inspired by the example of Czechoslovakia, the MSZMP leadership had by then initiated a series of major reforms intended to increase the productivity of the struggling Hungarian economy. Beginning in January 1968, economic planning was partially dismantled, allowing a wider degree of autonomy for enterprises in managing their salaries and production. In deliberately vague terms, this economic experiment was labelled 'New Economic Mechanism', and as such it avoided the fate that befell Czechoslovakia in August 1968, when Soviet tanks moved into Prague. By 1972, however, the Hungarian economy encountered severe problems and the left-wing opposition within the party succeeded in bringing the reforms to a standstill.

Within the Institute of History, Hont quickly grew dissatisfied with the Marxist academic milieu and acquired a reputation for being intellectually rebellious, which caused him significant problems as a student. Importantly, his undergraduate years coincided with the clandestine circulation of a highly influential *samizdat* book, whose formal title translates as *Is Critical Economics Possible at All?*, but which in the contemporary Marxist vernacular was simply referred to as 'Überhaupt'.[20] The three authors – György Márkus (1934–2016) and his students György Bence (1941–2006) and János Kis (1943–) – were associated with the Budapest school of Marxism (also known as the Lukács school), which emerged in the 1960s as part of the Hungarian New Left, and which was highly critical of the Soviet invasion of Czechoslovakia and the general 'dictatorship over needs' in the Eastern bloc.[21] Aside from György Márkus, another prominent member was the philosopher Ágnes Heller (1929–2019), whose study of Marx's concept of 'need' also had some influence on Hont.[22]

The discovery of the writings of the young Marx, especially the so-called 'Paris Manuscripts' of 1844, opened up the possibility of an

---

[20] The book was submitted for publication in 1972. Only in 1992, however, was it published in Hungary under the title *Hogyan lehetséges kritikai gazdaságtan?*.

[21] György Lukács named the school as such in his last article, published a few days after his death. György Lukács, 'The Development of a Budapest School', *The Times Literary Supplement*, no. 3615 (1971).

[22] Ágnes Heller, *Bedeutung und Funktion des Begriffs Bedürfnis im Denken von Karl Marx* (Budapest, 1974); English translation: *The Theory of Need in Marx* (London: Allison and Busby, 1976).

Introduction 11

alternative, humanist reading of Marx, one that emphasised the mutability of human needs and the role of human action and culture as agents in world history.[23] Armed with the philosophical anthropology of the young Marx, these critical Marxists of the 1960s were able to reject the dogmas and rigid determinism of orthodox Marxism, most notably the idea that all societies must follow the same path of development. In general, the school was characterised by a philosophical shift away from the answers of the mature Marx (and Engels) to the questions and intentions that had originally animated his critique of capitalism and political economy, especially the question of alienation.[24] More pragmatically, the authors of 'Überhaupt' sought to address the mutual estrangement that had emerged between socialists in East and West in the wake of the two defining events of 1968 – the Prague Spring and the mass student protests emanating from Paris. While East European socialists demanded economic and democratic liberties, prominent members of the New Left in the West exposed liberal democracy as a surreptitious form of oppression and denounced market reforms as an unconscionable departure from the socialist ideal.[25]

While retaining the young Marx's critique of alienation under capitalism, 'Überhaupt' exposed the contradictions and inadequacies of the conception of a future communist society that could be gauged from various key passages in *Capital*. In doing so, the authors sought to salvage the notion of critical economic theory by purging it of its reliance on the labour theory of value, which was shown to be predicated on the viability of Marx's outline for a market-less economy of pure use-value. An economy based on calculations of units of labour-time, however, was unable to eliminate alienation without also eliminating the economic dynamism brought about by capitalism. Moreover, the Marxian end-goal of a collective organisation

---

[23] The *Economic and Philosophical Manuscripts*, which Marx wrote in Paris in the summer of 1844, were discovered by Jacob-Peter Mayer and published in 1932, in two separate editions: S. Landshut and J. P. Mayer, *Der Historische Materialismus: Die Frühschriften* (Leipzig: A. Kröner, 1932) and *Marx-Engels Gesamtausgabe* [*MEGA*] 1/3 (Berlin: Marx-Engels-Verlag, 1932). However, the manuscript was considered so subversive of the dogmas of orthodox Marxism that it was initially excluded from the later German edition of Marx's *Werke* (1957–1968), published by the East German Institute of Marxism-Leninism, only to be included in a supplementary volume in 1985.
[24] On the Budapest school, see Douglas M. Brown, *Towards Radical Democracy: The Political Economy of the Budapest School* (London: Unwin Hyman, 1988); J. F. Dorahy, *The Budapest School: Beyond Marxism* (Leiden: Brill, 2019). See also János Kis, 'Preface', in György Márkus, György Bence and János Kis (eds.), *How Is Critical Economic Theory Possible?*, trans. John Grumley and János Kis (Leiden: Brill, 2022), pp. xi–xxviii; and György Bence and János Kis, 'On Being a Marxist: A Hungarian View', *Socialist Register*, ed. Ralph Miliband and John Savile, vol. 17 (1980).
[25] Kis, 'Preface', p. xxvi.

of society was shown to be predicated on the optimistic expectation that the productive powers of capitalism would produce a condition of material abundance. Such a condition, however, was not likely to materialise. In consequence, a state of relative scarcity had to be accepted as a fundamental fact of human existence. The task at hand for critical economic theory was thus to formulate a new conception of socialism that accepted a certain, unavoidable degree of alienation in exchange for a dynamic economy and an open-ended development of human needs.

Having lost the aura of protection following of the death of György Lukács (1885–1971), the Budapest school was publicly denounced at the Regional Conference on Agitation, Propaganda and Culture in January of 1973.[26] Bence and Kis were dismissed from their academic positions at the Academy of Sciences and, along with many others, prohibited from publishing in Hungary.[27] In solidarity with his dismissed colleagues, which included his wife, Márkus resigned from his position as well. While Bence and Kis continued their *samizdat* activity underground, Márkus eventually went into exile in the West, finding refuge in Australia along with Ágnes Heller and several other members of the Budapest school.[28]

Needless to say, Hont's sympathies with this school did not do him any favours within the Academy of Sciences, which set strict boundaries to research topics. However, he was fortunate to have access to the British Embassy library, which provided an indispensable sanctuary for his studies, allowing him to indulge in various academic 'heresies'. In retrospect, Hont described the academic environment in the Institute of History as having descended into orthodoxy and given up on the (Marxian) effort to combine theoretical thinking with historical research. In consequence, an intellectual and institutional divide between empirical and theoretical history had emerged. As he wrote in 1977:

---

[26] Brown, *Towards Radical Democracy*, pp. 20–22.

[27] A number of essays written by György Bence and János Kis between 1974 and 1976 were translated and collected in a book entitled *Towards an East European Marxism* (London: Allison & Busby, 1977). The book was published under the pseudonym Marc Rakovski.

[28] György Bence and János Kis were at the forefront of the radical opposition to the government of János Kádár in the 1970s, suffering further harassment after expressing their support for Charter 77. They later became active in liberal politics after the fall of communism. In time, Bence came to consider himself a heterodox kind of conservative, influenced in particular by the political thought of Hannah Arendt and Carl Schmitt. Kis, on the other hand, gravitated towards the liberalism of John Rawls and Ronald Dworkin. In November 2022, the ELTE Institute of Philosophy (Budapest) organised a conference to celebrate the fiftieth anniversary of 'Überhaupt', held in a venue named after György Bence. In that same month, 'Überhaupt' was also published in English under the title *How Is Critical Economic Theory Possible* (Leiden: Brill, 2022).

Introduction

Most Marxist historians in Hungary claim to accept the structural framework of the Marxian theory as valid, but in fact the actual historical research which is done lacks any explicit theory. The theoretical history practiced by the Marxist philosophy departments, on the other hand, contains a major flaw, in spite of its forceful explanatory powers. Instead of actually inspiring further theoretically oriented historical research, it has virtually replaced the historical inquiry itself.[29]

Such a disconnect between history and theory was something that Hont was unwilling to accept, and his MA dissertation was a first attempt to bridge the gap by applying, as he later explained, 'history itself to the study of this cleavage in historical understanding'.[30] Rather than studying Marx's historical materialism directly, however, Hont chose to approach the problem from the perspective of David Hume and the eighteenth century more generally.

I was convinced that one has to go back at least to the philosophical history of the Enlightenment period in order to acquire a sufficiently historical perspective to understand [the] 19th-century development. As the subject of my first inquiries I chose David Hume, as a major philosopher who also wrote theoretically relevant history.[31]

More specifically, Hont decided to focus on Hume's economic essays, examining the degree to which they were 'an expression of Hume's theoretical understanding of his own contemporary history'.[32] Far more than engaging merely with economic issues, these essays, it seemed to Hont, constituted a 'point of mediation' between the political theory of the *Treatise of Human Nature* and the political historiography of the *History of England*. In other words, they provided Hont with a historical example of the kind of historically informed theory – or theoretically informed history – that he was looking for. In his doctoral thesis entitled 'Hume and Scotland', completed under the supervision of the economic historian Professor Éva Balázs (1915–2006), Hont expanded his analysis of Hume by examining the theoretical significance of the fact that the provenance of 'classical' political economy was predominantly Scottish, being convinced that this had been more than a historical contingency. The specific historical vantage point of Scotland, which in contrast to England was a poor country, had profoundly shaped the philosophical perspective of Hume and his contemporaries in ways that had positively

---

[29] Letter from István Hont to David A. Perry, 29 September 1977, SC, The Papers of István Hont, p. 2.
[30] Ibid.
[31] Ibid.
[32] Ibid., p. 6.

enabled them to theorise a *generalisable* model of historical and economic development. As he explained:

> Any Scottish inquiry into the nature and causes of the wealth of nations had to be primarily an analysis of the economic experience of countries other than their own. Inasmuch as the Scottish effort to build a valid economic theory of contemporary society led to a genuine theoretical achievement, it formed a generalised understanding of the historical experience of the developed countries. Thus, it was not the content of the theory, but the living experience, the philosophical perspective and indeed the value choice behind it, that were Scottish.[33]

To emphasise 'Scottishness' as a positive influence, perhaps even a constitutive influence, on the development of classical 'bourgeois' political economy was, as Hont knew, to challenge the standard Marxian version of historical materialism, which saw theoretical development as a corollary of economic development.[34] As Hont pointed out, the fact that so many of the major contributors to eighteenth-century political economy resided in an economically backwards country meant that 'the *loci* of classical capitalist economic development and of classical bourgeois economic theory do not coincide'.[35] Moreover, by studying Scottish economic history as distinct from English economic history, Hont became convinced that the economic development of Scotland had in fact departed from the English 'model' that had informed Marx's understanding of capitalist development, which was principally based on the notion of 'so-called primitive accumulation'.[36] Scotland had instead followed its own path as a 'late starter', and the theoretical significance of this 'lateness' or 'backwardness' could in fact be demonstrated, he believed, by studying the particular Scottish preoccupation with banking, which had arguably functioned as a 'substitute' for the absence of English conditions.

---

[33] Ibid., p. 4
[34] Hont was influenced by Alexander Gerschenkron (1904–1978), the Harvard-based historian of Soviet industrialisation who emphasised the way in which the development of 'late starter' economies deviated from the English model. See Alexander Gerschenkron, *Economic Backwardness in Historical Perspective* (Cambridge, MA: Harvard University Press, 1962).
[35] Hont to David A. Perry, 29 September 1977, p. 3.
[36] In the mid 1980s, Hont wrote an unpublished critique of contemporary Marxist debates regarding Scotland's economic development and Scottish political economy, singling out in particular Andre Gunder Frank's 'development of underdevelopment' thesis, Robert Brenner's reading of Smith's so-called 'commercialisation thesis' and Eric Hobsbawm's account of the Scottish reformers as having resorted *tout court* to 'primitive accumulation' in their suggestions for agricultural improvement. The crux of Hont's argument was that the Marxian story of capitalist agriculture did not apply to Scotland, nor did it conform to Smith's reform proposals, since the consolidation of farms had occurred largely *in response* to economic improvement, and Smith was advocating for the virtues of small-scale agriculture. See Hont, 'Conjectural History'.

Introduction   15

The study of Scottish banking revealed the process in which the society tried to develop new institutional devices precisely as a substitute for these missing preconditions of capitalist economic development. Scottish banking was innovatory in this period, and there is a clear theoretical reflection of this in the economics of Hume and Smith. In that sense this feature of Scottish economic development, which is clearly related to the backwardness of the country, had a theoretical significance in the shaping of a specific approach to the problems of economic development.[37]

One of the major questions that this 'Scottishness' of classical political economy raised for Hont was the implications that it would have for the connection between Marx and his Scottish predecessors. That there was a strong affinity between Scottish conjectural history and historical materialism had been noted and explored by several scholars, most notably Werner Sombart, Roy Porter and Ronald Meek, but as Hont now realised,

these accounts are very much lacking in theoretical precision and historical understanding at both ends of the comparison. Both the philosophical history and political economy of the Scots and the development of Marx's views deserve a much more careful historical investigation.[38]

While in Hungary, Hont had merely broached this question. His preliminary approach had been that of deconstructing Marx's readings of the Scots such as these were recorded in Marx's notebooks and unpublished works. In the final chapter of his PhD, Hont had focused on Marx's criticism of Hume's views on monetary issues, criticising in particular Marx's reliance on James Steuart, whose special status within Marxist scholarship as a proto-Marxist he also questioned. But reassessing Marx's understanding of his predecessors was only a start, an opening of a terrain that needed much further exploration. What was needed was a thorough historical study of Scottish political economy on its own terms before its connection with – and influence on – Marx could be determined:

The point is not simply to indicate the similarity between the philosophical history attached to the classical Scottish political economy on the one hand and Marxian views on the other, but to explain their emergence and show how they were built into a coherent ideology.[39]

While he was still working on his PhD, Hont had – with the help of his father – acquired a set of visas for himself and his wife Anna Hont (née

---

[37] Hont to David A. Perry, 29 September 1977, p. 5. In 1981, Hont wrote a paper on Hume's changing view on banking and paper money. See Hont, 'David Hume and the Problem of Paper Money', Unpublished manuscript [1981], SC, The Papers of István Hont.
[38] Hont to David A. Perry, 29 September 1977, p. 6.
[39] Ibid.

Lovas) to visit England where he met Duncan Forbes, of Claire College, Cambridge, who at the time was the leading authority on Hume's political thought. On a second visit to England in 1975, as their new visas were about to expire, the couple made the difficult decision to defect, which they were able to do with the assistance of the economic historian Michael M. Postan (1899–1981).

Hont had befriended Michael M. Postan (later Sir Michael M. Postan) when the Academy of Sciences appointed him as Postan's designated driver during a visit to Budapest in the early 1970s. Having left Russia (now Ukraine) after the October Revolution, Postan was a vehement anti-communist who had been granted British citizenship in 1926 and subsequently rose to the position of Professor of Economic History at Cambridge in 1938, serving also for more than twenty years as editor of the *Economic History Review* – a journal which Hont was intimately familiar with since his duties as Research Officer included the rather laborious task of summarising its articles in Hungarian.[40] In spite of his antipathy to communism, Postan was very well-read on Marx and able to discuss his work in great detail. According to one distinguished student he was 'the only man in Cambridge who knew Marx, Weber, Sombart and the rest of the great central and East Europeans, and took their work sufficiently seriously to expound and criticize it'.[41] Hont's own encounter with Postan proved to be life-changing. Noticing his discontent in Hungary, Postan had encouraged him to emigrate to Britain and even promised to help in whatever way he could – a promise on which he delivered. Through his guidance and connections it was arranged that Hont would be enrolled at Oxford under the supervision of Hugh Trevor-Roper, then Regius Professor of History.[42] In this way, Hont came into close contact with the two scholars, Forbes and Trevor-Roper, who had been principally responsible for drawing scholarly attention to the Scottish Enlightenment, which only emerged as an independent field of study in the 1960s.[43] Naturally, this meant that he was now ideally placed to continue his work on Scottish political economy, having also gained access to the archival material of the Bodleian Library and with various Scottish archives within reach. And with the help of an Austrian relative, Hont even managed to smuggle out of Hungary his own 1802 edition of Hume's *History of England*.

---

[40] John Robertson, 'István Hont (1947–2013)', IHA/Hont/312.
[41] Eric Hobsbawm, *Interesting Times: A Twentieth-Century Life* (London: Allen Lane, 2002), p. 283.
[42] Robertson, 'István Hont (1947–2013)'.
[43] Max Skjönsberg, 'Hume and Smith Studies after Forbes and Trevor-Roper', *European Journal of Political Theory* 19/4 (2018): 623–635.

Introduction 17

At Oxford, Hont was appointed to a Research Fellowship in Intellectual History at Wolfson College. There he attended the classes of Sir John Hicks (1904–1989), the co-creator of the so-called IS-LM model in Keynesian economics, whose lectures gave him a firmer grasp of the history of economic thought, supplementing the already extensive knowledge he had acquired in Budapest.[44] At Wolfson College, Hont produced his first paper in English, the manuscript of which is dated March 1977 and entitled 'David Hume and the Paradox of Scottish Improvement: The Hume–Tucker Debate'.[45] This paper, which is an early version of his article on the 'rich country–poor country debate', was then submitted as part of his application to a fellowship at the King's College Research Centre in Cambridge, which at the time was directed by John Dunn and Gareth Stedman Jones. Following a successful interview, Hont received the position in 1978, acquiring also a leading organisational role alongside Michael Ignatieff in the advertised project on 'Political Economy and Society, 1750–1850', which lasted from 1979 to 1984. From its earliest conception the project was intended as an attempt to subject the history of economic thought to proper contextual analysis, thus providing a more historically accurate alternative to the prevailing modes of historiography, not least Marxist historiography. 'The conventional approach to political economy', as the earliest purpose statement said,

> has been to extract out of it those elements which could in some sense be construed as anticipations of modern economic analysis, or else to treat it reductively simply as the ideological expression of a particular class. Both tendencies have tended to accentuate its modernity.[46]

When invitations to the first series of seminars began to circulate, J. G. A. Pocock expressed his bewilderment to the fellow invitee Nicholas Phillipson, not so much about the project's intentions but about the people who had been placed in charge. Two questions in particular demanded answers: 'who are Ignatieff and Hont, as nobody here seems to know? [And] how large a role may one expect Duncan [Forbes] to play?'[47] Phillipson responded that he too was 'a bit puzzled' by the whole affair, but his first impression of Hont was highly positive:

---

[44] Robertson, 'István Hont (1947–2013)', IHA/Hont/312.
[45] Hont, 'David Hume and the Paradox of Scottish Improvement: The Hume–Tucker Debate', IHA/Hont/549.
[46] 'Society and Political Economy, 1770–1850' [c. 1978], IHA/Hont/537.
[47] Letter from J. G. A. Pocock to N. Phillipson, 28 November 1978, SC, The Papers of Nicholas T. Phillipson.

Hont is an extremely intelligent and quite delightful Hungarian refugee who began life as a philosopher, decided that Marx and philosophy had their limits and that intellectual history and Hume was the thing. When he defected Trevor-Roper took him up and he has now found his way into the Kings Institute. I am sure you will like him and no doubt everything will be made clear in due course. Though what Kings, who wanted to set up a program on the History of Economic Thought will make of it I daren't think.[48]

When the first seminar series kicked off in January of 1979, the focus was on 'Scottish Society and Political Economy, 1750–1800'. Among the speakers were a wide range of historians such as T. C. Smout, T. M. Devine, Rosalind Mitchison, Andrew S. Skinner, Peter Jones, David Lieberman, T. D. Campbell, George Davie, Michael Postan, Aladár Madarász and Donald Winch.[49] However, the culminating event was the colloquium scheduled for the final weekend of May, which brought together J. G. A. Pocock and Duncan Forbes – along with a select few mediators and supporters from either side[50] – to discuss what everyone realised was the central issue of contention, namely the question of whether the language of civic humanism or natural jurisprudence should be given prominence as the context of Scottish political economy. The tensions created by this intellectual tug-of-war, as Hont later commented, 'defined the Cambridge ground in 1979', and its reverberations can be seen in the resulting volume of articles entitled *Wealth and Virtue: The Shaping of Political Economy in the Scottish Enlightenment* (1983).[51]

In his own article on the 'rich country–poor country debate', which he delivered a version of at the colloquium in 1979, Hont explored the theoretical implications of Hume's Scottishness further, taking the opportunity to correct Duncan Forbes, whose recently published book *Hume's Philosophical Politics* (1975) had avoided any serious engagement with Hume's economic thought and, as a consequence, had perpetuated a misunderstanding of Hume's comments about the existence of 'necessary checks' to wealth, interpreting this as a rare reversal to a cyclical view of

---

[48] N. Phillipson to J. G. A. Pocock, 11 December 1978, SC, The Papers of Nicholas T. Phillipson.
[49] 'Seminar Series 1979: Lent Term' [1979], IHA/Hont/539.
[50] Nicholas Phillipson, John Robertson, Franco Venturi, István Hont and (possibly) Donald Winch.
[51] In a talk given in 2005 at Chiba University (Japan), Hont described his own intellectual development in Cambridge, emphasising the centrality of Forbes and Pocock. 'In 1975 Forbes published *Hume's Philosophical Politics* and Pocock published *The Machiavellian Moment*. For the late seventies and beyond, this was the "Cambridge School".' See 'The Cambridge Moment: Commerce and Politics in 18th century Political Thought', Unpublished manuscript [2005], SC, The Papers of István Hont, pp. 3–4. Notably, the book *Wealth and Virtue* was dedicated to the memory of Sir M. M. Postan, who died in Cambridge on 12 December 1981.

history of a civic humanist kind.[52] Hont convincingly showed that Hume, far from holding a pessimistic view of progress, was simply insisting on the capability of a poor country like Scotland to catch up with a rich country like England by exploiting the advantages of its backwardness, primarily its low wage costs. But aside from this minor criticism, Hont was thoroughly appreciative of Forbes' line of argument. The designation of Hume and Smith as 'scientific' or 'sceptical' Whigs established the framework for understanding their political position as one that stood at an intellectual remove from contemporary party politics, demolishing both Tory and 'vulgar Whig' fallacies regarding liberty and its history by asserting that its true origin was modern, a result of the rise of commerce, and that civil liberty held primacy over political liberty.[53] Moreover, the distinction between 'vulgar' and 'scientific' Whiggism was one that Hont especially appreciated, not just because it was a play on the distinction between 'utopian' and 'scientific' socialism but because it conveyed a serious point as well, namely that the rejection of the (vulgar) 'Whig interpretation of history' in favour of a more materialist interpretation of history needed not entail a denigration of politics or human agency, such as was the case with orthodox Marxism.[54] Nevertheless, it also suggested that Smith and Marx had something in common politically, notably the criticism of various forms of anti-modern utopianism which failed to take account of the economic or 'material' limitations to modern politics. In addition, Forbes had also persuasively argued that the natural jurisprudence of Hugo Grotius and Samuel Pufendorf, as taught in the Scottish universities, constituted 'the matrix of the social theory of the Scottish Enlightenment'.[55] Natural jurisprudence was thus the essential linguistic context for understanding the moral and political philosophy of Hume, whose theory of justice as an 'artificial virtue' was nothing short of a modern theory of natural law, derived exclusively from human nature.[56]

In his second article, published as the introduction to *Wealth and Virtue* and co-authored with Michael Ignatieff, Hont followed Forbes' example

---

[52] Hont, 'The "Rich Country–Poor Country" Debate', p. 288n58.
[53] Duncan Forbes, '"Scientific Whiggism": Adam Smith and John Millar', *Cambridge Journal* 7 (1954): 643–670; "Sceptical Whiggism, Commerce, and Liberty", in Andrew S. Skinner and Thomas Wilson (eds.), *Essays on Adam Smith* (Oxford: Clarendon Press, 1975), pp. 179–201; *Hume's Philosophical Politics* (Cambridge: Cambridge University Press, 1975), ch. 5: 'Scientific and Vulgar Whiggism', pp. 125–192.
[54] Hont, 'The Cambridge Moment: Commerce and Politics in 18th Century Political Thought', p. 3.
[55] Duncan Forbes, 'Hume and the Scottish Enlightenment', *Royal Institute of Philosophy Supplements* 12/3 (1978): 97.
[56] Forbes, *Hume's Philosophical Politics*, ch. 2: 'A Modern Theory of Natural Law', pp. 59–90.

and interpreted Adam Smith's work in the context of European natural jurisprudence, again intending to rectify Forbes' reluctance to venture into the domain of economics.[57] What he proposed was that the core of Smith's political economy was his contention that modern commercial society, despite exhibiting an extremely unequal distribution of property and goods, was nonetheless able to satisfy the needs of the least advantaged better than primitive or 'savage' societies, which were far more equal but also wretchedly poor. In other words, Smith had employed economic arguments to justify the inequality of commercial society, and in doing so he had transposed, Hont argued, the question of the legitimacy of exclusive private property rights from the jurisprudential domain and into the domain and language of political economy. As he wrote:

> [I]t is essentially in the natural jurisprudence tradition, rather than in the 'economic' pamphleteers usually described as Smith's predecessors, that the central question in the *Wealth of Nations* was set up. Moreover, it was within that tradition that we can see the preparation of a specifically 'market' solution to the paradox, and to its key problem: how to enjoy the benefits of exclusive dominion without excluding the propertyless wage-earners from the means of subsistence.[58]

What was distinctive about the trajectory of the natural law tradition, as it had developed from Aquinas to Grotius, Pufendorf and Locke, was the progressive elimination of residual rights on the part of the propertyless, derived from God's original grant of the earth to mankind in common. Whereas Aquinas had maintained that those in need retained a right to subsistence enforceable by law, Grotius and in particular Pufendorf had weakened this right to the point that the needy held only an 'imperfect right', which did not entail an enforceable reciprocal obligation on the part of the wealthy. To obtain access to subsistence goods, the poor had to either sell their labour on the market for a wage or appeal to the charity of the rich. Behind this transformation lay an increasing confidence in the power of trade and private property to increase the productivity of the soil and, more importantly, an altered conception of the nature of God's grant of the earth to mankind. Instead of conceiving the original community of goods as a 'positive community', belonging to everyone as a shared right to the earth held in collective stewardship, Grotius and Pufendorf redescribed the original community as a 'negative community', the earth belonging to no one in particular, but to anyone permissively, open for appropriation by all of mankind. This change had profound implications

---

[57] Hont, 'The Cambridge Moment: Commerce and Politics in 18th Century Political Thought', p. 4.
[58] István Hont and Michael Ignatieff, 'Needs and Justice in the *Wealth of Nations*: An Introductory Essay', in Hont and Ignatieff (eds.), *Wealth and Virtue*, p. 42.

for the conception of rights. On the one hand, the elimination of rights from the state of nature meant that rights were transformed into a human convention, into a socially mediated man-to-man relationship in which there was a strict correlativity of rights and duties. On the other hand, it also meant that rights, especially in Pufendorf's jurisprudence, came to be downplayed and stand in relation to the historical dynamic of developing human needs, being only called forth by necessity once the original condition of natural abundance was replaced by scarcity because of population growth. In this way, the concept of 'negative community' laid the foundation for a jurisprudential theory of history, which was essentially a history of the development of civilisation, and which became the foundation for the conjectural histories of the Scots and their four stages theory of development. As Hont wrote in conclusion:

> As long as Western thought on property was dominated by the idea that the world had originally been given to mankind in common, each account of the actual private property of the modern world had been forced to provide a conjectural history which both accounted for and legitimated exclusive individuation.[59]

Natural Law and Civic Humanism

Although *Wealth and Virtue* became a classic work, helping to define the field of intellectual history for decades to come, especially for the study of Scottish political economy, the project itself ended in an impasse. As J. G. A. Pocock's contribution to the volume made explicit, the participants had in fact failed to find common ground on a shared conception of the identity of political economy, applying two rival interpretive paradigms to the Scottish Enlightenment. Whereas Hont – following Forbes – emphasised the importance of natural jurisprudence, Pocock and in particular Nicholas Phillipson interpreted the Scottish thinkers in light of the classical and Florentine 'civic humanist' tradition, the British and American reception of which Pocock had detailed in his magisterial *The Machiavellian Moment* (1975). There was, however, no obvious way to integrate the two paradigms, as Pocock explained, given what appeared to him as

> a marked hiatus or discontinuity between the vocabulary or language of civic humanism and that of civil jurisprudence (...) The basic concept in republican thinking is *virtus*; the basic concept of all jurisprudence is necessarily *ius*; and there is no known way of representing virtue as a right.[60]

---

[59] Ibid.
[60] J. G. A. Pocock, 'Cambridge Paradigms and Scotch Philosophers: A Study of the Relations between the Civic Humanist and the Civil Jurisprudential Interpretation of Eighteenth-Century Social Thought', in Hont and Ignatieff (eds.), *Wealth and Virtue*, p. 248.

Aside from this incongruity between historical vocabularies, lurking behind the schism was also, to a significant degree, the question of the 'Scottishness' of political economy. The continental, protestant natural law tradition was almost exclusively taught in Scottish universities and could thus be claimed as an especially Scottish language in the British context. By contrast, civic humanism had largely flourished in England as a 'country' discourse ideologically opposed to the 'corrupt' Whig government of Robert Walpole, restoring to prominence ancient anxieties about public debt, political patronage and the integrity of the virtuous citizen in an increasingly commercial and transactional world. As Pocock wrote, perhaps especially with the Scot Duncan Forbes in mind:

> It may do something for nationalist sentiment by laying emphasis on Scottish cosmopolitanism rather than provincialism, on membership in Europe rather than on self-doubt and self-affirmation in an age of involvement within Britain.[61]

What Pocock claimed for his rival 'paradigm' was, on the one hand, that Scottish social theory was predominantly constructed as an ideological defence of the Whig regime and its reliance on patronage and credit to solidify the parliamentary monarchy of the Revolution Settlement. As such, it was to be understood as a response to the challenge posed by the civic humanist conception of ancient virtue and its ideal of an active and armed, land-owning citizenry. On the other hand, Scottish social theory, as emphasised by Phillipson, did not simply reject virtue outright, Pocock claimed. In the aftermath of the Union of 1707, and as a substitute for Andrew Fletcher's (defeated) virtuous patriotism, a concerted effort was made – influenced by the rapid adoption in Scotland of an (English) Addisonian culture of moralism – to cultivate and defend new, non-classical versions of virtue such as 'civility', 'refinement' or 'politeness', conceived in opposition to ancient virtue and the undiversified personality of the citizen soldier – more so than to the austere religious mores of Scottish Presbyterianism. Two opposing forms of virtue were thus pitted against one another in eighteenth-century Scotland – civic virtue against civil sentiments.

The rise of the 'social' as a substitute for the 'political' was thus not to be confused with the rise of 'possessive' or 'bourgeois' individualism, such as both proponents and detractors of liberalism maintained, but rested in Scotland on 'a psychology of sentiment, sympathy, and passion, better equipped to account for politeness, taste and transaction than was the rigorous individualism of self-interest'.[62] In this regard, Pocock

---

[61] Ibid., pp. 246–247.
[62] Ibid., p. 244.

Introduction   23

shared with Forbes and Hont the desire to replace the prevailing Marxist (and Straussian) interpretation of the eighteenth century, and for this reason he was eager to facilitate some kind of compromise between the two Cambridge paradigms, consolidating shared interpretive advances and making sure that 'the needle does not return to its starting point'.[63] As he wrote to Phillipson in late 1979, he was determined 'to make a resolutely eirenic effort to accommodate the civic humanist and natural law interpretations, which indeed don't strike me as in any way incompatible. I don't think this will do Duncan's neuroses much good, but I'd like to be on record as having made the effort.'[64] A month later, Phillipson wrote to Donald Winch that Pocock was 'quite right', there 'isn't a serious problem here and if I'm right, a sensible civic humanist reading will take care of the natural law problem on the way'. Nonetheless, such a 'sensible' reading, Phillipson acknowledged, had to account for the fact that 'the modes of participation which shape the moral personalities of citizens and work for the happiness of a country at large are infinitely more complex than anything the classical republicans ever dreamed'.[65] Some years earlier, Winch had received a word of warning from Duncan Forbes, advising him on how (not) to approach Adam Smith:

[D]on't sell yourself to the 'civic humanism' business. John Pocock used to have a bee in his bonnet about it. I am prepared to do so, provided lots and lots of other bees are given total license to buzz also. And anyway, the 'civic humanism' in the context of Smith, Ferguson and whomsoever *becomes* something else again. That is why I am so suspicious of 'traditions' of thought. (Smith is BIG!)[66]

In an article from 1981, circulated among the participants of the 'Political Economy and Society' project, Pocock presented his conciliatory response in the form of a 'model for historians'. Although the languages of *virtu* and *ius* could not be reconciled, they nonetheless shared a preoccupation with 'manners' and thus could be seen as overlapping in a joint discourse that he characterised as 'commercial humanism', encompassing both the *study* of manners (natural jurisprudence) and the *practice* and *refinement* of manners (civic humanism).[67] Thus, if classical virtue persisted into the eighteenth century, transformed by its encounter with

---

[63] J. G. A. Pocock, 'Virtues, Rights, and Manners: A Model for Historians of Political Thought', *Political Theory* 9/3 (1981): 353.
[64] Letter from J. G. A. Pocock to N. Phillipson, 18 December 1979, SC, The Papers of Nicholas T. Phillipson.
[65] Letter from N. Phillipson to D. Winch, 28 January 1980, SC, The Papers of Nicholas T. Phillipson.
[66] Letter from D. Forbes to D. Winch, 25 April 1975, The Donald Winch Papers, University of Sussex Library.
[67] Pocock, 'Virtues, Rights, and Manners', pp. 366–367.

commerce into softer, civil, non-classical alternatives, the jurisprudential paradigm now remained prominent in Pocock's model as 'the social science of the eighteenth century, the matrix of both the study and the ideology of manners'. In exchange, Pocock insisted that this concession be reciprocated. No longer could the history of natural jurisprudence be traced without any recognition of its 'ideological need to defend commerce against ancient virtue'.[68] This was the essence of 'commercial humanism', the eighteenth-century rejection or adaptation of the politics of the ancients in favour of the shift to the social in the sense of refined manners and the diversified personality. Pocock's model, however, with its suggestion of 'manners' as the organising concept of Scottish political economy, failed to persuade anyone (perhaps except for Phillipson) that the issues of interpretation had been properly settled.

In 1981, Hont co-organised another conference at King's College in an attempt to drive the discussion along by chronologically moving it forward to the 'final period of the Scottish Enlightenment and its aftermath in the work of Dugald Stewart and the *Edinburgh Review*, as well as in the early 19th century English political economy and radical political thought'.[69] For Hont, this entailed studying Malthus' *Essay on the Principle of Population* (1798) and determining the relative influence exerted on his populationist argument by both the English country-party discourse and Scottish political economy. He also wrote a paper on Dugald Stewart detailing his reading of the economic aspects of Hume's *History* and assessing the influence Stewart might have had on his many eminent students at the University of Edinburgh.[70] But this conference resulted in yet another unsatisfying impasse, and Hont concluded that the decision to extend the avenue of research beyond the Scottish Enlightenment had been premature. Consequently, the planned volume of articles, provisionally entitled *After Adam Smith: Political Economy and Theories of Commercial Society in the Early Nineteenth Century*, never saw the light of day.[71]

---

[68] Ibid., p. 366.
[69] Hont, 'Invitation to the workshop "The Identity of Political Economy"' [1 October 1983], IHA/Hont/532, p. 2.
[70] Neither of these two papers was ever published, but an updated version of the latter paper was presented at a workshop held as part of the 'Institutionalisation of Political Economy' project. See Note 6 in this Introduction. A third paper projected by Hont, but seemingly never written, was entitled 'Between Adam Ferguson and Marx: Dugald Stewart and the Critique of the Capitalist Division of Labour'.
[71] Another potential title was *After Adam Smith: Crossroads in Early 19th-Century Political Economy*. Among the contributors were Nicholas Phillipson, Pietro Corsi, Neil de Marchi, Biancamaria Fontana, Gilbert Faccarello, Gregory Claeys, Gareth Stedman Jones, Keith Tribe, Ursula Vogel and Evert Schoorl.

Introduction

On our own, obviously, we lacked the resources to carry out a range of detailed studies of the 19th century idioms comparable to the work which has been done on the 18th century; nor could we rely on a secondary literature similar to that which has been generated by recent scholarship on the 17th and 18th centuries. Perhaps even more importantly, we found great difficulty in communicating this new understanding of the 18th century to 19th century scholars, or in convincing 18th-century scholars about the direct relevance of early 19th-century developments.[72]

But this second impasse had the positive effect of clarifying for Hont what the essential problem was. It was the result of a seemingly paradoxical aspect of the way in which Cambridge school contextualism had been practiced so far, namely that the organising key categories, as employed by historians working on individual thinkers and specific periods, were insufficiently historical, thus rendering the transition between contexts an extremely difficult historiographical exercise. Lumping categories such as 'Liberalism' or 'Ricardian socialism' were often contrived and superimposed on the past rather than derived from the historical actors and texts themselves. As such, they could rarely be employed without much heavy-handedness to intellectual developments beyond those for which they had originally been invented. As Hont wrote:

The situation at present strikes us as somewhat paradoxical. On the one hand, great store is set on understanding each period in terms of its own language, style and idiom, by teasing out meanings from the dialectic of historical debates and paying special attention to minor thinkers, as well as those of greater intellectual stature of presumed 'influence'. While this approach has been deployed with an awareness that the ensuing relativity and fragmentation constitute a price well worth paying for genuine historical understanding, it is quite blatantly the case that some of the key organising categories of this variety of scholarship have not been derived from the historical language of the period studied. Categories like 'civic humanism', 'scientific whiggism' (...) are organising rubrics of our own. They were assuredly not those of our putative historical subjects.[73]

The limited scope and ahistorical nature of these organising categories suggested to Hont that the price hitherto paid for Cambridge school contextualism – the price of historiographical fragmentation – could be reduced if such categories became less artificial and more comprehensive. Only a rigorous historical approach, which nonetheless remained focused on the *longue durée*, could make possible a history of political economy that could trace its trajectory through multiple contexts, and especially into the nineteenth century, without becoming parochial

---

[72] Hont, 'Invitation to the workshop "The Identity of Political Economy"', p. 2.
[73] Ibid., p. 4; The same point is made in Hont, 'Commercial Society and Political Theory in the Eighteenth Century', p. 55.

and discontinuous. Hont, in short, was unwilling to accept so readily 'such radical fragmentation in our historical understanding, preempting any effort to comprehend intellectual history in a larger and more synoptic sense'.[74]

To remedy this situation, he used the remaining funds of the 'Political Economy and Society' project to organise one final workshop at the King's College Research Centre with the stated intention of finding 'a common language in which to discuss our fragmented historical knowledge'.[75] The workshop was held on 1–3 July 1984 under the heading 'The Identity of Political Economy: Between Utopia and the Critique of Civilisation, 1688–1845'.[76] For Hont this became an opportunity to provide his own answer to the problem and to present some of the work he had been doing on his *Culture, Needs and Property Rights* project. In fact, the papers that he delivered over the course of these summer days amount to a comprehensive exposition of the ideas that would have formed the content and argument of that book.

Culture and Civilisation

Hont's first paper, reproduced as Chapter 3 in this volume, laid out the framework for the discussion by engaging critically with Pocock's prior proposal of a compromise between the two Cambridge paradigms. He began by noting that Pocock had committed at least one crime of anachronism: the term 'commercial humanism' was nowhere to be found in either the eighteenth century or later. Aside from this, Hont agreed with Pocock that eighteenth-century natural jurisprudence, including Adam Smith's jurisprudential thought, was indeed characterised by an ideological need to defend commerce against ancient virtue. What struck Hont as odd about Pocock's argument, however, was the sense of optionality that his model conveyed regarding civic virtue and its civil alternatives. It was as if the advent of modern commercial society had left political and moral thinkers the option to choose between ancient and modern virtue. In other words, the question of why the civic humanist tradition had undergone a reversal of strategies regarding commerce had been left

---

[74] Hont, 'Invitation to the workshop "The Identity of Political Economy"', p. 5.
[75] Ibid.
[76] Among the contributors were John Dunn, Mark Goldie, James Moore, John Robertson, Richard Tuck, Quentin Skinner, Michael Ignatieff, Sylvana Tomaselli, Hans-Erich Bödeker, Judith Shklar, Biancamaria Fontana, Stephen Holmes, Pasquale Pasquino, Keith Tribe, Ursula Vogel, Aladár Madarász, Gregory Claeys, Gareth Stedman Jones and Jörn Rüsen.

Introduction 27

unanswered.[77] Similarly, Pocock had also been unable to account for the fact that, after the brief flourishing of 'commercial humanism' in the eighteenth century, another reversal of strategies had taken place sometime after the French Revolution when 'the mantle of humanism passed from the defenders of commerce to its critics'.[78] For these reasons, the concept of 'manners' could not express the true essence of political economy according to Hont. To divest the discourse of this 'optionality' and properly convey the causal impetus behind the modernist defence of commerce against ancient virtue, Hont suggested that the organising key concept of political economy had to be found instead in the popular mid eighteenth-century neologism 'civilisation' and its implied normativity. In short, Hont argued that 'to be a political economist entails the comprehension, however crudely, that modern civilisation is a system with definite boundaries, the transgression of which, from whatever intentions, can precipitate the system's relapse into barbarism'.[79] Thus, it was not simply two forms of virtue, ancient and modern, that were pitted against one another in Scottish political economy but a much starker choice between civilisation and barbarism.

Although the word 'civilisation' was not coined until the middle of the eighteenth century, its first usage being ascribed to the physiocrat Victor Riqueti, Marquis de Mirabeau (1715–1789), Hont was convinced that the intellectual rudiments of the theory of mankind's rise from rudeness to refinement were to be found in the natural law tomes of Grotius and Pufendorf. We have already seen how the concept of 'negative community' made a jurisprudential theory of history possible and, indeed, necessary. But Hont also sought to demonstrate that the theory of sociability underlying the eighteenth-century defence of civilisation ultimately derived from the modern natural law tradition, beginning with Grotius' attempt to counter moral scepticism by grounding natural law on a conception of man as having an appetite for society (*appetitus societatis*) and a blameless interest in his own self-preservation. By reinterpreting Grotius' social appetite as itself a function of man's

---

[77] Hont provided his own answer to this question in 'Free Trade and the Economic Limits to National Politics: Neo-Machiavellian Political Economy Reconsidered', in John Dunn (ed.), *The Economic Limits to Modern Politics* (Cambridge: Cambridge University Press, 1990), pp. 41–120. This paper was originally intended as (part of) a larger monograph by Hont, focusing especially on Charles Davenant (1656–1714), provisionally entitled *High Wages, Empires and Public Virtue: Free Trade and Conflict among Nations in Neo-Machiavellian Political Economy*. See letter from Hont to Keith Tribe, 21 May 1988, SC, The Papers of István Hont.
[78] Pocock, 'Virtues, Rights, and Manners', p. 367; Hont explored this transition in Chapter 6, this volume.
[79] See Chapter 3, this volume.

interest in self-preservation, Pufendorf then simplified this anti-sceptical foundation, creating a theory of human sociability that accounted for man's need for society not by reference to an innate social propensity but by seeing it as a result of man's unique and paradoxical position in nature as the only animal whose needs were neither fixed nor accompanied by a corresponding ability to satisfy them. While animals came into the world equipped with a natural aptitude for self-preservation, man emphatically did not, being the most helpless of God's creations. However, this weakness or indigence – man's natural *imbecillitas* – made human cooperation utterly necessary. And given the fact that human desires did not terminate with mere self-preservation but developed and multiplied with the refinement of man's mind and taste, humans were able to far surpass animals in the structure of their needs-satisfaction. This paradox of being both inferior and superior to animals – a paradox that was later invoked by Smith, Kant and Hegel – was precisely what enabled Pufendorf to imagine mankind's departure from the state of nature as a gradual development through *cultura* (i.e. culture or cultivation) as opposed to an abrupt, Hobbesian transition into a contractually constituted state. Society thus came before the state as an independent organisational form, held together by mutual need and certain precepts of obligation, underpinned by God, but founded on the dictates of reason by men interested in their own survival. This theory of human sociability, based on individualist and universal assumptions, later earned Pufendorf the title as founder of a 'socialist' school of natural law – as Hont was always keen to point out[80] – not only because it established the origin and theory of society as distinct from that of the state but also because it emphasised the necessity or duty of man to cultivate sociableness in himself.

The crucial thing for Hont to emphasise was that the driving force of historical progress was provided by the dynamic between human needs-satisfaction and the material environment, and that the institutional development of the state and private property was a consequence of this dynamic rather than its precondition. Moreover, even after the introduction of private property and the state, it was still needs that ultimately held society together, given that the legitimacy of private property was predicated on the continuous expansion of commerce, which provided the excluded members of society with the means to their own self-preservation. Pufendorf's theory of sociability thus explained not only the origin of society but also its ultimate preservation through

---

[80] Hont traced the source of this designation to Gottlieb Hufeland's *Lehrsätze des Naturrechts und der damit verbundenen Wissenschaften* (Jena, 1790).

the introduction of monetary exchange. As such, Pufendorf's theory of sociability was a 'commercial' sociability, and it was in this regard that Pufendorf had provided, according to Hont, the foundation for Adam Smith's economic legitimation of private property and inequality and for the conception of a stage of development beyond agriculture – the commercial stage – in which there is an extensive division of labour and where everyone becomes, as Smith wrote, 'in some measure a merchant'.[81]

Marxian Marxism

Having established the link between natural law and political economy in the concept of 'negative community' and in the conjectural historicisation of needs and property rights serving as a defence of civilisation, Hont then proceeded to examine the further connection with Marxism in the second paper that he submitted to the 1984 workshop on the 'Identity of Political Economy'. The paper fell in two parts, published as Chapters 4 and 5 in this volume. While the first part sought to establish the context of Marx's early communist writings, especially through an analysis of the 'Paris Manuscripts', the second part was a close textual analysis of the concept of 'use-value' in *Capital*, broadly understood to include all the proximate works and 'notes' such as the *Grundrisse* and the *Theories of Surplus Value*.

As the starting point of his analysis of the later Marx, Hont took it as given that historical materialism was a continuation of the jurisprudential theory of history whose trajectory and 'philosophical anthropology' he had discussed in his previous paper. However, he also knew that the absence of any theory of rights from Marx's thinking – and *a fortiori* his hostility to bourgeois notions of right – constituted a problem that needed to be addressed head-on. Moreover, this problem was perhaps particularly topical in Cambridge given that the King's College Research Centre had hosted a seminar in November of 1981 at which 'The Theory and Practice of Socialism' had been discussed, notably with a contribution by the Oxford-based political and social theorist Steven Lukes, who had given a paper entitled 'Can a Marxist Believe in Human Rights?'.[82] On that occasion, Lukes had argued that Marxism stood outside the tradition of modern political thought because Marx, by excluding considerations of rights from his theory of communism, had rejected the key element of European and American political theory.

---

[81] Adam Smith, *Wealth of Nations*, I.iv.1.
[82] 'King's College Cambridge, Seminar on the Theory and Practice of Socialism – Michaelmas Term 1981', IHA/Hont/540.

This was an unfortunate lacuna, Lukes believed, rendering Marxism virtually silent on most issues of topical relevance.[83] Contrary to Lukes, Hont wished to demonstrate that Marx did in fact belong to the same tradition of thought as Pufendorf and the eighteenth-century Scottish political economists since their jurisprudential theories of history were in essence less about rights than about needs. To strengthen his argument, Hont pointed to a key aspect of Marx's thought that theorists such as Lukes had neglected to take proper notice of, namely the fact that Marx, although he had indeed been highly critical of the anachronistic and Robinson Crusoe-like conceptions of early mankind often expounded by political economists and bourgeois rights theorists, had in fact also been highly dismissive of rights-based notions of man's early community advanced by what he called 'crude communism', which equated communism with communal property or co-proprietorship. If the broader context for understanding Marx was thus to be found in seventeenth-century natural jurisprudence and eighteenth-century political economy, the more immediate and narrower context, Hont argued, was to be located in Marx's persistent hostility towards contemporary versions of utopian socialism or communism, a hostility which was informed by arguments provided by 'bourgeois' political economy.

The germ of this interpretation, it would seem, lay in Hont's discovery of a central passage in the 'Paris Manuscripts' in which Marx dismissed the crude communism of his fellow socialists as 'merely a *manifestation of the vileness of private property, which wants to set itself up as the positive community system*'.[84] The specific wording of this dismissal suggested to Hont that Marx had been aware of the natural law distinction between 'negative' and 'positive' community from his earliest conception of communism, or at the very least that there existed a structural similarity between Marx's rejection of all conceptions of communism based on co-ownership and the natural lawyers' rejection of any 'positive' community of goods beyond the confines of small close-knitted groups. Furthermore, the absence of rights from Marx's notion of communism made it evident that the communist future he envisioned was best understood as that of a return to the negative community of man's early past such as it had been conceived by Pufendorf, namely a return to a condition of abundance in which the satisfaction of human needs no longer required any social mediation through property rights and

---

[83] See Steven Lukes, *Marxism and Morality* (Oxford: Oxford University Press, 1985). Aside from Steven Lukes, another important interlocutor of Hont's was Norman Levine. See Chapter 1, this volume.
[84] Marx, 'Economic and Philosophical Manuscripts 1944', *MECW* 3, p. 296 (emphases in original).

Introduction 31

monetary exchange. The strict correlativity of rights and duties, which had emerged as a necessary constraint on human nature because of the progress of civilisation and the onset of scarcity, could be suspended with the re-emergence of material abundance produced by capitalism. Consequently, a distributive principle of each-according-to-their-needs could reassert itself on a higher stage of history, preserving – or going beyond – the level of culture and civilisation achieved by capitalism.

Viewed as such, Marxian communism constituted the natural culmination of Western rights theorising such as this had been developed by Pufendorf and the political economists of the Scottish Enlightenment in particular.[85] In contrast, by conceiving communism as a return to communal co-ownership, Hont suggested that it was in fact the crude communists who had negated the entire trajectory of the modern natural law tradition towards a historicisation of human needs and property rights, ironically by remaining – as Marx had pointed out – within the 'bourgeois' ideological domain of property rights. Moreover, because they saw private property as a pathological expression of supposedly 'natural' human needs, their vision of a communist society had to be one that supressed human needs to what Marx had described as a 'preconceived minimum'. Their crucial mistake, Hont emphasised, was their failure to grasp the paradoxical and dynamic nature of human needs, which had been the anthropological starting point of the jurisprudential history of man's rise from barbarism to civilisation.

As suggested, Hont's reading of the 'Paris Manuscripts' was probably the source of his realisation that the Marxian conception of communism was that of a 'negative community'. However, it is also plausible that it was Hont's study of Hume that initially made him aware of the fact that Marxism represented the realisation of a theoretical possibility that had existed within modern natural law theory since Pufendorf at least, but which Hume had been the first to make explicit. In his *Treatise of Human Nature* (1740), Hume had hinted that communism was a legitimate outcome of the jurisprudential theory of rights and needs, provided that a condition of abundance was to (re)emerge. As Hume wrote:

Increase to a sufficient degree the benevolence of men, or the bounty of nature, and you render justice useless, by supplying its place with much nobler virtues, and more valuable blessings. The selfishness of men is animated by the few

---

[85] In effect, this constituted a correction of the idea that it was Hume who represented the culmination of the modern theory of natural law, such as Forbes had suggested. Following Forbes, Steven Buckle later claimed that Hume 'completed' natural law and 'fulfilled' its 'bold ambitions' by grounding moral obligation 'firmly in the soil of human nature itself'. See Stephen Buckle, *Natural Law and the Theory of Property* (Oxford: Oxford University Press, 1991), p. 298.

possessions we have, in proportion to our wants; and 'tis to restrain this selfishness, that men have been oblig'd to separate themselves from the community, and to distinguish betwixt their own goods and those of others.[86]

It was in this regard that Marx was, as Hont 'somewhat frivolously' stated, an eighteenth-century type thinker – someone who breathed the same air as Hume and Smith. And properly understood in this way, Marxism could in fact contribute something relevant to contemporary political thinking in the sense that it could help elevate the discussion about 'property and community in terms of rights theories appropriate to the present day, both in the context of the welfare state and in the context of the current reforms in really existing "socialist" societies'.[87] More specifically, the concept of 'negative community' constituted for Hont a theoretical recovery which held the potential of unsettling the fixed dichotomy between state and private ownership, and which provided a shared ideological vantage point from which to re-examine the ossified ideological positions of the Cold War. On the one hand, it drew attention to the manifest disparity between Marx's original conception of communism and that of existing socialist societies, which Hont strongly implied resembled more the crude notion of communism that Marx had so vehemently scorned for its repressiveness and its civilisational regression towards an 'unnatural simplicity' of needs. And indeed, several socialist governments in Eastern Europe had by 1984 embarked on cautious reform efforts, including in Hungary, where the 'New Economic Mechanism' had been partially reintroduced since 1980. On the other hand, it also served as a reminder that the theoretical primacy of human needs over property rights was not just characteristic of socialism but was in fact a defining feature of the Western 'rights' tradition – the tradition that in time came to be known as liberalism. But the problem was larger than the mere bifurcation of the discourse on rights and needs. As Hont concluded his paper in 1984: 'Instead of the familiar choice between two competing languages of political theory we find ourselves facing a single core problem: Are the inherited categories of Western political thought – the discourse of rights and needs – adequate for understanding the relationship between economy and polity in the 20th century?'[88]

In regard to Marxism, the question was answered promptly by Hont. In fact, it was precisely because Marx belonged to the same discourse

---

[86] David Hume, *A Treatise on Human Nature* [1739–40], ed. L. A. Selby-Bigge (Oxford: Oxford University Press, 1888), second edition by P. H. Nidditch (Oxford: Oxford University Press, 1978), Bk. III. Part II. sect. ii., pp. 494–495.
[87] See Chapter 4, this volume.
[88] See Chapter 5, this volume.

Introduction 33

of rights and needs as Hume and Smith that the Marxian solution to the 'riddle of history' could be shown to be self-contradictory. In the second part of his 1984 paper, reproduced in this volume as Chapter 5, Hont took his analysis further both chronologically and thematically and explored the challenges that the later Marx faced in reintroducing the concept of use-value to the centre of political economy and in defining it in such a way that an economy based on the direct use of material resources became conceivable. Building on the work done by Márkus, Bence, Kis and to some extent Ágnes Heller, the question which Hont tried to answer was essentially epistemological in nature: given the absence of property rights and exchange values (i.e. prices) from this final stage of civilisation, was an economic theory of Marxian communism possible at all? Hont centred his analysis on the semantic duality that the concept of 'use-value' conveyed as being both independent of market exchange yet also in some regard an economic notion. This duality had been crucial to Marx, Hont claimed, because it suggested that it could potentially provide the basis for a post-capitalist or 'critical' economic theory. In fact, the economic analysis of use-value was the central aspect of Marx's critical political economy, the key contribution that in his own mind distinguished him from bourgeois political economy. The practical viability of Marxian communism – the 'administration of things' in negative community – thus in an important sense depended on the epistemic potential of this compound concept, on the theoretical usefulness of use-value, so to speak, in conceiving and operating a non-market economy, and for that reason it was worth examining how well Marx himself had succeeded in his attempt to analyse and define it.

In volume one of *Capital*, Marx had defined use-value as an object in its physical particularity, either natural or man-made, which satisfies human needs in a way capable of being realised without exchange, that is, in a socially unmediated way. As such, use-values formed the material content of the total wealth of a given society or, indeed, of the world, but they were nonetheless impervious to the degree of civilisation reached by that society whose wealth they comprised. A use-value thus expressed a direct and immediate relationship between man and thing, yet at the same time it was an object of human needs, which Marx – like Pufendorf and Smith – believed evolved historically along with mankind's progress through the various stages of development. By implication, use-values had to be historically determined in some regard. This socio-historical aspect of use-value constituted for Hont the primary philosophical problem that Marx had struggled to solve – a struggle in which Marx ultimately failed, Hont concluded. Despite his many ingenious attempts to define and distinguish his way out of the problem, the naturalistic definition of use-value that he advanced in *Capital* was fundamentally at odds with the philosophical anthropology that Marx had espoused regarding man's historical 'species being'.

Given Marx's commitment to a historical conception of human nature, for a communist society to avoid imposing a preconceived limit on human needs, the development of new needs within a communist economy had to be somehow anticipated. A communist 'administration of things' thus had to be epistemologically superior to a market economy, which only coordinated production with needs retrospectively, leaving a wasteful trail of bankrupt producers whose productive activity was shown to be based on a mistaken estimation of demand. However, Marx's own research in *Grundrisse* showed that there was no historical precedent for how such an anticipatory or immediate harmonisation of production and needs could occur. All pre-capitalist societies, such as the ancient *polis*, which had operated with a near harmony of production and needs, were in reality based, as Hont emphasised following Marx, on an implicit, 'political' suppression of needs through custom. The ultimate contradiction of Marxian communism was thus that it sought to retain the dynamism of a market economy while dispensing with both the epistemic delay of market corrections and the epistemic deceit of political constraints masquerading as 'natural' determinations of need. But since there could be no natural determination of needs if needs kept evolving as civilisation progressed, continuously pushing a state of abundance further into the future, then a communist society was forced to develop a 'rationally' planned economy, which could hardly be described as a mere administration of things. Moreover, the tradition of thought to which Marxism belonged was one that distinguished society above politics and prioritised the historical rationality of unintended consequences over human rationality and design. This was indeed a contradiction that Marx had left unresolved.

From Marx to Smith

In arguing in this fashion, Hont thus showed that, although Marx's conception of communism was not to be conflated with state- or co-ownership, the antinomies of his concept of use-value nonetheless made the disparity between Marx's 'avant-garde vision' and the reality of real existing socialism a rather predictable one. It would thus be wrong to suggest that Hont was attempting to rescue the idea of communism from its association with a Soviet-style planned economy. Instead, what he showed was that anyone attempting to do so had to move beyond Marx and succeed where he had failed in theorising how an economy of direct use could in fact be conceived and realised by means – theoretical as well as practical – not yet imagined. Leaving this problem to be solved by the progress of civilisation itself, by the logic of unintended consequences, was to misunderstand the challenge altogether.

In many ways, *Culture, Needs and Property Rights* can be seen as an intellectual history of what Hont at one point called the 'old socialist tradition', which began with Pufendorf and which both culminated and reached its limit with Marx, who appeared in Hont's interpretation as 'the only major modern author who was a socialist both in the old and the new sense'.[89] The core characteristic of this tradition was the view that both needs and property rights had to be understood as socially mediated relationships in a modern commercial society. The redescription of mankind's original community as a 'negative community' transformed property rights into socially constituted rules of conduct, rendered necessary by the moral or political (or divinely ordained) imperative to preserve peace and promote sociableness among selfish individuals in an environment of material scarcity. And the idea of human sociability as a function of man's natural inability to survive without the help of others meant that it was needs that established society among human beings, a society of reciprocal assistance and exchange, which in turn facilitated an endless development and refinement of human needs to be satisfied by an increasingly complex web of commercial relationships. Human beings were thus neither sociable nor unsociable, but something in between. The best and most accurate term for the 'old socialist' theory of sociability was Kant's purposely oxymoronic term 'unsocial sociability', representing an alternative to both the natural unsociability of Hobbes and the natural or positive sociability of various Christian or Aristotelian traditions as well as many modern socialists.[90] As Hont explained in 1994, the essential characteristic of an 'old socialist' was

---

[89] See Chapter 6, this volume.
[90] In 1989, Hont devised (with Hans-Erich Bödeker) an ambitious research programme focusing on the concept of 'unsocial sociability'. It was to be a study of the development of natural law from Grotius to Kant, emphasising in particular the challenge posed by various strands of scepticism in the transformation of natural law from the early to the late Enlightenment. This research programme was presented at an international workshop that Hont co-organised at the Max Planck Institute for History in Göttingen, 26–30 June 1989. The workshop was entitled 'Unsocial Sociability: Modern Natural Law and the 18th-Century Discourse of Politics, History and Society'. See Hans Erich Bödeker and István Hont, 'Naturrecht, Politische Ökonomie und Geschichte der Menschheit. Der Diskurs über Politik und Gesellschaft in der Frühen Neuzeit', in Otto Dann and Diethelm Klippel (eds.), *Naturrecht – Spätaufklärung – Revolution* (Hamburg: Meiner, 1995), pp. 80–89.

somebody who had accepted Pufendorf's emendation to Hobbes's theory of the state of nature as a state without society and accepted commercial reciprocity as the real foundation of man's ability to form a common social life and provide foundations for politics. A 'socialist' opposed natural sociability and the Christian idea of sociability based on love, and hence accepted that the basis of modern politics was the 'unsocial sociability' described in such critical terms in Rousseau's *Second Discourse*. A 'socialist' was a supporter of the idea that the *état social* was commercial society built on the reciprocal satisfaction of human needs through the division of labour.[91]

By seeing Hont's project in this way, it becomes clear that the continuity that he sought to establish between seventeenth-century natural law and nineteenth-century Marxism rests on two principal moves – on two more or less accurate 'translations' – which together serve to define the parameters of the old socialist tradition in such a way as to include both Pufendorf and Marx, as well as a whole host of authors in between, authors such as Hume, Smith, Kant, Hegel and Sieyès. The first is the projection of the idea of a 'negative community' forwards to Marx; the second is the projection of the idea of 'unsocial sociability' backwards to Pufendorf. In regard to the first move, Hont's reading of Marx has been supported by the subsequent work of Gareth Stedman Jones and Michael Sonenscher, both of whom have expanded upon Hont's analysis and explored the various ways in which the young Marx could have absorbed the idea of negative community.[92] Incidentally, Sonenscher has also followed Hont's suggestion about the centrality of the concept of civilisation, arguing that this concept most accurately captures the normative content of Montesquieu's *The Spirit of Laws* (1748) as well as the subsequent debates about the perceived impending crisis in pre-Revolution France.[93] In regard to the second move, Hont's reading of Pufendorf has been questioned by subsequent scholarship, disputing that Pufendorf's concept of *socialitas* should be understood as a mechanism that sets up a (teleological) historical process of social development. Instead, Pufendorf's theory of sociability should be understood, it is argued, as a morally mandated conduct that demands individual

---

[91] Hont, 'The Permanent Crisis of a Divided Mankind: "Contemporary Crisis of the Nation State" in Historical Perspective', *Political Studies* 42 (1994): 193n49.

[92] Gareth Stedman Jones, 'Introduction', in Karl Marx and Friedrich Engels, *The Communist Manifesto* (London: Penguin Books, 2002), pp. 162–176; Michael Sonenscher, *Capitalism: The Story behind the Word* (Princeton, NJ: Princeton University Press, 2022), pp. 78–95.

[93] Michael Sonenscher, *Before the Deluge: Public Debt, Inequality, and the Intellectual Origins of the French Revolution* (Princeton, NJ: Princeton University Press, 2007), pp. 174, 218. Another scholar who also explored the concept of civilisation in the eighteenth century is Anthony Pagden, 'The "Defence of Civilisation" in 18th Century Social Theory', *History of the Human Sciences* 1/1 (1988): 33–45.

self-discipline and, as such, requires reinforcement in the form of institutions such as marriage, private property and civil government. On this reading, Hont's interpretation of *socialitas* is criticised for being an echo of various eighteenth-century expounders and critics of Pufendorf, notably Jean Barbeyrac and Rousseau, whose interventions have obfuscated the true meaning of Pufendorf's notion of *socialitas*. Central to this reinterpretation of Pufendorf has been the work of Fiammetta Palladini, who presented her Hobbesian interpretation of Pufendorf at a conference on natural law in Göttingen in 1989, a conference that Hont co-organised.[94] Hont was greatly appreciative of Palladini's work and seemed to suggest that her reading of Pufendorf was consonant with his own, as can be seen in Chapter 6 in this volume.[95] However, while some scholars, notably Robert Wokler, have seen Hont and Palladini as compatible, others have insisted on incompatibility, most prominently Ian Hunter and Knud Haakonssen.[96]

Although these disagreements are interesting, what is important here is to understand the reason why Hont attributed such significance to the concept of 'unsocial sociability' and to the recovery of the 'old socialist' tradition more generally. What it provided was a way to transcend the usual, binary categories of modern political discourse, both historical and contemporary, and thereby arrive at a better understanding of the problems facing the politics of commercial society in our own time. Perhaps it might be helpful to see Hont's reconstruction of the 'old socialist' tradition as intended to serve a purpose similar to Quentin Skinner's well-known recovery of a third concept of liberty, the neo-Roman concept of liberty as non-domination, offering a critical perspective on both negative and positive liberty.[97] In both cases, intellectual history was put to

---

[94] Fiammetta Palladini, *Samuel Pufendorf, Disciple of Hobbes: For a Reinterpretation of Modern Natural Law* [1990], trans. David Saunders (Leiden: Brill, 2019). The central chapter, presented in extract to the conference in 1989, was subsequently published in English as 'Pufendorf Disciple of Hobbes: The Nature of Man and the State of Nature: The Doctrine of Socialitas', *History of European Ideas* 34 (2008): 26–60.

[95] For an overview of the issues involved, see the special issue on 'Sociability in Enlightenment Thought' in *History of European Ideas* 41/5 (2015). See also Hont, 'Introduction', in *Jealousy of Trade: International Competition and the Nation-State in Historical Perspective* (Cambridge, MA.: Harvard University Press, 2005), pp. 38–39.

[96] Robert Wokler, 'Rousseau's Pufendorf: Natural Law and the Foundations of Commercial Society', *History of Political Thought* 15/3 (1994): 387–393; Knud Haakonssen and Ian Hunter (eds.), *The Cambridge Companion to Pufendorf* (Cambridge: Cambridge University Press, 2022). See especially Knud Haakonssen, 'Receptions, Contestations and Confusions', in Haakonssen and Hunter (eds.), *The Cambridge Companion to Pufendorf*, pp. 362–385.

[97] Quentin Skinner, 'The Idea of Negative Liberty: Philosophical and Historical Perspectives', in Richard Rorty, Jerome B. Schneewind and Quentin Skinner (eds.), *Philosophy in History* (Cambridge: Cambridge University Press, 1984), pp. 193–221.

the task of disrupting the ideological orthodoxies of the Cold War and going beyond the repetitive nature of debate which had come to characterise political theory. But while Quentin Skinner remained within the framework set out by Isaiah Berlin and suggested that what distinguished political discourses from one another was their theory of liberty, Hont insisted that political discourses were first and foremost distinguished by their theories of community and sociability.

What the concept of 'unsocial' or 'commercial' sociability captured was the predicament that had befallen modern politics in the wake of the rise of international commerce in the seventeenth century. As Hont wrote in 1990, the essential problem was that there was 'enough commercial sociability in modern society to make the politics of virtue impossible, but not enough to keep the peace'.[98] In other words, while Hobbes' natural unsociability produces a crisis that is brought to an end with the creation of the state, and while positive or 'social' sociability produces a society that is naturally human, benevolent and social, unsocial sociability produces a society that is in perpetual crisis, even after the creation of the state, and which is only social in an indirect and oftentimes brutal way. As Hont aptly stated in a talk from 1996, published as Chapter 7 in this volume, rather than being 'specifically humane' it is 'human only in the worst sense of the word'. Most importantly, the kind of society that unsocial sociability gives rise to is *our* society, a commercial society, and as it has grown and haphazardly expanded, eventually producing the modern market economy, individuals can survive only if they become a means to the satisfaction of another's need, and the state can survive only if it adapts and pays close attention to the unruly dynamic of society, to the whims and workings of the market, and to the unintended consequences of civilisation. In this regard, we are still contemporaries of Hume, Smith, Kant and Hegel. In fact, when viewed through the prism of the 'old socialist' tradition, the long eighteenth century emerges, Hont believed, as an extensive debate about commercial sociability and the viability of a society based on mutual needs-satisfaction:

> Hobbes had rejected the idea that man was a *zoon politikon* and replaced it with a project of pure politics without social foundations. Pufendorf, in answer, substituted a theory of sociability drawn from the idea of utility-led cooperation for the satisfaction of human needs and desires for the Aristotelian moral project of friendship. This genealogy of socialism can be turned into the starting point of an extremely illuminating historical inquiry. First, it is clear that Hegel and Marx's System of Need is a direct progeny of Pufendorf's socialist amendment to Hobbes. Second, by tracking the debate on Pufendorf's theory

---

[98] See Chapter 6, this volume.

Introduction

of utilitarian sociability one can reconstruct the political thought of the century between Hobbes and Hegel. In this mirror, the Enlightenment appears as a grand controversy between market sociability (socialism in this old sense) and its enemies.[99]

Broadly understood, the concept of 'unsocial sociability' thus provided a third concept of sociability with the potential to unsettle the usual dichotomy between liberalism and socialism, between individualism and society, much like the concept of 'negative community' presented an alternative to both private and communal property. What is more, just as the concept of 'negative community' enabled Hont to expose the antinomies of Marxian Marxism, antinomies related to the theory of sociability espoused by Marx, it also enabled him to identify the core inadequacy of the language of rights and thus expose the core weakness of modern liberalism. Despite emerging as the seeming ideological victor at the end of the twentieth century, liberalism had little cause for self-gratulation or complacency according to Hont:

> Although the question of private property appears to have been settled for the time being and no longer constitutes the sort of great ideological divide which it was whilst socialism was still powerful as a theory and as a historical movement, it is perhaps useful to remember that this outcome has been due less to a victory of the theory of private property over its rival, than to a practical failure of economic regimes based on its alternative.[100]

The fact that private property had its ultimate origin in a propertyless 'negative community' meant that its legitimacy, especially property in land, could never be a truly settled question. Moreover, if private property is always in need of justification, then the same is *a fortiori* the case for the property on which private property is based, namely the property that the state holds over its national territory.[101] Within the natural law discourse, this weakness had indeed been recognised and frequently expressed in the idea that states exist among each other in a state of nature.[102] In other words, the territorial claims of national communities could never be given any solid *de jure* basis in international law but only ever receive recognition as *de facto* possession. This meant that the relationship between sovereign states was always that of a latent state of war,

---

[99] Hont, 'Unsociable Sociability: The Morals and Politics of Markets in Enlightenment Thought', Leverhulme Major Research Fellowship Application, 2001–2002, SC, The Papers of István Hont.
[100] Hont, 'The Permanent Crisis of a Divided Mankind', pp. 173–174.
[101] Ibid., p. 175.
[102] On this topic, see especially Richard Tuck, *The Rights of War and Peace: Political Thought and the International Order from Grotius to Kant* (Oxford: Oxford University Press, 1999).

and as such it inevitably generated a politics of necessity – a politics of national survival – that carried over into the modern world in the form of commercial rivalry. In what was arguably intended as a spoof on the Marxist notion of 'permanent revolution', Hont described this predicament as the 'permanent crisis' of a divided mankind.[103] But while the term was a play on Marxist terminology, the joke was at the expense of the prevailing liberal optimism and the hope that international trade would generate a world of *doux commerce*, a prospect which Hont believed was no less utopian than the communist expectation of a radiant future beyond the state. The Janus-faced nature of the nation state, being both the guardian of justice domestically and an actor operating in an anarchic realm of power politics, meant that the reciprocal logic of trade was continually inflected by the zero-sum logic of war. As a result of the military revolution and the rise of international commerce in the seventeenth century, a bridge had been formed between the state's outward might and the administration of its internal resources, a bridge that became treacherous in the eighteenth century with the advent of public debt financing, which enabled the state to exceed its natural power through borrowing but possibly also exceed its ability to pay, thus jeopardising the prosperity, liberty and future survival of the very community whose interest it had been raised to promote. What Hume had called 'jealousy of trade', in short, was ultimately the result of the inherent weakness of national territorial legitimacy.

The problem with the modern discourse of rights and needs – with both liberalism and socialism – was that it was ideologically disposed to perceive this 'crisis' of the nation state as a pathological crisis, as a crisis which invoked a solution, either in the form of nation states ultimately exiting the state of nature and acquiescing to international law or simply exiting history altogether.[104] But between the utopia of a perfect solution and the dystopia of a total war, there was a third option which had no real name but which could be described as 'a happy escape from death, which falls short of achieving a utopian return to real health'.[105] The language of this third option, Hont believed, was 'reason of state', a discourse that had migrated from Renaissance republicanism to modern natural jurisprudence, and which had been an integral part of the political economy of both Hume and Smith. As Hont wrote in his introduction to *Jealousy of Trade* in 2005:

---

[103] Hont, 'The Permanent Crisis of a Divided Mankind', p. 169.
[104] On the influence of Reinhart Koselleck on Hont's thinking regarding the crisis of the nation state, see Lasse S. Andersen, 'Hont and Koselleck on the Crisis of Authority', *Journal of the Philosophy of History* 17/3 (2023): 357–379.
[105] Hont, 'The Permanent Crisis of a Divided Mankind', p. 169.

Introduction   41

Hume, Smith and their contemporaries wanted to explain how the conflation of the logics of war and trade arose in the seventeenth century and why it was so difficult to exorcise them afterward. They also hoped to discern the future of international economic competition. Their explanations of the past and projections for the future proceeded hand in hand. Hume and Smith's denunciation of jealousy of trade is still interesting because it is neither hysterically realist nor smugly utopian. The *Wealth of Nations* is a book not about perpetual peace but about competitive economic strategy. In his book Smith weighed the odds for national survival in global markets.[106]

Much like Hume's original essay, *Jealousy of Trade* was both a restatement and a reassessment of earlier ideas. As such, the book's long introduction was largely the result of Hont turning his attention to the language of 'reason of state', which he did in earnest in the spring of 1993, when he organised a major conference in Cambridge on 'The Politics of Necessity and the Language of Reason of State'.[107] In his opening address to the attendees, Hont likened the present-day political situation to the state of acute anxiety that prevailed in Europe after the First World War. It was in this ominous atmosphere that Friedrich Meinecke had written his classic account of *Die Idee der Staatsräson in der neueren Geschichte* (1924).[108] The subsequent marginalisation of the 'reason of state' tradition, largely a result of the utopian dreams of the twentieth century, was a problem that urgently needed to be remedied as the century drew to a close:

At the end of the century we have no good reasons to be more complacent than he [Meinecke] was. History is not at an end, the problem of the Janus-faced nation state is still with us and it is a noticeable feature of the current political climate that reasons of state are yet again moving closer to the centre of our intellectual attention. Purely domestic conceptions of political order are poor devices for the dilemmas of modern states. This, of course, is regarded as a truism by specialists in international relations theory. What is startling, however, is that these concerns became marginalised in the history of political thought and that no history of reason of state on a comparable scale of theoretical and historical ambition has been written since Meinecke's book.[109]

---

[106] Hont, 'Introduction', *Jealousy of Trade*, p. 8.
[107] The conference was intended to 'consider the historical idiom of "reason of state" and the analytical problems it housed in relation to the historiographical gains made in "Cambridge School" studies of republicanism, natural jurisprudence and political economy'. See Hont, 'The Politics of Necessity and the Language of "Reason of State"', p. 4.
[108] Hont refused to use the book's chosen English title, *Machiavellism*, which he considered misleading and indicative of the historical sidelining of the 'reason of state' discourse.
[109] Hont, 'The Politics of Necessity and the Language of "Reason of State"', p. 2.

Completed after a decade of scholarly labour, *Jealousy of Trade* was Hont's attempt to deliver such an ambitious history, placing his earlier work more directly in the context of the language of reason of state – a language that compromised the tunnel-walls of Cambridge historiography and therefore held the potential to realise the kind of synoptic, historical vision that Hont had sought to restore since his time as a student in Budapest.[110] The result would not have been the same, however, if he had not first explored the contours and limitations of the 'old socialist tradition', an intellectual recovery that he hoped – as do we – would make an impact and cause people to 'ponder on the meaning of such a term as "socialist"'.[111]

---

[110] See Hont's preface to the Japanese translation of *Jealousy of Trade*, IHA/Hont/520.
[111] See Chapter 7, this volume.

1 Theoretical History and Natural Law in the Scottish Enlightenment

First of all I want to say thank you to Professor Rüsen and the University of Bochum for the invitation to give a lecture about our work in Cambridge. I understand from Professor Rüsen that the interest of this seminar is in theories of history and historiography. I also understand that you have a special interest in current interpretations of the theoretical and historiographical achievement of the so-called Scottish Enlightenment, that is, the achievement of those two generations of brilliant Scottish historians and political economists in the eighteenth century whose catalogue would stretch from Francis Hutcheson to Dugald Stewart and Lord Lauderdale and in between would include such names as David Hume, Adam Smith, William Robertson, Sir James Steuart, Lord Kames, Adam Ferguson, John Millar and Thomas Reid. Every single one of these authors had something important to contribute to the shaping of modern European consciousness; they were all influential in their own time, both home and abroad. Their contribution would add up to an extraordinarily comprehensive enterprise in the founding of modern philosophy, history writing and what nowadays we call the social sciences, including economics, or political economy. A proper lecture on the character of their historical *Weltanschauung* (worldview) should thus give an account of their moral epistemology, their historicised theory of human nature, or philosophical anthropology, their jurisprudence, their theory of citizenship and the forms of government, their philosophy of religion, their political economy and last, but not least, their extensive historiographical writing, including their theory of history in the narrower sense. Such an exercise would take up not one lecture but a whole lecture course. Instead of trying to do the impossible, the present lecture will be devoted to the problem of the ideological origins of one particular bit of their theory of history, the so-called four stages theory of history, or more precisely the four stages theory of the history of property.

What is the four stages theory? Somewhat loosely defined, it is the following. The formation of modern property relationships went through four stages of social organisation, that of (1) hunting and gathering,

(2) pasturage, (3) agriculture and, finally, (4) commerce. These stages of social development depict four major types of the mode of subsistence in human societies. The legal mirroring of each major mode of subsistence appears in different degrees and kinds of property ownership. This is the primary version of the four stages theory. On this fundamental mode of subsistence – and type of property system correlate – several further steps of the four stages theory were built. Each mode of subsistence and property system possesses its characteristic system of justice, its characteristic system of manners and moral psychology, its characteristic mode of government and, finally, its characteristic type of military organisation. The stages are types of societies and, as sort of ideal types, represent a sequential order, starting from hunting and gathering and concluding in commercial society. Each stage is represented as comprehensively different from the others, but in the analysis of any of the stages no strong prioritisation of causal determination can be demonstrated. The various facets of a stage, the mode of subsistence, the system of property, the system of justice, the form of government and military organisation are represented to be corresponding to each other, rather than determining each other in an ascending order. All the facets were perhaps comprehended as the particular manners of a society. Nonetheless, the mode of subsistence, the way a society advanced in the conquest of the material environment, was seen as the clearest indicator of the overall limits of each of the stages.

It is not difficult to see why this eighteenth-century theory caught the attention of modern theorists. It seems to be quite clearly a theory of history which puts great emphasis on the material foundations and economic organisation of societies. Its affinity to the historical materialism of the Marxists was increasingly highlighted by historians of social theory, from Werner Sombart to a number of present-day Anglo-Saxon authors, most prominently by the New Zealander and Marxist economist Ronald Meek.[1] Some, such as Roy Pascal before the Second World War, claimed the so-called Scottish School as the direct progenitors of Marx.[2] Others, such as Norman Levine, tried to prove that there was a radical break between the type of historical theory involved in the

---

[1] Ronald L. Meek, 'The Scottish Contribution to Marxist Sociology', in Meek, *Economics and Ideology and Other Essays* (London: Chapman & Hall, 1967), pp. 34–50; *Turgot on Progress, Sociology, and Economics* (Cambridge: Cambridge University Press, 1973); *Social Science and the Ignoble Savage* (Cambridge: Cambridge University Press, 1976); 'Smith, Turgot, and the "Four Stages" Theory', *History of Political Economy* 3/1 (1971): 9–27, republished in *Smith, Marx and After: Ten Essays in the Development of Economic Thought* (London: Chapman & Hall, 1977), pp. 18–32.
[2] Roy Pascal, 'Property and Society: The Scottish Historical School of the Eighteenth Century', *The Modern Quarterly* 1/2 (1938): 167–179.

four stages theory of property and the historical materialism, or socio-economic determination of history, espoused by Karl Marx himself.[3] There is a teleology – or inverse teleology – involved somewhere in these claims, therefore I would not like to accept their framework of argument, but if I had to put my money on a thesis in this context, I would choose continuity rather than discontinuity between the eighteenth century and Marx. Somewhat frivolously, but nonetheless not without some truth, one can fruitfully see Marx as the major eighteenth-century-type thinker of the nineteenth century. Be that as it may, a more general perspective of continuity cannot be denied. In the rise of the four stages theory one can spot an apparent shift in Western theorising from a more 'political' to a more 'economic' or, if you want, a more 'sociological' conception of modern society. This is a common feature of economic liberalism – a primarily eighteenth-century product, whose 'manufacture', so to speak, was helped greatly by such Scottish theorists as David Hume and Adam Smith – and of Marxism of virtually any *bona fide* variety. Thus, in a longer perspective, the rise of the four stages theory heralded the eclipse of *sui generis* political theorising, at least in those paradigms of social thought in which it came to figure at all. And, not unimportantly, these paradigms became the dominant socio-political discourses of our age and the preceding century. Quite bluntly, any political discourse which takes the economic sphere as explained first by political economy and later by economics will end up with serious problems. It will have great problems in explaining the limits of the political. Hence, I would contend it would be sooner or later found to be based on some sort of four-stages-theory-of-history type of historical theory. In this sense, economic liberalism and Marxism are in the same boat. Any enquiry, therefore, which tries to shed light on the origins of the four stages theory of history will help us in clarifying the simultaneous crisis of liberal and Marxist political theory and perhaps will hold the key to the exit from this unhappy impasse.

This perspective would not make sense on the basis of our old understanding of eighteenth-century economic liberalism, or of the eighteenth century in general for some, as fundamentally anti- or a-historicist. The commonplace view of classical political economy, shaped so strongly by the Scottish Enlightenment, is that it was based on a concept of

---

[3] [Norman Levine attended a King's College Research Centre seminar in 1980 at which he presented a paper on 27 November entitled 'The Disjunction between Marx and Scottish Historical Theory'. Levine resided in Cambridge at the time, and on 17 March 1981 he gave a similar talk, this time entitled 'The Disjunction between Marx and the Scottish Historical School'. Levine published the results of his research in 'The German Historical School of Law and the Origins of Historical Materialism', *Journal of the History of Ideas* 48/3 (1987): 431–451.]

human nature which lacked any meaningful historical dimension. My assumptions are precisely the opposite. We owe a substantial chunk of our modern historical consciousness to political economy. Any historical sensitivity which is roughly of the same kind or of the same order as that of Marxism – and nowadays the social sciences are all based on such types of historical theories – is a historical sensitivity which was first nurtured by the political economy of the Enlightenment. Four stages theories abound in the historiography of the second half of the eighteenth century; nonetheless, when it was used by a Robertson or a Gibbon, and many others, it was applied theory. It is simply the case empirically that the best expressions of the four stages theory are to be found in the work of leading political economists: Adam Smith, Anne-Robert Jacques Turgot, Simon-Nicholas Henri Linguet, Pietro Verri, Antonio Genovesi and others. The four stages theory was inherently the theory of its last stage, commercial society. Evidently, the discourse of commercial society is political economy. Economics, however, the merchant or commercial discourse, as it were, was only one part of the classical synthesis of political economy, just as it is only a part of Marxism. For simplicity's sake, one can look at political economy as consisting of two major components. Undoubtedly, it is an explanation, indeed the explanation *par excellence* of commercial society, or capitalism if you want. It may be dynamic in its internal explanatory framework, but it is essentially an uncovering of the logic of the structure of market society. Without an intent for such a causal explanation no theory of modernity can exist. The other major component of political economy is a theory of how and why this structure came into being. In the political economy of Adam Smith, just as in the straight historiography of David Hume, William Robertson and Edward Gibbon, this genetic explanation or discourse had two components. One part of their effort went into a straightforwardly historical explanation of the development of modern Europe since the fall of the Western Roman Empire, traversing the history of feudalism, the rise of the cities and the new trade routes up to the formation of the new commercial order and its various trade and credit institutions in the sixteenth, seventeenth and eighteenth centuries. Book III of the *Wealth of Nations* is a prime example of such an exercise.

Another part of this historical component of political economy was invariably a historical theory of the four stages type. The essential element of this was the comparative intent built into it. There was no other way of defining what was – and what was not – commercial society without comparing it to other socio-economic systems. The main types of human activity directly comparable to living from commerce, that is, from marketing products, was to live from agriculture or from shepherding or from hunting and gathering. To explain systematically and causally how commercial society worked meant showing why it was different from other, logically anterior stages of social organisation. This exercise was no less historical than historical materialism. You may say that neither of them constitutes genuine history, and in some sense I might agree, but you will nonetheless have to show what can be taken then as a genuine theory of history, that is, a conceptual grid designed to explain historical phenomena, if this cannot. This theoretical or philosophical history was essential for the eighteenth-century political economist in order to provide an assessment of modernity. Assessment does not mean condemnation or legitimation; what it means is an opening up of the field for controversy by providing an understanding of each system on its own, suggesting that history traversed these choices not only sequentially but also in a parallel fashion. What is of crucial importance here is not the coexistence of societies or sub-societies belonging to different stages of organisation and manners. This mattered too. But what made the four stages theory cardinally important for the eighteenth-century political economist and philosophical historian was the coexistence (in their own highly civilised fourth stage) of ideologies extolling the property system, the manners, the mode of government, the personality structure, or whatever, of societies other than fourth-stage commercial regimes. Thus, the theory of stages was not simply a logical derivative of the analytical discourse of markets, which was, to a large extent, already in existence in Scholastic 'just price' theories and seventeenth-century merchant and governmental civil servant pamphleteering. Scottish political economy was the heir of at least three different major languages of social discourse for assessing commercial modernity, the anti-protectionist, free-trade pamphleteer's tradition being only one of them. The other two – as it was demonstrated convincingly by the previous generation of intellectual historians on the Enlightenment and on the Scottish eighteenth century – were the tradition of modern Protestant jurisprudence and the discourse of what John Pocock has named 'civic humanism', the post-Renaissance political language of the activist republican citizenry.

The distinctive Scottish contribution was to take the problems of justice and virtue posed in these two languages and propose a unified interpretation – sometimes that of reconciliation, sometimes that of a hard and cruel choice – of the value preferences in the language of markets and the market division of labour. Thus, in the four stages theory, or perhaps in its contextualisation in political economy, economic, jurisprudential and moral-political discourses were tightly interwoven in a richly synoptic insight. As a consequence, the four-stages-theory type of historical consciousness was deeply built into all of these facets of their theory and served as a general vehicle of historicisation for the general discourse on society. This general historicisation was as distinctive and persuasive as that of Marx and, given the hard facts of historical chronology, it had to be, in some way or another, the origin of the Marxian total-historical discourse of capitalism. Nor was the eighteenth-century version apologetic of capitalism, or commercial society, in a way Marx was not. In fact, both the discourse of justice and the discourse of Aristotelian–Machiavellian citizen activism were laden with heavy criticism of the emerging new social order and its market-oriented underpinnings. Both the ancient *polis* ideal of the citizen and the gothic ideal of the warrior husbandman left deep echoes in the minds of those who shaped the four stages theory. They knew that the specialisation of the division of labour worked against the ideal of the unified personality, and they could see the damage done by commercial society to time-honoured institutions of justice and political participation. The awareness of these tensions in fact helped to underline the historicisation of the moral-political-economic discourse. What could a four-stages-theory type of historical vision answer to these critics?

Their answer was that these values, ideals, principles or institutional mechanisms cannot be applied in any society at any time by will but that they had to fit in with the mode of subsistence and the manners governing the society in question. This last keyword which I mentioned, manners, contains the answer to the charges issuing from the defenders of ancient citizenship. The political economists and their fellow historians redefined the notion of virtue involved in the republican discourse with the aid of the concept of manners. The farmer warrior of earlier times may have been free, the citizen of the ancient *polis* may have been heated by feelings of patriotism, but their manners were rude and unrefined. In the new commercial society, on the other hand, people interacted far more with their fellows, came into contact with far more objects, in fact products of those other people, and in general lived more complex and variegated lives, developing more and more aspects of their moral and psychological personality. In potentiality, if not yet in actuality as they well knew, commercial society could compensate the subject for the loss of ancient or gothic virtue by a perhaps infinite enrichment of their personality, the product of a multiplying and ever-more complex interaction with other persons and things. Modern manners were preferable to the ancient and feudal ones. Thus, there was a humanist core to the political economist's application of the four stages theory. It defended the position of the modern person against, if not the personal ideals of the past, then against their actual past *persona* as uncovered by theoretical history. In one of the most famous and relevant applications of the four-stages-theory perspective, Adam Smith argued that the labouring poor of commercial society, despite the oppressive inequality surrounding them, were significantly better off enjoying the minimal comforts of life required by a decent way of living than the equal and free savages, or even their master, the savage king, the ruler of 10,000 lives.[4]

There is no time here to tell how political economists and historians developed a typology of human passions appropriate to the four stages, or how they explained the human destiny in commercial societies. Essentially the language of manners, the key language of the social discourse of the second half of the eighteenth century, gave them a neat framing which helped to develop their arguments with compelling rhetoric. Modern manners were said to be civilised or cultured, humane and polite. Thus, the top end of the chronology encompassing the four stages theory was occupied by civilisation. The beginnings were described as the age of savagery, barbarism, the age of rude society. The story was told as an ascent, even if contradictory ascent, from rudeness to refinement, from barbarism to culture or civilisation. This framework was perhaps the most general idiom for eighteenth-century theorists. Adam Ferguson, who evacuated the terrain of political economy in favour of David Hume and Adam Smith, wrote his history of refinement, as it was first titled, or his history of civil (i.e. civilised) society, precisely in these terms. While *he* attacked, Smith defended some of the institutions of civilised society, such as the standing army, but Smith framed the version of the four stages theory that appeared in the *Wealth of Nations* in the same language of barbarism, rudeness and civilisation. There was nothing especially Scottish about this framing. It is well known how strongly Ferguson plagiarised Montesquieu, and of course Smith was also familiar with the language of Montesquieu and Rousseau, just to mention these two users of the language of civilisation. The barbarism/civilisation framing of the four stages theory gave enormous rhetorical power to this idiom. Choices relating to the institutions of commercial society ever since, and I believe up to now, are presented as choices between barbarism or civilisation. In the name of the systemic explanations of the four stages theory, critics of civilisation are always shown to lack understanding of the barbaric consequences of their critique. Because of the close correlation between the four stages theory and the analytical part of political economy, economics appears as the science of the internal logic of the key institution of modern civilisation, the market, while the four stages theory itself appears as the theory of the rise of civilisation. The kind of historicism associated with this kind of historical theory became

---

[4] Smith, *WN*, 'Introduction and Plan of the Work', 4; *LJ*(A), vi.26–27; *LJ*(B), 212, 287.

firmly embedded in the barbarism versus civilisation choice. Yet again I would like to call attention to the fact that this is a crucial feature of Marxian Marxism as against all other kinds of socialism and communism which are feeding on pre-Marxist roots. It was the young Marx of the 'Paris Manuscripts' who accused the crude socialists and communists that their levelling aims would only create universal poverty (remember Adam Smith here) and would destroy *'Bildung und Zivilisation'*.[5] Marx's notion of the future cannot be understood without realising that it was firmly built on the civilisation option rather than on a primary critique of civilisation. What he wanted was rather a synthesis of the two, built on the primacy of preserving civilisation. This, however, is not the place or time to discuss the merits or demerits of his own positive theorising. The upshot of this present discussion is rather this. Yet again we see that classical economic liberalism and Marxian Marxism share a common paradigm of concepts. The one cannot really be used to criticise the other. Rather, one should try to understand the origins and nature of the unified idiom as such. Any step forward, if such a step is possible at all, should build on such a focused understanding of the historicised stages theory underpinning the economics of market civilisation.

Now I turn to the second part of my title, natural law. We should ask the following: where can we find the origins of the four-stages-theory type of theoretical history that was practised in the Scottish and other Enlightenments? Strict four-stages theories, that is, the ones that explicitly nominated a fourth stage and called it the commercial one, appeared only in the 1750s. Even then, very explicit discussions of the theory were rather rare. This sudden emergence of such a basic theory is strange and calls for an explanation. Ronald Meek, who tried to explain the origins of the theory, did notice that the first appearances of the theory in Scotland were in legal treatises and textbooks and that in general he suspected that Smith borrowed the fundamentals of the theory from Grotius, Pufendorf and Locke, the natural jurists.[6] Meek's view was that these juristic anticipations were so vague that they could not have constituted the origins of the theory. Some other external factor, Meek assumed, must have sensitised Smith and Turgot before they could see these scattered passages in natural law compendiums. I think Meek is wrong here. We are coming up against a difficulty similar to the one related to the notion that classical political economy is inherently anti-historical. The twin notion of this is that modern – that is, early modern, or to use a now unfashionable word, baroque – natural law was also fundamentally ahistorical. Such a

---

[5] Marx, *MECW* 3, p. 295; *Paris Manuscripts*, p. 346 ('Private Property and Communism').
[6] Meek, *Social Science and the Ignoble Savage*, pp. 99–130.

belief would obviously prevent anybody from seeing the natural law origins of the four stages theory.

To reconstruct the role of a theory of history in modern natural law is not all that simple a task. For the sake of simplicity, I would like to identify two key moves in the ideological structure of the natural law of Grotius, Pufendorf and their contemporaries. Let us see first why they think that natural law as a concept was necessary. I think it is important to realise that seventeenth-century Protestant natural law was designed to combat scepticism. Anti-Aristotelian scepticism, whose most influential representative was perhaps Pierre Charron, and whose symbol was seen in the ancient sceptical philosopher Carneades, argued for a wholly relativistic notion of justice and law. For them, actual right was just might, law was a matter of opinion, and its actual codification was created by crafty individuals. In their view, the multiplicity of human social organisational types, of religions, of laws, proved that no such thing as a general natural law could exist. Since the Aristotelian moral code could not save universality and morality, as it did for Renaissance humanists and Spanish Scholastics, Grotius and his followers had to find a new way of combating radical moral scepticism. The solution that wise and virtuous man had nothing to rely upon except the customs and manners of their own society did not seem, in Grotius' eyes, to safeguard justice. Grotius – and later a group of thinkers who gathered in France around Marin Mersenne (Descartes, Gassendi and Hobbes among them) – thought of a new way of combating scepticism by taking seriously their fundamental starting point. Grotius was looking for an empirical not an *a priori* metaphysical foundation of general morality, and he found it in the favourite argument of the sceptics. Every human being in society cared about his self-preservation, argued Grotius, and this fact made self-interest the primary basis of man's moral existence everywhere. What this entailed was that man was required to abstain from harming others. This was a minimalist theory of sociability. Both characteristics of Grotius' new intermediary level natural law are important. It started from a fact of life, that is, generally observable interest in self-preservation and sociable life, and it was also minimalist in its core content. It was this minimalist content of natural law which made it an intellectual successor to the moral relativists inside the natural law tradition. If there were no basic natural laws outside the minimalist core discussed in the 'Prolegomena' to *On the Law of War and Peace* (1625), all starting from the fact of law rather than from reason, then the natural world which man inherited from God had to be without social institutions.

Men possessed property in themselves and in the immediate necessaries of life, but every other type of property and institution had to be the result of human bargaining processes. The consequences of such a model appear as contradictory to the modern mind. On the one hand it entailed that the type of rights which existed before government was the same type which later societies with governments had, and thus governments were seen to have arisen from the society of the state of nature in order to protect these pre-government rights. At the same time, building on the supposition of pre-government sociability and organisation, every later step was seen as man-made and justified by long custom, by the fact of sustained empirical existence. Within the minimalist core constraints of the self-preservation dictate, the miraculous variety of human institutions could all be seen as proper subjects for the natural law theory of society. We can see in the moral sceptic tradition the parallel structure for any argument attacking total historical relativism. Montesquieu and his Scottish followers argued repeatedly that the stages theory was a tool to organise the multiplicity of social experience observable in history and that without it disciplined social argument would be impossible. Similarly, Marx's answer to the *Rechtsnihilismus* (rights nihilism) of the German historical school of law was eventually his historical materialism, his stages theory of history with their appropriate legal representation.[7]

The other reason for Grotius and his followers to introduce theoretical history to natural law was also connected with their tendency to start from observable empirical reality. The world they lived in was the world of individualism and of private property. Was this legitimate or illegitimate in natural law? This question had to be asked because of the great relevance of the communitarian tradition for theorists of the natural law of property. The basic axiom of Christian natural law was the one which was enshrined in the biblical Book of Genesis: God gave the Earth to Mankind in Common. Thus, if somebody took the position that God's law was immutable, then it followed, as it was argued by all sorts of radicals and at least on a theoretical level by Catholic theorists, that God's gift of the Earth to mankind in common actually prescribed an access to property for everybody forever. This kind of logic was turned on its head by the radical right-wing arguments of Robert Filmer and a few other thinkers in Europe. If the presence of private property was a fact, and God's law was immutable, then private property had to rule mankind's fate effectively from day one of the creation. This argument, although sometimes described by historians as traditionalist, was a distasteful innovation for most seventeenth-century natural jurists. Grotius had good reasons to develop his theory on quite different tracks. In the

---

[7] Marx, *MECW* 1, p. 203 ('The Philosophical Manifesto of the Historical School of Law' [1842]).

Mare liberum (1609) he wanted to prove that the oceans were of a common nature, free for each and any nation to use. On a more intellectual level, he well knew that history suggested that early societies indeed were in some sense communitarian and lacked the institution of modern property rights. The solution he provided, which Pufendorf, Locke and many others later developed further, can be explained in two steps.

First, he wanted to avoid the conclusion that the communitarian utopias of his time were derivatives of primeval communism; he argued that the real historical record of early societies, to the extent that they were accessible through the ancient poetic tradition, proved that those societies did not exhibit the analytical features of the modern system of private property or the modern system of group communal property. Whatever those early societies had as serving the place of modern property, it was not property in the same sense. This move entailed the design of a new language of social description for early societies and highlighted how different modern societies were from that of the primeval and ancient world. What Grotius and Pufendorf could leave in place was, however, that these societies were communitarian in some non-modern sense. The new notion of community was that of a 'negative community', a society operating on the basis of treating its natural endowment as *res nullius*, as no man's land. Men were quite rightfully using nobody's property by creating possession only, not exclusive property.

The second major step of Grotius' intellectual strategy then could start off from this reinterpreted version of the traditional communitarian origins of mankind and show, by invoking the tools of a theoretical history, how from a stage of no property mankind could reach historically the stage at which property could come into existence. This account was governed by the technical construction of the Roman law of property. In a full sense, only God had 'property', since only he was the maker of the earth. The rule was that the maker, the person whose labour created something, was by definition its owner. When men only consumed the natural products of God's creation, they only used God's property through possession. This was the stage of gathering natural fruits and hunting animals but not creating new objects through labour. What is more, each of these acts were on-off possessions. Usufruct means the sustained and repeated use of the products of a natural asset without owning the asset itself. The shepherds had such a use of the environment and the animals. They could enclose pasture for their herd, for example. Property means the right of use and usufruct of the asset itself for a humanly unlimited time. The crucial asset for any human society is land itself. Property appears when land can be taken into permanent individuated use. This is the stage of agriculture. In a primary sense, this theory of the history of the origins of property rights could run through three stages: the use, usufruct and ownership of the natural endowment of man. We, too, live in this last stage, when food is produced for self-preservation by agriculture based on the legal rights and economic incentives provided by private or group communal property. The fourth stage is parasitical on this third. It appears when not everybody can have access to land anymore. These people could only own their body and their labour and could access provisions only through exchanging the artisanal products of their labour for food. When this process is inaugurated as a mode of subsistence for a significant group in society and their survival is absolutely dependent on this exchanging activity, then we can talk about a fourth stage, the stage of exchange or commerce, or if you like, a *Verkehrsgesellschaft*. The natural jurists did not explicitly call this the fourth stage. Rather, they simply described it as the process of the rise of cities, the division of labour, the emergence of luxury and artificial, new needs. Quite clearly, the discourse about the origins of capitalism was inaugurated.

The intellectual strategy of mitigating moral and cultural scepticism and the need to fight communitarian utopias thus produced a sort of theoretical history within the corpus of modern natural law. In the concept of 'negative community' they could find the option of a flexible beginning for history, so to speak. The process of leaving the negative community beginnings of mankind took a long time, natural jurists, like Pufendorf, argued, and their description of the stages in mankind's development through time was by definition a 'theoretical history'. The theory of the origins of property which served as the backbone of this history was the occupation theory of property. Occupation through labour was an important element in it. The natural law theorists explained how the growing needs of man led to the invention of new labour processes, new types of 'occupations' of God's gift to mankind. The emphasis shifted from contracts to the theorisation of the forms of labour which created property and to the underlying moral psychology of motivation. A new, civil jurisprudence emerged, focusing on man's sociability and division of labour, making it possible to carve out this theoretical history from its juristic and theological framing. The concept which provided the new frame for these histories was the concept of *Kultur* or 'civilisation'. The Latin concept of *cultura*, defining the direction of mankind's ascent from rudeness to refinement, was invented and first properly theorised by Samuel Pufendorf. Politeness, refinement, taste – all the eighteenth-century keywords of theoretical history emerged from this comparative concept of *cultura* versus barbarism. The discourse on primeval communism and the rise of private property, a discourse revolving around the contrast between possession and property and various ways of occupying through labour, took on board the complex eighteenth-century theory of passions and interests and at the end emerged as the philosophical history of *Kultur* and civilisation. From then on it lived a separate life in political economy and later in Marxism and the rising social sciences. Nevertheless, we should not forget about its origins in Roman law, its theory of property, and the Aristotelian theory of exchange, markets and prices, which complemented it. Both the advantages and the limitations of stages theories of civilisation (currently the most popular of these is historical materialism) are the advantages and limitations of the original Western theory of property and markets, a theory of very ancient lineage and very ancient contradictions built into it. The same, in a narrower sense, applies to our understanding of the theoretical history of the Scottish Enlightenment. Largely but not exclusively, it was a fruit of the Scottish encounter with seventeenth-century natural jurisprudence and with its eighteenth-century follow-up debates on primitivism, sociability, passions, interests and the artificial foundations of property rights. Yet again, scepticism and relativism found an answer there in a systematised, philosophical vision of history, designed as a guidance for clear-headed theoretical vision.

Note on Chapter 1

This paper was given at the University of Bochum (Ruhr-Universität, Bochum) in West Germany at some time during the King's College Research Centre project on political economy, probably after July 1984. Professor Jörn Rüsen, who had invited Hont to West Germany, served as professor of modern history at the University of Bochum from 1974 to 1989 and was himself a contributor to the 1984 workshop on 'The Identity of Political Economy: Between Utopia and the Critique of Civilisation'. The paper introduces many of Hont's ideas related to the *Culture, Needs and Property Rights* project, and for this reason it serves as an ideal introduction – as Hont's own introduction in fact – to the subsequent papers in this volume.

2   Samuel Pufendorf's Jurisprudential Theory of History

The Nature of the Link between Natural Jurisprudence and Classical Political Economy

In recent writings on the sources and origin of eighteenth-century political economy a great emphasis has been laid on the contribution of republican political science to the understanding of the mechanism and dangers of credit creation. Civic humanism is said to be the discourse which pushed the concerns of the modern money economy into the limelight of English political pamphleteering. Be that as it may, not even the most extreme partisans of the civic humanist interpretation of the formation of political economy would deny the existence of a conceptual link between the mobile property theories of Augustan political economists and the natural law foundations of the property theory of classical political economy. The civic humanist contribution to the new discourse cannot, in fact, be understood without a clarification of this link.

Property and political economy are notions closely wedded in virtually all histories of eighteenth- and nineteenth-century political and economic thought. Similarly, the idea that the historical origins of political economy ought to be sought in the natural jurisprudence tradition of the seventeenth century and in its Scholastic antecedents has gained wide currency in modern historiography. An important exponent of this view was the late Joseph Schumpeter (1883–1950), who in his monumental *History of Economic Analysis* (1954) highlighted his assessment of the relative unoriginality of Adam Smith's political economy by a demonstration of the close anticipation of its chief arguments in modern natural law. 'It will suffice to advert to the well-rounded presentation in Pufendorf's treatise', he wrote:

> Distinguishing value in use and value in exchange (or *pretium eminens*), he [Pufendorf] lets the latter be determined by the relative scarcity or abundance of goods and money. Market price then gravitates toward the cost that must normally be incurred in production. (...) He goes on to discuss various problems of public policy, such as the repression of luxury by sumptuary laws, the

regulation of monopolies, craft guilds, inheritance, entails, population. Good sense and moderation are invariably in evidence as is also a sense of the historic flux of things. The welfare aspect is always kept in view. Again, we behold an embryonic *Wealth of Nations*.[1]

Schumpeter was right in pointing to the existence of such 'economic' elements in Pufendorf's jurisprudence and highlighting the similarity between them and certain preoccupations in the *Wealth of Nations*. Nonetheless, we cannot accept the all too easy identification of these aspects of Pufendorf's jurisprudence, as well as the *Wealth of Nations*, as an early form of economics. The underlying argument in Schumpeter is quite clearly the assertion that in Pufendorf we already encounter a bounded set of propositions about an autonomous economy. What he implies is a continuous 'economic' tradition stretching back to the natural jurists of the seventeenth century and even further. In Schumpeter we encounter a teleological historian of a continuous and incremental economic tradition.

In order to avoid putting such a construction on our explanation of the natural law foundations of classical political economy, it is worthwhile to investigate briefly how this teleological discourse of an incremental 'economic' tradition is constructed in the histories of political economy. Historians of economic thought who have considered this question of the boundary of economic argument within political economy have argued that its autonomy was constituted basically by three 'bracketing operations' which, while not explicitly stated in the texts themselves, nonetheless served as the effective and discernible procedures structuring them.

First, the political economists modelled economic behaviour on the simplifying assumption of rational self-interest, excluding the consideration of the deeper levels of human motivation from the field of economic analysis by taking human needs and specific preferences as given. While they did not use the term themselves, 'economic man' makes its appearance in their pages, notably, it is argued, in Smith's passage about our dinners depending not on the 'benevolence of the butcher, the brewer or the baker' but on their self-interest.[2] Furthermore, Smith, Hume and James Steuart distinguished implicitly between their technical analysis of economic man's behaviour within given income and price constraints and their moral assessment of his narrow and mean self-absorption. Thus, the fact that they evidently disapproved of his ignoble selfishness made no effective difference to the content of their economics. This procedure

---

[1] Joseph A. Schumpeter, *History of Economic Analysis* (Oxford: Oxford University Press, 1954), p. 122.
[2] Smith, *WN*, I.ii.2.

was not original to Adam Smith and the Scottish School; it is also to be found in the economic discourse of Nicholas Barbon and Dudley North in the 1690s and, as a bracketing operation, it paved the way for the establishment of the full autonomy of economic from moral discourse within the texts of political economy. At the same time the political economists assumed that economic man's propensities to truck, barter and exchange were innate characteristics of the species. Both Marxist critiques of political economy and standard histories of economic thought agree that this starting assumption enabled the political economists to bracket the question of how capitalist motivation was engendered historically as an issue extraneous to the economic modelling of contemporary behaviour.

The constitution of economic man as a historical constant was connected in turn to the second major 'bracketing operation', which was to distinguish economic theory from economic history. The deductive modelling of a static circulation and production process was kept distinct from the empirical history of the origins of the economy. The synchronic and diachronic dimensions were kept apart. There was plenty of empirical history in political economy, used as validation of certain deductive arguments, and there was in Book III of the *Wealth of Nations* a history of the natural progress of opulence in Europe since the fall of Rome, but it served a subsidiary and digressive role in relation to the economic core. This was so because political economists distinguished analytically between the shape an economic process could be predicted to take 'in the natural course of things' and the shape it actually assumed under different historical circumstances or in response to contingent political interventions. The deductive modelling of the former was the proper domain of economic analysis, while the empirical reconstruction of the latter was the domain of politics and history. The idea of 'natural' economic processes, therefore, was constitutive of the boundary between economic argument, political disquisition and historical excursus within political economy.

According to the histories of economic thought it was the continuity of these bracketing operations which gave unity to the classical economic tradition through all its subsequent debates and differences over the economic content of the Smithian inheritance. In his *Principles on Political Economy and Taxation* (1817), David Ricardo simply took for granted Smith's historical and political account of the origins of markets and their political and legal prerequisites, concentrating his analysis on an exclusively synchronic economic terrain. This terrain had already been constituted in the *Wealth of Nations* by Smith's modelling of 'natural' long-term economic processes in abstraction from contingent, short-term political and historical 'distortions'.

This argument that the economic core was structurally autonomous from other discourses in political economy depends on the contention that the economic core stood within and descended from a discrete tradition of economic discourse. Yet the economic tradition described by historians of economic thought was never the only, nor even the principal, site of discussion of human behaviour in its economic dimensions as far as the Scottish political economists were concerned. Besides the economic discourse on national economic policy, there were 'additional' sites like natural jurisprudence, for instance, in which the Scottish political economists encountered the questions they were trying to answer with the economic arguments of their political economy.

As a young professor in Glasgow, Smith transformed the jurisprudence curriculum he had inherited from his predecessor and former teacher, Francis Hutcheson, by importing the French rubric of 'police' and by considering under its heading those 'economic' regulations of the state, dictated not by natural laws of justice but by 'expediency'.[3] Smith's economic arguments were thus first presented to the world within a jurisprudential system. Even at the end of his life, Smith said that the purpose of the *Wealth of Nations* had been to give 'an account of the general principles of law and government, and of the different revolutions which they had undergone in the different ages and periods of society (...) in what concerns police, revenue and arms'.[4] The significance of this self-description on Smith's part becomes apparent if we also consider his observation that political economy was to be considered as a 'branch of the science of a statesman or legislator'.[5] At the very least, these remarks raise the question whether Smith considered the economy analytically separable from its legal and political structure. As a branch of the science of the legislator, political economy would seem to have been intended as an attempt to establish the rules of law and the policies of economic administration which would reconcile the 'natural liberty' of economic actors with the demands of strict justice.

In his jurisprudence lectures, Smith also sought to give his students a more plausible historical account of the origins of law and government than the hypothesis of the 'original contract' in the state of nature offered by certain strands of natural jurisprudence. In place of this highly rationalistic account of law and government originating as an act of deliberate choice by a hypothetical collectivity, Smith drew on William Temple, Bernard Mandeville, Montesquieu and Hume to construct an account of

---

[3] Smith, *LJ*(A), i.2; *LJ*(B), 5.
[4] Smith, *TMS*, VII.iv.37.
[5] Smith, *WN*, IV.1.

human institutions evolving as the willed but unconcerted consequence of the passage through four stages of human subsistence – hunting and gathering, pastoral, agricultural and commercial. Law was then understood as taking the shape required by the particular forms of acquisition, possession and exchange, which emerged at each stage. This conjectural history, it has been argued recently, came to serve as the 'frame of reference' for the economic argument in the *Wealth of Nations*.[6]

Because Smith located modernity within this conjectural paradigm, his task was not merely that of explaining the functioning of a capitalist economy in its static, synchronic dimension but also of accounting for its historical possibility in time. Moreover, the theoretical object of political economy was not the mode of subsistence within the fourth stage but the whole stage itself, that is, the interaction of mode of subsistence with manners, law and government. Its object was not an economy as such but 'commercial society' as a social formation, as a stage in history.

On this reading, therefore, Smith's political economy emerged within Scottish jurisprudence, taking up its conjectural history as the theoretical matrix with which to transform a narrowly economic discourse into a 'science of commercial society'. This 'science', in its Scottish form, retained the conceptual imprint of its jurisprudential origins, continuing to treat the economy as embedded in a structure constituted by its legal and political relations. However, a note of caution is in order here. An unthinking attempt to trace the derivation of classical political economy may easily miss its target if the crucial questions to be answered are not focused properly. By denying the validity of a teleological history of the incremental rise of early 'economics' we do not wish to obliterate the relevance of what is analytically 'economic' within political economy itself.

The currently fashionable, interpretative line on the *Wealth of Nations* as an element in a system of 'the science of the legislator' shows where the economic arguments were positioned within the *Theory of Moral Sentiments* and the Glasgow jurisprudence lectures before their final form in the *Wealth of Nations*. But it does not really explain what difference their original placement within other parts of the Smithian 'system'

---

[6] [It is unclear precisely whom Hont is referring to here, but a likely candidate is Duncan Forbes. From 1954 onwards, Forbes argued that 'The idea of the progress of society can be described as the historical frame of reference of the *Wealth of Nations* – a fact that seems to have been ignored in the long debate as to how far Smith's method is really deductive or empirical.' Duncan Forbes, 'Scientific Whiggism: Adam Smith and John Millar', *Cambridge Journal* 7 (1954): 648. Another likely candidate is Ronald L. Meek, see *Social Science and the Ignoble Savage* (Cambridge: Cambridge University Press, 1976), p. 219.]

made to their ultimate appearance in the *Wealth of Nations*, especially since, according to Smith's own memorandum of 1755, the key elements of 'the system of natural liberty' were formed in his mind before either the *Theory of Moral Sentiments* or the jurisprudence lectures.[7] The mere fact that Smith first taught 'economics' within jurisprudence does not resolve the vexed question of whether his 'natural price' modelling owes anything to the idiom of natural jurisprudence. As a matter of fact, contemporary readers of Smith and readers in the period after his death did not feel they had to read the *Theory of Moral Sentiments* in order to recover his assumptions about economic behaviour. These were clear enough in the *Wealth of Nations* itself. Nor does the fact that he, as well as Steuart, understood the modern economy as a stage in a conjectural history of progress necessarily mean that he did not distinguish the domain of economics from the domain of theoretical history.

Thus, the claim that political economy was a historicised discourse of 'commercial society', derived from the natural law tradition, does not resolve the question of the boundary and status of the 'economic'. Instead, it raises the question in a new and more interesting form. Without revising our view of where to look for the linkages between jurisprudence and political economy our interpretation can easily remain inconclusive, leaving the dominance of the old interpretations intact. The result might be a simple historiographic stand-off.

In repositioning the central questions connected with the issue of the jurisprudential origins of classical political economy we should ignore Schumpeter's references to the Pufendorfian formulations of price and value. We should rather return to his suggestion that Pufendorf had shown a strong interest in issues of welfare coupled with a strong sense of historical change. In Schumpeter's economic language, concentration on welfare comes very close to meaning that Pufendorf's strength was in the close attention he paid to issues of economic justice, to the issues of 'economic distribution' (although, of course, not to 'distributive justice' in its Aristotelian sense, which Pufendorf, following Grotius, excluded from the compass of natural jurisprudence).

That the issues of economic distribution and welfare in a historical perspective were also central to Smith's *Wealth of Nations* must be quite obvious to any careful reader of the opening pages of the book. As I have argued elsewhere, it was the distributional welfare paradox of commercial society that Smith identified – in his theory of morality, in his jurisprudence lectures and in the *Wealth of Nations* – as the central question to

---

[7] [The content of Smith's 1755 memorandum was partially published in Dugald Stewart's *Account of Smith*, IV.25.]

be explained, above all other purposes he might have had in mind.[8] The essence of the 'paradox' was the acute perception that commercial societies were more unequal ('unjust' in some sense) in their distribution of property and income than any other previous stage of society, and yet they remained capable of satisfying the necessary needs of those whose labour maintained and produced the wealth of society at a significantly higher level than any hitherto known society (i.e. they were 'just' in a historical perspective). Smith saw as his task the explanation of the historical 'fact' that inequality in property holding and in the distributive hierarchy was compatible in commercial societies with an adequate satisfaction of the necessary needs of wage earners within a free market system.

If it was in this compatibility that his claim for the 'justness' of commercial society was anchored, then we ought to look for the link between natural jurisprudence and classical political economy in the theoretical foundations which made the 'historical fact' of the ultimately beneficial distributive features of commercial society a possible object of explanation. We have to ask the question whether the welfare preoccupations of natural jurisprudence were, and if so in what way, the original *loci* from which the theoretical ramifications of Smith's solution for the paradox emerged. In other words, we have to clarify the debt which Smith's theory of the paradox of commercial society owed to the fundamental shape of natural jurisprudence's understanding of the history of property rights. In particular, we have to ask questions about the boundaries of Smith's theory of the 'justness' of commercial societies and about the history of the conceptualisation of the boundaries of welfare considerations in the property theories of natural jurisprudence.

We called Smith's statement a 'paradox'. The *Oxford English Dictionary* defines the relevant meaning of the word paradox as a 'statement contrary to received opinion, belief or expectation'. Smith's views would appear as a paradox only if they are, as indeed they were, set against the background of an expectation claiming that a society based on exclusive private property cannot be 'just' in the most general sense of the word; or at least that such a system cannot be expected to possess a system of welfare distribution which could be 'just' and at the same time be wholly in accordance with the jurisprudential boundaries of a system of exclusive private property at a historical stage where not everybody could expect to be an owner of private property in anything except his life, bodily strength and labour.

---

[8] István Hont and Michael Ignatieff, 'Needs and Justice in the *Wealth of Nations*: An Introductory Essay', in István Hont and Michael Ignatieff (eds.), *Wealth and Virtue: The Shaping of Political Economy in the Scottish Enlightenment* (Cambridge: Cambridge University Press, 1983), pp. 1–44.

In our effort to locate the link, or at least a fundamental link, between jurisprudence and political economy in the basic shape of their conceptions of justice, welfare and exclusive property rights, we are not without historical antecedents. It was not Schumpeter, nor Marx for that matter, who first argued that the shape of natural jurisprudence determined the boundaries of classical political economy. Shortly after the death of Adam Smith it was Dugald Stewart who first attempted to locate the origins of Scottish political economy in the jurisprudence tradition of the seventeenth century, in Grotius and particularly in Pufendorf's theory of the laws of nature and nations.[9] Nor do we strike out an entirely new path when we argue that the essence of this link should not be sought in the anticipation of the economic arguments of the *Wealth of Nations*. In his review essay on Stewart's dissertation on seventeenth-century moral and legal thought, James Mackintosh had already pointed to the way Stewart's theory of the jurisprudential origins of political economy can be best understood. 'The natural jurists', he wrote, indeed

> became, as Mr. Stewart states, the forerunners of the beneficent science of political economy, – spreading the same spirit which it breathes, and reaching, with a sort of practical coarseness, some of its results, – though their reasonings did not, we conceive, lead by any logical process to the establishment even of its first principles. The connection is rather historical than philosophical.[10]

Alternative Foundations: Aquinas and the Scholastic Tradition

The story begins not with the seventeenth-century Protestant natural law theorists whom the Scots explicitly claimed as their forebears but with the medieval Scholastic formulations, which the Protestant theorists, however reluctantly, had to engage with. It was Thomas Aquinas who set the initial terms of the debate on the origins and limits of property rights, and it is with Aquinas that we must begin, as many eighteenth-century participants in the grain debates, Condorcet for example, were aware. It is important to pay attention to this awareness of an alternative tradition in property right theorising throughout the eighteenth century. This can give a historical dimension to a debate which is usually seen as simply

---

[9] Dugald Stewart, 'Dissertation Exhibiting a General View of the Progress of Metaphysical, Ethical and Political Philosophy, since the Revival of Letters in Europe [1815–21]', in *The Collected Works of Dugald Stewart, Esq., F.R.S.S.*, ed. Sir William Hamilton, 11 vols. (Edinburgh, 1854–61), vol. I., pp. 170–187; See also 'Outlines of Moral Philosophy – Part III', *Lectures on Political Economy*, vol. 1, in *The Collected Works of Dugald Stewart*, vol. VIII., p. 5.

[10] James Mackintosh, 'Art. 9', *Edinburgh Review* (Sept. 1816), p. 237.

fought between radicals and the defenders of the order of exclusive private property rights. However, an emphasis on the radical opposition to private property would be misplaced in this context. The reference to an older tradition by Condorcet was directed against Jacques Necker, by no means a radical, and Condorcet's point was precisely to push the origins of the radical and paternalist position into the limelight. It was precisely the historical lineage of the debate which was shown up dramatically in his outraged accusations against Necker's *La legislation et le commerce des grains* (1775). 'What is certain', argued Condorcet, 'is that his principles on property lead to the legitimation of pillage, just as the Jesuit principles on compensation lead to the legitimation of theft. The charming thing is that his reasons are the same as those of the Jesuits.'[11] This historical reference was not spurious. The Jesuits had a long-standing reputation as 'defenders of theft'. Blaise Pascal's famous polemics against the Jesuits in the widely read *Provincial Letters* (1657) preserved the memory of the mid seventeenth-century debate between the Jesuits and the Jansenists on the obligation of charity. Pascal insisted that the Jesuits' justification of theft in times of necessity was simply intended to relieve the rich from the obligation to give alms. It made a joke of religion in order to gratify men's passions. Against the Jesuit endorsement of stealing even in 'grave, though not extreme, need', Pascal argued that

> there is hardly anyone who does not think his need is grave, and whom you therefore enable to steal with safe conscience. And even if you limited this licence solely to people who are genuinely in that state, it means opening the door to innumerable thefts, which judges would punish notwithstanding such grave need, and which you ought to repress all the more, bound as you are to uphold among men not merely justice but charity too, which is destroyed by this principle.[12]

The theoretical formulations giving rise to an organised system of almsgiving were the work of the early medieval church and its most authoritative statement, in Thomas Aquinas' *Secunda secundae* (second part of the second part) of the *Summary of Theology* (1485), which built a whole theory of property around the problem of satisfying the needs of the poor in times of necessity. For Aquinas the world was properly speaking God's property since he was the one who created it. He accepted that in a full sense 'dominion connotes power', and thus man does not naturally

---

[11] Marquis de Condorcet, 'Condorcet à Suard, 1775', in Theodore Besterman (ed.), *Studies on Voltaire and the Eighteenth Century*, Vol. 1 (Oxford: The Voltaire Foundation, 1955), p. 55. See also Keith Michael Baker, *Condorcet: From Natural Philosophy to Social Mathematics* (Chicago: Chicago University Press, 1975), p. 61.

[12] Blaise Pascal, *Provincial Letters*, trans. A. J. Krailsheimer (London: Penguin, 1967), pp. 124–125.

possess external goods: 'man has no power over external things, since he cannot change their nature'.[13] Therefore the rich man in the Bible was justly criticised for 'thinking that external goods were his absolutely as if he had not first received them from another, namely God'.[14] In the second step of his analysis, Aquinas allowed that Aristotle was right in his view that 'the possession of external things is natural to man' in the sense of use.[15] Material objects, he argued, 'can be looked at from the point of view of use and management, and in this regard man has a natural dominion over external things, for he has a mind and a will with which to turn them to his own account. They seem to be made for him in so far as imperfect things are for the sake of the more perfect.'[16] This allowed that the whole external world of man could be subsumed under the collective stewardship of the human species as a positive community.

When Aquinas turned to the problem of individual possession (*proprietas*) of goods, he qualified the radical line in earlier Church thinking which, in the work of St Basil for example, had denied that it was legitimate to preclude others from the use of common property.

> Basil says, *Rich people who regard common property as their own simply because they have been the first to occupy it are like those who prevent others from coming to the public games by arriving at the arena first and so appropriating what is meant for common use*. But it is not legitimate to preclude others from the use of common property.[17]

Basil's appearance in Aquinas' text had more relevance than a simple example of radical argument. Basil was actually opposing there the explanation of the origin of property from the principle of first occupation, favoured by Roman law, and used the framework of Cicero's famous metaphor of the public theatre to develop his Christian counterargument. In answer to that, Aquinas stressed his agreement with the idea that individuals should be only trustees of the world's resources. This enabled him to maintain a radical position on the question of theft in times of necessity. But recoiling from the full consequences of Basil's position, Aquinas qualified man's dominion over the use of external things by talking about man's two different competences in this respect. In the spirit of his main radical line, he again upheld the thesis that the 'use and management of property' was only legitimate 'in the common interest'. Individuals should only be trustees and stewards of the world's

---

[13] Aquinas, *ST*, 2a2æ.q.66.a.1.
[14] Ibid.
[15] Ibid.; Aristotle, *Politics*, 1256a.
[16] Aquinas, *ST*, 2a2æ.q.66.a.1.
[17] Aquinas, *ST*, 2a2æ.q.66.a.2.

resources, thus 'no man is entitled to manage things merely for himself, he must do so in the interest of all, so that he is ready to share them with others in case of necessity'.[18] But he also stressed man's competence 'to care for and distribute the earth's resources'. This second competence of man rendered private possession legitimate, for three reasons:

> First, because each person takes more trouble to care for something that is his sole responsibility than what is held in common by many – for in such a case each individual shirks the work and leaves the responsibility to somebody else, which is what happens when too many are involved.
> Second, because human affairs are more efficiently organised if each person has his own responsibility to discharge; there would be chaos if everybody cared for everything.
> Third, because men live together in greater peace where everyone is content with his task. We do, in fact, notice that quarrels often break out amongst men, who hold things in common without distinction.[19]

Aquinas was quoting here almost verbatim from Aristotle's *Politics*. He and Aristotle both construed individual property as deriving from a compact between members of society:

> Community of goods is said to be part of the natural law not because it requires everything to be held in common and nothing to be appropriated to individual possession, but because the distribution of property is a matter not for natural law but, rather, human agreement, which is what positive law is about (...) The individual holding of possessions is not, therefore, contrary to the natural law; it is what rational beings conclude as an addition to the natural law... (...) provided he is ready to share it; he sins only if he unreasonably prevents others from using it.[20]

Aquinas was in fact prepared to go with Aristotle a long way but not the whole way. When he set up the target thesis for refutation, Aristotle himself appeared in the dock:

> Aristotle says that *the very words for certain acts imply malice*, and he includes theft amongst them. But what is intrinsically evil cannot become good just because of some good end. Nobody may, therefore, steal to supply his basic needs.[21]

The tension created by introducing man's two competences was still present in Aquinas' answer, but on the whole he held to the opposite position to Aristotle:

---

[18] Ibid.
[19] Ibid.
[20] Ibid.
[21] Aquinas, *ST*, 2a2æ.q.66.a.7; Aristotle, *Nicomachean Ethics*, 1107a. [Hont has altered the translation by substituting 'basic needs' for 'basic necessities'.]

The dictates of human law cannot derogate from natural or divine law. The natural order established by God in his providence is, however, such that lower things are meant to enable man to supply his needs. A man's needs must therefore still be met out of the world's goods even though a certain division and apportionment of them is determined by law. And this is why according to natural law goods that are held in superabundance by some people should be used for the maintenance of the poor.[22]

This obligation to cater for the needs of the poor in cases of ordinary necessity could still allow and indeed made necessary a system of individual property for the already stated reasons of efficacy. There had to be a responsible management of the property held in trust to discharge the obligation of almsgiving: 'At the same time those who suffer want are so numerous and they cannot all be supplied out of one stock, and this is why it is left to each individual to decide how to manage his property in such a way as to supply the wants of the suffering.'[23]

However, in cases of extreme necessity, such as famines, human law was to be overruled altogether. In such situations, Aquinas' radical position of the original (positive) community of ownership re-established itself:

If, however, there is so urgent and blatant a necessity that the immediate needs must be met out of whatever is available, as when a person is in imminent danger and he cannot be helped in any other way, then a person may legitimately supply his own needs out of another's property, whether he does it secretly or flagrantly.[24]

Accordingly, the rich man who took prior possession of something that was common before was not at fault, providing he was ready to share it. He sinned only if he unreasonably prevented others from using it. Moreover, Aquinas argued that it was precisely the individuation of the world which made possible a responsible and productive management of God's estate. It was private individuation, in other words, which made it possible to adequately supply the needs of the distressed. Aquinas also explained that his position on the legitimacy of 'theft in necessity' was not to be regarded as a simple 'exception'. Any endorsement of private property systems was conditional on the acceptance of a priority of the needs of the whole community of mankind.

The history of modern European natural law can be understood as a series of attempts to rearrange the elements of the puzzle left by Aquinas. It was possible either to insist on an original positive community of goods and then to limit individual property rights according

---

[22] Aquinas, *ST*, 2a2æ.q.66.a.7.
[23] Ibid.
[24] Ibid.

to this first premise or, alternatively, to insist on the necessity of private property as a guarantee of the responsible management of man's resources and of peace in conditions of scarcity. The logical corollary of the first position was that men should restrict their needs to what is natural and necessary in order to always have a superfluity to distribute to the needy in times of scarcity, while the corollary of the second position was that private property created the incentives for raising the productivity of God's dominion in such a way that everyone's needs could be satisfied without a system of austerity.

Grotius: The Freedom of the Oceans and the Simplification of the Language of Scholastic Jurisprudence

At the beginning of the seventeenth century, Hugo Grotius, the 'founding father' of modern natural jurisprudence, took up and transformed these polarities in the Aristotelian and Thomist tradition. As we have seen, Aquinas had developed his property theory as an answer to the problem of theft in conditions of necessity. This too was an essential problem for Grotius. Swallowing some of his Protestant antipathy to Catholic doctrine, he agreed with Aquinas that 'if a man under stress of such necessity takes from the property of another what is necessary to preserve his own life, he does not commit a theft'. Grotius explained:

> The reason which lies in the back of this principle is not, as some allege, that the owner of a thing is bound by the rule of love to give to him who lacks; it is, rather, that all things seem to have been distributed to individual owners with a benign reservation in favour of primitive right. For if those who made the original distribution had been asked what they thought about this matter they would have given the same answer as we do.[25]

What made it possible for Grotius to argue the thesis that 'men in general possess any right over things which have already become the property of another' was the hypothesis that when men originally divided the goods and resources given to them in common, they had intended a 'benign reservation' according to which the rights of individual ownership were subordinated to the claims of natural equity in times of extreme necessity. As Grotius put it:

> Some perchance may think it strange that this question should be raised, since the right of private ownership seems completely to have absorbed the right which

---

[25] Grotius, *DJBP*, 2.2.6.4.

had its origin in a state of community of property. Such, however, is not the case. We must, in fact, consider what the intention was of those who first introduced individual ownership; and we are forced to believe that it was their intention to depart as little as possible from natural equity. For as in this sense even written laws are to be interpreted, much more should such a point of view prevail in the interpretation of usages which are not held to exact statement by the limitations of a written form.[26]

In effect, Grotius sought to historicise Aquinas' conception of man's two competences. In the original community of goods, man's competence as trustee of resources held in common was to the fore. In the historical development of human society and the unfolding of human needs, his second competence, the exclusive possession of scarce goods became necessary. In the original community of goods, Grotius argued,

each man could at once take whatever he wished for his own needs, and could consume whatever was capable of being consumed. The enjoyment of this universal right then served the purpose of private ownership; for whatever each had thus taken for his own needs another could not take from him except by an unjust act.[27]

If the whole purpose of using external goods was to satisfy human needs, it was obvious that the stability of any such arrangement of use depended on the stability of the needs structure underpinning it. No stable arrangement was possible if needs changed over time. A true common ownership of the external world was possible only through a natural or imposed constraint on human needs:

This primitive state might have lasted if men had continued in great simplicity, or had lived on terms of mutual affection such as rarely appears. Of these two conditions, one, exemplified in the community of property arising from extreme simplicity, may be seen among certain tribes in America, which have lived for many generations in such a condition without inconvenience. The second, again, exemplified in the community of property arising from affection, was formerly realized among the Essenes, afterward among the first Christians at Jerusalem; at the present time, also, by a goodly number who live an ascetic life.[28]

In this primitive stage of communal ownership, men were free from 'wicked excess of passion' and lived in a state of 'incorruption' and 'simplicity'. No toil burdened man. 'They lived easily on the fruits which the earth brought forth of its own accord.'[29]

---

[26] Grotius, *DJBP*, 2.2.6.1.
[27] Grotius, *DJBP*, 2.2.2.1.
[28] Ibid.
[29] Ibid.

'Men did not, however, continue to live this simple and innocent life', Grotius went on, beginning to historicise the picture.[30] The brutish life was succeeded by a passion for pleasure, by the emergence of new needs which could only be satisfied by labour: '[M]en were not content to feed on the spontaneous products of the earth, to dwell in caves, to have the body either naked or clothed with the bark of trees or skins of wild animals, but chose a more refined mode of life; this gave rise to industry, which some applied to one thing, others to another.'[31]

Grotius then proceeded to link the history of private property to the history of the passage of primitive peoples from the productive activities of hunting and gathering to pasturage and agriculture. First moveable objects were hived off from common ownership and lands for grazing became the property of different tribes. In the second step immoveable property became individuated by families within the same tribe. As men applied their industry to the land, disputes developed over the soil which each had occupied, and primitive harmony degenerated. A compact or agreement, either tacitly through acceptance of existing occupations or explicitly through formal collective division of communal land, became necessary to put an end to disputes.

> In fact, as soon as community ownership was abandoned, and as yet no division had been made, it is to be supposed that all agreed, that whatever each one have taken possession of should be his property. 'It has been granted', says Cicero, 'that each may prefer to acquire for himself, rather than for another, whatever contributes to the advantage of life; and in this there is no conflict with nature'. To this should be added the sentence of Quintilian: 'If this is settled, that whatever has come into a man's possession is the property of the possessor, certainly what is rightfully possessed is not taken away without injustice'.[32]

After this first compact, Grotius insisted that the division of property could not be repeated. It had to remain a unique act. Anything which had not yet been divided could afterwards only be turned into private property by occupation. As we have seen with reference to the 'interpretative charity' principle embedded in the 'benign reservation' formula, however, Grotius tried to reconcile private property rights with God's original intention to give the world to mankind to ensure the survival of each individual. Another such 'rider' on property rights was the obligation to allow freedom of the high seas and freedom of commerce in general. 'No one, in fact, has the right to hinder any nation at a distance. That such permission be accorded is in the interest of human society and

---

[30] Grotius, *DJBP*, 2.2.2.2.
[31] Grotius, *DJBP*, 2.2.2.4.
[32] Grotius, *DJBP*, 2.2.2.5.

does not involve loss to any one.'³³ Even in his early work on the freedom of the ocean, Grotius already recognised that a serious obstacle in the way of gaining acceptance to his theory of property rights was a confusion in the language of jurisprudence (and in everyday speech). The same vocabulary was used to describe all stages of the history of property regardless the distinct legal qualifications property assumed at each historical stage as mankind left its original simplicity. 'Owing to the poverty of human speech', he argued, 'it has become necessary to employ identical terms for concepts which are not identical. Consequently, because of a certain degree of similitude and by analogy, (...) expressions descriptive of our modern customs are applied to another right, which existed in early times.'³⁴

The most serious confusion was precisely between the jurisprudential description of primeval community arrangements and modern exclusive systems of property rights. The difference in the structure of 'rights' involved was fundamental. He highlighted the difference in very clear conceptual terms:

For in the present age, the term 'ownership' connotes possession of something peculiarly one's own, that is to say, something belonging to a given party in such a way that it cannot be similarly possessed by any other party; whereas the expression 'common property' is applied to that which has been assigned to several parties, to be possessed by them in partnership (so to speak) and in mutual concord, to the exclusion of other parties.³⁵

While

it must be understood that, during the earliest epoch of man's history, ownership (*dominium*) and common possession (*communio*) were concepts whose significance differed from that now ascribed to them (...) Thus, with reference to that early age, the term 'common' is nothing more nor less than the simple antonym of 'private' (*proprium*); and the word 'ownership' the power to make use rightfully of common (i.e. public) property.³⁶

Again, we can see the fundamental historicisation of concepts to which Grotius turns as a device. First of all, he was not denying at all the existence in the past of widespread communal ownership and use of land and even of moveable objects. His concern was rather to make it clear that this was a 'concept of fact but not of law'. It was nonsense to use the words property and ownership in more than one sense in the legal

---

³³ Grotius, *DJBP*, 2.2.13.5.
³⁴ Grotius, *Prædæ*, p. 227.
³⁵ Ibid.
³⁶ Grotius, *Prædæ*, pp. 226–227.

discourse. Whatever the 'fact' of arrangement was in the primeval community, it was not useful to describe it in terms of modern legal concepts:

> A certain form of ownership did exist, but it was ownership in a universal and indefinite sense. For God had given all things, not to this or that individual, but to the human race; and there was nothing to prevent a number of persons from being joint owners, in this fashion, of one and the same possession. But such a concept would be completely irrational if we were giving to the term 'ownership' its modern significance, involving private possession (*proprietas*), an attribute which did not reside in any person during that epoch. In fact, it has been most aptly observed that,
> ... All things belonged to him
> Who put them to his use ...[37]

However, when he first attempted to develop his theory of property, Grotius realised that the breakaway from the Thomist universe also implied a change in terminology. The temporalised model of the 'history' of property then was pressed into the service of this conceptual clarification:

> [T]he significance of these different terms will be very easily explained if, in imitation of the method employed by all the poets since the days of Hesiod as well as by the ancient philosophers and jurists, we draw a chronological distinction between things which are perhaps not differentiated from one another by any considerable interval of time, but which do indeed differ in certain underlying principles and by their very nature.[38]

The ploy which Grotius had used suggested that the older, medieval and ancient terminology of property, the language of common property, was in fact a true conceptual mirror of the life of early mankind, while the modern terminology of strict property was appropriate to describe the modern world only. The hitch was that the verbal terms in fact remained the same, while their meaning has changed fundamentally. Accordingly, the very question which presented itself to Grotius was to explain this rightful use of the common without invoking the modern concept of (exclusive) property. That 'there was no private property under the primary law of nations, to which we also give the name "natural law"', from time to time was the accepted view of the ancients, and Grotius repeated Horace's dictum that 'Nor he, nor I, nor any man, is made / By Nature private owner of the soil'.[39]

As a consequence, the term 'use' applied by the Scholastics in this context was 'a concept of fact but not of law', modern law that is. The

---

[37] Grotius, *Prædæ*, p. 228.
[38] Grotius, *Prædæ*, p. 226.
[39] Grotius, *Prædæ*, p. 227.

modern exclusive notion of use would have made complete nonsense of the term common as joined to it. Thus, argued Grotius, what the actual use of common property meant differed according to the nature of the thing used. Use involved individuation:

For there are some things which are consumed by use, either in the sense that they are converted into the very substance of the user and therefore admit of no further use, or else in the sense that they are rendered less fit for additional service by the fact that they have once been made to serve. Accordingly, it very soon became apparent, in regard to articles of the first class (for example, food and drink), that a certain form of private ownership was inseparable from use. For the essential characteristic of private property is the fact that it belongs to a given individual in such a way as to be incapable of belonging to any other individual.[40]

Thus, common property could accommodate individual appropriation in a natural way without the source of the consumed thing passing into private dominion.

Thus Athenaeus depicts the master of the feast as maintaining that the sea is common property, whereas fish become the property of the persons who catch them. And again, in Plautus' play entitled *The Rope*, the fisherman assents when the young slave says,
    The sea's most certainly common to all;
but when the slave adds,
    'Tis common property, found in the sea,
the fisherman justly objects,
    Whatever is caught by my net and hook
    Is mine in the truest sense ...[41]

Grotius then presented the freedom of trade as a derivative of natural law:

In harmony with this is the statement of Libanius: 'God did not bestow all products upon all parts of the earth, but distributed His gifts over different regions, to the end that men might cultivate a social relationship because one would have need of the help of another...' (...) In Florus are the words: 'If you destroy commerce, you sunder the alliance which binds together the human race'.[42]

Freedom of trade, however, was not supposed to transgress the boundaries set by natural equity. In particular, the freedom to trade in grain was limited by the requirement that prices should remain within the reach of the poor: 'We affirm, therefore, that all men have the right to buy such things at a fair price, unless they are needed by the person from

---

[40] Grotius, *Prædæ*, p. 228.
[41] Grotius, *Prædæ*, p. 232.
[42] Grotius, *DJBP*, 2.2.13.5.

whom they are sought; thus in times of extreme scarcity the sale of grain is forbidden.'[43]

In the context of international trade this meant that grain should not be exported in times of dearth. It had to be offered for consumption in the province where it was produced. Similarly, Grotius would not allow free rein to the right of engrossing. Although as far as natural law was concerned it was enough to demand that the monopoly buyers of grain should have an intent to sell it at a fair price, Grotius believed positive law should set limits to natural liberty. And once municipal law has laid down a rule,

the law of nature itself prescribes that this must be obeyed. For although municipal law cannot enjoin anything which the law of nature forbids, or forbid what the law of nature enjoins, it can nevertheless set limits to natural liberty, and forbid what by nature was permitted; thus, through exercise of the power which belongs to it, municipal law can by anticipation prevent an acquisition of ownership which by the law of nature might have been permitted.[44]

As the long string of qualifications to private property right has shown us, Grotius placed great stress on the role of justice in the regulation of social life. But he took society as it was, operating beyond the constraints of either natural equity or artificial simplicity.

A similar procedure of linguistic and conceptual clarification was applied by Grotius to the various meanings of justice, as inherited from earlier discourses. Aristotelian distributive justice, for example, had no place within his paradigm. Distributive justice, as Grotius explained, was concerned with

the rational allotment to each man, or to each social group, of those things which are properly theirs, in such a way as to give the preference now to him who is more wise over the less wise, now to a kinsman rather than to a stranger, now to a poor man rather than to a man of means, as the conduct of each or the nature of the thing suggests. Long ago the view came to be held by many, that this discriminating allotment is a part of law, properly and strictly so called; nevertheless law, properly defined, has a far different nature, because its essence lies in leaving to another that which belongs to him, or in fulfilling our obligations to him.[45]

The proper domain of justice, or *expletive justice* as Grotius called it, concerned 'perfect rights': rights of usufruct, possession, contract. Distributive justice, or *attributive justice* as Grotius called it, had as its domain those 'imperfect rights', those virtues 'which have as their purpose to do good to others, as generosity, compassion, and foresight in

[43] Grotius, *DJBP*, 2.2.19.
[44] Grotius, *DJBP*, 2.2.5.
[45] Grotius, *DJBP*, 'Prolegomena', §10.

matters of government'.⁴⁶ The crucial distinction between these two rights, perfect and imperfect, is that the latter did not entail a strict, reciprocal obligation:

[F]or counsels and instructions of every sort, which enjoin what is honourable indeed but do not impose an obligation, do not come under the term statute or law. Permission, again, is not, strictly speaking, an operation of law; but a negation of operation, except in so far as it obligates another not to put any hindrance in the way of him to whom permission is given.⁴⁷

A perfect right, moreover, was one which could be defended by force, while an imperfect one was merely a claim of a potential virtue in the behaviour of others. Yet Grotius insisted that the legitimacy of private possession did not derive from the human institution of force but was based itself in natural law. Any concession to the opinion that might makes right would be the end of justice itself, as far as Grotius was concerned. He also strongly opposed that historicisation and relativisation of justice according to which human laws of exclusive possession simply ratified man's natural selfishness:

What the philosopher here says, and the poet reaffirms in verse, 'and just from unjust Nature cannot know', must not for one moment be admitted. Man is, to be sure, an animal, but an animal of a superior kind, much farther removed from all other animals than the different kinds of animals are from one another; evidence on this point may be found in the many traits peculiar to the human species. But among the traits characteristic of man is an impelling desire for society, that is, for the social life – not of any and every sort, but peaceful, and organized according to the measure of his intelligence, with those who are of his own kind; this social trend the Stoics called 'sociableness'. Stated as a universal truth, therefore, the assertion that every animal is impelled by nature to seek only its own good cannot be conceded.⁴⁸

Thus, Grotian property theory did not proceed from a shift in the moral evaluation of contemporary European property. He remained within a paradigm of moral scepticism and hostility towards the selfishness of individual possession and sought, through the idea of a 'benign reservation', to preserve a place for the poor in a world of exclusive private dominion. The distinctive feature of his jurisprudence, however, lay in so reducing the scope of distributive justice that the right of theft under necessity, or the right to buy grain at a fair price – rights of desert and claims of need – became conceptualised as exceptions rather than as a priority case and a rule, such as they had been under Aquinas. A man

---

⁴⁶ Grotius, *DJBP*, 1.1.8.1.
⁴⁷ Grotius, *DJBP*, 1.1.9.1.
⁴⁸ Grotius, *DJBP*, 'Prolegomena', §6.

only had a right to what was his own. He had no perfect right to what was his due. His imperfect right to be treated with humanity only hardened into a perfect one under conditions of gravest necessity.

Samuel Pufendorf's Conjectural History of Property

The Shift from Rights to Obligations: The Natural Law of Humanity or Charity

Pufendorf began by granting the Grotian argument that natural law allowed the needy to appease that 'gnawing of hunger' which 'carries the right to do many things which, apart from it, were held to be forbidden', whatever the prevailing system of property prescribed in normal times.[49] He also recognised that modern positive law actually enforced men's imperfect obligations of charity, making them duties, in times of necessity. Yet the question remained: were such positive laws consonant with natural law? And what did the poor have the right to do in cases where no positive laws required charity? Pufendorf's question was not merely theoretical, and his rhetoric shows that he was fully aware of the practical relevance of the issue:

[I]f such a precaution is not taken for the poor in some particular commonwealths, and if the obduracy of men of means cannot be overcome by prayers, while there is no means whereby a person may come to the aid of the man who is in want either of money or assistance, would you have him die of hunger? Can any human institution have such power that, if another neglects to do his duty toward me, I must perish rather than depart from the customary and usual manner of procedure?[50]

In answer to these questions, Pufendorf began by granting the Grotian position that natural law indeed gave dispensation to the needy to satisfy their hunger and gave an excellent *précis* of Grotius's theory:

Grotius, Bk. II. chap.ii. §6, has undertaken to solve this difficulty in the following way: Those who first introduced the distinct ownership of particular things are understood to have added to it the limitation that the force of ownership whereby others are excluded from the use of a person's own property, should expire, in case the other person cannot be kept alive without the use of the same; and so, in a case of such necessity, private property, without which another must surely die, is understood to revert to original common ownership. Or, in other words, when men first instituted distinct ownership, all individually entered into agreement to keep their hands off the property of others, except in so far as the owners allow

---

[49] Pufendorf, *DJNG*, 2.6.3; 2.6.1.
[50] Pufendorf, *DJNG*, 2.6.5.

them, with the reservation, however, that at the urge of extreme necessity any one's possession, without which a person's life could not be preserved, was to be used as if it belonged to all. For since written laws must be allowed that interpretation, which varies as little as possible from natural equity, the same must be done all the more in the case of customs which are maintained only by tacit agreements. And it is certainly just for every one to have the right to preserve his life with the means which at the time constitute his sole hope.[51]

But he insisted that this natural law was not based on Grotius's 'benign reservation', that is, on the hypothesis that in times of necessity the 'community of goods' returns. He believed that this hypothesis was both inconsistently argued and dangerous; inconsistent because Grotius granted the right to the poor and then insisted that they make restitution after the crisis had passed, and dangerous because the right of the poor might reduce society to a complete state of lawlessness even in times of moderate plenty. At the same time, Pufendorf believed that both humanity and common prudence required that the rich should provide for the needs of the poor in times of adversity. How then was Pufendorf to theorise this obligation?

To start with, he argued that the original establishment of private property gave occasion for the exercise of benevolence:

Certainly property was not distinguished with the purpose of allowing a man to avoid using it in the service of others, and to brood in solitude over his hoard of riches, but so that each man might be able to dispose of its use according to his pleasure, and that when he was minded to share it with others, he might at least have the opportunity to put another person under obligation to him. Therefore, after the introduction of the ownership of things, men were given the ability not only of carrying on commerce with signal advantage to all mankind, but also, after securing such means, of making a richer display of humanity and kindness to others, while before that time they could aid others only by their own personal service.[52]

If we listen carefully to what Pufendorf is saying here, it becomes clear that he did not put an obligation to charity on private property as such, but rather on the owner of the property as a person. Private property was owned on the basis of a perfect right. Its role was to put its owner in the position of having the superfluity to be charitable. While property itself was owned on the basis of a 'perfect right', that is, one strictly enforceable at law, the property owner as a person was under an 'imperfect obligation' to be charitable to the distressed. Against Grotius' theory

---

[51] Pufendorf, *DJNG*, 2.6.6.
[52] Pufendorf, *DJNG*, 2.6.5.

of 'benign reservation', the return to a state of positive community, Pufendorf argued that

> this matter is better explained on our theory, if we say that a man of means is bound to come to the aid of one who is in innocent want, by an imperfect obligation, which no one should, as a rule, be forced to meet; and yet the urge of supreme necessity makes it possible for such things to be claimed, on the same ground as those which are owed by a perfect right, that is, a special appeal may be made to a magistrate, or, when time does not allow anything of the sort, the immediate necessity may be met by taking the thing through force or stealth.[53]

By this distinction between 'perfect rights' and 'imperfect obligations', Pufendorf managed to find a way to provide for the poor consistent with natural law without granting them, as Grotius did, a sort of property right in the goods of the rich in times of necessity. In his theory, the poor simply came into a right by default of someone else's obligation. This obligation in turn derived not from the laws but from regulating property benevolently. Property owners had an imperfect obligation as men, deriving from a merely voluntary law of humanity, or law of charity.

In his distinctions of 'perfection' and 'imperfection', Pufendorf was merely following Grotius, although putting them to a new use. The idea of 'imperfect right' was identical to Grotius' concept of 'aptitude'. Both concepts stressed the idea that the obligation correlative to this imperfect right was merely voluntary. If the obligated person denied his obligation, he would, indeed, be acting unfairly and yet the injured party would by no means be receiving a wrong which would furnish him with an action against the injurer. These 'imperfect rights' were the rights to be treated with respect, gratitude, kindness or generosity. These were the rights comprehended within the Aristotelian concept of distributive justice, and like Grotius, Pufendorf argued that this realm – giving to each man his relative due – was more properly an area of voluntary moral behaviour than of jurisprudence proper.

Following the same distinctions as Grotius, between distributive and expletive justice, Pufendorf argued that natural jurisprudence was concerned with the rules necessary to the very existence of society, that its proper domain was in 'perfect rights', those rights of ownership, usufruct and contract which were absolutely central to the existence of society. What was due to the poor through the imperfect obligation of the rich to be charitable was a matter of distributive justice and was a voluntary rather than obligatory question, since it was not absolutely essential to

---

[53] Pufendorf, *DJNG*, 2.6.6.

the maintenance of society, merely something conducive to its improvement. Only when actual starvation loomed and the very existence of society was at stake did the right of the poor become 'perfect', giving them right of appeal to magistrates.

In both Grotius and Pufendorf, perfect rights implied strictly correlative obligations. Yet in the case of imperfect rights, the correlation was looser, for the poor did not have the right to force the rich to discharge their obligations to be charitable and generous according to Pufendorf, except in the exceptional case of necessity. Even in the primitive stage of natural liberty, Pufendorf argued, there obtains from the precepts of natural law an inequality of obligation.

For such things as natural law commands one man to show another, before any agreement has passed between them, such as the duties of charity and humanity, can be required only by peaceful means, as by persuasion, admonition, request or entreaty. But it will not be allowable to use force against a person who persists in his refusal, unless it happens that extreme necessity impels us. The reason for this seems to lie in the fact that, without such duties, the intercourse of men cannot be sufficiently peaceful, and so nature is understood to have put them to one side, as a means by which men may bind others to themselves by a special exhibition of good will; since things which may be extorted by force have no such power to win the hearts of others, as those which may be denied without fear.[54]

Pufendorf insisted that it was precisely this asymmetry, the lack of correlation between the rights of the poor and the obligations of the rich, which gave occasion to the exercise of the moral quality of generosity. The whole relationship lost its quality of humanity if coercion was implied.

For it was this very reason that moved me to do another some favour, that is, I did not require the return of what I did for him, in order that he might have an opportunity to show that he was grateful from a love of uprightness, not from a fear of coercion, and in order that I myself might seem to have favoured him, not from the hope of gain, but from a desire to show humanity, in that I was unwilling to provide that I secure an equal return.[55]

What the needy owed to the rich in such a gift relationship was gratitude, since

The counterpart of beneficence is a grateful mind, by which he who is the recipient of the benefit, shows that he received it, is kindly disposed to the giver because of it, and seeks an opportunity to return its equivalent, so far as he can.[56]

---

[54] Pufendorf, *DJNG*, 3.4.6.
[55] Pufendorf, *DJNG*, 3.3.7.
[56] Pufendorf, *DJNG*, 3.3.16.

This analysis of imperfect rights as a 'gift' relationship obliterated the idea that the poor could claim relief from their sufferings on the basis of 'distributive' justice. Pufendorf's theory created a sort of jurisprudence of paternalism, by shifting natural law theorisation from the rights of the poor to the voluntary obligations of the rich. This rhetoric of moral sentiments obliterated the theoretical possibility that the poor had rights of desert unrelated to the products of their own labour. Instead of looking to the law as grounds for protection, the poor were henceforth to look to God, for the obligation of the rich was strictly speaking not to the poor themselves but to God:

> And so a natural obligation is that which binds only by the force of natural law; a civil obligation that which is reinforced by civil laws and authority. The efficacy of each is considered, either in him in whom it resides as the subject of the obligation, or in the other person, who is its object. From the point of view of the subject, the efficacy of a natural obligation consists principally in the fact that it binds the conscience of a man, or that a man realizes, when he has not fulfilled it, that he is disobeying the will of God, whose law all men recognize that they should obey, just as they are indebted to Him for their very existence. And although penal sanctions are not to be found so expressly defined in natural law, there is no reason to feel that it lacks every kind of sanction, and that the man who breaks its obligation should expect no greater punishment from the hands of its author than he who fulfils the same.[57]

The Concept of Beginning in Pufendorf's Theory of Property: Negative Community

While the shift from imperfect rights to imperfect obligations in formulating a natural law to govern the poor's right to subsistence in necessity pushed Pufendorf to move away from Grotius' theorisation of the same problem, his effort to draw out all the possible consequences of this shift helped to revitalise some fundamental assumptions of the Grotian general theory of property. For Grotius to claim that in times of necessity the primitive communal use of the earth's resources could be re-established, he had to ground his whole account of the origin of property in the primitive existence of such common property in the first place. When Pufendorf mounted his attack to remove even this last vestigial foundation of the Grotian 'benign reservation' theorem, he also opened the way for a more coherent and complete historicisation of the justification systems of private property.

---

[57] Pufendorf, *DJNG*, 3.4.6.

The manipulation of the natural rights–natural obligations correlativity proved itself in many ways troublesome when applied to the reciprocal relationships of men within the natural law framework. But it was a very sharp intellectual weapon to slice away confusion from the language of rights in those parts of the discourse where man's relationship to his environment was at issue. In a significant sense, Pufendorf claimed, this relationship – man versus his natural habitat – was the very basis of all theorising of society.

> Such is the constitution of man's body that it cannot live from its own substance, but has need of substance gathered from outside, by which it is nourished and fortified against those things which would destroy its structure. Nay, nearly all nature serves man to the further end that he may live his life more advantageously and easily. (...) It is in view of all this that so many transactions pass between men, and the way is opened to many controversies as well as contests. To see that these shall not disturb the peaceful association of mankind is the task of natural law, and the civil laws of most peoples are chiefly concerned with the same end.[58]

If 'man to man' relationships somehow had their origin in man's relationship to non-human objects via the agency of human needs, then it was an issue of some importance whether the language of rights was directly applicable to this primary field of human experience or not. Pufendorf insisted that if a right presupposed a simultaneous obligation arising from the very same relationship which gave rise to it, then the use of the word 'right' would lead to an inconsistency when applied to non-human objects. 'It must be recognized', he argued, in a celebrated argument against Hobbes,

> that not every natural faculty to do something is properly a right, but only that which concerns some moral effect, in the case of those who have the same nature as I. Thus, as in the fables, the horse had a natural faculty to graze in the meadow, and so had the stag as well, yet neither of them had a right to this because their respective faculties did not concern the other. In the same way, when a man takes inanimate objects or animals for his use, he exercises only a purely natural faculty, if it is considered simply with regard to the objects and animals which he uses, without respect to other men. But this faculty takes on the nature of a real right, at the moment when this moral effect is produced in the rest of mankind, that other men may not hinder him, or compete with him, against his will, in using such objects or animals. Of course it is absurd to try to designate as a right that faculty which all other men have an equal right to prevent one from exercising.[59]

This insight then yielded a whole series of formulations, all contributing to a conceptual historicisation of mankind's relationship to his habitat, to

---

[58] Pufendorf, *DJNG*, 4.3.1.
[59] Pufendorf, *DJNG*, 3.5.3.

his 'property'. First of all, if the rights–obligations correlation was to be strictly upheld, it was impossible not to treat property relations as artificial, as results of human action. For Pufendorf, property presented itself as a purely human relationship, since, as he explained:

> proprietorship and community are moral qualities which have no physical and intrinsic effect upon things themselves but only produce a moral effect in relation to other men; and that these qualities, like the rest of the same kind, owe their birth to imposition. Therefore, it is idle to raise the question whether proprietorship in things is due to nature or to institution. For it is clear that it arises from the imposition of men and there is no change in the physical substance of things, whether proprietorship is added to or taken away from them.[60]

It was important then to see clearly what was 'natural' about property relationships; in what sense, if any, did they belong to the domain of natural law. Pufendorf here tried to demolish both the religious and the more secularly phrased versions of some sort of absolutely primary system of property stemming directly from 'nature'. Reaching back to the traditions of Scholastic natural law theories he of course upheld the notion that in the strict sense only God had complete dominion over the world:

> Without doubt the most Good and Great God, since He is the creator and preserver of this universe has, as it were, complete dominion over all things, which therefore belong so strictly to Him that no man against His will can pretend to any right over them.[61]

But then God, and only God, had a 'natural' dominion over any part or, indeed, over the whole of his creation. However, it was wrong to infer from this that a man, a human being, could receive a specific right of dominion deduced directly from God's ways to man. Property rights had no authority from God alone: 'That donation of God, described in the Sacred Scriptures, sets forth not a definite form of dominion, but only an indefinite right to apply things to uses which are reasonable and necessary', argued Pufendorf and continued:

> But it is incorrect to infer that men received a right from the donation of God: therefore, proprietorship did not come from appropriation and division. For the donation of God only made man secure, on the assumption that God wished him to consume upon his necessities the things which He had created.[62]

Nor was another formulation of the same dogma acceptable, namely that somehow 'proprietorship and dominion belong to natural law taken in

---

[60] Pufendorf, *DJNG*, 4.4.1.
[61] Pufendorf, *DJNG*, 4.3.2.
[62] Pufendorf, *DJNG*, 4.4.10.

its strict sense, and as it is engraved upon the minds of men'. This interpretation was simply based on a play on the word 'natural' in the phrase 'natural law'. For, attacked Pufendorf,

> Here it should be observed that the expression, 'this or that belongs to natural law,' has a different meaning, according as it is applied either to some command, in the strict sense of the word, or to some institution introduced into human life. In the former sense it means that the law of nature commands that this be or not be done; in the latter, that sane reason, upon a consideration of the general state of social life, advises that this be set up and established among men. For whatever institutions have been introduced, because of their special advantage to this or that state, are said to belong to civil or positive law. Therefore, when the question is raised, whether dominion traces its origin to natural law, the latter and not the former sense of the word is to be taken.[63]

This understanding of the nature of the system of property required Pufendorf to work out his own definitions of the two distinct conceptual stages involved in its construction. First, he had to explain how to understand man's relationship to his habitat in the beginning – since no theory of human institutions could do away with some concept of beginning – and then, second, he had to develop an account of the rise of property not as a man–nature relationship but as a man–man relationship. As one would expect, this second relationship was to be a contract, tacit or explicit, but the contract had to be based on the theoretical work done on the first step of the 'historical' model.

Pufendorf's conceptualisation of the 'beginning' stemmed directly from his understanding of the rights–obligations correlation. A doctrine which deduced the system of property from the first man, in singular, from Adam, would simply overlook the requirement of the man–man nexus in the establishment of a right:

> The right of Adam to things was different from that dominion, which is now established among men; one may call it indefinite dominion not formally established, but only conceded, not actually, but potentially so. It has the same effect as dominion now has, that, namely, of using things at one's own pleasure; but it was not, properly speaking, dominion, because no other man was then on earth to whom it could oppose its effect; although, upon the increase of men it could pass into dominion. Therefore, so long as Adam was the only man, things to him were neither common nor proper. For community implies a sharer in the possession, and proprietorship connotes the exclusion of another's right to the same thing, and so neither is intelligible before more than one man has come into being.[64]

[63] Pufendorf, *DJNG*, 4.4.14.
[64] Pufendorf, *DJNG*, 4.4.3.

The concept of community in Pufendorf's theory of rights was therefore a concept expressing a potency, an indeterminacy. The key term in this equation was that of a negative community:

> The term community is taken either *negatively* or *positively*. In the former case things are said to be common, according as they are considered before the interposition of any human act, as a result of which they are held to belong in a special way to this man rather than to that. In the same sense such things are said to be nobody's, more in a negative than a positive sense; that is, that they are not yet assigned to a particular person, not that they cannot be assigned to a particular person. They are, furthermore, called 'things that lie open to any and every person'. But common things, by the second and positive meaning, differ from things owned, only in the respect that the latter belong to one person while the former belong to several in the same manner. Furthermore, proprietorship or dominion is a right whereby the substance, as it were, of something belongs to a person in such a way that it does not belong in its entirety to another person in the same manner.[65]

As Pufendorf argued, this was also the basic concept of community inferred in the Grotian theory, but the use of the 'benign reservation' clause by Grotius confused his commentators as to the nature of the primeval community – whether it was positive or negative – involved in his theory of property. It is crucial to see that Pufendorf's case for a negative community in the beginning was not an argument excluding any later development of specific positive communities but rather a transposition of a temporal grid over the history of property systems in such a way that the beginning should and could not predetermine the outcome. The concept of negative community did not allow the direct and crude 'naturalisation' of private property in any way. Pufendorf laid great emphasis on this polemical point:

> Most recent writers differ entirely from us on the origin of dominion. Let us see what force there is in their argument. Now they acknowledge that community is taken in a double sense, either as that which, while undivided and proper to several, furnishes a common use to each person; or as that which acknowledges no proprietorship whatsoever, and serves the general use of all. But they deny things not only the first kind of community at the beginning, as we also do, but also the second; and so they deny that at the beginning, when proprietorship was entirely lacking, all things lay open to common use, denying as well the consequence of this, namely, that individual dominions arose originally from division and occupation.[66]

Now, once Pufendorf argued that no credit should be given to any such idea that God at the beginning instituted a positive community, from

---

[65] Pufendorf, *DJNG*, 4.4.2.
[66] Pufendorf, *DJNG*, 4.4.10.

which men later withdrew on their own initiative, he had to 'humanise' the whole account of the rise of the system of private property in such a way that it was based on the known attributes of men. Private property had to appear as an outcome of human decision-making, as the result of a human choice:

> [T]he grant of God, by which He allowed men the use of the products of the earth, is not the immediate cause of dominion, as it has its effect in relation to other men (a proof of which is to be found in the fact that brute creatures use and consume things as if it were God's will, although no dominion is recognized among them); but that dominion presupposes absolutely an act of man and an agreement, whether tacit or express. It is true that God allowed man to turn the earth, its products, and its creatures, to his own use and convenience, that is, He gave men an indefinite right to them, yet the manner, intensity, and extent of this power were left to the judgement and disposition of men; whether, in other words, they would confine it within certain limits, or within none at all, and whether they wanted every man to have a right to everything, or only to a certain and fixed part of things, or to be assigned his definite portion with which he should rest content and claim no right to anything else.[67]

This account brings together in an organic way the two pillars of the Pufendorfian theory. Choices between systems of human community and property are made by men; there was no direct 'natural' determination. This necessarily invokes the interaction of men as rational beings in the explanation of the genesis of rights to external objects. Interaction of rational beings was to be seen as a contract. The emphasis on human choice naturally led Pufendorf to argue that

> the law of nature approves all conventions which have been introduced about things by men, provided they involve no contradiction or do not overturn society. Therefore, the proprietorship of things has resulted immediately from the convention of men, either tacit or express. For although after God had made the gift, nothing remained to prevent man from appropriating things to himself, yet there was need of some sort of convention if it was to be understood that by such appropriation or seizure the right of others to that thing was excluded. But the fact that right reason suggested the introduction of separate dominions does not prevent them from going back to a human pact.[68]

This side of the argument thus allowed him to articulate the theory of property as a theory of rights, while maintaining the force of his basic insight about the correlativity of rights and obligations. It explained how a general choice leading to private property could have been made. However, the reader is well advised to pay due attention to all the

---

[67] Pufendorf, *DJNG*, 4.4.4.
[68] Ibid.

consequences of this model. If property rights were the work of human convention, Pufendorf had to answer a normative question: whether such conventions were the result of God's exercise of design, that is, whether they were consonant with natural law; and a historical one: how it was that humans had transformed the usufruct of God's creation into a system of private property. In order to answer these questions, Pufendorf first had to explain the nature of God's original grant of the world for the use of men. Had God granted the world to man 'preceptively', that is, with specific injunctions in natural law as to how it was to be used and individuated, or had he granted it to man 'permissively', without express natural law stipulations? Or to pose the question another way, was the natural law in relation to property 'preceptive' or 'permissive'?

The Scholastic Foundations of the Negative Community Theory: A Digression on Suarez and the Primeval Community of Property

By invoking the notion of 'negative' community, Pufendorf availed himself of an interpretative tradition which was perhaps best articulated in the early seventeenth century by the Jesuit Francisco Suarez in his seminal work *On Laws and God the Lawgiver* (1612). Suarez accepted Aquinas' suggestion that, although justice can be applied to every virtue, the 'primary basis and significance of *ius*' is that special virtue of justice which 'renders to another that which is his due'.[69] However, he argued, when one refers to *ius* in this strict sense, it was not enough to say that *ius* was what had been 'prescribed or measured by lex',[70] law being in this context 'a measure of rectitude, viewed absolutely'.[71] *Ius* derived from strict justice in the *Digest* is an expression of 'the virtue that renders to every man his own right (*ius suum*), that is to say, the virtue that renders to every man that which belongs to him'.[72] Accordingly, *ius* was a certain 'moral power, which every man possesses in respect to his own property or with respect to a thing which in some way pertains to him'.[73] This double set of references built into the notion of 'subjective' rights had an equivalent couplet of linguistic expressions going back to the Bible. An already established right is that of 'the owner of a thing' who is said to have a 'right *in* that thing'. Another acceptation of the term right is what 'the labourer is said to have (...) to his wages',

---

[69] Suarez, *De Legibus*, 1.2.4; *ST*, 2a2ae.q.57.a.1.
[70] Ibid.
[71] Suarez, *De Legibus*, 1.1.6.
[72] Suarez, *De Legibus*, 1.2.5.
[73] Ibid.

the 'rights of servitude or rights of rural and urban estates, rights of use or enjoyment, and similar rights'. This is expressed by the expression 'a right *to* a thing'.[74] Summing up: Suarez transformed the Thomist terminology in such a way as to make it clear 'that *ius* sometimes signifies *lex*; while at times it means dominion or quasi-dominion over a thing, that is, a claim to its use'.[75]

This distinction becomes vital for Suarez's general framework for the understanding of property rights. His problem was the following: 'by natural law all things were [originally] held in common, and nevertheless a division of property was introduced by mankind'.[76] Does this mean that natural law 'may be changed by means of human law'?[77] A voluntarist answer to the question would have opened the gates for absolutism, while a negation of the legitimacy of the system of private property would have meant a radical denial of the world as Suarez knew it. To free himself from the difficulty, Suarez set out to restore the Thomist position on the status of natural law and gave strong support to the position that 'in so far as its precepts are concerned', natural law 'is by its very nature unchangeable' and in any case since 'in the case of every precept of natural law, God is the Lawgiver; and man cannot change a law that God has established, since an inferior cannot prevail against his superior'.[78] However, Aquinas also was understood to endorse the view that the specific form of the law can undergo a change if 'the matter dealt with by the law' can change.[79] There was no contradiction in this position, since

such a mode of change is not inconsistent with the necessary and unchangeable character of the natural law; and that, for the rest, it is convenient and frequently necessary for men, in accordance with the various changes of estate which befall them. In this connexion, too, one may fittingly apply the familiar illustration drawn from Augustine, namely, that just as the science of medicine lays down certain precepts for the sick, others for the well, certain precepts for the strong and others for the weak, although the rules of medicine do not therefore undergo essential change but merely become manifold, so that some serve on one occasion, and others, on another occasion; even so, the natural law, while it remains [in itself] the same, lays down one precept for one occasion and another, for another occasion; and is binding [in one of its rules] at one time, though not binding previously or subsequently, and this without undergoing any change in itself but merely because of a change in the subject-matter.[80]

---

[74] Ibid.
[75] Suarez, *De Legibus*, 2.14.16.
[76] Suarez, *De Legibus*, 2.14.2.
[77] Suarez, *De Legibus*, 2.14.1.
[78] Suarez, *De Legibus*, 2.14.8.
[79] Suarez, *De Legibus*, 2.13.6.
[80] Suarez, *De Legibus*, 2.14.12.

Suarez thus had to clarify the meaning of the phrase that 'a matter may fall under the natural law'.[81] There is a positive sense, in cases when something is prescribed by natural law, and 'when any thing is prohibited thereby, the thing thus prohibited is said to be positively opposed to natural law'.[82] But there is also another sense:

> According to another manner of speaking, however, a thing is said to pertain to the natural law merely in a permissive, negative, or concessive sense, to put the matter thus. Under this classification many things fall which, from the standpoint simply of natural law, are permissible, or conceded, to men – such things as the holding of goods in common, human liberty, and the like. With respect to these things, the natural law lays down no precept enjoining that they shall remain in that state; rather does it leave the matter to the management of men, such management to be in accord with the demands of reason.[83]

Suarez evidently took it that property rights did not fall under natural law in the positive sense, since the 'division of property is not opposed to natural law in the sense that the latter absolutely and without qualification forbids such division'.[84] He enlisted the argument of Aquinas that 'ownership in common was part of natural law in the sense that, by virtue of that law, all property would be held in common if men had not introduced any different provision'.[85] In light of his extension of the meaning of rights to include subjective rights Suarez then further developed his notion of 'negative' natural law.

According to Suarez, subjective rights, that is, natural laws concerning dominion and quasi dominion (*iure naturali dominativo*), 'even if positively given by nature itself, may be changed, and may at times be licitly and validly abolished by human agency' and 'when this change has been made, it may be said that the natural law is changed in an extrinsic sense, inasmuch as the prior law lapses when the subject-matter has changed and another law becomes binding', 'whereas the preceptive natural law may not be thus changed'.[86] This difference between the natural law undergirding 'objective' rights and 'subjective' rights could not have been more explicit than in the following passage:

> The general reason, however, for the difference between the preceptive law and the law concerning dominion is that the former kind comprehends rules and principles for right conduct which involve necessary truth, and are therefore immutable, since they are based upon the intrinsic rectitude or perversity of

---

[81] Suarez, *De Legibus*, 2.14.14.
[82] Ibid.
[83] Suarez, *De Legibus*, 2.14.6.
[84] Suarez, *De Legibus*, 2.14.16.
[85] Suarez, *De Legibus*, 2.14.14. *ST*, 2a2ae.q.66.a.2.
[86] Suarez, *De Legibus*, 2.14.18; 2.14.19; 2.14.18.

their objects; whereas the law concerning dominion is merely the subject-matter of the other preceptive law, and consists (so to speak) of a certain fact, that is, a certain condition or habitual relation of things. And it is evident that all created things, and especially those which are corruptible, are characterized through nature by many conditions that are changeable and capable of being abolished by many causes. Accordingly, we say of liberty and of any similar lawful right, that even if such a right has been positively granted by nature, it may be changed by human agency, since it is dependent, in the individual persons, either upon their own wills, or upon the state, in so far as the latter has lawful power over all private individuals and over their property, to the extent necessary for right government.[87]

Suarez was clearly aware of the absolutist implications of treating the 'subjective' rights to liberty or property as subject-matters of preceptive natural law which come under natural law only negatively speaking. The mistake of those who had thought that there was a voluntarist gap in the argument was that they could not understand that the natural laws of dominion, while they were in force, always had to have positive precepts as 'carriers' of a precept of immutable natural law. In this sense it would appear that

liberty rather than slavery is a precept of the natural law, for this reason, namely, that nature has made men free in a positive sense (so to speak) with an intrinsic right to liberty, whereas it has not made them slaves in this positive sense, strictly speaking. Similarly, nature has conferred upon men in common dominion over all things, and consequently has given to every man a power to use these things; but nature has not so conferred private property rights in connexion with that dominion.[88]

However, Suarez's statement here must be understood carefully. What he meant was not a prescription for personal liberty and common property where everybody has a claim to the use of common property. Even liberty was alienable for him, since – he argued – 'for the very reason that man is lord of his own liberty, it is possible for him to sell or alienate the same'.[89] His discussion of positive precepts under the laws of dominion were framed in such a way as to defend rather than concede the possibility of their change. In connection with property rights his answer to both 'immutable natural law' theorists and voluntaristic absolutists was that their arguments were

incompatible with this positive law of dominion which nature has given either to all collectively, or to individuals separately. Therefore, although nature may not have prescribed that things should always be owned in common (in which

---

[87] Suarez, *De Legibus*, 2.14.19.
[88] Suarez, *De Legibus*, 2.14.16.
[89] Suarez, *De Legibus*, 2.14.18.

sense it is said that community of property comes negatively under natural law), nevertheless, while that condition of common ownership did exist, there was a positive precept of natural law to the effect that no one should be prohibited or prevented from making the necessary use of the common property. This positive precept in its own fashion is even now in existence with regard to those things which are common, and for so long as they are not in any way divided; for no one may be prohibited from the common use of such things, generally speaking – apart, that is, from cases involving special necessity or a just cause. Moreover, in the same way, and arguing conversely, although division of property may not be prescribed by natural law, nevertheless, after this division has been made and spheres of dominion have been distributed, the natural law forbids theft, or the undue taking of another's property.[90]

How each positive law of dominion then operated with respect to subjective property rights was not discussed in these parts of Suarez's work in any detail. However, it was clear that Suarez wished to articulate the notion of mankind as community along lines similar to his distinction of negativity and positivity. The 'multitude of mankind' as a recipient of subjective rights had also been understood 'in two different ways'.[91] In one sense mankind could be regarded 'simply as a kind of aggregation', without constituting 'an unified whole, whether physical or moral'. The power of dominion in this case did not exist 'properly and formally', but 'it is understood to dwell in them at most as a fundamental potentiality [*radicaliter*], so to speak'.[92] On the other hand, mankind can be thought of as a unity if there is a 'special volition, or common consent' to form such a community proper. Furthermore, Suarez explained, there was no need to think of this community as embracing 'the entire species, or entire aggregate, of men existing throughout the whole world', such a 'whole assemblage of mankind' either 'never existed' or 'it so existed for an exceedingly brief period'.[93] 'Domestic' dominion first existed in families and it became 'political' only when 'many families began to congregate into one perfect community'.[94] This in fact happened 'soon after the creation of the world' and from then on 'mankind began to be divided into various states' each of which forming his own law of dominion 'in a distinct form'.[95] In any case, the operation of common ownership of all in the initial period under a positive precept of the laws of dominion did not seem particularly problematic for Suarez. In a brief remark he noted that 'without prejudice to the rectitude of their conduct, men could in

[90] Suarez, *De Legibus*, 2.14.17.
[91] Suarez, *De Legibus*, 3.2.4.
[92] Ibid.
[93] Suarez, *De Legibus*, 3.2.5.
[94] Suarez, *De Legibus*, 3.2.3.
[95] Suarez, *De Legibus*, 3.2.5.

that state of innocence take possession of, and divide among themselves, certain pieces of property, especially those which are movables and necessary for ordinary use'.[96]

Pufendorf's Conceptual Apparatus in His Account of the Origins of Property Rights

It is difficult to say how closely Pufendorf used Suarez to shape his own position. He certainly did not quote him, but then he did not quote Aquinas even once in his large tome, not to mention Molina, Vitoria and the other Spanish jurists. His formulation nonetheless seems to be a true mirroring of Suarez's doctrine, and it is obvious from the context that Pufendorf was attempting to block the absolutist consequences of a voluntarist interpretation of pacts along the same defensive lines as his Spanish forerunner. He was anxious that his concept of exclusive subjective property right should not be caught up in a confusion between concepts of 'law' and 'right':

[S]ince the term 'right' often signifies the same thing as law (...), care ought to be taken that we do not use it in the place of law itself, when it means the power, given or left by laws, to do something. (...) The word 'right' in this usage, means merely liberty, while the word law denotes some bond by which our natural liberty is restrained.[97]

It was in the very nature of subjective rights that they could only refer to 'the faculty of acting, and what a person can do without injury, and therefore it cannot be properly inferred that a person ought necessarily do everything he has the right, in this particular sense, to do'.[98] Pufendorf's theory of the state of nature was constructed so as to accommodate this distinction in complete unison with his parallel theorising of property rights. His listing of natural precepts interpreted as *lex* extended only to a strictly defined core area. He envisaged man not as 'some animal, which is directed by the forces and tendencies of the senses', guided by 'his base passions', but as a creature whose 'chief adornment and master of the other faculties is reason'.[99] Man he regarded as naturally sociable and he looked at the idea of the 'solitary individual' as merely the starting point of social theorising, although admitting that such an idea 'may seem tolerable in a way' as a tool of analysis; as in Hobbes' attempt in *De cive* (1642) to 'consider men as if now sprung out of the earth, and suddenly,

---

[96] Suarez, *De Legibus*, 2.14.13.
[97] Pufendorf, *DJNG*, 1.6.3.
[98] Pufendorf, *DJNG*, 2.2.3.
[99] Pufendorf, *DJNG*, 2.2.9.

like mushrooms, come to full maturity, without all kind of engagement to each other'; as only 'thrown out as a kind of hypothesis'.[100] Pufendorf was adamant that one should be concerned 'with a state of nature, not as may be conceived in the abstract, but as it actually is'.[101] On that basis he still argued that there were 'absolute duties, which obligated all men even before the formation of any human institution', and that the first and foremost of these was that 'no one should hurt another'.[102] The other commands, which he logically connected to this precept of immutable natural law, all centred around the notion that among creatures endowed with reason 'the natural state of men (...) is not one of war, but of peace'.[103]

But no natural law of property, common or private, could be regarded as a *lex*, as a precept. Accordingly, Pufendorf was now indeed committed to interpret the logical beginning of mankind as a 'negative community'. This was the only logical basis of his presentation of what did and what did not amount to exclusive property right. Thus,

the donation of God, described in the Sacred Scriptures, sets forth not a definite form of dominion, but only an indefinite right to apply things to uses which are reasonable and necessary ...[104]

For that divine gift only rendered men more certain at the mercy of God towards them, and assured them that it was with His approval that they turned other creatures to their use and service.[105]

Accordingly, in the beginning the situation was such that things were lying 'open to any and every person', Pufendorf maintained:

In the same sense such things are said to be nobody's, more in a negative than a positive sense; that is, that they are not yet assigned to a particular person, not that they cannot be assigned to a particular person.[106]

Negative community ultimately, but as we shall see only ultimately, was the abstract situation when 'considered before the interposition of any human act'.[107] Originally the whole world was *res nullius*. God had thus given the usufruct of his dominion to mankind in negative common but left it open to them to establish human dominion over any part of this conceded usufruct. Before we follow the unfolding of this

---

[100] Pufendorf, *DJNG*, 2.2.7. Pufendorf's quotation of Hobbes is from *De cive* (1642), ch. viii. §1.
[101] Pufendorf, *DJNG*, 2.2.7.
[102] Pufendorf, *DJNG*, 3.1.1.
[103] Pufendorf, *DJNG*, 2.2.9.
[104] Pufendorf, *DJNG*, 4.4.10.
[105] Pufendorf, *DJNG*, 4.4.4.
[106] Pufendorf, *DJNG*, 4.4.2.
[107] Ibid.

creative process of human dominion, we have to realise that Pufendorf here faced the same problems of language that Grotius had encountered in his attempt to create a natural law justification of the modern system of exclusive private property rights. But unlike Grotius in *Mare liberum* (1609), Pufendorf did not discuss the existence of two languages of right and the difficulty of translation between them. Rather, Pufendorf unambiguously chose the language of exclusive private property rights as the only system of reference concerning *ius*, and then asked what the origins were of such a right. Faithful to his earlier jettisoning of distributive justice, Pufendorf declared that, for him, dominion and proprietorship were 'one and the same thing', both being 'a right whereby the substance, as it were, of something belongs to a person in such a way that it does not belong in its entirety to another person in the same manner'.[108] Apart from the special rights of grave necessity, there were no immediate limitations on such a proprietorship. 'Such is the force of dominion', argued Pufendorf, 'that we are able to dispose of things, which belong to us as our own, at our pleasure, and to keep all others from using them, unless they have acquired for themselves a special right from us by pacts'.[109] Thus, 'the power of a man to alienate a thing of his or to transfer it to another, comes from the nature of full dominion'.[110] It was easy to comprehend that such a state of human affairs in which dominion became general only came into being at a certain historical moment. It was hard luck on latecomers, but Pufendorf quoted Pliny to the effect that exclusion could have been the result of personal indecision: '[I]n a state where everything is seized upon by the man who can get hold of it, it is staying much too late to wait till precisely the proper time.'[111] However, he claimed the possibility of alienation could still facilitate a deal between those who owned property and those who did not. 'Since things were not divided among men with the purpose that there should be an end to all sharing together of property', one could allow for the theoretical and indeed historical possibility of some men acquiring rights over the property of others.[112] Thus, there was a plethora of derivative property rights grafted upon any established system of private exclusive dominion. An understanding of these derivative rights seems to be necessary in order to clarify the analytical boundaries of Pufendorf's concept of property. It was precisely the gist of Grotius' complaint about terminological confusion that the projecting of a language describing these derivative

[108] Pufendorf, *DJNG*, 4.4.2.
[109] Ibid.
[110] Pufendorf, *DJNG*, 4.9.1.
[111] Pufendorf, *DJNG*, 4.6.2.
[112] Pufendorf, *DJNG*, 4.8.1.

rights on the period preceding the completion of the system had confused many legal philosophers. Three categories are of special interest to us here: the transfer of dominion, usufruct and use, which represent different degrees of alienation in a descending order. Usufruct and use were not full *dominia*. They came into existence because: 'Most of the things subject to dominion of men have this characteristic, that they do not remain in the same state, but abound in different increases.'[113] Some of these new accessions come 'from the mere nature of these things without the agency of man' and these are called 'natural fruits'.[114] Other substances could be 'increased in value' and their 'natural fecundity or aptitude must be procured by the labour of men in making it more fruitful and productive'. These fruits which 'are produced entirely or in part by the agency and labour of men' were usually called 'the fruits of industry'.[115] Now, it was 'the very nature of dominion and the purpose for which it was first introduced' that the owner should own the 'substance' of his property, the possession of which would be 'in vain if their fruits belong to others'.[116]

According to this legal definition 'usufruct is the right to use and enjoy the things without impairing their substance'.[117] It follows from this that usufruct is really applicable only to such cases where the substance of the property is 'not exhausted by use'. Apart from those 'things which furnish some use beyond that of their substance', usufruct 'is not to be found in a thing which was only of use when it was being consumed, since the body of the thing, and so dominion over it, is understood to belong to him who can rightfully consume anything at his pleasure'.[118] Use was defined by Pufendorf according to the tradition as a weaker condition than usufruct. 'It is called *use*', he argued, 'when a man secures only a daily and necessary advantage from another's property without impairing its substance; and this involves less than usufruct, since he who has use of a thing can only take as much as will suffice for himself and his dependants.'[119]

A further qualification of Pufendorf's language of property is to be found in his discussion of transfers of dominion, that is, their complete alienation by their owners. When the owner actually joined his dominion physically, he was in possession of it. This was to be distinguished from

---

[113] Pufendorf, *DJNG*, 4.7.1.
[114] Ibid.
[115] Ibid.
[116] Pufendorf, *DJNG*, 4.7.2.
[117] Pufendorf, *DJNG*, 4.8.7.
[118] Ibid.
[119] Pufendorf, *DJNG*, 4.8.8.

a 'mere retention of a thing, such as, for instance, a guardian, an administrator, a borrower, or a usufructuary, has over a thing which belongs to another'.[120]

Accordingly, dominion could be divided into two moments. It 'may be considered, either as it denotes merely a moral quality, according to which a thing is understood to belong to some one and necessarily to be the subject to his disposal, or as it is accompanied by some further physical faculty', which makes it a possession.[121] In a transfer of property both of these steps had to be completed. 'It appears that dominion, according as it is considered as a moral quality, and as it derives from possession, can in every case pass only by means of pacts', but to complete the transfer 'delivery of possession was also required in addition to pacts'.[122] Since it was conceivable that the two steps were temporally separated while the transaction was completed, Pufendorf conceded that 'the Roman laws maintain that by contracts which are concerned with the alienation of things, only a right to the thing is secured, as if before delivery of possession a man were as yet outside the thing, as it were, although he still has a right to join it with him'.[123] When the transfer was actually completed, the physical element has then been added to the moral one, and 'they say that a right has been established *in* the thing'.[124]

Such a split between a right *to* and a right *in*, however, was not conceivable for Pufendorf as legitimate during the original acquisition of dominion. It was a definitional feature of his notion of property right that 'in original acquisition, such as occupancy, the title or cause, and the manner of acquisition, concur'.[125] While, as we have seen, 'a dominion already established over things may pass from one citizen to another', to 'establish dominion for the first time, and to pass it on when once established, are different things'.[126] Having defined stringently what could and what could not be dominion or strict property, Pufendorf had not left much room for choice for himself in the further definition of what steps could legitimately lead originally to such an acquisition of property. He had to define logically what constituted the moral faculty and then how physical possession could result in exclusive ownership in things at the beginning. Dominion was a moral quality 'which had no physical or intrinsic effect upon things themselves'. Such

---

[120] Pufendorf, *DJNG*, 4.9.7.
[121] Pufendorf, *DJNG*, 4.9.6.
[122] Pufendorf, *DJNG*, 4.9.8.
[123] Ibid.
[124] Ibid.
[125] Pufendorf, *DJNG*, 4.9.5.
[126] Pufendorf, *DJNG*, 4.6.6.

96 Political Economy from Pufendorf to Marx

a moral effect could conceivably come into being only 'in relation to other men'; that is, by the exclusion of other men. That is why the qualifying feature of property was that it was due to human institution, due to 'the imposition of men'.[127] Property was a man–man relationship, and it is inconceivable that all individuals could have a man–nature type of 'right' simultaneously as it seemed to be the case in Hobbes' theory. Rights as defined by Pufendorf could not be mere natural faculties because of the logical requirement of a right–duty correlation which we have already discussed in connection with Pufendorf's solution to the charity problem.

Men have similar natural faculties which make them capable of using things and animals. The fact that 'an original right over things' with effect of exclusion could be morally constituted only through a pact was simply an analytical consequence of the supposition that all men were equal, that is, that 'human nature belongs equally to all men'.[128] Assuming this 'original equal faculty of men over things', argued Pufendorf, 'it is impossible to conceive how the mere corporal act of one person' – that is, a man–thing relationship – 'can prejudice the faculty of others, unless their consent is given, that is unless the pact intervenes'.[129] Man has to have his fellow men's 'consent, expressed or presumed', to have 'a proper right to a thing' as his very own.[130] That the pact can be express or tacit – Pufendorf always cared to emphasise – presumed understanding under the term of tacit consent, a pact which is 'clearly to be gathered from the nature of the business and other circumstances'.[131] It is important to remember that Pufendorf was careful not to talk about a renunciation of rights for the sake of a new type of right; what 'all other men expressly or tacitly renounce [is] their faculty to use a thing',[132] which cannot be a right because 'things are under no obligation to present themselves for man's use'.[133]

The physical possession element of Pufendorf's definition of the original acquisition of a strict exclusive property right is equally important. It was this which constituted the limits of what could or could not be agreed upon in the first pact establishing property, either expressly or tacitly. Men could renounce their use of their natural faculties only over such objects which somebody else had already taken into his use using his own natural faculty; 'for the establishment of possession it is always required

[127] Pufendorf, *DJNG*, 4.4.1.
[128] Pufendorf, *DJNG*, 3.2.1.
[129] Pufendorf, *DJNG*, 4.4.5.
[130] Pufendorf, *DJNG*, 3.5.3.
[131] Pufendorf, *DJNG*, 3.6.2.
[132] Pufendorf, *DJNG*, 3.5.4.
[133] Pufendorf, *DJNG*, 3.5.3.

that a man (...) has physical contact with a thing'.[134] This corporeal act was a strong condition in Pufendorf's eyes. In case of moveable things the actual 'approach with our body' had to amount to a bodily seizure 'in such a way (...) that the things are moved from the spot where they had been placed, and transferred into some place of our own'.[135] This act in the case of moveables was usually effected 'by the hands', 'merely to have seen a thing, or to know its location, is not held to be sufficient to establish possession'.[136] In the case of land, however, bodily seizure had to be accompanied by 'the intention of cultivating it and of establishing boundaries either exact or with some latitude'.[137] This activity was obviously constrained by the natural faculties of the occupier which were his title to enter the moral contract of acquiring property:

> Any single individual is held to have occupied land when he undertakes to cultivate it, or marks out its boundaries. Yet it is understood that he will not embrace more than what one family, even though it includes many members, can probably defend. For if, for example, a single man together with his wife should be cast upon an unoccupied island which would support myriads of inhabitants, it would be imprudent of him to claim it all upon the plea of occupancy, and to attempt to expel all others who might have landed on another part of the island.[138]

This argument has the additional relevance of also setting out the procedure for the later extension of the first pact establishing dominion. Pufendorf accepted Grotius' logical construct, which suggested that since the first pact amounted to a general moral endorsement of the principle of physical occupation, in the future all further first physical occupations of things not yet under somebody's dominion carried with them a moral endorsement by the way of a tacit extension of the first pact.[139] In connection of these exertions of man's natural faculty in order to acquire dominion by occupation, Pufendorf was keen to emphasise that the process of first occupation had to have its own natural boundaries:

> Such was the generosity of God towards men that He supplied them abundantly with what serves their needs. But reason prescribed to men such bounds of possession, as would leave them content upon acquiring what would be likely to meet the needs of themselves and of their dependants. Nor yet does it want them to take no thought for the future, provided their envy and craving for more than they need do not prevent others from providing for their own necessities. If any person ranges too far afield and heaps up superfluous wealth by the oppression of

---

[134] Pufendorf, *DJNG*, 4.9.7.
[135] Pufendorf, *DJNG*, 4.6.9.
[136] Pufendorf, *DJNG*, 4.6.8.
[137] Ibid.
[138] Pufendorf, *DJNG*, 4.6.3.
[139] Pufendorf, *DJNG*, 4.4.9.

others, the rest will not be blamed if, when opportunity affords, they undertake promptly to bring him into line.[140]

Thus, dominion of land in the first instance had to be acquired by a physical act, and this had to be accompanied by the express intent of cultivating. The boundaries were set by the family's 'real' needs for such fruits as nature and man commonly produced on the land and by the family's ability to defend the territory in question.

The relevance of this characterisation of the criteria of occupation becomes apparent when we consider the difficulties Pufendorf had to solve in rescuing the Grotian heritage from the opposition. The two-step Grotian conceptual definition of a first division and then a continuous temporal process of occupation naturally emphasised only the gradual spatial expansion of dominion as men multiplied and started to occupy the whole extension of land on earth. This model appeared to suggest a multiplication only of *dominia* of the same quality, that is, property in the same substance. Although Grotius also suggested a 'conjectural history' in which the objects of dominion were also arranged along a temporal sequence, Pufendorf was alerted by the criticism levelled at Grotius in the post-Grotian debate to the need for a more stringent theorising of the temporal model as a sequence of successively more substantial objects being appropriated in an exclusive manner.

While according to Pufendorf's definition of God's gift of the world to mankind this in itself could not be 'the immediate cause of dominion, as it has its effect in relation to other men', in a less immediate sense in negative community all things lay open to all men for use, and indeed they could have made use of things in the way animals did. Animals used the resources promiscuously, since being animals, 'no one of which, of course, can claim a special right above others to anything, but every one takes for his own nourishment everything he first happens upon'.[141] In some sense a similar 'promiscuous use' was also possible for men.[142] What was actually grasped and consumed by somebody was his own. The problem only started when 'any one of them has stored up some things for future use', since on the level of purely natural animal existence he could do that only if 'others were prevented from seizing them, for the reason that there is no convention among animals which confers a special right over a thing to the one that first got it'.[143] Nonetheless, if this activity was carried on by humans and not by animals, an interpretative

[140] Pufendorf, *DJNG*, 4.5.9.
[141] Pufendorf, *DJNG*, 4.4.5.
[142] Pufendorf, *DJNG*, 4.4.6.
[143] Pufendorf, *DJNG*, 4.4.5.

problem has clearly presented itself. If it appeared that this system of promiscuous or 'universal use' of things had temporally preceded the pact of the first division then it could be easily regarded as the cause of the pact. Pufendorf conceded the point but asked for terminological clarity:

> [I]f any one wishes to designate by the name of proprietorship that right, given men by the Creator, of using things, it might be admitted that 'proprietorship is the cause of division and occupancy', that is, men were allowed to claim things for themselves by occupancy and division, because God had allowed them to apply things to their use. But if we wish to take proprietorship in its proper sense, as denoting the exclusion of all others from a certain thing allowed one person, it is quite true that division and occupancy are the causes of proprietorship.[144]

What is more, this first promiscuous use was not only 'first property' but also 'common property' in this special sense of the word 'property'. Pufendorf conceded this as well: 'Here we will have no quarrel with any one over mere terms, and will allow common dominion to be what is for us the right, belonging to men by virtue of the gift of God, to use creatures; provided that common dominion, considered by itself, has no effect in relation to men.'[145]

This concession on Pufendorf's part, however, could easily cause him a lot of trouble. The notion of common dominion which was at stake was a difficult one. On the one hand he was now in a strong position to quickly eliminate some of the confusion which already bothered Grotius and became quite acute in the decades preceding his own writing. The concept of 'negative community' as a sharp razor sliced away those new theories which tried to short-circuit the apparent ambiguity of jurisprudential rights theories by directly stipulating private dominion from the act of God at the beginning of mankind's career. Pufendorf particularly despised that insipid variety of this argument which attempted to originate private dominion from the solitary Adam as the personal agent of divine will. This interpretation not only misunderstood the nature of God's gift of things to man but missed also the necessary logical connection between rights and obligations in the concept of private dominion. But by successfully demolishing these individualistic theories his troubles were not yet over and indeed a new set of problems presented itself which he found very difficult to tackle within the linguistic constraints he set for himself.

This part of his polemic concerned community theorists. In part they could be also caught out by the clarification between 'right as law' and 'right as human institution' sanctioned by dominative natural law.

[144] Pufendorf, *DJNG*, 4.4.12.
[145] Ibid.

Despite all linguistic appearances, however, exclusive property rights did not have a single individual as their sole reference point, as Pufendorf well knew. If the physical act of occupation, or individuation was a common act of several people, then the moral endorsement lent to it by express or tacit consent of others created common property, that is, 'common dominion'. The relationship between the joint owners was governed by their own decisions and could conform to distributive justice as defined by Pufendorf within the realm of strict justice. When a thing is held 'by several in an undivided manner, in such a way that each one has an equal right in it according to his share', then in Pufendorf's language one was talking about a 'positive community'. The right involved here was a full right in Pufendorf's sense; that is, it was exclusive of everybody outside the group. As Pufendorf argued:

Such community differs from proprietorship, not in the manner and force of dominion (for several persons may have the same right over a common thing that one man has over a proper thing; and just as the proprietorship of a thing which concerns but one man excludes every other man from an equal right in that thing, so from a common thing all are excluded but those for whom the thing is said to be common), but it differs only in the subject in which it terminates, because a proper thing belongs to one man, a common thing to several. And since none of these has a right extending, as it were, over the whole thing, but having power only over a part of the thing, such part still remaining undivided, it is obvious that one person cannot of his own right dispose of the entire thing, but only of his share; and that if any decision is to be reached on the whole thing, the consent and authority of each person concerned in it must be secured.[146]

This sub-species of dominion, this 'positive community', of course was not a symmetrical counterpart of 'negative community'. The main distinction between negative community and dominion was that of potency and actuality, while positive community was common dominion contrasted to individual, private dominion. According to Pufendorf it was as nonsensical to believe that God had given a natural precept to hold things in common dominion as in private. To use an analogy, Pufendorf argued negative community implied that a man naturally had 'the power to acquire some right' similar to his capacity 'to be a potential musician', while if an actual member of a positive community kept his right temporally suspended as a mere potentiality one was talking about a 'right itself inhering by habit, yet without operation and exercise' like when one chooses 'not to sing when one has been musically trained'.[147]

[146] Pufendorf, *DJNG*, 4.4.2.
[147] Pufendorf, *DJNG*, 4.4.10.

Pufendorf did not seem to think that holding property partly or wholly in positive community was unimportant, *a priori* undesirable or impossible. However, he could maintain this view only if he could avoid any confusion between his concession of a communal quasi-dominion in primeval negative community and positive community proper (in his terminology). This concession brought him into dangerous territory. Absolutist property theories of the Filmer-type, which sought to derive modern property rights from Adam's dominion, also sought to argue that a community of goods was impossible because it could not find any way to legitimise the individual appropriation of things necessary to human survival. In such communities, so it was argued, each man would have the right to pull food out of another man's grasp or even his mouth. In view of this, some commentators of Grotius, notably Boecler, already protested against such a concession as the one Pufendorf was just about granting, since it was quite absurd to accept that 'on this theory proprietorship is established in community'. Pufendorf, however, replied that the solution to the problem was easy if due attention was paid to the actual process that was meant to be theorised:

Here a difficulty is uselessly created where there is none. For primitive community is one thing, before any deed of man and the use of any thing, when each thing merely belongs no more to one man than to another, and in this way belongs quite as well to neither; but it is another thing when men begin to make use of things open to all. For then, whatever each man has seized for his own uses becomes proper to him by a previous pact, since without such men would have to refrain from the use of all things. Therefore, in this, as it were, limited community the bodies of things belong to no one, but their fruits after gathering are proper. Such a tempering of primitive community with proprietorship, I feel, is comprehensible even by men of ordinary intelligence. An oak-tree belonged to no man, but the acorns that fell to the ground were his who had gathered them.[148]

Pufendorf also reminded his learned readers that his own interpretation followed the spirit of the ancient Stoic metaphor of the public theatre. He quoted the relevant passage the following way:

The comments of Seneca, *On Benefits*, on the different kinds of community are not irrelevant to our subject: 'For I have not everything in common with a friend in the same manner as with a partner, where one part belongs to him, and another to me, but rather as a father and a mother possess their children in common, when they have two, not each parent possessing one child, but each possessing both (...) The knights' seats in the theatre belong to all the Roman knights; yet of these the seat which I occupy becomes my own, and if I yield it up to any one, although I only yield him a thing which we own in common, still I

---

[148] Pufendorf, *DJNG*, 4.4.13.

appear to have given him something. Some things belong to certain persons under particular conditions. I have a place among the knights, not to sell, or to let, or to live in, but simply to see the spectacle from; wherefore I do not tell an untruth when I say that I have a place among the knights' seats. Yet if, when I come into the theatre, the knights' seats are full, I both have a seat there by right, because I have the privilege of sitting there, and I have not a seat there, because my seat is occupied by those who share my right to those places.'[149]

It was only later, with the consent of the state, that a citizen could secure a seat for himself 'for all the time'. Pufendorf could argue in this way in apparent harmony with the language of rights as he defined it, because the first pact he assumed, he allowed to be a tacit one. The grasping of a fruit, or occupying a seat in the theatre, was a consequence of a human act, a corporeal act, as required by the legal act of occupancy. Thus, he declared,

no credit should be given to any such idea as that God at the beginning instituted a positive community, from which men later withdrew on their own initiative, but rather, so far as it concerned God, such things were left open to the uses of men. Now so long as the actual bodies of things were not yet assigned to certain individuals, there was a tacit convention that each man could appropriate for his own use, primarily of the fruits of things, what he wanted, and could consume what was consumable. And such a universal use of things in some way took the place of proprietorship, while, what a man had taken in this way, another could not take from him without doing him an injury.[150]

For the operation of the primeval system all that was needed was to indicate the corporeal occupation 'in order that others might know what belonged to another, so as to be able to keep their hands off it'.[151] This was, of course, not at all as obvious as he claimed. 'For, if the sum total of things had been given to all mankind, there appears no consideration', argued Ziegler, another leading Grotius commentator,

by which individuals might by occupancy make any of these things their own, (...) such is the nature of things in common, which have their parts not divided but undivided, that there is not even an atom of them in which the community is not indivisible, while if it is taken by an individual for his own use alone, it will be severed from the community, and an injury done the latter. Yet those who defend a primitive community confess that individuals upon occupancy acquired such a right over the things thus taken that the right of all others to any particular thing in question was excluded.[152]

---

[149] Pufendorf, *DJNG*, 4.4.2; Seneca, *On Benefits*, Bk. VII. ch. xii.
[150] Pufendorf, *DJNG*, 4.4.9.
[151] Pufendorf, *DJNG*, 4.4.10.
[152] Pufendorf, *DJNG*, 4.4.11.

But for Pufendorf this was not a problem. Short of a positive community stipulating such an unreasonable pact for itself, individuation from negative community or from a deliberately indefinitely owned part of a positive community was validated by the occupation criteria of his definition of dominion, by the physical, bodily, occupation of the thing in order to satisfy the legitimate needs of the occupier and his family. Pufendorf's real problem was rather to show how and why people actually left the 'negative community' and ended up in a world where the just norm was to have the earth divided into exclusive private properties of land and productive assets.

Since Pufendorf was committed to the denial of the utility of demonstrative models which only constructed a 'state of nature' in order to demonstrate the process of leaving it, he had to look 'into the state of nature, not as may be conceived in the abstract, but as it actually is',[153] that is, to a reconstruction of mankind's decision of choosing the type of dominion which was most conducive to peaceful life in historical terms. Such a history – a 'conjectural history' as it was called in the eighteenth century – required that he should underpin the language of rights with a theory of human nature as unfolded in real history. Furthermore, this theory of human nature had to concentrate in particular on man's relationship to objects on which relationships among men were based, that is, on man's needs.

Needs and Property: Against Positive Communities of Simplicity and the Ideology of the 'Golden Age'

No contract theory (in a narrow sense) could give an account of the prior reasons which led to the contract itself in terms of the rights which followed only from the contract. Since Pufendorf cancelled the possibility of construing the pre-contract appropriation as rightful dominion, he needed a dynamic principle which could introduce the element of temporal causation into his theory of the origins of property rights. He once hinted at the solution earlier. The solution was connected to the time-honoured commonplace of all criticisms of property theories, namely that it was human greed which made the commonality of the world into a domain ruled by a right for the few. Here was a cause for dynamic change. The theory which explained it had to be a theory of needs, not of rights. Rather, rights at every stage were now conceived as constraints called forth by the dynamism of human needs. Rights were a static and consolidating element in the system, parasitical on an

---

[153] Pufendorf, *DJNG*, 2.2.7.

underlying dynamic of desires and passions. The theory of needs had a further advantage over a theory of primeval community operating with original 'distributive' rights. A needs theory, unlike the theoretical construct of rights, could break out from the straitjacket of the correlativity theorem. It could also introduce the necessary element of individuality into the community theory of the beginnings of mankind's appropriation of God's gift of the world for human use. As a theory of these beginnings, the idea of negative community was still pronouncedly a 'community theory' since it was relating all its arguments to the theoretical object of mankind, the human species. Since the 'negative community' theory attempted to draw a picture of mankind at its earliest stages, the community element in it was entirely credible in historical terms. In Pufendorf's needs theory, individuality appeared in community in the following way. Although men lived in 'community', the use of nature by any person could nonetheless happen in no other way than as a process of individuation: '[S]o long as the actual bodies of things were not yet assigned to certain individuals, there was a tacit convention that each man could appropriate for his own use, primarily of the fruits of things, what he wanted, and could consume what was consumable.'[154] At the level of elementary needs, none but a strictly individual use was in fact possible:

[S]ince things are of no use to men unless at least their fruits may be appropriated, and this is impossible if others as well can take what we have already by our own act selected for our uses, it follows that the first convention between men was about these very concerns, to the effect that whatever one of these things which were left open to all, and of their fruits, a man had laid his hands upon, with intent to turn it to his uses, could not be taken from him by another.[155]

Given the fact that men were living in community but by definition were also individuals, it made it easy to supplement the theory of community with a theory of individuality. The theory of negative community as such could not yield such a theory of individuality, but it allowed a choice, as we have seen, at least in the sense that it left the theoretical space for it indeterminate. Here the occasion presented itself to Pufendorf to gather the fruits of his elaborate critical transformation of the joint heritage of Grotius and Hobbes and clarify the compatibility of community and individuality even further. For Pufendorf mankind began in family units, or as an absolute beginning, first perhaps in one family, the family of Adam and Eve. Distributive relationships inside the families, however,

---

[154] Pufendorf, *DJNG*, 4.4.9.
[155] Pufendorf, *DJNG*, 4.4.5.

did not necessitate any division or pact. The members of the family received their share from paternal authority. The boundary line emerged only when the natural multiplication in the family resulted in the setting up of new 'secondary' family units. Pufendorf insisted that men existed in a social state from the beginning; he could not attribute meaning to the hypothesis that 'in the beginning, a multitude of men, in no way related to one another, suddenly sprang into being'.[156] He also insisted on the point that man was a uniquely feeble animal, less capable of naturally maintaining himself than any other animal, particularly in the beginning. He characterised the condition of early man as *imbecillitas*. 'A man left in the open, away from any assistance of his fellows', he argued, would be 'a miserable animal':

A dumb and ignoble creature, with no power other than to dig up plants and roots, to slake his thirst at any spring, river or pool, he may happen upon, to crawl into caves so as to avoid the inclemency of the weather, to cover his body with moss or grass, to pass his time in intolerable inactivity, to tremble at every sound or at the passing of another animal, and finally to perish of hunger and cold or to be torn to pieces by some wild beast. [Thus] (...) man owed it to his intercourse and relations with other men that he did not pass an existence more miserable than that of any other living being.[157]

In fact, mankind's prolonged existence in *imbecillitas* would have precluded, for all practical purposes, the use of man's natural faculties, like reason, since 'there would be little or no use of all such faculties in a life lawless, brutal and unsociable'.[158] However, by establishing mutual assistance men could realise their potential superiority over animals. The needs of animals were easily satisfied by nature's bounty and they had no other needs than hunger and lust guided by the necessity of procreation. The needs of animals were 'simple and uniform desire' and 'the different kind of animals have in general similar inclinations, (...) if you know one you know them all'.[159] Man's desires were, on the other hand, manifold and varied:

[M]an is filled through and through with a great conglomeration of affections and desires unknown to beasts. A craving for luxuries, ambitions, honours, and the desire to surpass others, envy, jealousy, rivalries of wit, superstition, anxiety about the future, curiosity, all these continually trouble his mind, none of which touch of the senses of brutes.[160]

---

[156] Pufendorf, *DJNG*, 2.2.7.
[157] Pufendorf, *DJNG*, 2.1.8.
[158] Pufendorf, *DJNG*, 2.1.5.
[159] Pufendorf, *DJNG*, 2.1.7.
[160] Pufendorf, *DJNG*, 2.1.6.

Pufendorf's vision of historical development was based on this fundamental tension between animal and civilised existence. The main polemical message of Pufendorf in the raging debate about the origins of the modern exclusive system of dominion was that there had to be a temporal process, a history, traversing the space between the two extreme polarities of man's condition, primitive rudeness and modern civility, since it would be near absurd to think that 'the whole earth was at once divided between that handful of mortals, or that all things once and for all passed under proprietorship' at the time of the first establishment of boundaries between families.[161]

How could this idea of a passage from miserable simplicity to refinement be squared with Pufendorf's concession that early mankind lived in community, albeit a negative one, but already tempered by a certain kind of property? The starting points of his theory were already defined in terms of *imbecillitas* and a basic network of family units. But this point of departure still had to be worked out in the terms suggested by the community theories of jurisprudence. As Pufendorf already had shown, the Stoic metaphor of the public theatre, frequently used by Grotius and by himself, met the need of illustrating how community could be tempered with individuality without conflict. Now, however, a further step had to be taken. The same type of model had to be reformulated also in terms of the dynamic needs theory. What should be the proper historical model here? One point was clear to Pufendorf:

[T]he example of the Aborigines, as Justin describes them, is not to the point. For the words of that author picture some positive community, such as that primitive state was not, as if that entire country belonged to a people, but had not yet been divided into private estates, because those men were content with fruits that grew of themselves, which the expanse of forests and fields brought forth in profusion for a small population. But it does not seem likely that those fruits were collected unto a common store. Yet Grotius rightly maintains that if this negative community was to continue without disturbance to the common peace, men had to live in great simplicity, content to subsist upon natural fruits, to live in caves, and to go about with bodies either bare or else covered with the bark of trees and the skins of animals; while if they wanted a more refined kind of life, the advantages of which had to be secured by industry, property in things was necessary.[162]

What Pufendorf emphasised here was a certain amount of choice open to such communities. Every community had to choose to enforce its own form of 'distributive justice'. His point was this: those communities which did – and Pufendorf cited as contemporary examples 'the

---

[161] Pufendorf, *DJNG*, 4.4.11.
[162] Pufendorf, *DJNG*, 4.4.9.

barbarous and simple peoples' of the primitive world discovered by contemporary travellers – could only maintain their distributive principles intact as long as the population remained stable, and as long as needs remained limited to the same common standard. He insisted that such an arrangement was not 'a purely imaginary hypothesis'. However,

> that community, considered as thoroughgoing, could not persist, unless men were willing always to go hungry and to wander about naked; but, so long as men were not too numerous and led a simple life, nothing prevented its existence with a certain degree of proprietorship. Yet it is certain that the more the number of men increased, and the more refined life became, the greater necessity there was for things in increasing numbers to pass under proprietorship. Those people who to this day are but barbarous and simple; such, for instance, as exist on herbs, roots, the natural fruits of the earth, by hunting, and fishing, with no other property than a shed and some rude furniture.[163]

There were two confusions here, which Pufendorf decided to fight with all the rhetorical prowess he could muster. Community theorists, opposing the system of exclusive private property, were fond of two particular arguments. On the one hand they argued that models of early simplicity could be, and in fact were, reintroduced, and pointed to certain experiments in modern times which were considered a success. Secondly, they tried to argue that the primitive negative community with its relative simplicity was a 'good world' which had been lost but which retained a normative relevance for modern thinking on property and society as an ideal model. Pufendorf rightly pointed out, with some dismay, that even Grotius had made some concessions on the first point. Thus, he elaborately argued that Grotius,

> when he adds that community could have endured 'if men had lived on terms of mutual affection such as rarely appears', confuses negative community with positive, such as was practised formerly among the Essenes (...), the early Christians in Jerusalem, and among those who follow an ascetic life. (...) For such a community can be instituted and maintained only by a small group, which is also endowed with singular humility of mind. When men are scattered to distant places it would be a labour of folly to gather products into one place, and then distribute them from a common store; while among a large number of men many must necessarily be found who from a defective sense of justice and from greediness would be unwilling to maintain due equality either in labour or in consumption of food. And Plato, in *Laws*, Bk. V, suggests this very thing in assigning to the gods and their offspring this same state where there is a community of all things. But it is foolish to believe that after men had separated into several families, they ever established or wanted to establish such a community.[164]

---

[163] Pufendorf, *DJNG*, 4.4.13.
[164] Pufendorf, *DJNG*, 4.4.9.

Such a positive community of simplicity must by nature be limited and had to be suffused by an extraordinarily strong sense of distributive justice. Growth was inimical to its very existence. But growth there was, all the time, as Pufendorf never tired of pointing out again and again. The system of private property in the end was thus the result of the growth of the population in a world of scarce resources. It was a mistake to believe that mankind could be modelled after small group behaviour. Pufendorf heavily relied here on authoritative sources in his polemic, primarily on Aristotle's refutation of 'the Platonic community of property'. However, he was also aware of the vitality of the Platonic utopian tradition:

I confess, however, that these arguments have not prevented Thomas More and Thomas Campanella from introducing community of property, the former among the inhabitants of his *Utopia* and the latter in his *City of the Sun*, probably I suppose because perfect men are more easily imagined than found. But this also shows the falsity of the old saying: 'Mine and thine are the causes of all wars.' Rather it is that 'mine and thine' were introduced to avoid wars.[165]

If one saw the world as it was, then the system of private property was not an 'expression' of human nature but rather an artificial constraint on it. The voluntarism underlying visions of utopian communities presupposed not men as they were but as they could be imagined. Pufendorf was also adamant in his opposition to any romanticisation of the early primeval period. He clearly pointed to the ideological origins of this veneration of the 'simple' past:

Some quite aptly point out that, to understand this tradition of a Golden Age, we should bear in mind the disposition of unlettered and agricultural peoples, which is so clearly inclined to ease and sluggishness, and averse to labour. And that the more unrefined and simple the life of any people, the less place they hold, while a richer and more refined manner of life requires great industry and extended endeavour. (...) Finally, that it is a common failing of old men to be 'praisers of the past time when they were young' (Horace, *Art of Poetry*, 173f.), almost consistently scorning the present and praising what is old and time-worn, and that, therefore, it seems likely that when those simple folk were forced by legislators to labour and a more refined life, they took such a change of habits very hard, and many a time longed for their nuts and their idleness. From this complaint of their forbears later generations then created those dreams about a Golden Age.[166]

It was not the case, he added, as the tradition had it, that it was the vices of 'greed and avarice' only which forced these happy people into the transition from one stage to another. Pufendorf's argument was that

[165] Pufendorf, *DJNG*, 4.4.7.
[166] Pufendorf, *DJNG*, 4.4.8.

these 'unlettered and agricultural peoples' were not virtuous but simply stood at an early stage of development with an appropriately undeveloped structure of needs: 'For they were probably not as yet so given over to avarice, because they were still unacquainted with wealth, and the earth furnished them, still ignorant of the enticements of the appetite, an easy living, while there do not appear to have been any resources for liberality, when there was no occasion to collect wealth.'[167]

In opposition he clearly stated his own ideological intentions: 'I myself believe that the complaint of the masses about the burdens and drawbacks of civil states could be met in no better way than by picturing to their eyes the drawbacks of a state of nature.'[168]

The foundation of these mythological theories of positive communities simply overlooked the basic facts prevailing through most of mankind's history in man's relationship to his environment; 'Ovid's perpetual spring, the choice of fruits produced spontaneously, and rivers running over with nectar and milk' were pure fable, argued Pufendorf. The truth was rather sombre and disappointing. Instead of abundance, the basic fact of human life was an ever-present scarcity:

The causes for things passing into proprietorship, and the order which they followed can, I think, be understood on these considerations: Most things which are of use to men immediately and are employed to nourish them and protect their bodies, are not produced everywhere by nature and without cultivation in such abundance that they fully suffice for every one. Therefore, an occasion for quarrels and wars lay ready at hand, if two or more men needed the same thing, and individuals tried to appropriate for themselves the same thing, when it was not enough for all. (...) Moreover, most things require labour and cultivation by men to produce them and make them fit for use. But in such cases it was improper that a man who had contributed no labour should have right to things equal to his by whose industry a thing had been raised or rendered fit for service. Therefore, it was advantageous to peace among men that, as soon as men multiplied, there should be introduced dominion of mobile things, especially such as require labour and cultivation by men, and, among immobile things, dominion of those which are of immediate use to men, such as places for dwelling; that, in other words, the substance of these objects might belong separately to individuals, or, when several were concerned, to those who by special convention had agreed to a positive community in such things.[169]

Man's habitat was a world of scarcity, and the only means mankind had to improve the lot of the species was labour. The conquest of nature by labour was, of course, not a process which could be depicted in the static

---

[167] Pufendorf, *DJNG*, 4.4.8.
[168] Pufendorf, *DJNG*, 2.2.2.
[169] Pufendorf, *DJNG*, 4.4.6.

terms of the community theories of simplicity, and Pufendorf had to insist again and again that the process of leaving the primitive negative community ought to be modelled as a 'historical' process in time:

> [M]en left this original negative community of things and by a pact established separate dominions over things, not, indeed, all at once and for all time, but successively, and as the state of things, or the nature and number of men, seemed to require. Thus, the Scythians used to allow property in flocks and household goods, but their fields were held in original community. And truly the peace and tranquillity of mankind, the maintenance of which is the first concern of the law of nature, made no uncertain suggestion as to what might be the most salutary arrangement by men in this regard. For after the human race had multiplied and acquired a cultured mode of life, the peace of men did not suffer that there should remain for every man an equal power over all things, that is, that all things should lie open to all for the promiscuous use of every man. Since innumerable conflicts could not avoid arising from the rivalry of many persons over the same thing, which could not suffice for all of them at one time, especially in view of the fact that such is the nature of the vast majority of things, that they can be of service to but one person at one time.[170]

Pufendorf's Conjectural History of the Stages of Property

The conception of human nature which underpinned utopias and of positive community theories presupposed men not as they were but as they wished to be. Pufendorf, on the other hand, wanted to consider mankind's lot, as we have seen, not as it 'may be conceived in the abstract, but as it actually is'. What had to be explained was not why some men remained content with the barbarous simplicity of positive community but why most others had chosen to institute rules of exclusive private property, and why in doing so they had been able, on the one hand, to control the 'avarice of men' which 'burns to overleap the bounds of "mine and thine"', and on the other, to secure, through property, a 'more refined kind of life'.[171] In other words, having shown that the world was given to man neither as a positive community nor as exclusive private property from the beginning, and having committed himself to an account of property as a human institution, Pufendorf was led towards the construction of a conjectural history of property in which human needs were the driving dynamic. In the polemic over the origins of property and the related polemic over the relative merits of the vanished 'Golden Age' of primitive communism versus modern private individuation, Pufendorf's chief message was that the whole debate had to

[170] Pufendorf, *DJNG*, 4.4.6.
[171] Pufendorf, *DJNG*, 4.4.7; 4.4.10.

be posed and understood in historical terms – in terms of the transformation of rules of individuation in the passage of mankind from primitive rudeness to modern civility. The key problem in this conjectural history was to explain how God's original grant of a right to use the things of the world was gradually converted into a right *in* – a property *in* – the things of the world. It was as absurd to argue that 'the whole earth was at once divided between that handful of mortals' as it was to maintain 'that all things once and for all passed under proprietorship'.[172] Instead, the process was historical: '[A]s mankind multiplied and living conveniencies were increased by industry, the necessity of preserving a social life led to the introduction of dominion, yet so that not all things passed into proprietorship at one time, but successively, according as considerations of concord seemed to require.'[173]

Pufendorf now historicised property relations vertically, so to speak, that is, in terms of their progressive application to more and more objects as these came to be the basis of human subsistence. It was essentially a three-stage theory. As the objects of people's activity changed, that is, as man passed from depending on fruit and game in the hunting and gathering stages of society to dependence on agricultural land, and as this land was progressively filled up by population and rendered relatively scarce, so then the principle of individuation changed from 'promiscuous use' to property. This account, in other words, linked the evolution of types of individuation – the passage from the quasi rights *to* of negative community to rights *in* – to the development of new modes of procuring subsistence, to population growth and to the expansion of human needs. The tension between abundance and scarcity was constantly operating throughout this process, explained Pufendorf, since both notions were only relative ones. The scarcity constraints were never rigid. Human labour could change the constraints themselves by pushing the limits of productivity further and further. Differential labour inputs then produced differential access to the goods which could satisfy needs. Initially, of course, the opportunity to find proper objects for labour to transform was equal and all men had the option open to exercise their diligence. While the historical process was in theory open-ended, Pufendorf put the initial emphasis on the fact that at any given moment of human existence, at any level of production, a conflict could arise between men's needs and desires and the relative abundance in immediate available means for their satisfaction. This gap was the cause of introducing private dominion:

---

[172] Pufendorf, *DJNG*, 4.4.11.
[173] Pufendorf, *DJNG*, 4.4.12.

The causes for things passing into proprietorship, and the order which they followed can, I think, be understood on these considerations: Most things which are of use to men immediately and are employed to nourish them and protect their bodies, are not produced everywhere by nature and without cultivation in such abundance that they fully suffice for every one. Therefore, an occasion for quarrels and wars lay ready at hand, if two or more men needed the same thing, and individuals tried to appropriate for themselves the same thing, when it was not enough for all.[174]

In the first period of human existence, which Pufendorf theorised as a hunting and gathering stage, no contractual delineation of exclusive dominion was required for individuation. There was 'a tacit convention that each man could appropriate for his own use, primarily of the fruits of things, what he wanted, and could consume what was consumable'.[175] The fruit of the earth and the wild animals were tacitly recognised to be rightly appropriated for use by the first person who harvested or took them. Thus, 'an oak tree belonged to no man, but the acorns that fell to the ground were his who had gathered them'.[176] In things like game and wild fruit, which perish in their consumption, use coincided with dominion. Yet such a tacit convention to 'promiscuous use' could only continue 'without disturbance to the common peace', Pufendorf argued, so long as men lived in 'great simplicity, content to subsist upon natural fruits, to live in caves and to go about with bodies either bare or else covered with the bark of trees and the skins of animals'.[177] After the stage of gathering natural fruits and hunting wild animals, *dominia*, or exclusive use rights, were extended to 'mobile things' such as domestic animals and then also to land. The modes of subsistence associated with these stages in the completion of property rights were shepherding and agriculture:

> It was enough at first that those things should be made proper which are either immediately and indivisibly of use to several persons, such as clothing, habitations, and fruits gathered for food, or which require some labour and care, such as implements, household furnishings, herds, and fields. Little by little what remained came under proprietorship, according as the inclination of men or their increasing numbers directed. Thus for a long time pasture lands remained in primitive community, until, has herds multiplied and quarrels arose, it was to the interest of peace that they also be divided.[178]

Initially, too, men simply appropriated land for their habitations and fields by a 'tacit convention of rights of first occupancy'. No formal

[174] Pufendorf, *DJNG*, 4.4.6.
[175] Pufendorf, *DJNG*, 4.4.9.
[176] Pufendorf, *DJNG*, 4.4.13.
[177] Pufendorf, *DJNG*, 4.4.9.
[178] Pufendorf, *DJNG*, 4.4.11.

or contractual delineation of exclusive private property was required because land was still in abundance relative to population:

[R]egarding the immobile things produced by nature without the labour of man, such as fields, they were so extensive that they abundantly provided for the small number of early men, and for that reason at first only so much of them was occupied as men judged to be suitable for their uses, while the rest was left in a state of original negative community, so that every man who wished to was free in the future to take it. And hence it is understood that a pact was agreed upon, to the effect that such fields as had been assigned to one person by the express convention of the rest of men, or such as the rest could be held tacitly to have withdrawn from, in view of the fact that one man alone had been allowed to enjoy them in peace, while they had claimed for themselves other fields on the same basis – that such fields should belong to those who cultivated them. And finally, that what was left should pass to those who would hereafter occupy the fields.[179]

It is important to recognise that this first division of lands in Pufendorf's conjectural history was still in the condition of 'negative community'. Here the community aspect of the notion of 'negative community' was to the fore, although the technical meaning, originating from Roman law, was also relevant. These fields were no one's at the point of occupation, they were *res nullius*. But once a group of people occupied a piece of land, they used it amongst themselves 'promiscuously' – in common. Pufendorf's construction of this history was conjectural; nonetheless he tried to use 'real' history to support the view that the first common property in land was in the mould of the modern village common:

But when a group of men have together occupied some portion of land, this has usually been done either as a whole or by sections. It is an instance of the former kind of occupancy, when a group of men take under possession some desert tract of land, the bounds of which have been fixed either by nature or by the decision of men. Portions of this are then allowed each member of the group to occupy as he pleases (a method rarely followed) or they are assigned to each person of the group by the whole body, which is the best way to avoid quarrels and confusion. For that a promiscuous occupancy gives rise to confusion is suggested by Livy, where he describes Rome as 'more like a city taken up by individuals, than regularly portioned out by commissioners'.[180]

He described the way ancient people actually managed the common. Their method was that of the 'system of natural lot', which definitely did not confer to individuals any rights in the substance of land itself. The spirit of equality among ancient tribes required that

---

[179] Pufendorf, *DJNG*, 4.4.6.
[180] Pufendorf, *DJNG*, 4.4.3.

in case the thing to be distributed cannot be divided among several, it should, if possible, be used in common by those who have equal rights in it, on the understanding that if the quality of the thing permits, they may use it as much as they wish. But if the thing does not permit this, they may employ it in a limited degree, and in proportion to the number of those who use it; for any other way of observing equality cannot be imagined.[181]

The first primitive tribes of agricultural peoples, Pufendorf reasoned, would have acted like the German tribes mentioned by Julius Caesar, who did not assign a definite quantity of land or estate to each individual. The chiefs of the tribes simply designated the tracts of land which ought to be cultivated and then ordered the tribe to move on once it was used up, leaving to each individual what portion they should cultivate. This system maintained 'the simplicity of their life' and avoided 'avarice and luxury'. In such a loose system of use rights, no individual was excluded from the land of another. In this system of equality, Pufendorf argued, no 'sufficient proof, indeed, can be advanced why something that I feel to be proper for myself, I should feel to be improper for others who are my equals, other things being equal'.[182] Selfishness, manifesting itself in the desire of retaining 'a special share in things which are the common property of all', Pufendorf thought was despicable. He used strong language to condemn those greedy men, 'who, in their miserliness, rob others of the necessities of life by keeping more than they can use, and who cannot be changed in their way, such is the stubbornness of their make-up, and constitute a permanent menace and burden upon society'.[183]

Exclusion and the creation of absolute property right in land began to occur in the agricultural stage only when land became relatively scarce, and occupiers sought to push back these scarcity constraints by applying the labour of improvement to their plots. The reason for this division of land, he explained, was primarily the virtually unstoppable multiplication of mankind, that is, population growth. It was this exogenous reason which forced men to accept the change in land tenure systems, not some principle inherent in the legal reasoning of property right. Here Pufendorf again encountered the residue of Grotius' concession to communities of property. He made it clear that mankind, when pressed by population growth, had to introduce the enclosure of fields, while the same pressure did not apply to the oceans, whose original holding by mankind in negative community could thus survive the rise of civilisation:

---

[181] Pufendorf, *DJNG*, 3.2.5.
[182] Pufendorf, *DJNG*, 3.2.4.
[183] Pufendorf, *DJNG*, 3.2.5.

it is surely contrary to reason that a thing which is open to all mankind and sufficient to meet any use of every man should be divided into shares. So great, indeed, is the size of the earth, that it is sufficient for all people in every use, yet it would not be so if it were kept undivided by so great a multitude of men as now inhabit it. It could in no way sustain them without cultivation and improvement. This, therefore, is a further reason why the size of the earth is no obstacle to its being divided, and yet this reason would make a division of the ocean ridiculous.[184]

Pufendorf's position on labour creating entitlement to exclusive dominion was derived from Aristotle's *Politics*. There, Pufendorf said, Aristotle had argued that if 'all men should labour in common and should lay up their earnings in common, and should they be maintained from a common store, quarrels could not help arising by reason of the inequality of their toil and its product'.[185] The introduction of property did away with such quarrels and enabled each man to devote himself to the improvement of his portion and 'to show liberality to others out of his own store'.[186] Quite clearly, Pufendorf argued, 'it was improper that a man who had contributed no labour should have right to things equal to his by whose industry a thing had been raised or rendered fit to service'.[187]

Yet if it was labour which constituted the principle of desert for exclusive appropriation, it did not grant occupiers the right to exclude others from the means of subsistence. Apart from the imperfect obligation to display 'liberality' to others, exclusive dominion in land was constrained initially at least, by the fact that, in an economy still without money, men had no interest in appropriating land which they could not cultivate and improve themselves. They could not appropriate more than they needed and, as a result, could not infringe on the right of others to subsist on God's dominion. Man's natural faculty to acquire dominion through occupation, in other words, had its own natural boundaries.

In an economy without money, moreover, 'envy and craving for more than they need' had no means to develop. It was not the case, in other words, that greed and avarice were innate to human nature and hence the 'essentialist' dynamic driving mankind from one stage of subsistence to another. The fact that men now had to labour the land, improve it, was the first step towards a fully agricultural stage in history, a stage in which the substance of the land was owned as full exclusive dominion. However, beside labour, a second new element

---

[184] Pufendorf, *DJNG*, 4.5.4.
[185] Pufendorf, *DJNG*, 4.4.7. Aristotle, *Politics*, 1263a.
[186] Pufendorf, *DJNG*, 4.4.7.
[187] Pufendorf, *DJNG*, 4.4.6.

had to enter history before the transition could be completed. This second element was money. But faithful to his principles of historical motivation, Pufendorf had explained the introduction of money not by recourse to the hypothesis of innate greed but by recognising man's unique sociability as a species: his dependence on other men to meet his needs and the dynamics of these needs once stimulated by the new material possibilities opened up by human labour. In these arguments, Pufendorf was again closely following Aristotle, using his arguments about the origin and functions of money in order to theorise the transition from 'promiscuous use' in negative community to exclusive dominion in the agricultural stage.

Initially, mutual needs could have been met by simple barter of natural produce, but since natural produce perishes, barter could not provide means for preparing for and avoiding future scarcities. Pufendorf repeated both of Aristotle's initial arguments in favour of exchange and money. First, exchange was a kind of bond between people; it was an underlying agent of natural sociability. Second, people were individuals, with different needs, living in regions with various natural endowment. If needs and the natural endowment of mankind were homogeneous, instead of heterogeneous, no exchange could have taken place and the original community would have survived forever. Need in the Aristotelian theory, which Pufendorf took over wholeheartedly, was a bonding, rather than a dividing agent:

> For that *chreia* or need 'which, as it were, holds together all things' and supports them, is (...) the sole foundation (...) of exchange or of commerce. For if men had need of nothing, or of another thing no more than what they have, there would be no commerce and no exchange, since each man would keep what was his own and enjoy that. For Aristotle expressly says in that same passage [*Nicomachean Ethics*, Bk. V. chap. viii]: 'The fact that it is demand which is like a principle of unity binding society together, is evident because, if there is no mutual demand on the part of two persons, if neither of them or one only needs the services of the other, they do not effect an exchange.' The same point is illustrated in his *Politics*, Bk. I, chap. vi (9): 'The art of exchange extends to all possessions and it arises at first in a natural manner from the circumstance that some have too little, others too much. For they were forced to use exchange until they had enough.'[188]

The introduction of money to satisfy men's *chreia* (or *indigentia* or need) then led to complex new developments. As Aristotle had explained in Book V of the *Nicomachean Ethics*, money was introduced in order to guarantee exchange in the future, that is, to ensure that exchange shall

---

[188] Pufendorf, *DJNG*, 5.1.4. Aristotle, *Politics*, 1257a.

be possible when a future need arises. Yet once introduced, money broke through the constraint on unequal accumulation which had been provided by the fact that natural produce spoils if unused. It was for this reason that money transformed human nature, creating first the possibility and then the desire of avarice:

> But it is certain that (...) avarice increased with the use of money. For so long as wealth lay only in stores of grain, herds, and the like, the desire for unlimited gain was ultimately quenched by the work involved in such things, the difficulty of handling and keeping them, and the further fact that they were easily destroyed. But now, upon the introduction of gold and silver money, it is easy for avarice to amass even millions.[189]

There were two sides, negative and positive, to the introduction of money, the negative being the emergence of 'avarice' and inequality, the positive being the incentive which money offered to men to exert their labour to improve themselves, trade their surplus with others and expand their own needs. Pufendorf held both of these positions, refusing golden-age jeremiads about the loss of the pre-money age of primitive society but also refusing to deny that modernity – commerce – had brought with it luxury, avarice, restlessness and inequality. Given this ambiguous nature of societies based on private property of land and monetised commerce, Pufendorf was obliged to show how the just principles which created the system of private dominion according to his model could retain at least a basic level of justice in the distribution of goods. He was first of all intent on showing what the logic of the new monetised exchange system entailed. Two processes combined in forming the inevitable logic of the full agrarian stage; of the stage in which exclusive dominion of land was first allowed and then generalised. This was, of course, all premised on one thing, on the fact that the age of simplicity was left behind and the dynamics of needs and desires took over the shaping of social progress. The first major factor which influenced the working of such societies was the limitless nature of the desires which became liberated from their earlier constraints. Needs bred other new needs, the satisfaction of these new needs made it necessary that the exchange process should expand, and this expansion then called forth more and more ingenuity to find new arts that could produce a sufficient quantity of various goods which this expanded exchange could carry. Secondly, once population pressure grew to such an extent that some people could have no access to the land at all, these people were left with no other choice but to try to earn their livelihood through this expanded exchange of ever more luxurious and

---

[189] Pufendorf, *DJNG*, 5.1.14.

118   Political Economy from Pufendorf to Marx

'unnecessary' products. These people, who were naturally congregating in the cities, became entirely dependent on the new system of ever reproduced and newly created needs:

> Now after most nations had given up their primitive simplicity they easily appreciated the fact that the old ordinary price no longer sufficed to carry on the business and commerce of men as these increased from day to day. For commerce used to consist only in the exchange of goods, and the work of others could be paid for only in work or in kind. Yet when our luxurious desires led to a lack of so many things, in that we no longer were content with what was produced at home, but yearned for the delights of other climes, it was not easy for a man to secure such things as another would be willing to exchange for what we wanted, or which were equivalent to another's goods. And in civilized states where citizens are divided into different social orders, there must needs be several classes of men who cannot subsist at all, or else with the utmost difficulty, if this simple exchange of commodities and labour persists.[190]

By describing this inevitable development in the fundamental structure of the agrarian stage, Pufendorf introduced a new fourth stage in his considerations. Technically speaking, strictly in the terms of Pufendorf's concept of property rights, the history of property had its culmination in property of land, the fundamental productive asset donated by God to mankind. Men first made nature's own products their own, then moveable things, and finally land. By doing this they completed the occupation of the earth, and any further development was restricted to a refinement of the agrarian stage. The natural completion of the agrarian stage was when everybody had some property in land and society was a community of landed proprietors. Population growth, however, ensured that after a certain point some people could not own land in their own country; they became excluded from exercising their natural faculties in labour on their own plot derived from God's original gift. They could obtain a livelihood only from exchanging the products of their labour in artefacts for natural products of the earth whose production was assisted by the landowner's agricultural labour. While the exchange process was happening, they both could benefit from the products of the land for their subsistence, in effect exchanging labour for labour – equal effort for equal effort. Once such a class of excluded people came into existence, Pufendorf argued, the process of exchange – commerce – became a necessity for the justice of society. What is more, given the presence of further population growth, this commerce had to be an expansionary one. As Pufendorf argued insistently: 'In civilised states where citizens are divided into different social orders, there must needs be several

[190] Pufendorf, *DJNG*, 5.1.11.

classes of men who cannot subsist at all, or else with utmost difficulty, if this simple exchange of commodities and labour persists.'[191]

Yet Pufendorf did not leave his assessment of commercial society there. Given the starting premise of his whole theory of property, that is, that God had granted the world to mankind for his use in such a way that no one should be denied the means of subsistence, Pufendorf had to show how it was that in a civilised division of labour, where the population was divided into proprietors and landless labourers, those without land could continue to enjoy the means of subsistence. For men would never have allowed exclusive property in land in the first place if it were to result in the exclusion and starvation of others or themselves. This was the burden of Pufendorf's insistence that the passage to exclusive property in land had been a process of consent. The fact that 'an original right over things' with effect of exclusion can be morally constituted only through a pact was simply an analytical consequence of Pufendorf's supposition that all men are equal, that is, that 'human nature belongs equally to all men'.[192] Assuming this 'original equal faculty of men over things', Pufendorf argued, 'it is impossible to conceive how the mere corporal act of one person – one man's appropriation of a thing – can prejudice the faculty of others, unless their consent is given, that is, unless the pact intervenes'.[193] One had to have one's fellow man's 'consent, expressed or presumed', to have a proper right to a thing as one's very own.[194] Yet how was it, in a commercial society, that the extension of exclusive property right in things and land could remain compatible with providing a subsistence for the have-nots, the excluded? Jurisprudence, in other words, required a consistent and conscientious theorist to engage not only with modern property relations as such but also with the question of the legitimacy and humanity of the money system within which the 'have-nots' laboured and subsistence goods were priced. The justice of the commercial stage, and thus ultimately the legitimacy of property in land, now appeared as a question of how the products of the land were priced. From the point of view of completing his theory of justice, Pufendorf had to develop a theory of price in money terms in such a way as to ensure the operations of the law of humanity in this civilised system of the division of labour where the population was divided into two great groups, people with land and people without land, both groups catering for each other's needs.

[191] Ibid.
[192] Pufendorf, *DJNG*, 3.2.1.
[193] Pufendorf, *DJNG*, 4.4.5.
[194] Pufendorf, *DJNG*, 3.5.3.

Obviously, not all goods had the same function in the maintenance of human life. At first, the commercial system seemed to 'deviate from right reason', looking only at the 'enormous values' which 'overweening luxury' led men to place upon goods they could easily do without.[195] The price men put on various objects was paradoxical and subject to their fancy, the change in fashion and the insatiability of their newly developed desires. Luxury was one of the consequences of civilisation, yet such prices sustained the artisans who worked up such goods. Moreover, these artisans were not simply at the mercy of the price system, in the ordinary operation of the market. As scarcity in supply relative to demand determined market prices, 'the abundance or scarcity of workmen' was also a basic factor. What is more, 'the price of labours and actions is raised by their difficulty, the dexterity required in them, their usefulness, necessity, the scarcity of workers, their renown or position, their freedom to work when they choose and similar considerations'.[196] In Pufendorf's eyes the price which these workmen set on their products could justly include their profit too: '[I]t would surely be inhuman, and likely to destroy the industry of men, to try to allow a man for his business, or any other sort of occupation, no more profit than barely permits him to meet his necessities by frugality and hardships.'[197]

But what about the other key price in a labourer's maintenance: the price of bread and other subsistence commodities? Pufendorf could not and in fact did not even wish to turn a blind eye to the problem that, although 'the price of manufactured articles is usually raised not only by their rareness but because of their workmanship', the price movements of basic necessities had a fundamentally more severe effect on the well-being of consumers. A scarcity in basic necessities had identical moral consequences as what was required when the preservation of life was at issue in necessity:

But things of daily use and such as concern primarily food, clothing, and arms, experience the greatest rise in price when scarcity of them is joined with necessity, such as is seen in times of famine, and in sieges, and delayed voyages, when hunger and thirst must be appeased and life preserved at any price.[198]

Pufendorf's treatment of this problem thus takes us back to our starting point – the problem of the boundary of property rights in cases of necessity. What was the 'just price' at which subsistence goods ought to exchange in a free market? The question was inevitably posed by any

---
[195] Pufendorf, *DJNG*, 5.1.6.
[196] Ibid.
[197] Pufendorf, *DJNG*, 5.1.11.
[198] Pufendorf, *DJNG*, 5.1.6.

serious jurisprudential consideration of the justice of a society divided into haves and have-nots. Pufendorf made it clear that in a market of free agents the just price is the price which the market would bear. The market price of goods was decided by the men who entered into the exchange and ultimately, at least in normal circumstances, no single individual was in the position to set the price arbitrarily of any of the products which he produced for others:

> And even if I should set an outrageous price upon a thing of mine, no one can complain about it, since it is no one's else affair how wealthy my fancy makes me, while others who feel my price too high, have the very simple course left them of leaving me in possession of what is mine. Therefore, if a man wants to have anything of mine, he must give the price I have decided upon, just as, on the other hand, if I want to force my wares upon someone else, I have to take whatever price a fastidious purchaser chooses to give.[199]

But Pufendorf knew that this statement could not be left unqualified in cases when the commodity in question was one of basic necessity. Thus, he added a 'rider' to the previous statement on the formation of the 'just' price. Men could legitimately demand a profit in the commerce of subsistence goods, but they could be charged with inhumanity if they tried to fix the market against the basic interests of the consumer:

> There can, therefore, be just cause for complaint only when a man, through inhumanity or out of hatred and envy, either refuses to sell to one in need, things of which he enjoys a superfluity, or else is willing to part with them only upon very hard terms. From this it follows that in a state of nature the prices of all things are fixed by agreement between the parties concerned, and that a man cannot be charged with a sin against the rules of commerce, if he does not overlook a chance for profit, provided he show no inhumanity toward the needy.[200]

In the end, values could not be set arbitrarily, because of the basic non-commensurability in the fundamental utility of products created by land on the one hand and manufacturing on the other. The primacy of subsistence needs and thus of the land asserted itself in the long run, and the regulation of the market had to be put on such a footing that the landless artisan class in the big cities could be in a position of equal partnership with the landed proprietors with exclusive access to food production. If men 'wanted a more refined kind of life, the advantages of which had to be secured by industry', then 'property in things was necessary' and money and the valuation of goods in money terms was the

---

[199] Pufendorf, *DJNG*, 5.1.8.
[200] Ibid.

necessary instrument which made this system operational.[201] In these circumstances the requirements of justice demanded that the price system should conform with the legacy of God's gift of the world to mankind in common. The only way to ensure justice as between haves and have-nots in a commercial economy, Pufendorf believed, was to guarantee the productivity of agricultural land by keeping market prices of agricultural commodities high. Since 'land meets this end best of all, since from it comes, mediately or immediately, most of the things by which human life is sustained', the consequence was that modern commercial societies had to be kept in an exchange equilibrium:

[I]n the hands of private individuals, land is the general basis of all wealth, it is fair that the value of money should rise or fall according as it is found to be scarce or plentiful in respect to land. For since in the more civilized states there are in general two classes of men, that which devotes itself to cultivating the soil, and that which in different occupations looks after the convenience of life, if in a time of great abundance of money the price of land and its products should be low, the cultivators of the soil must needs be ruined, while if money is scarce and the price of land high, the other class of men must labour in want.[202]

Given the inevitability of natural fluctuations in harvest yields, the only mechanism capable of maintaining justice in a society based on private property in land was one which set the level of all market prices in accordance with the price obtainable for basic agricultural products in lean years. Hardship was easily caused if the whole price system was allowed to fluctuate with the natural cycle of the climate:

This we see happen when there is a good harvest and so a low price of food, but the labour of the artisans and of all others who live upon the work of their own hands, remains at the same scale as prevailed in less productive years. For under such circumstances the farmers find little help from the bountiful harvest on their lands. And the same hardship rests upon the artisans, when, with food high, their labour draws the old price. Since, therefore, in years of moderate yield the trade of artisans and farmers seems capable of the best comparison, and then the minimum of recriminating is heard between them, it is clear that in fixing the price of money the greatest regard should be given to land, especially in case some district subsists not on trade alone but chiefly upon its own products.[203]

In a commercial society, justice could only be observed when the price of the products of land was

sufficiently fixed by a full year compensating for a lean one, these are understood to have a fairly stable price, on which the prices of everything else, which

---

[201] Pufendorf, *DJNG*, 4.4.9.
[202] Pufendorf, *DJNG*, 5.1.15.
[203] Ibid.

has so far not received a valuation from the luxury or foolishness of men, are based. For it is highly agreeable that the prices of things which come from or are supported by land, should in general be raised or lowered according to the price of land itself.[204]

Note on Chapter 2

This text originated as a paper written during the King's College Research Project 'Political Economy and Society 1750–1850', co-directed by István Hont and Michael Ignatieff from 1979 to 1984. In its earliest form it was entitled *What Is Political Economy? I. Understanding the Natural Law Foundations of Political Economy*. Subsequently, Hont changed the title to *Samuel Pufendorf's Jurisprudential Theory of History* and envisioned it as 'Part I' of his larger research project *Culture, Needs and Property Rights*.

---

[204] Ibid.

3 Natural Jurisprudence, Political Economy and the Concept of Civilisation
Samuel Pufendorf's Theory of *Cultura*

> Now, however, it is also the subject of the inquiry what are the desires and needs of men; and these are accepted as the inner foundations of private and public law.
>
> Hegel on Pufendorf in his *Lectures on the History of Philosophy*, 1836

This paper has been written as an introduction to a more complex discussion of the origins of political economy than what is presentable within its constraints. In the context of the present workshop the production of this complexity and historical balance should be the task of the overall discussion of all the papers together. In the present paper, by giving a detailed and historically precise anatomy of Samuel Pufendorf's theory of *cultura*, two of the simplified, introductory tasks of this larger discussion can hopefully be fulfilled.

On a more general level, I would like to discuss briefly how we might go about understanding the discursive origins and the discursive 'meaning', as it were, of political economy. It will be suggested that in the notions of *civilisation* and *culture* we can find historically legitimate and at the same time cognitively potent tools for understanding the history of political economy and also for a modern causal analysis of commercial society, as it exists today.

Once the rudiments of such a theoretical perspective are sketched out, it will be suggested that a discussion of the merits of this proposition cannot possibly take place in ignorance of how and when the notions of civilisation and culture were played out first in modern European philosophical thinking in a directly relevant way for the understanding of the history of political economy and for the history of the distinction between civil society and the political state. Without realising that this, in fact, seemed to have happened within the framework of natural jurisprudence and, furthermore, without knowing precisely what – and with the help of what vocabulary – was said about culture and civilisation in the seventeenth century, we cannot possibly hope to discover what the relevant structural continuities and discontinuities are in the history of political economy and modern political theory.

I

It may or may not be the most fruitful way of discussing the identity of political economy by focusing on its 'discursive origins'. Nonetheless, recent debates, which were in fact framed in such a way, can provide us with a convenient starting point. In the debates of the past few years, discussion got bogged down repeatedly by encountering two persistent and interrelated difficulties. It was impossible to reach a working arrangement on what, in the contexts of the seventeenth, eighteenth and early nineteenth centuries, should be legitimately called political economy, that is, what is the historical identity of political economy, and partly as a consequence of this, but only partly, those who were interested in such problems also could not agree on the intellectual procedure which would show up political economy as either a derivative of natural law or the derivative of what John Pocock calls 'civic humanism'. Let me not repeat the content of our past arguments here. Some of the parties have moved a long way from the entrenched positions of the late 1970s anyway.

Perhaps a brief look at John Pocock's important article on 'Virtues, Rights and Manners' would be helpful here to restart the discussion on the level of the more sophisticated analysis which he set out there.[1] The three key words in Pocock's title indicate the three main discourses he wanted to discuss in a comparative framework: 'virtue' stands for the key word of humanism, 'rights' that of jurisprudence and 'manners' apparently occupied the centre of the 'discourse of the eighteenth century', as it were, which Pocock on this occasion christened as 'commercial humanism'. Some of Pocock's important arguments concern the discontinuity and theoretical incompatibility between classical republicanism based on humanism and the kind of political thought which was based on natural rights. Virtue and rights, he argues, were singularly incompatible as springboards for constructing political discourses.

As far as the discourse of 'manners' in the eighteenth century was concerned, Pocock left no doubt in the minds of his readers that he had no wish to deny that it was historically heavily reliant on jurisprudence. In his words, talking about this period,

---

[1] J. G. A. Pocock, 'Virtues, Rights, and Manners: A Model for Historians of Political Thought', *Political Theory* 9/3 (1981): 353–368.

we are now in the era of a revived and modernized natural jurisprudence, based on the notion that an intensive study of the variations of social behaviour throughout space and time would reveal the underlying principles of human nature on which diversities of conduct were based and from which *lois* took their *esprit*. Jurisprudence, whatever it was like as the formal study of law, was the social science of the eighteenth-century, the matrix of both the study and ideology of manners.[2]

Nonetheless, as Pocock rightly points out, although the 'ideology' of the eighteenth century was based on jurisprudence, it was not simply a kind of jurisprudence. This becomes clear, he argues, when one realises that the key word in the operational vocabulary of the eighteenth century was *manners* rather than laws or rights, a concept, Pocock argues, which although it was 'enormously advanced by and through the natural and civil law, particularly *jus gentium*', was not in fact a jurisprudential word. The new jurisprudence-based discourse of the eighteenth century, or at least the idiom Pocock has in mind, was not simply modernised natural law but a kind of 'legal humanism, or humanist jurisprudence, whose roots were in [Donald] Kelley's "civil science of the Renaissance".' Others, though not Pocock in the first instance, combined these terms together and talked of the origins of the eighteenth-century discourse of manners in terms of 'civil jurisprudence'.

If I understand him well, Pocock's explication of the civil or humanist character of the jurisprudence-based discourse of the eighteenth century takes the following route. First, one has to note that a most conspicuous feature of this idiom was its 'complex historical schemes and the nascent historicism which make Adam Smith's *Lectures on Jurisprudence* a theory of the progress of society through the four stages of production'.[3] Second, this historicism, and here Pocock returns to a leitmotif of *The Machiavellian Moment*, ought to be accounted for by the 'ideological need to defend commerce against ancient virtue', without which eighteenth-century jurisprudence cannot be properly understood.[4] The ideal of ancient virtue was antithetical to the world of commerce because the multifarious transactional relationships it gave rise to were only so many opportunities for the virtuous citizen of the republic to catch the infection of corruption. Corruption could be kept at bay only if virtue was guarded against temptation, hence the 'austerely civic' nature of republican virtue.[5] As is well known, the eighteenth-century civil jurists regarded the virtuous *persona* of ancient times as archaic, rigid, austere and impoverished

[2] Ibid., p. 366.
[3] Ibid.
[4] Ibid.
[5] Ibid., p. 365.

because, though unified, it was unrefined and unsophisticated. Third, one has to realise that the historicised attack on ancient virtue upheld by the humanists followed a sort of humanist strategy itself to the extent that it attempted to redefine virtue in terms of the richness of human personality. It was argued that the loss of ancient virtue was compensated 'by an indefinite and perhaps infinite enrichment' of the modern personality, forged in ever multiplying relationships with both things and persons.[6] Furthermore, the rise of this new personality was connected to the notion of commerce, since it was argued that the new humanism was brought about by commerce, the division and diversification of labour, and the ensuing general increase of sociability. The new personality may have been lacking a pronounced political profile, but it was endowed instead with new manners, which were polished and refined. Fourth, through the nexus with commerce the new cultural humanism remained jurisprudentially based, 'largely in consequence of', as Pocock argues, 'the jurist's fascination with the universe of *res*'. Thus, Pocock concludes,

> Now, at last, a right to things became a way to the practice of virtue, so long as virtue could be defined as the practice and refinement of manners. A commercial humanism had not been unsuccessfully constructed.[7]

For our purposes, this interesting argument has at least one obvious blemish. While he resolutely tries to be historical, Pocock allows his argument to culminate in a key term which is part of no historical, or for that matter contemporary, vocabulary. Perhaps the coining of the new term is part of his effort to confront an excessive bias towards natural jurisprudence in the writing of the history of modern political thought. As Pocock explained,

> recently (...) and in pursuit of a now prevalent technique of discovering and recapitulating the vocabularies and idioms in which political thought has been articulated in the course of history – there have arisen presentations of that history in which the natural-law paradigm occupies only a part of the stage, and we learn to speak in idioms not reducible to the conjoined languages of philosophy and jurisprudence.[8]

In his effort of clarifying the gap between natural law and the discourse of the second half of the eighteenth century, Pocock obviously started off from the same technique and homed in on the vocabulary of 'manners'. But somewhere, at the point of finding a name for the 'discourse', this fruitful technique has failed and been cast aside. The problem which

---

[6] Ibid.
[7] Ibid., p. 367.
[8] Ibid., p. 354.

Pocock encountered here is unfortunately not unique. Terms describing 'discourses', such as 'civic humanism', 'mercantilism' or 'protestant Aristotelianism' are notoriously not to be found in the vocabulary of historical texts.

It would serve no good purpose here to enter into a discussion of the methodological problems, all too well-known to the audience of the present workshop, which such 'artificial' discursive names create. The point I want to make here is rather this. In relation to the historical period under discussion – the second half of the eighteenth century – we are in a better position concerning the availability of names for dominant discourses than in most earlier periods. There is one conspicuous new discourse which has emerged in this period and fortunately also received a name from its practitioners. Obviously, what I have in mind is 'political economy'. Political economy, besides being an eighteenth-century fashion word and fashion discourse, also seems to fit the interpretative bill of Pocock's commercial humanism. If commercial humanism was a natural law-based discourse, or at least a theory of property rights, which was not in itself straightforwardly juridical, concentrating on the modern personality as surrounded by *res* and as shaped in interaction with others in the process of the enrichment of man's social and material environment, then most people would not hesitate to call this idiom of social thought 'political economy'.

Why did Pocock shy away from using the term 'political economy' in his attempt to recover the meaning of the eighteenth-century discourse? One cannot but guess some of his reasons. But one problem he encountered seems to be obvious. Political economy is a term which has been in continuous existence ever since the eighteenth century and is still part of our vocabulary. Its use in the discussion of the specificities of the eighteenth-century discourse of manners would have burdened the discussion with unwanted modern meanings and connotations. Pocock insists that the period specificity of commercial humanism is important. According to his account,

about 1789, a wedge was driven through this burgeoning universe, and rather suddenly we begin to hear denunciations of commerce as founded upon soullessly rational calculation and the cold, mechanical philosophy of Bacon, Hobbes, Locke, and Newton. How this reversal of strategies came about is not at present well understood.[9]

This reversal of strategies (whose strategies?) is, yet again, not quite the proper subject of this paper. However, one thing is clear. The two

[9] Ibid., p. 367.

strategies, as it were, cannot be understood without each other. If in fact what is alluded to here is that sometime around the turn of the eighteenth and nineteenth centuries the mantle of humanism passed from the defenders of commerce to its critics, then to comprehend this apparent shift we ought to try bringing into focus the eighteenth-century discourse, still warm and humanistic, very precisely indeed. Leaving the issue of discursive names on the side for a moment, we should ask the question how much Pocock's focusing on the language of manners in the eighteenth-century discourse can help us in comprehending this apparent shift in the discursive location upholding 'humanism'. Are we facing here a genuine discontinuity or merely a discursive optical illusion? There is something deeply disconcerting in this shift – if it indeed can be seen as such. The attack on ancient virtue and the birth of the new 'commercial' humanism coincided with the move of the whole society from its former stage to a commercial one. It is far more difficult to then accept that once this commercial system more or less was installed, humanism could shift away from those who based their moral and social philosophy on its continued existence and became the property of its critics. What sort of 'humanism' was expressed in this critique? A repeat of the older, pre-commercial notion of virtue? If so, why was this humanism, if indeed it was based on a replay of ancient virtue, not pre-empted by the historicised defence of commercial man worked out in the eighteenth-century discourse? If it was not simply a replay of ancient against modern virtue, what virtue and what humanism could it possibly be? The grid of ancient versus modern manners leaves precious little room for further options, unless this option seems to be projected away from the past and present and into the future.

What I try to argue here is this. While the concept of manners was indeed a keyword in the eighteenth-century discourse of commercial humanism, it does not express fully the centre of gravity at the heart of this discourse. Unquestionably the discourse worked out a matrix of modern manners as a substitute for ancient virtue; 'politeness', 'refinement', 'taste' and 'sociability' were indeed specified as the content of commercial humanism, precisely as Pocock argues. That one could conceive an ideal of man in these terms, and that such an idea could be termed humanistic, is equally plausible. But something is missing here if one stops at the level of the language of manners. One ideal of virtue is pitted against the other, one set of manners against another set.

What seems to be missing are the hard edges of the discourse of commercial humanism. It is terribly important to emphasise its humanistic content, but it is also important to explain why one should choose modern humanism over the ancient. The discourse as a whole, even in

Pocock's own description, reads much harder than to allow loose optionality motivated by desires of being humanistic in one way or another. It seems to have offered a reasoned and cogently argued choice between various options of virtue and manners. The notion of manners most of the time operated as a connecting category in the eighteenth-century discourse between historical and political circumstances and the morality and system of social life which was compatible with it. Different periods and also different forms of government had a set of manners that suited them. Thus, the choice was not simply between ideals of humanism or virtue but also between social and political systems within which they could flourish or, to put it more pessimistically, survive. Now, the choice between ancient virtue or the 'refinement-politeness-transactional diversity' ideal of commercial humanism may appear as optional in certain circumstances. But the choice becomes considerably harder when one asks the question whether commercial society was optional or not? Without asking this question the choices argued in terms of manners by commercial humanism hardly seem to be intelligible. Only then could one ask the question whether commercial society could exist with any other manners than the modern ones, whether the existence of commercial society could still leave moral thinkers and moral agents with a choice between ancient and modern virtue, ancient and modern manners.

It seems to be a correct perception that the concept of 'manners' acted as a linking agent in the eighteenth-century discourse between the jurisprudential base, the theory of commercial society, the doctrine of the forms of government, the historicised scheme of stages of history and the moral theory of personality. But if this discourse can indeed be seen as an elaborate defence against, or perhaps attack on, ancient virtue, mobilising a whole new set of historical arguments as well as the jurists' elaborate theory of property, then perhaps the keyword of 'manners' signifies the presence of the new discourse but could hardly be the concept in which these various facets were fused together in a causal theory of modernity. Looked at in isolation, modern manners could appear as optional, as one ideal of virtue amongst others, but taken in the context of the whole causally interlinked discourse of commercial society it became invested with a determining force, whose logic thinkers, who took the trouble to follow through the thread of causal determination built into it, found hard to escape.

What I try to suggest is the following. What was defended in commercial humanism against ancient virtue was not simply the humanistic ideal of manners, which could be described by the word 'civility', but a more total and causally articulated vision of modernity, which can be captured by the keyword 'modern civilisation' or simply 'civilisation'. This concept not only can act as the carrier of the humanistic moral intent of the discourse but also encapsulates the causal force dictated by its jurisprudential foundations and, significantly, its historicised theory of the stages of society from rudeness to refinement. This word, or concept, cannot even be imagined or comprehended without the type of historicism present in the eighteenth-century discourse. For it does not stand alone; it is one of those concepts which gains meaning only if seen together with its mirroring counter-concept. Civilisation always goes together with its contrasting opposite, barbarism. Understood in this way it indeed expresses a stark choice which the concept of manners cannot. What it suggests is that the choice between ancient and modern virtue in the context of modern commercial society entails a choice between civilisation and barbarism. Thus, it is with the help of the concept of civilisation that the defence of modernity *qua* defence can be conducted, and in fact has been since the birth of commercial humanism.

It is perhaps unnecessary to argue in front of the present audience that this is not merely an interpretative suggestion. It would be difficult to find a newly coined term which could be more characteristic of the social thought of the second half of the eighteenth century than the word 'civilisation'. With its twin brother, 'civil' or 'civilised' society, it can be found everywhere in the language of the various European Enlightenments. In the 1770s, Dr Samuel Johnson was not yet willing to accept it as a legitimate expression in the English language. But famously his Scottish companion Boswell could reproach him for not following the fashionable thought of his time. In his *Dictionary*, Johnson acknowledged 'manners', in the plural, as meaning a 'general way of life; morals; habits'.[10] In a more pejorative sense, he also noted its meaning as 'ceremonious behaviour' or 'studied civility' or simply 'civility'. 'Civility' could mean politeness, elegance of behaviour, but primarily Johnson noticed its meaning as 'freedom from barbarity; the state of being civilised'. Similarly, while 'civil' could simply mean 'complaisant, civilised, gentle, well bred, elegant of manners, etc.', he put the meaning 'civilised, not barbarous' in front of the former. In verb form, 'to civilise' meant for him the act of reclaiming 'from savageness and brutality; to instruct in the arts of regular life'. Under 'civilisation' he only noted a 'law, act of justice (...) which renders a criminal process civil'.[11] Boswell could legitimately complain in 1772:

---

[10] Samuel Johnson, *A Dictionary of the English Language* (London, 1755).
[11] Ibid.

He would not admit *civilisation*, but only *civility*. With great deference to him, I thought *civilisation*, from to *civilise*, better in the sense opposed to *barbarity* than *civility*; as it is better to have a distinct word for each sense, than one word with two senses, which *civility* is, in his way of using it.[12]

Boswell seems to have been better informed of intellectual fashion in this case than his much older intellectual master. 'Civilisation' was almost certainly a word which came to Britain from the French, where it was one of the small number of neologisms with the ending '-isation' which came to be introduced after the middle of the century. Its first serious user seems to have been the 'Friend of Man', the elder Mirabeau, in the 1750s.[13] But from the late 1760s its usage suddenly exploded and it became a word used naturally and with great frequency by virtually all French writers on social theory and politics.

If it is indeed true that the word 'civilisation' was coined in the 1750s and then spread with great speed through all the Enlightenment circles of Europe in the 1760s, then our case of trying to establish, or more properly re-establish, the concept at the heart of the eighteenth-century discourse on society can be seemingly easily turned again towards the issue of discursive names which I have already touched upon once in this discussion. If 'civilisation' was one fashionable keyword of this period, then 'political economy' was certainly another. Starting with the Marquis de Mirabeau we would be hard put to find a political economist from Naples to Milan, from Milan to Paris, and from Paris to Scotland, who did not list up quickly amongst the users of the word and concept of 'civilisation'. Hence, focusing on the concept of 'civilisation' as lying at the heart of the commercial humanist discourse, we can also find a convenient way of arguing that the historically proper name of the discourse which Pocock has presented to us as modern humanist jurisprudence was political economy.

Pocock argues that a paradigmatical example of his commercial humanism can be found in Adam Smith's four stages theory of the history of the modes of subsistence, in which modern eighteenth-century jurisprudence was clearly pushed in the service of a historicised defence of modern manners against ancient virtue. If so, then it is easy to call attention to the liberal use of the word 'civilisation' in the *Wealth of Nations*, particularly when the four-stages-theory idiom appears on its pages. Smith's historical scheme was a picture of mankind's ascent from

---

[12] James Boswell, *Boswell's Life of Johnson* [1791], ed. Sydney Roberts, 2 vols. (London: J.M. Dent & Sons, 1960), vol. 1, p. 414.
[13] [Victor de Riqueti, Marquis de Mirabeau (1715–1789), author of *L'ami des hommes : ou, Traité de la population* (1759).]

rudeness to civilisation. In the context of the defence against, or attack on, ancient virtue, Smith clearly articulated his conceptual matrix with the help of the notion of civilisation. Talking about the role of militias he phrased his defence the following way: 'It is only by means of a standing army, therefore, that the *civilisation* [my emphasis – I. H.] of any country can be perpetuated or even preserved for any considerable time.'[14] And in the 'Introduction and Plan of the Work', which (as I have argued in *Wealth and Virtue*) must be seen as the key for the understanding of the whole of the *Wealth of Nations* as a single programmatic intervention in the debate about modernity, the contrast between the equality of poverty and the historically far superior lot of the poor labourers in modern societies was clearly set up as between 'savage' nations on the one hand and '*civilised and thriving nations* [my emphasis]' on the other.[15]

The line of historical inquiry and interpretation advanced here commits us to see the concept of civilisation rather than the concept of a pure market 'economy' as the core of political economy. This creates less of a problem concerning the vexed question of the 'identity' of political economy than one would first imagine. First of all, those who have argued that the concept of a pure economy was the hallmark of the birth of political economy understood as 'economics' had to put the date of its birth forward to the nineteenth century – to the time of Ricardo – and had to abandon Adam Smith as a mere forerunner. Secondly, this way of approaching the discursive definition, through the historical vocabulary of civilisation, also can help to deflate the opposite argument, that is, the idea that the core of political economy can be conceived without its anatomy of markets, containing only its historicised schemes of the rise of commercial society and the humanist defence of modern manners against ancient virtue, which was built upon this history. Recently, both of these approaches were effectively countered with the 'discovery' of large systematic intentions in the work of virtually all the major political economists of the eighteenth century. Unfortunately, sometimes this systematic intent is explained complacently as an ambition of multidisciplinarity. However, if we readmit the concept of civilisation into the centre of political economy, then this comprehensiveness and systematic vision appears as an inner structural necessity of the discourse. As I have argued, the concept of civilisation is precisely the concept which helps us to understand how the various facets of modernity interlink and form a causally determining totality. In this sense, political economy necessarily contains both the historicised scheme, which explains to us in the

---

[14] Smith, *WN*, V.i.a.39.
[15] Smith, *WN*, 'Introduction and Plan of the Work', 4.

language of the twin terms of civilisation versus barbarism what modern civilisation is and how it came about, and also the anatomy of civilisation in its own synchronic terms, that is, how it operates and how its operation draws a boundary for human actions, including political actions, which helps us in deciding what course of action helps us to preserve civilisation, or indeed to foster it, and what actions would carry the danger of a relapse into barbarism. It seems to be true that to be a 'true' political economist requires the comprehension of this mutual system of determination and constraints operating on civilisation from both directions, and that is why we still celebrate Adam Smith's achievement. He has done both, not out of an ambition of system-building but by understanding what a serious effort to understand modern civilisation requires from a thinker who cares about causality.

Thus, to be a political economist entails the comprehension, however crudely, that modern civilisation is a system with definite boundaries, the transgression of which, from whatever intentions, can precipitate the system's relapse into barbarism. The emphasis is on the systematic character of the links between the fundamental concepts of political economy, not on the extent of systematic detailing of any of its various constitutive elements. The shape of what is and what is not possible in civilisation remains encoded into the *Weltanschauung* of political economy, even if individual practitioners of political economy, whether liberal political theorists or 'economists', cannot themselves see the linkages with sufficient clarity. A modern economist may or may not comprehend that he is engaged in working out the systematic logic of the economy simply along the guidelines suggested by the concept of modern civilisation. Or he may possess an understanding of civilisation only at the level which every 'civilised' person would 'know' instinctively. Nonetheless, the very conceptual tools which he uses are predicated on the existence of the fundamental choice between civilisation and barbarism which I have been talking about.

We should perhaps stop here for a moment in order to notice that, although our discussion started off from a rethinking of the eighteenth-century idiom of commercial humanism, the attempt to use the concept of civilisation as an organising category resulted in arguments which are rather Hegelian in their shape. It was Hegel who argued that political economy is a subset of the theory of civil society, starting from its categories and systemic assumptions. Hegel was at pains in the *Philosophy of Right* to point out that the characteristic feature of modernity was its interlinked systematic nature. In the 'system of needs', individuals found themselves in a position where they could attain what they wanted only within the constraints of the overall system. In Hegel's words:

In the course of the actual attainment of selfish ends (...) there is formed a system of complete interdependence, wherein the livelihood, happiness, and legal status of one man is interwoven with the livelihood, happiness and the rights of all. On this system, individual happiness, &c. depend, and only in this connected system are they actualised and secured.[16]

When Hegel historicised the 'system of needs' and tried to functionally position it in mankind's history, he operated with the concept of *Bildung*, a concept closely related to the notion of civilisation. Hegel was engaged in a joint defence of *Bildung* and the 'system of needs' against ancient and austere virtue and attacked those who showered disfavour on *Bildung*. These people he accused of shying away from the hard struggle which civilisation and *Bildung* entailed. 'The idea' – he explained – 'that the state of nature is one of innocence and that there is a simplicity of manners in *ungebildeter* (the English translation here is "uncivilised") peoples, implies treating *Bildung* as something purely external, the ally of corruption.'[17] This single quote can show us, and if required it can be proven through elaborate textual analysis, that when Hegel talks about the system of needs he articulates what I called the theory of modern civilisation, and that the retranslation of Hegel's notion of *bürgerliche Gesellschaft* into civil society – that is, civilised society – is on the whole a legitimate one.

In the next step of his analysis, when Hegel tried to link political economy to the theory of the 'system of needs', he argued that political economy was the analysis of the 'infinitely complex, criss-cross, movements of reciprocal production and exchange' which characterise the operation of the 'system of needs' lying at the heart of civilisation as a whole.[18] He saw political economy as contained within the conceptual boundaries of the system of needs. Political economy started off from the concepts of civilisation to explain the 'mass relationships and mass movements' occurring in civilisation 'in their complexity and their qualitative and quantitative character'.[19] This was a form of knowledge, Hegel argued, which had 'arisen out of the conditions of the modern world'. It could give modern man the chance to reconcile himself with civilisation by demonstrating the rationality and order lying at the core of the system. Or, he remarked to his students, if one wished to look at it from the opposite point of view, 'this is the field in which the

---

[16] G. W. F. Hegel. *Elements of the Philosophy of Right* [1820–1821], trans. T. M. Knox (Oxford: Oxford University Press, 1971), Part III. Sub-section 2: 'Civil Society', §183.
[17] Ibid., §187.
[18] Ibid., §201.
[19] Ibid., §189.

Understanding with its subjective aims and moral fancies vents its discontent and moral frustration'.[20]

I have no intention here to minimise the relevance of the causal understanding of the internal working of the economy, which ought to form a part of any serious theory of modern civilisation. But instead of trying to analyse further the internal relationship between the 'theory of civilisation' or 'theory of civil society' part of political economy and the more narrow discourse on the logic of the market, I would like to turn back to the issue which is really at stake here, that is, to the divide between those who understand modern society in the light of the boundaries of the concept of civilisation and those other idioms of thinking about society and politics which are incompatible with the acceptance of these boundaries. The real divide is between those who try to understand and defend modern civilisation and those who first and foremost are its critics. I would now like to return to some of the themes in Pocock's account of commercial humanism with the help of Hegel's text. One theme in Hegel's text which needs explanation is his use of the concept of *Bildung*. This leads us back to the notion that political economy was born out of a defence against ancient virtue and that in general the humanistic motivation of this defence should not be forgotten. The other point which must be taken up is the discrepancy between Hegel's use of the term 'political economy' and the wider one which has been suggested in this paper.

Hegel restricted the discursive definition of 'political economy' to a definite intellectual mode of looking at the operations of the system of needs and civil society, while I tried to suggest that the whole theory of civilisation can be meaningfully called political economy. The difficulty here is only apparent. Again, it can be shown by textual analysis that the concepts which Hegel used to describe the system of needs were to be found in the works of those political economists he had in mind. Hegel, in fact, at least partly, derived his own theory of the system of needs from precisely these books on political economy. However, from the point of view of placing the whole theory of civil society in context, one should not miss the point that Hegel's entire discussion is contained in his elaboration of jurisprudence in his *Rechtsphilosophie*. Paying attention to this fact brings us back to the idea that commercial humanism, or political economy, was an idiom of social thought based fundamentally on jurisprudence or, more precisely, on natural law. Hegel argues that the theory of the system of needs can be identified as that part of the philosophy of law where the subject of discussion is not the 'person', the explanandum of the theory of abstract rights,

[20] Ibid.

nor the subjectivity of the individual, the explanandum of moral theory, nor man as a member of a family, which belongs to the discussion of simple societies, nor the *bourgeois*, which is the fundamental concept of the whole of the theory of civil society, including the theory of the administration of justice. In the theory of the system of needs, the theorist looks at the 'concrete idea which we call *man*'.[21] It can be argued that this particular type of idiom within the philosophy of law, which looks at its subject matter as 'man' in the abstract and tries to position 'man' in the structure of society, again in the abstract, is a very important proprietary feature of natural law or *Naturrecht*. If this is indeed the case, then, on this Hegelian evidence, we can obtain a continuous history of natural law and political economy held together by the concepts of civil society and civilisation.

I hope I can carry on better with the joint analysis of these two themes – the theme of *Bildung* and the natural law origins of the theory of civilisation – if I bring Kant's work into the discussion. Since a number of arguments which are presented to this workshop turn on a notion of a Kantian break in the history of natural jurisprudence, it may be helpful if Kant is present in my account too.[22] As I have argued, Hegel presented his theory of the system of needs as an attack on ideologies of austere and ancient virtue. The use of the concept of *Bildung* in his discussion, however, does present a difficulty to an interpretation centring exclusively around the concept of civilisation. It would be a mistake to overlook the existence of a powerful critical idiom in modern thought in which civilisation itself is seen as a target of a specifically humanist critique, a critique developed from the concept of culture or *Kultur*. In this critical idiom, civilisation may mean something which is indeed useful but nevertheless only the bearer of humanist values of the second rank. Civilisation in this idiom is understood as the process which is usually described in the everyday language under the name of progress. Culture, on the other hand, is understood not as a process but rather as an ideal, a target which represents inner and moral achievements for individual persons or for the whole human species. Culture as a category stands in contrast with the existing as a norm, instead of being a defence of the existing against the past. The problem for us is the following: the concept of *Bildung*, in this context, is usually associated with culture rather than

---

[21] Ibid., §190.
[22] [This was in particular the case with Richard Tuck's contribution 'Histories of the "Science of Morality" in the Eighteenth Century', an early version of the article 'The "Modern" Theory of Natural Law', in Anthony Pagden (ed.), *The Language of Political Theory in Early-Modern Europe* (Cambridge: Cambridge University Press, 1987), pp. 99–119.]

with civilisation, while the system of needs and political economy are invariably regarded as archetypal theories of civilisation.

There can be no doubt that such a contrasting usage of the concepts of 'culture' and 'civilisation' has been widespread in the social and moral thought of the nineteenth and twentieth centuries. Remembering Pocock's problem of the shift in the humanist discourse in England at the turn of the eighteenth century, one can readily recall that the English romantics, particularly Coleridge, indeed made distinctions along these lines. In his *On the Constitution of Church and State* (1830), Coleridge built up the contrast between civilisation and culture in the following way:

[T]he permanency of a nation (…) its progressiveness (…) and personal freedom (…) depend on a continuing and progressive civilisation. But civilisation is itself but a mixed good, if not far more a corrupting influence, the hectic of disease, not the bloom of health, and a nation so distinguished more fitly to be called a varnished than a polished people, where this civilisation is not grounded in *cultivation*, in the harmonious development of those qualities and faculties that characterise our *humanity*. We must be men in order to be citizens.[23]

However, the distinction which Coleridge made between civilisation and cultivation did not necessarily and always take this linguistic form. The evolving usage of these terms was so ambiguous that Wilhelm von Humboldt could use the distinction precisely the opposite way, nominating the progressive development of manners as cultivation and the moral concept relating to more inner personal values as civilisation.[24] Or John Stuart Mill could distinguish between these concepts as two meanings of the same term, civilisation. To his mind the narrower sense of the word civilisation referred to 'that kind of improvement only, which distinguishes a wealthy and powerful nation from savages and barbarians'. In a larger, second sense, however, he noted civilisation describing a country 'if we think it more improved; more eminent in the best characteristics of Man and Society; farther advanced in the road to perfection; happier, nobler, wiser'.[25]

By citing these variations in the historical usage of the words 'civilisation' and 'culture', I do not want to deny the significance of distinguishing between these various critical meanings. Rather I want to distance myself from a conservative German political philosophy built around the distinctions of culture and civilisation, which gained currency during and

---

[23] Samuel Taylor Coleridge. *On the Constitution of Church and State* [1830] (London: J.M. Dent & Sons, 1972), pp. 33–34.

[24] Wilhelm von Humboldt, *The Limits of State Action* [1792] (Cambridge: Cambridge University Press, 1969).

[25] John Stuart Mill, 'Civilisation' [1836], in *The Collected Works of John Stuart Mill*, Vol. XVIII (Toronto: University of Toronto Press, 1977), p. 119.

after the First World War, a philosophy of civilisation which acquired a second lease on life recently through the delayed reception of the work of Norbert Elias.[26] The history which Elias presents as centring around a sharp distinction between *Kultur* and *Zivilisation* may have its philosophical merits, but I doubt that it can give us reliable guidance in unravelling the meaning of past idioms in a historically precise manner. Elias' own material, sometimes hidden in his footnotes, itself casts doubt on the historical accuracy of his insights. On Elias' own evidence, the 1897 edition of Meyer's popular *Konservationslexicon* still gave the current relative meaning of the terms *Zivilisation* and *Kultur* as follows: '*Zivilisation* is the stage through which a barbaric people must pass in order to attain higher *Kultur* in industry, art, science, and attitudes.'[27] Hence there is no good reason to suppose that the concepts of *Kultur* and civilisation were always conceived in the strong contrasting manner as Elias suggests.

The relevance of calling attention to the historical fact that culture and civilisation were conceived by many as connected notions encompassed within a larger understanding of the theory of civilisation, as in Mill's case, is that it helps us in avoiding the mistake of positioning these two key words in two separate discourses occupying opposite positions along the divide between the defenders and critics of civilisation. The acceptance of such a divide in historical terms would give credence to Pocock's tentative suggestion that the mantle of humanism has changed hands after the short flowering of humanist political economy in the eighteenth century. On the other hand, if we see the two meanings of civilisation as contained within the same discursive space, then this would give credit to our assumption that the systematic character of – and the extremely sharp choices dictated by – the notion of civilisation does not easily allow us to see the connection between the historical and jurisprudential 'base' of the discourse and its humanistic content as a temporary and tenuous one.

Elias has asserted that the opposition of *Kultur* to *Zivilisation* has received an early authoritative formulation in the hands of the great Immanuel Kant. 'It seems to have been Kant', he argues, 'who first expressed a specific experience and antithesis of his society in these related concepts'.[28] Elias quotes what Kant wrote in 1784 in his *Idea for a Universal History from a Cosmopolitan Point of View*:

---

[26] [Norbert Elias' two-volume work *Über den Prozess der Zivilisation* (Basel: Verlag Haus zum Falken, 1939) was largely unknown until it was republished after the war and translated into English, the first volume in 1969, the second in 1982.]
[27] *Meyers Konversations-Lexikon* (1897), quoted from Norbert Elias, *The Civilising Process, Vol. 1: The History of Manners* (Oxford: Oxford University Press, 1978), p. 289.
[28] Elias, *The Civilising Process*, p. 8.

140   Political Economy from Pufendorf to Marx

To a high degree, we are, through art and sciences, *cultivated* (*cultiviert*). We are *civilised* (*civilisiert*) perhaps too much for our own good – in all sorts of social propriety and decorum. But to consider ourselves as having reached *morality* (*moralisiert*) – for that, much is lacking. The ideal of morality belongs to *culture* (*Cultur*), its use for some similitude of morality in the love of honour and outward decorum constitutes mere *civilisation* (*civilisierung*).[29]

Kant was certainly developing here a critique of a notion of civilisation understood as civility or politeness. The critique of the courtly ideal of politeness is an aspect of most serious theories of civilisation. This we should not lose from sight. For Kant, true virtue and morality had to be intentional. 'Everything good that is not based on a morally good disposition' – he went on to criticise the politeness of the courts – 'is nothing but pretence and glittering misery.'[30] He also called attention to the fact that while the courts were indulging in polite manners, the international political scene was dominated by warmongering and by aggressive foreign policy. As long as this chaotic state lasted in the international state system, he pointed out, 'human nature must suffer the cruellest hardships under the guise of external well-being; and Rousseau was not far wrong in preferring the state of savages, so long, that is, as the last stage to which the human race must climb is not attained.'[31]

It was this encounter with Rousseau's critique of civilisation which was the immediate textual context of Kant's distinction between culture and civilisation, as quoted by Elias. However, Kant's overall argument in the essay was an only slightly qualified rebuttal rather than an endorsement of Rousseau's critique. For Kant the difference between civilisation and culture, at one level, was in their different relationship to morals. Morality for Kant entailed intentionality, that is, conscious, goal-directed activity, and thus the 'unintended consequences' logic of civilisation did not satisfy his requirement. At any rate, civilisation was investigated here by Kant in the context of a 'universal history', the history of the whole human race. For this universal history, the history of the species, *Cultur* had a very special relevance indeed. *Cultur* was the *telos* of mankind's history, the fulfilment of man's potentials generally and not only for the few 'wise and virtuous' men who sporadically rose above the level of the masses to partake in *Cultur* on an individual basis. The difficulty for Kant, however, was not in the perception that civilisation as a process did not produce *Cultur* directly but rather in the

---

[29] Immanuel Kant, *Idee einer allgemeinen Geschichte in weltbürgerlicher Absicht* [1784], trans. L. W. Beck et al. as *Idea for a Universal History from a Cosmopolitan Point of View*, in Kant, *On History*, p. 18 (7th thesis); quoted in Elias, *The Civilising Process*, p. 8.
[30] Kant, *On History*, p. 18.
[31] Kant, *On History*, p. 21.

opposite problem, that is, in the explanation of how the folly, vanity and sheer destructiveness produced by the civilisatory process could be meaningfully related to mankind's universal history which, according to Kant, was to culminate in *Cultur*. In order to determine this relationship, Kant had to go back and investigate the determinants of the history of man as man in the abstract. Kant drew up the following theses to define human nature and human destiny:

1st thesis: All natural capacities of a creature are destined to evolve completely to their natural end.
2nd thesis: In man those natural capacities which are directed to the use of his reason are to be developed only in the race, not in the individual.
3rd thesis: Nature has willed that man should, by himself, produce everything that goes beyond the mechanical ordering of his animal existence, and that he should partake of no other happiness than that which he himself, independently of instinct, has created by his own reason.
4th thesis: The means employed by Nature to bring about this development of all the capacities of men is their antagonisms in society, so far as this is, in the end, the cause of lawful order among men.[32]

The central moral category of civilisation, which Kant developed from these assumptions, was his famous thesis of the 'unsocial sociability' of man. Man was naturally destined to live in society, because that was the only way man could develop his God-given capacities. But, when man has found himself, by necessity, in society, he developed a natural inclination to behave unsocially and in a selfish manner, wanting 'everything to go according to his own wish'. The consequences of this unsocial selfishness were indeed regrettable and definitely unpleasant, Kant admitted. But – he went on – those who do not cease to lament this, seem to have forgotten that

without those in themselves unamiable characteristics of unsociability from whence opposition springs – characteristics each man must find in his own selfish pretensions – all talents remain hidden, unborn in an Arcadian shepherd's life, with all its concord, contentment, and mutual affection. Men, good-natured as the sheep they herd, would hardly reach a higher worth than their beasts; they would not fill the empty place in creation by achieving their end, which is rational nature. Thanks be to Nature, then, for the incompatibility, for heartless competitive vanity, for the insatiable desire to possess and rule. Without them, all the excellent natural capacities of humanity would forever sleep, undeveloped. Man wishes concord; but Nature knows better what is good for the race; she will discord.[33]

Kant's message could not be clearer. Man's life in society was destined to move through antagonistic oppositions. Without unsocial sociability man

---

[32] Kant, *On History*, pp. 12–15.
[33] Kant, *On History*, p. 15.

could not fulfil himself as man. With its help the central activity in which man could fulfil his destiny was labour. It was the will of the Creator that

> man (...) was not to be guided by instinct, not nurtured and instructed with ready-made knowledge; rather, he should bring forth everything out of his own resources. Securing his own food, shelter, safety and defence (for which Nature gave him neither the horns of the bull, nor the claws of the lion, nor the fangs of the dog, but hands only), all amusements which can make life pleasant, insight and intelligence, finally even goodness of the heart – all this should be wholly his own work.[34]

Kant thus clearly placed his model of unsocial sociability in the context of the assumed ascent of the species towards *Cultur*, the highest state of skill and mental perfection as well as of happiness. The beginnings now were said to belong to 'lowest barbarity'.[35] Although man lived in society even in this barbarous state, Kant argued, the sociability which has manifested itself in this state was not of true morality, since it was not based on the voluntary feeling which can make a society a moral whole. But without this 'unsocial sociability' man could not conquer his own laziness and would have been destined to remain barbarous forever. Without social unease, the motivations of 'vainglory, lust for power, and avarice, to achieve a rank among his fellows whom he cannot tolerate but from whom he cannot withdraw', Kant argued, not even the first steps could have been taken from 'barbarism to *Cultur*'.[36]

The relationship between civilisation and culture which emerges from Kant's fundamental argument is quite different from the civilisation/culture division presented by Elias. The humanism of Kant's discourse is precisely predicated on the intricate interplay between culture and the civilisatory process. *Cultur* does not stand here in an external critical relationship to civilisation but is a necessary part of the explanation why the choice between barbarism and civilisation has to be made and why no amount of moralising can make this choice easier.

What was the discourse that Kant was making use of in his far-reaching arguments about the character of modern civilisation? What theoretical language was he talking? If nothing else, the concept of 'unsocial sociability' should give us some direction. I think it would be difficult to make a mistake and identify Kant's discourse as anything else but an almost pure idiom of natural jurisprudence. He started off from the fact that man was a special animal, created in imbecility but with reason, and followed this up with the statement that as the only animal endowed with reason, man must, by obligation, try to fulfil his destiny through labour

---

[34] Kant, *On History*, p. 14.
[35] Ibid.
[36] Kant, *On History*, p. 15.

and effort. These ideas, just as the notion of sociability, belonged to the idiom of the natural jurists. The discursive continuity with Hegel's *Rechtsphilosophie* is unbroken here. It seems to me that Hegel's theory of the system of needs as a necessary stage in mankind's struggle for *Bildung* simply echoed Kant's text. We encounter here at the core of the theory of civilisation a recognisably 'juristic' philosophical anthropology, which seems to rely emphatically on the intellectual constructs of the seventeenth-century natural jurists. If I understand correctly Richard Tuck's arguments about the birth of modern natural law as located in Grotius' desire to counter moral scepticism, then the philosophical anthropology which we recover here seems to me a direct derivative of precisely that common 'anthropological' core of the modern moral science of man on which both the sceptics and their natural law opponents seemed to agree.[37] In this sense we may argue that what allowed Grotius to counter scepticism was his reliance on the rudiments of the concept of civilisation founded on the notion of man as a social animal interested in his own self-preservation. In any case, my arguments about the identity of political economy are now thrown back, if I am not mistaken, to a question about the identity of natural jurisprudence.

I have tried to approach the juristic anthropological core of the theory of civilisation through the texts of Kant and Hegel in order to show that both some of Kant's works and Hegel's theory of civil society naturally belong to this idiom; to show that the vocabularies of civilisation and cultivation or culture can be seen as continuous and interrelated and that commercial humanism was a far more durable product than it is sometimes assumed. I have also ventured to open an argument which suggests that the 'philosophical anthropology' which seems to be the driving force of the theory of civilisation is a characteristic product of the modern natural law tradition. Now I would like to turn to the second task of this paper as outlined in my introductory passages and would like to make the connection between the concept of civilisation and natural jurisprudence much tighter and more strictly historical.

II

The way I would prefer to show the historical and theoretical connection between natural jurisprudence and the theory of civilisation in political economy is through also making a connection between the theoretical languages of these discourses. If, however, the word civilisation gained

---

[37] Richard Tuck, *Natural Rights Theories: Their Origin and Development* (Cambridge: Cambridge University Press, 1979).

currency only in the second half of the eighteenth century – as I have argued when I wanted to demonstrate the coincidence of the rise of the word 'civilisation' and the rise of political economy – then such an exercise faces considerable difficulties. Clearly, one has to recover the thread of historical connection by other types of textual interpretation.

One such way would be to follow the dialectic of the debate between thinkers developing the vocabulary of culture and civilisation. We have seen that Kant's use of these terms was connected to his controversy with Rousseau. It is well known that Rousseau's *Discourse on Inequality* (1755) develops its argument from a direct encounter with the civilisation theory of the natural jurists, chiefly using the texts of Grotius and Pufendorf. The emphasis can be put here on the meaning and message of these texts rather than on their vocabulary. Kant used the terms *Cultur* and *civilisierung* to construct his answer, but Adam Smith's very similar answer to Rousseau in the *Theory of Moral Sentiments* used neither of these terms. Nonetheless, even a brief glance at his text shows how similar the idea presented was. Talking about the notions of wealth and greatness that captured men's minds despite the toil and anxiety attendant to the effort of obtaining them, he declared, using a rhetoric similar to Kant's, that:

> it is well that nature imposes upon us in this manner. It is this deception which rouses and keeps in continual motion the industry of mankind. It is this which first prompted them to cultivate the ground, to build houses, to found cities and commonwealths, and to invent and improve all the sciences and the arts, which ennoble and embellish human life; which have entirely changed the whole face of the globe, have turned the rude forests of nature into agreeable and fertile plains, and made the trackless and barren ocean a new fund of subsistence, and the great high road of communication to the different nations of the earth. The earth by these labours of mankind has been obliged to redouble her natural fertility, and to maintain a greater multitude of inhabitants.[38]

The vocabulary which Smith used in this passage and in its textual environment was the standard eighteenth-century vocabulary of refinement, politeness, taste, manners, virtue, propriety, luxury, the passions and so on. The term which comes closest in this passage to the vocabulary of culture and civilisation is 'cultivation'. However, Smith used the word here not as a technical term but in its proper everyday meaning related to agriculture. However, there was another Scottish tradition of social and moral theory, also heavily reliant on natural jurisprudence, which made use of the term cultivation and its derivative, 'culture', in a more technical sense.

[38] Smith, *TMS*, IV.1.

Thomas Reid, who brought the discursive language of Aberdeen with him to Glasgow when he took over Adam Smith's chair, also developed a critique of Rousseau on similar lines to that of Smith and Kant. 'That the Earth would be more fruitful without Cultivation' – Reid explained to his students of 'pneumatics' – 'and more abundant in the things that are necessary for human Life, is one of Rousseau's paradoxes.'[39] In the technical language of Aberdeen moral philosophy, the word cultivation was transformed into 'culture' and was used in various contexts, such as the 'culture of the understanding', or the 'improvement or culture of our rational powers'. In this discourse it was possible to talk about the 'culture of nature' as contrasted to the 'culture of society, & education'. When Reid wanted to explain to his students that, in his view, Rousseau's system was that of corruptibility rather than perfectibility, he played upon the various shades of the term 'culture' available to him in the following way:

It is a Law of the human Constitution that we Receive at first (...) from the hand of Nature only the Seeds as it were of those Faculties which distinguish us from Brute Animals; That those Seeds by proper Culture may grow up so as to produce the Noble fruits of Wisdom & Virtue and every human Excellence; on the other hand by neglect & want of Culture may be checked in their growth or totally destroyed; nay by bad Culture they may produce Monsters of the human Species more odious & more mischievous than the worst of Wild beasts.[40]

An interesting point concerning this use of the word 'culture' in the moral philosophy language of the Aberdeen school is its relatively early timing in the eighteenth century. It is usually believed that the source of using the term culture in a theoretically pronounced way is a German invention. Kant's use of it would give support to such an idea. This does not seem to be the real historical case. In his *Versuch einer Geschichte der Cultur des menschlichen Geschlechts* (1782), the Leipzig historian Johann Christoph Adelung (1732–1806), writing at about the same time as Kant in Konigsberg, claimed that it was him who coined the word *Cultur* for the Germans. For Adelung, *Cultur* was a property of *Menschheit* in the sense of 'human nature', in particular the property of human nature which was the main agency from mankind's ascent from a more animal kind of existence to proper life in society. The difference between the state of nature and social life was precisely the

---

[39] Thomas Reid, The Birkwood Collection, Aberdeen University Library, MS. 2131/4/I/30, p. 11.
[40] Thomas Reid, The Birkwood Collection, Aberdeen University Library, MS. 2131/4/I/30, p. 17.

gradual evolution of *Cultur*, the gradual articulation of the human body, the human mind, human sociability and, at the end, human taste. Full culture, according to Adelung, was only possible on the basis of fully developed sociability; it was a concept which expressed the comprehensive nature of the latest stage of mankind's development, although in some sense it was a characteristic of anything human which was more than man's lot in the state of nature. As he explained, it was a comprehensive category describing the qualities of man's universal history, and no existing German word could substitute it. 'Refinement' (*Verfeinerung*), 'Enlightenment' (*Aufklärung*), the 'Development of Potentials' (*Entwicklung der Fähigkeiten*) could all describe some aspect of *Cultur*, but not the whole thing itself. *Cultur* for Adelung, just as in the language of Aberdeen moral philosophy, was a direct Latin borrowing. It did not belong to the polite, vernacular vocabulary of either the Germans or the Scots (or the French for that matter). I suspect it survived in Aberdeen as a Latinism because of the much later changeover from Latin to English in university teaching there and because of the more old-fashioned intellectual culture of Scotland's North-Eastern province compared to Edinburgh and Glasgow.

The thesis of this second part of the paper is that expressions such as the 'culture of the mind' or *die Cultur des Geistes*, as well as the idea of using the term 'culture' to describe the opposite of the state of nature, were borrowed from the last great moral philosophy system of modern Europe that was still written and conceived in Latin, that is, late seventeenth-century natural jurisprudence. More specifically, the historical evidence seems to suggest that the coinage of the word *cultura* in modern Latin can be attached to the name of the most influential of all the late seventeenth-century natural jurists, Samuel Pufendorf. If an investigation of the textual context of his use of the term proves that its introduction was connected to the theoretical idiom of modern civilisation, then we can make a significant step forward in clarifying the discursive connection between natural law and political economy as successive contributors to the theory of civilisation.

Pufendorf's text is relevant for the writing of such a history from more than one point of view. Not only were his works amongst the most widely read and debated Latin textbooks of natural jurisprudence; they were arguably *the* most published and read. This very popularity meant that these were also among the first major jurisprudential works to be translated into the main vernacular languages of Europe. This gives a unique opportunity to check the translation procedure of the cardinally important (for the seventeenth century) theoretical language of jurisprudence into French, English and German simultaneously.

Only the rudiments of these two reconstruction processes will be presented in this paper as a preliminary report on work in progress. However, the findings of this work can already be summarised reasonably clearly and authoritatively. First, it seems that the terms that were derived from the Latin verb *colere* or *excolere* – producing two major groups of expressions, one around the concept of *cultura animi*, the other around the concept of *cultus* or *cultura vitae* or briefly *cultura* – indeed occupy the centre of a crucially important theoretical space in natural jurisprudence and can be seen as part of the working out of the theory of modern civilisation. Secondly, it seems to be clear that the terminology of *cultura* was lost in the translation process to polite, late seventeenth-century and early eighteenth-century vernaculars, but when looked at more closely it can be seen to be replaced by a matrix of terms which include improvement, refinement, politeness, civilising, luxury and taste as opposed to rudeness, savagery, barbary, lack of discipline and a number of other terms producing similar meanings. Thus, it seems that *cultura*, in a somewhat diffuse way, became replaced in the translation process with the language of commercial humanism. In that way the circle of historical continuity around the term *cultura* seems to be closed, since, as I have mentioned already, when it reappears in late eighteenth-century Enlightenment German, it is claimed to be a synthetic reconstitution of precisely that particular vocabulary in the eighteenth-century discourse which was the natural language of political economy, understood as a theory of civilisation, and from which the word 'civilisation' itself has also emerged.

Let us start this survey with a discussion of Pufendorf's use of the concept of *cultura animi*, the 'culture of the mind'. This notion was not yet present in a pronounced way in the first edition of Pufendorf's *magnum opus*, the *De jure naturae et gentium*, when it first appeared in 1762. But when it later received extensive treatment in the second and later editions and in the textbook companion to the *De jure*, the popular *De officio hominis et civis juxta legem naturalem* from 1673, it appeared as if it were a necessary component of Pufendorf's jurisprudence, without which it could not work as a moral philosophy. Once it was in place, the culture of the mind appeared as an integral element of Pufendorf's theory of sociability. In this theory of sociability, we also find that Pufendorf introduces new terms and enriches the language of jurisprudence. *Socialitas* was also a technical term which gained currency through Pufendorf's texts. He was here following the Stoic tradition and Grotius, who already made use of such terms as *appetitus socialis* or, in the *Mare liberum* (1609), the negative term of *insociabilis*. When Pufendorf made the social nature of man the cornerstone of his theory of obligation, he used the term *socialitas* as the key term to express the *socialis* in human nature. *Sociabilitas* occurs only once in *De jure*.[41] *Socialitas* (or in English, sociableness) was at the heart of the human obligations which men owe to other men. 'This then will appear a Fundamental Law of Nature', Pufendorf argued, that 'Every Man ought, as far as in him lies, to promote and preserve a peaceful Sociableness (*socialitatem*) with others, agreeable to the main End and Disposition of the Human Race in General'.[42] Contemporary and later debate focused on the possible secularising implications of Pufendorf's formulation of the natural law of sociability, but this is not the central issue for us here. It is more to the point to look at the preconditions of sociable behaviour as commanded by this law. Sociableness essentially related to the quality of human interactions in society. However, society as such was not an operative category of the discourse; in the moral discourse it was duties and obligations which mattered. Duties were the duties of individuals. Thus, Pufendorf had to find a fundamentally individualistic starting point for developing the moral category of sociability as relating to society. The operation of the law depended on the availability of men who in themselves were willing and capable of sociable life. Before men could relate to others, they had to relate to themselves in a sociable way. In Pufendorf's words:

We said it was the Duty of every Man to promote and to practice Sociableness as far as in him lies; because, for as much as it is not in our Power to oblige all other Men to behave themselves towards others as they ought, we have done our Duty when we have omitted nothing which we were able to perform, in moving and engaging them to exercise the like Sociableness towards us.[43]

The notion of sociableness as governing the relationship between men was thus essentially predicated on a duty which mankind owed to themselves. It was at this point that the fundamental notion of sociability and '*culture*', or more precisely *cultura animi*, became strongly linked. *Socialitas* was possible in reality only if every man took the trouble to study his own nature, his own self (*sui*) and also, on this basis, attempted a 'culture' of the self. In this way, the new notion – *cultura animi* – appears at the very heart of the fundamental natural law of sociability:

The Culture of the Mind which all Men are oblig'd to undertake, and which is absolutely necessary for the Performance of human Duty, consists chiefly in these Particulars; that we obtain true Opinions concerning all such Things as

---

[41] Pufendorf, *DJNG*, 2.3.18.
[42] Pufendorf, *DJNG*^{K}, 2.3.15.
[43] Ibid.

our Duty bears any reference to, that we set a right Judgment and Price on those Objects which commonly excite our Appetites, and that we temper and regulate our Passions by the Direction of sound Reason.[44]

The introduction of the phrase itself – *cultura animi* – was not Pufendorf's innovation by any means. The phrase comes from Cicero, whose *Tusculan Disputations* was quoted in the *De jure* several times. The Ciceronian usage – *anima cultus* – cropped up regularly in modern writing, from Thomas More to Pufendorf's contemporary Richard Cumberland. But more direct influences on Pufendorf can also be found. When Pufendorf added the fourteen new sections to the chapter discussing man's duties to himself, a new source also appeared in his footnotes. Bacon's essays, or rather their Latin version, the *Sermones fideles* (1638), were quoted here by Pufendorf with some frequency. Although none of the citations relate to Bacon's theory of *cultura animi*, it is quite likely that Pufendorf was aware of Bacon's use of the term. Bacon, who introduced *cultura animi* in his *The Advancement of Learning* (1605), used it as a number of metaphors expressing self-cultivation. The 'cure', the 'medicine', the 'husbandry' of the mind, the 'Georgics of the mind' or *Georgica animi* were the variations of the metaphor. Bacon's idea was not simply a loose mirroring of the necessities of moral education. The 'culture of the mind' for him was a technical term describing a new branch of the moral science which he wished to develop. It was contrasted by him to the doctrine of the virtues. Extending his metaphor of 'culture', he explained the difference in the following way: the doctrine of the virtues, the *doctrina de exemplari bonum*, described the 'fruit of life', while the new branch of moral knowledge, the *doctrina de cultura animi*, had to speak about the 'husbandry that belongeth thereunto'.[45] *Cultura animi* for Bacon was practical ethics, a doctrine about moral means as applied in everyday life, rather than a philosophy of moral aims. As an eighteenth-century translator put it, *cultura animi* as moral knowledge was the science of the 'Culture of our Manners'.[46]

Another possible source of Pufendorf could have been Hobbes, whose ideas and works were always there in the background of Pufendorf's thinking. In *Leviathan* (1651), Hobbes actually supplied a derivation procedure of the word *cultura* from the much more widely used Latin term *cultus*. Talking about men's feelings about God, he remarked that

---

[44] Pufendorf, *DJNG*^{K}, 2.4.2.
[45] Francis Bacon, *The Advancement of Learning* [1605], Bk. II, ch. XXII.
[46] Francis Bacon, *Lord Bacon's Essays, Or Counsels Moral and Civil: Translated from the Latin by William Willymott, in Two Volumes* (London: Henry Parson, 1720), vol. 2. ch. 26, p. 355.

the externall signes appearing in the Words, and Actions of men, are called *Worship*; which is one part of that which the Latines understand by the word *Cultus*: For *Cultus* signifieth properly, and constantly, that labour which a man bestowes on any thing, with a purpose to make benefit by it. Now those things whereof we make benefit, are either subject to us, and the profit they yeeld, followeth the labour we bestow upon them, as a naturall effect; or they are not subject to us, but answer our labour, according to their own Wills. In the first sense the labour bestowed on the Earth, is called *Culture*; and the education of children a *Culture* of their mindes.[47]

The single use of the phrase *cultura animi* in the first edition of *De jure* in fact followed the spirit of this Hobbesian definition. Here Pufendorf argued that no parent would entirely neglect the 'culture' of his or her child and let the child to grow up like a beast. In this case Kennett added the explanatory words 'culture or education' to make the meaning clear. But when Pufendorf in the second edition of *De jure* and in *De officio* stretched the meaning far beyond simply meaning education, the translation procedure broke down. The Latin title of Pufendorf's new section on man's duties towards himself as connected to the law of sociability used the word *cultura* in a very exposed way. But now the title, *De praestationibus hominis adversus seipsum, tam circa culturam animi, quam curam corporis et vitae*, appeared in English as *The Duties and Performances of Man towards himself; as well in Regard to the improvement of his Mind, as to the Care of his Body and his Life*.[48] *Cultura* was translated as 'improvement' and *cura* as 'care'. This translation procedure was not accidental. From the title of the first section of the chapter, *Homini cultura sui est necessaria*, the word *cultura* again disappeared, the sentence appearing in Kennett's bland English as the dictum that 'Every Man is to take Care of himself'.[49]

The intellectual effects of dropping the word culture from the translation, substituting it with various words which the translator deemed to be appropriate in the context, were quite serious. This becomes visible if we look briefly at the comprehensive character of Pufendorf's discussion of *cultura animi*. Pufendorf divided *cultura* into two parts along the divide of the body/mind dualism and positioned *cultura animi* higher than the culture of the body, that 'subordinate instrument'.[50] Certainly, the 'care and improvement' (*cura et cultura*) of the former came first. Since God has endowed man at a qualitatively higher level than animals, man was 'more capable of fruitful culture and useful improvement' (*fructuosam culturam admittentia*) than any species of animals. As

---

[47] Hobbes, *Leviathan* (1651), ch. 31.
[48] Pufendorf, *DJNG*^{K}, 2.4.1.
[49] Ibid.
[50] Ibid.

a consequence, man had a duty to 'brighten and quicken his faculties by good exercise' (*cultura*) in such a way that 'the labour which Man spends on his own Improvement' (*opere circa seipsum excolendum*) should help 'in his Endeavours to fulfil the Laws of Society, to which he is by his Creator directed and designed'.[51] A 'rightly cultivated Mind' (*animo rite excolendo*) first of all had to worship God (*cultus Divini*) and then when 'this principal care is over' (*post haec cuique cultura sui*) he had to examine 'his own nature, and to study *to know himself*'.[52] This was primarily a moral duty, Pufendorf argued, since morality was 'about the Improvement of Men's Minds, and the Advancement of Social Life' (*circa culturam animi, ac sociali vitae promotionem*).[53] 'Another necessary part of Human Improvement' (*illa cullturae pars maxima necessaria*) was what Pufendorf described as the ability 'to set a just Price on those things which are the chief in moving our Appetites'.[54] *Cultura animi*, he explained, required that

We must not on any account give too loose Reins to our desire of Getting (...) And those Things which we have fairly made our selves Masters of, we are to account no otherwise, than as Helps to our Necessities, and Instruments to make us deserve well of Mankind. But the Mind must by no means fix and enslave itself, to possess and to preserve them merely for their own Sake; or to be perpetually employ'd in them in the endless Labour of increasing them.[55]

Cultura animi included also the cultivation of the sciences, mathematics and the languages, or at least those men who were endowed with sufficient ability had to practice them 'for the Garniture and Ornament of Human Improvement' (*condimenti atque ornamenti vicem in cultura hominis habent*). He realised that the abstract arts and sciences might have to be defended from anti-intellectualism, that at least there was one part of this 'more peculiar Culture of the Mind, consisting in the various Knowledge of Things, and of Arts and Disciplines' which was beyond reproach: 'as far those Arts which administer to the Necessities and to the Conveniences of human Life, no Man can raise a Doubt about their Excellency and Use'.[56] And finally, Pufendorf added, 'although the principal and the most laborious part of human Improvement is concern'd about the Mind' (*animum cultura*), one should also strive to avoid 'Effeminacy and Idleness' and try to culture one's bodily strength and health.[57]

[51] Ibid.
[52] Pufendorf, *DJNG*^{K}, 2.4.5.
[53] Pufendorf, *DJNG*^{K}, 2.4.13.
[54] Pufendorf, *DJNG*^{K}, 2.4.9.
[55] Pufendorf, *DJNG*^{K}, 2.4.10.
[56] Pufendorf, *DJNG*^{K}, 2.4.13.
[57] Pufendorf, *DJNG*^{K}, 2.4.14.

152   Political Economy from Pufendorf to Marx

Pufendorf's taxonomy of the elements of *cultura animi* or *cultura hominis* was quite extensive and if read systematically it defined the broad meaning of the word culture. This comprehensive vision of what was required from men who wanted to live according to the laws of sociability was easily lost once the unitary linguistic underpinning of the discourse disappeared in the vernacular translation. 'Culture' described a system of moral ideals and duties; 'improvement', 'care', 'exercise' read more like the rhetorical tools of an exhortatory discourse. While in the subject index of the Latin edition, *cultura* was indexed under *cultura animi*, in the vernacular translations the word simply disappeared from the index and the vocabulary. In fact, Kennett was not even the worst offender in this respect. He used the word culture with some frequency. Barbeyrac, on the other hand, had written out the word *cultura* from his French translation altogether. 'Homini cultura sui est necessaria' in his translation simply read as 'L'Homme est indispensablement obligé de prendre soin de lui-même', and he contrived not to use the word culture in any of the above-mentioned contexts.[58] The situation was quite similar in German. In Immanuel Weber's German translation of *De officio*, culture was simply substituted by *Erbauung*, thus the sentence quoted above read as 'Hiernechst muss der Mensch zur Erbauung seiner Seelen sich ausserst angelegen lassen dass er sich und seine Natur genau erkennen lernte.'[59]

The fragmentation in the language of *cultura* as concerning the 'culture of the mind' perhaps was not so damaging for the reception of Pufendorf's overall system of jurisprudence. It was argued by a number of his commentators, such as Gottlieb Treuer, that

the doctrine of *cultura animi* has no interest in the law of nature and in the attainment of peace in the world except insofar as it cultivates good appearances of character and behaviour. For the principles of justice require that you harm no-one, give each his own property and keep the peace insofar as it lies with you to do so. In the court of natural justice, it is not asked whether an action was performed with a cultivated and improved mind, or at peace with yourself; it is

---

[58] Pufendorf, *Droit de la Nature et des Gens, ou, Système Général des Principes les Plus Importans de la Morale, de la Jurisprudence, et de la Politique. Par le Baron de Pufendorf, traduit du Latin par Jean Barbeyrac...* (Amsterdam: Pierre de Coup, 1734), Tome I. Livre II. Chap. IV. §1. (p. 249).
[59] Pufendorf, *Einleitung zur Sitten- und Stats-Lehre, oder, Kurtze Vorstellung der schuldigen Gebühr aller Menschen ... aus dem Lateinischen übersetzet durch Immanuel Webern* (Leipzig: Johann Friedrich Gleditsch, 1691), Bk. 1, ch 5. § 1. [In the preface, Weber claims that he has followed word for word Pufendorf's original Latin edition, except for this chapter, 'On the Duties of Man to Himself', where, on Pufendorf's request, he has inserted several additional paragraphs from *De jure naturae et gentium*, and in some cases has sought to assist the understanding with a paraphrase.]

enough that your duties have been carried out in accordance with the laws of justice and the requirements of peace in the world.[60]

On the other hand, once Treuer (correctly) positioned the discourse on manners framed by the concept of *cultura animi* as belonging to the discourse on the 'principles of honour', he reiterated its importance. If peace was to be preserved in the world, then men's understanding of their duties towards themselves and then towards others required that 'the mind should be shaped according to the life of the society in which it lives'.[61] In precisely this respect, in describing the quality of life in each and every society, according to which the culture of the mind is adjusted, we encounter another theoretical idiom which is expressed in the language of culture. The concept in question is that of *cultura vitae*, the culture of life. In the vernacular language of jurisprudence this connection is not visible through the interfaces in the vocabulary of culture, and the linkages in the theory of civilisation disappear from the surface. In Pufendorf's Latin discourse, however, this connection was still visible, and it is to the examination of this connection I would now like to turn.

The Pufendorfian concept of *cultura vitae* is a development of Hobbes' first meaning of *culture* as discussed in *Leviathan*, culture *tout court*, without a designated object, or at least without a more specific object than 'life' in general. As Hobbes explained, and this is the most significant meaning of the metaphor of 'culture' for the theory of civilisation, culture in this general sense describes everything which is somehow the result of conscious, human, creating activity, or in other words, everything that is a specific product of human labour. This use of the word culture brings out the meaning at the root of culture, hidden in the dynamic verb form, as 'cultivation' or 'improvement'. It expresses the advance which the application of human labour through mankind's history ever caused; it includes everything that was modified from its original natural condition. From the point of view of *cultura animi* this reference field of culture paradoxically appears as a specific one, focusing on labour as an activity directed towards the material environment. Within *cultura animi* the culture of life is subsumed under the cultivation of those arts which administer to the 'Necessities (...) and Convenience of Human Life'.[62] In this particular instance, perhaps the translation of 'culture' as 'improvement' indeed captured a crucial aspect of its meaning. However, it is perhaps

---

[60] Pufendorf, *De officio hominis et civis secundum legem naturalem libri duo. Adnotationibus illustrati quibus principia ... Gottlieb Samuele Treuer* [1717] (Leipzig: Christ. Meisner, 1734), I.5.ii (note 1).
[61] Ibid.
[62] Pufendorf, *De Officio*, 1.5.9.

better to see the hierarchy, as it were, of the two concepts of culture the other way round and regard the whole of *cultura animi* as a partial product or accompanying phenomenon of the culture or improvement of the whole of human life.

The notion of *cultura vitae* appears at the very core of Pufendorf's whole natural jurisprudence. It is a key concept in his discussion of the state of nature as opposed to the adventitious state of mankind. Pufendorf's discussion of the concept of the state of nature was not an ordinary one. First of all, it was a methodologically sophisticated discussion. He was perfectly aware of the fact that he was engaged in an exercise of conjectural, historical model-building and realised the advantages and disadvantages of using counterfactual models. He discussed the various shades of meaning which one could attach to the notion of 'being natural'. He discussed what the concept of a 'state' meant and made it clear that he understood both the actual condition and the process leading to its formation as necessary components of such an idea. Nor were there religious undertones to his discussion, at least not in the sense of any revealed religion. 'I set out to deal with the study of natural justice as a universal, in other words, as it pertains to the character of all men and races, whatever their position on religious matters' – he answered his critics.[63] For him the use of the concept of the state of nature was a necessary methodological tool in establishing those 'first principles (...) which would be appropriate to the character of all men, and whose truth all men could recognise with the help of reason alone'.[64]

Pufendorf took great care to disaggregate the model of the state of nature as it was used in natural jurisprudence and introduced a tripartite division into the theory. 'The Natural State,' he explained, 'by the Help of the Light of natural Reason alone, is to be considered as Threefold, Either as it regards *God our Creator*, or as it concerns *every single Man* as to *Himself*, or as it affects *other Men*.'[65]

The first and third models are the ones which are more familiar from other theories of the natural state. According to the first model, man is contrasted to animals and appears as the only creature endowed with reason and allowed to possess the potential of perfectibility. The third model of the state of nature was conceived in contrast to the 'Civil State' and seen as a condition in which men live together only as fellows sharing

---

[63] Pufendorf, *Eris scandica, qua adversus libros de jure naturali et gentium objecta diuuntur* (Frankfurt: Friedrich Knoch, 1686) [Pufendorf, *Eris Scandica und andere polemische Schriften über das Naturrecht*, Gesammelte Werke, bd. 5, ed. Fiammetta Palladini (Berlin: Akademie Verlag, 2002), p. 288.]
[64] Ibid. [Pufendorf, *Eris Scandica und andere polemische Schriften über das Naturrecht*, p. 33.]
[65] Pufendorf, *De Officio*, 2.1.2.

the same human nature, without ordered and organised hierarchy, without a state. Where Pufendorf was innovative – at least in calling special attention to the need of distinguishing it separately – was in his second model of the state of nature.

The second model of the state of nature, Pufendorf argued, could be understood from a contrast of looking at man in isolation and in his real position in society, when he is in interaction and division of labour with his fellows. Man in isolation, on his own, was imbecile, weak, miserable and destined to poverty. 'Let us imagine' – Pufendorf argued –

> a man brought to maturity without any care and training (*curam & culturam*) bestowed upon him by others, having no knowledge except what sprang up of itself in his own mind, and in a desert, deprived of all help and society of other men. Certainly a more miserable animal it will be hard to find. Speechless and naked, he has nothing left him but to pluck herbs and roots, or gather wild fruits, to slake his thirst from spring or river, or the first marsh he encountered, to seek shelter in a cave from the violence of the weather, or to cover his body somehow with moss or grass, to pass his time most tediously in idleness, to shudder at any noise or encounter with another creature, finally perish by hunger or cold or some wild beast.[66]

On the other hand, he argued, 'whatever advantages now attend human life have flowed entirely from the mutual help of men'.[67] In this sense, Pufendorf defined the second model of the state of nature as 'opposed to a *Life not cultivated by the Industry of Men (vitae per industriam hominum excultae)*.'[68] Or, as he put it even more sharply in his defence of this idea in his *Eris scandica* (1686), 'in this second sense in which we discuss the natural condition of man, it is opposed to culture'.[69]

Pufendorf never claimed that the content of his theory of the state of nature as it appeared in the second model was innovative. He claimed rather the opposite. His meaning, he thought, was 'so clear that anyone who cannot understand it must be devoid of reason. And if anyone thinks that this is a revolutionary doctrine, he can find it stated in the passages of the Holy Scripture.'[70] Nonetheless, the clarity and systematic use of language gave a definite distinction to Pufendorf's theory. Once it was clear that the state of nature can be contrasted with a state of culture, certain continuities and organising principles in the history of mankind became more clearly visible.

---

[66] Pufendorf, *De Officio*^M, 1.3.3.
[67] Ibid.
[68] Pufendorf, *De Officio*^M, 2.1.4.
[69] Pufendorf, *Eris scandica* (1686). [Pufendorf, *Eris Scandica und andere polemische Schriften*, p. 134.]
[70] Ibid.

To gain a clearer sense of the role which this concept of culture played in Pufendorf's discourse, we should again look at the vernacular translations. In the sense of the nature/culture dichotomy, the word culture seemed to be redundant for Kennett. In Pufendorf's chapter on property, where the notion of culture played a key role, it rarely appears in the translation. Culture there was associated with products of human labour. '*Res per naturam citra industriam humanam productas*' did not cause a problem for the translator. It appeared as 'things which Nature produc'd without the concurrence of Humane Industry'.[71] But when Pufendorf put the same notion in the following way, '*res per naturam citraque culturam producuntur*', then the word culture was dropped from the sentence, the translation simply being 'things (...) not by bare unassisted Nature produc'd'. Thus, in the context of the property chapter, the link between culture and property virtually disappeared from the English text. At other places, it was replaced by interpretative translation. One such meaning for the translator was *cultura* as 'civility', thus *hominum cultiorem* appeared as 'man of Culture and Civility'.[72] In tune with this, '*incultior & simplicior ... vita*' was translated as the 'more rude and simple way of Life' and '*simplicem incultamque vitam*' appeared as 'simple unimproved way of living'.[73] While *cultura* was translated as 'civility', in cases where Pufendorf himself used the expression *civilis vitae*, this has been translated as 'decent Orders of Life'.[74] The dichotomy of *incultior/cultior* understood as rude/civilised gained further shades of meaning at other places in the English translation. Rude people living without '*nulla praevia cultura*' were described as existing 'antecedent to all Culture and Information', while when Pufendorf says that they lacked '*omni disciplina ac cultura*' this appeared in English as men 'stranger to all Institutions and Discipline'.[75] The opposite conditions, life with *cultura*, '*vitam cultiorem & labores*' appeared in English as a 'Life of Manners and of Industry'.[76] This translation of *cultura* as 'manners' was neither misplaced nor accidental. Pufendorf himself connected *cultura* with mores or manners in phrases like *cultura* or *cultus mores*. When this cropped up in the text, Kennett translated it as 'Civility and Improvement of Living'. People possessing *cultu morum* appeared as nations 'more polish'd in

---

[71] Pufendorf, *DJNG^K*, 4.4.6.
[72] Pufendorf, *DJNG^K*, 2.2.11.
[73] Pufendorf, *DJNG^K*, 4.4.8.
[74] Pufendorf, *DJNG^K*, 3.3.2.
[75] Pufendorf, *DJNG^K*, 2.2.1.
[76] Pufendorf, *DJNG^K*, 4.4.8.

their Manners', and '*gentes queis alique morum est cultura*' was translated as 'Nations of Manners and Civility'.[77]

It seems that Pufendorf successfully constructed a discourse of *cultura* which was centring around a notion of manners and whose polarities were barbarism on the one hand and politeness, civility, commodiousness on the other. We can see how powerful this unified reading of mankind's history was if we realise that the actual content of the theoretical and historical space stretching from man's first imbecility to the culture of polished and civilised nations was occupied by Pufendorf's theory and history of property. We have told the story of this property theory in the first chapter of *Wealth and Virtue*, of how the ideological fight against the idea of positive communities of property, which Pufendorf took over from Grotius, necessitated the demonstration of an ever-present choice between artificial simplicity and the further development of culture. We have also demonstrated that Pufendorf's stages theory of culture and property culminated in an argument for the necessity of commerce in any situation where part of the population became excluded from property in land and could only survive by exchanging the products of their labour for subsistence goods. With this outcome of Pufendorf's theoretical history of property in mind, we can argue that in Pufendorf's double theory of culture, as *cultura animi* and *cultura vitae*, a discourse leading to commercial humanism, or political economy, came into being.

From another point of view, we may notice the consequences of Pufendorf's triple theory of the state of nature for the general shape of natural jurisprudence. What the new division between the second and third model of the state of nature meant – that is, the separate construction of the state of nature first as opposed to *cultura* and then as opposed to the *civitas* – was that the growth of culture and the rise of the state could be told as separate stories. We may or may not be unhappy with this outcome, the duality of politics and the theory of civil society. One thing seems to be reasonably clear, however, from the present discussion of its origins. A joint understanding of the identity of natural law and of political economy can only help us in coming to terms with the choice between civilisation and barbarism if we do not wish to find refuge either in utopia or in the mere cultural critique of modernity.

Note on Chapter 3

This paper was presented to the workshop 'The Identity of Political Economy: Between Utopia and the Critique of Civilisation', which took

---

[77] Pufendorf, *DJNG^K*, 4.1.28.

place in King's College, Cambridge, 1–3 July 1984. This workshop was organised by István Hont as a 'final chance' to discuss the problems thrown up by the 'Political Economy and Society, 1750–1850' project, which was coming to an end by the close of 1983. In the invitation to the workshop, written by Hont in collaboration with John Dunn and Gareth Stedman Jones, the purpose of the event was described as follows:

> Our intention is to reconsider the results and language of recent historical research into past political, social and economic thought in a mode which makes possible a critical dialogue between historians of the different periods. In other words, we would like to try and find a common language in which to discuss our own fragmented historical knowledge. We are under no illusion that the time has come to construct a new synthesis, but without making a beginning, it is unlikely that such a time will ever come. Our hope is that if we begin to question ourselves and each other on the character of our own historical work in the light of the intellectual issues indicated above, a meeting of the kind proposed should be a catalyst in the process of promoting such integration. We are in no sense pessimistic about its prospects of success, and we are unconvinced that the task of integration would be better left to the working of an 'invisible hand'.[78]

---

[78] István Hont, 1 October 1983, 'Invitation to the workshop "The Identity of Political Economy"', IHA/Hont/532.

4 Negative Community and Communism
The Natural Law Heritage from Pufendorf to Marx

My paper has a double, though interrelated field of reference, as indicated by the title and subtitle: 'Negative Community and Communism: The Natural Law Heritage from Pufendorf to Marx'.[1] The central focus will be on an analysis of the key controversy about the nature of property rights, or rights in general, in the second half of the seventeenth century. The leading participants of the debate were familiar figures, Grotius, Hobbes, Locke and Pufendorf, as well as some less important, juristic theorists of society, all operating within the idiom of modern natural law. My aim is to demonstrate the significance of the now forgotten concept of 'negative community', a concept which stood at the centre of debates on individuality and community in Europe for the century between 1610 and 1710. In a broader sense I hope to shed some light on the origins of Marx's concept of communism and on the genesis and significance of his theory of historical stages. Since the connection between the debate on 'negative community' and historical materialism is one of the major ways in which the older debates about rights, needs and property gain their relevance for modern theory, I shall start by sketching out the Marxian, or rather post-Marxian, perspective which I wish to bring to bear upon my historical topic.

My argument in this context is roughly the following. The notion of community and its conceptual status is obviously central to socialist theory; indeed, the very word communism denotes a political preference for – and a demand of – 'community'. Marx's own brand of communist theory emerged through his critique of those radicals, socialists and communists of his own time who saw the future society as a system of communal, as opposed to individual, property. In his critique, Marx drew on political economy, and that, in its turn, drew on a long tradition of theorising about property in the natural jurisprudence tradition.

---

[1] I am grateful for the intellectual companionship of Julian Franklin, Judith Shklar and John Dunn who helped me when I was thinking through and writing this paper. Fredric Smoler and János Atkári also helped me in matters of style.

The natural jurists' critique of positive communities of property has the same analytical structure as that of Marx's critique of his own communist predecessors. Recognising this connection or morphological parallel can help us to develop modern arguments about property and community in terms of rights theories appropriate to the present day, both in the context of the welfare state and in the context of the current reforms in really existing 'socialist' societies. It also follows from this perspective that the promise of a way forward from the present difficulties of political theory lies more in considering the difficulties which face both liberal rights theories and Marxian theories of community (an unusual species of communitarianism) together and simultaneously, rather than in using the one tradition as a means to develop a critical perspective on the other.

I

I would like to discuss the connection between the origins of Marxism and the debate between individual and communal concepts of property in early modern Europe in three steps.

On the first and simplest level we should look at these seventeenth-century debates on common property as an important element in the emergence of historical materialism. The materialist conception of history is fundamentally the political economist's view of history, even if Marx regarded himself as a political economist who was also a radical critic of political economy (in its bourgeois idiom). Those earlier theorists in eighteenth- and early nineteenth-century Britain and France, whom Marx acknowledged as his predecessors in developing a theory of history that argued for a mutual determination of the 'mode of subsistence' and the 'superstructure' (both of these are eighteenth-century expressions), were all contributors to the political economy tradition in its wider sense. Early political economy as a theory of society and history was a product of seventeenth- and eighteenth-century natural jurisprudence. Thus, understanding how the historical theory of political economy emerged from the natural law discourse can contribute a great deal to the understanding of historical materialism and can help us to position Marx's contribution in a longer historical perspective. In this context, my argument is that it was the emergence of the notion of 'negative community' that made it possible for the natural jurists and the political economists, and thus also for Marx, to historicise the theory of property to such an extent that it could become the backbone of a largely secular theory of social development. The formulation and acceptance of an interpretation of mankind's early 'community' of property as 'negative' was a precondition of any thoroughgoing historicisation of the theory of property and modes of subsistence later.

In order to identify the second link between earlier rights theories and Marxian communitarianism we have to ask the following question. How can one argue at all for the analytical relevance of seventeenth-century debates on property rights in the shaping of historical materialism when, as is well known, Marx himself was strongly opposed to rights theories and juristic notions of history? It has been argued, most emphatically by Steven Lukes, that Marx's intellectual achievement stands outside the tradition of Western rights theories, and by excluding considerations of *Recht* from its theoretical edifice it constitutes a negation of modern European and American political theory.[2] What this perspective on Marx neglects is the fact that Marx's position was as much the result of his opposition to socialist and communist ideologies of his own time as it was of his critique of bourgeois theory. While Marx chose Hegel and political economy as the points of departure for the materialist view of history, he also used these ideas to develop a historicist critique of those contemporary socialist indictments of commercial society that were based on the concept of rights. Rights theories in the early nineteenth century figured prominently in socialist and communist theory, frequently with open reference to the older theories of the seventeenth century. The socialist and communist theory of rights developed its own versions of the history of private property in order to legitimise the critique of the prevailing system of distributive justice. This historical idiom was invoked as the underpinning of the opposition to capitalism – with reference both to communal property in the dawn of mankind and to the early history of European states as democracies based on shared systems of property. Marx did not object to this preoccupation with community. On the contrary, the 'Paris Manuscripts' and *The German Ideology* display an almost obsessive concern with the theory of community, and in his later writings, from the *Grundrisse* to the 'Zasulich Letters', Marx remained preoccupied with community, spending the last ten years of his life reading anthropological evidence to rework his theories.[3]

---

[2] Steven Lukes, *Marxism and Morality* (Oxford: Oxford University Press, 1985). [On 27 November 1981, Steven Lukes (Balliol College, Oxford) presented a paper at King's College, Cambridge, entitled 'Can a Marxist Believe in Human Rights?'. The paper was presented as part of a seminar on 'The Theory and Practice of Socialism'.]

[3] [The letters to Vera Zasulich, drafted by Marx in 1881 and written in French, concerned the possibility of Russia undergoing a direct transition from the system of peasant communes (*obshchina* or *mir*) to fully developed communism. For a recent discussion of these (draft) letters, see Gregory Claeys, *Marx and Marxism* (New York: Nation Books, 2018), pp. 134–135.]

Yet there was no more bitter critic in his own time of rights-based socialist theorising of community than Marx himself. In his view, the socialist and communist theorists of right, who argued for the establishment of some sort of system based on communal property, had remained prisoners of the worst delusions of natural law itself. Marx regarded his own communism as radically different. In his own theory of community, he wanted to eschew totally the 'ahistorical' and apparently static concept of rights.

If one accepts the fact that there was a direct and incremental continuity between seventeenth-century radical rights theory and early nineteenth-century theories of communal property, then the seventeenth-century critique of community under the aegis of 'negative community' theory can enable us to establish a pedigree for Marx's own attempt to formulate a historical materialist notion of communism. Perhaps more important, by uncovering the parallels between Marx and seventeenth-century natural jurists, we can recover the well-developed theoretical language of the latter and use it to clarify both Marxian theories of community and other current concepts of communitarianism. In this paper I do not offer a reconsideration of these theories. Nonetheless, by excavating the distinction between 'positive' and 'negative' community I hope to establish a point of departure for such an enquiry.

Let me consider more closely the nature of Marx's critique of socialist and communist theories of communal ownership rights. At first sight it might appear that Marx dismissed the whole issue as irrelevant. Natural law with its state of nature theorems was an ideological fallacy. Natural lawyers and political economists, who based their 'explanation in some imaginary primordial condition', Marx argued, were merely evading the real issues, an evasion which socialists should avoid. 'Such a primordial condition explains nothing', he declared, 'it simply pushes the question into the grey and nebulous distance'.[4] But since socialists were apt to commit the same mistake, Marx was compelled to investigate the issue further, and to criticise also the socialist version of an apparently imaginary and irrelevant primordial condition of mankind. For many radicals the model of primordial community was also the model of what Marx termed the ideal of 'crude communism', an ideal which had a strong hold over the minds of many early nineteenth-century communists. By defining communism as communal property, he fumed,

---

[4] Marx, *Paris Manuscripts*, p. 323. ('Estranged Labour'); *MECW* 3, p. 271. [Throughout this paper, the first-listed reference refers to the specific English translation of Marx used by Hont, whose choice of translation alternated from one quotation to the next, seemingly according to his estimation of its accuracy.]

the social imagination of these people had remained wholly inside the domain of a social model based on property rights. What is more, they had shown even less understanding of the historical origins of property than the earlier natural jurists. The latter at least understood that property was not a relationship between man and things but between man and man, thus seeing property as a historical product of specific systems of human labour.

Although early socialists contrasted communism with modern systems of private property, they still conceived communal man as a property-owning animal, albeit a co-owner of property. For this reason, they had to have a theory of property which proceeded along lines quite different from the theoretical histories of private property. The link between property and theories of human nature as developed in the seventeenth and eighteenth centuries had to be severed. As a consequence, the socialist theory of property – co-ownership – had to adopt an excessively simplistic view of human nature. The socialists maintained that private, as opposed to communal, property was based on envy and greed, pathological manifestations of need. Hence the communist aim was to reduce future members of the community of co-owners to a preconceived minimum of envy and desire. Instead of conceiving property as a complicated, historically evolved and interpersonally mediated relationship, they strove to understand man's relationship to the material environment as a simple issue of material needs. In their critique they lost sight of the crucial theoretical difference, well understood by the natural jurists, between the nature of animal and human need. Because of their primitive nature, communist theories of need depicted historically evolved wants as disguised, even supressed, but nonetheless universalised manifestations of greed, lust and desire. Their antithesis to private property was therefore fundamentally impoverished and vitiated. In Marx's words, 'crude communism' was 'therefore only a *manifestation* of the vileness of private property, which wants to set itself up as the *positive community system*'.[5]

This last phrase of Marx – 'positive community' – is important to us here. Marx was apparently a critic of communism conceived as 'positive community', which leads us to ask: what other notion of community can there be than positive community? What was wrong with the notion of communal property as a system of co-ownership? The answer is that there was once a time in the development of rights theories when theorists readily spoke of 'negative' as well as 'positive' communities. There was not one but at least two notions of community, and they were diametrically opposed. The theory of 'negative community', furthermore,

---

[5] Marx, *MECW* 3. p. 296; *Paris Manuscripts*, p. 347. ('Private Property and Communism').

was not simply an abstract possibility conceived for the sake of logical neatness inspired by Scholastic mentality. It consciously attempted to avoid those shortcomings of community theory which Marx was now condemning in nineteenth-century socialist or communist thought. Indeed, the seventeenth-century natural law theory of 'negative community' met Marx's deepest objection to positive community. In 'negative community' early mankind was not conceived as a community of co-owners of property but rather as a community as yet without any property at all. It was a community, but not a community of persons holding property in common. On such basis, one can readily see that a future communal (albeit 'negatively communal') society without any property rights at all was quite conceivable.

With this last remark we come to the third important facet of the connection between seventeenth-century debates about property and community and the deep foundations of Marxian thought. Marx's critique of the natural law notion of primordial community focused on the foolish circularity of state of nature theories. For him these were not serious attempts to discover man's early history, or man's 'pre-history' as it was called. State of nature theories were only projections backward of modern man. It would be a mistake to see this critique as a denial of the relevance of inquiries into pre-history or man's *Vorgeschichte*. Marx and Engels, and a long line of their followers afterwards, spent much energy on reconstructing the earliest history of property, family, community and the state. The reconstruction of primordial times was clearly quite relevant for them for reasons vaguely similar to that of the natural jurists and 'crude' communists. The latter wanted to show that their theories of human nature were a quasi-permanent fixture of human history. Marx also understood that the nature of early communities could offer a key for visions of a future stage of communality. This explains the vehemence of his critique, throughout his life, of vitiated notions of early community.

Marx's view of history was not inherently teleological or utopian. At least he made conscious efforts to avoid this. But it is almost an inherent feature of stage theories of history (and particularly the thesis-antithesis-synthesis theories of Hegelian provenance) that the definition of the beginning – the very first stage – holds the key to the definition of the last stage, however open-ended the scheme might be. The last stage does not have to be conceived as finite. But it has to rely on facets of human arrangements which could be deduced from actual human history. For Marx this meant that both the early stage and the as yet undefined and indefinite communist future had to be conceived purely in historical terms. Hence a static, structurally restrictive and pseudo-historical understanding of early community could foreclose the possibility of any future communism based neither on private property (institutionally sanctioned greed) nor communal property (institutionally suppressed greed) but on man 'rich in needs' (deinstitutionalised, liberated or *aufgehoben* 'greed'). Marx regarded capitalism as a revolutionary improvement on earlier times. The step forwards could not be, for him, a step backwards, to a dictatorship of the associated co-owners of communal property over the needs unleashed by capitalism. Such communism, Marx argued, only 'negates the *personality* of man in every sphere'.[6] The new, higher level of society had to base its communal character on a newly found identity between man and nature. The conception of future communism as a negation and progressive transcendence of 'crude communism', it seems to me, had to rely on a conception of early community as 'negative'. Without understanding the notion of 'negative community' one cannot seriously accept Marx's historical scheme as open-ended or indeed understand the true nature of his theoretical contentions.

II

Before turning to the analysis of the seventeenth-century debate on property rights and community, it is necessary to reiterate the key analytical features of the Marxian critique of positive communities of property. Such a conception, he believed, was a mechanical obverse of the regime of private property. By pitting itself against theories of private property as an alternative theory of property it remained the prisoner of the bourgeois idea of rights. Neither the primeval community nor indeed future communism, Marx claimed, can be imagined as a structure of property rights. Rather, they were both systems based on the direct satisfaction of needs. Marx thus developed his own theory of community, or communism, in terms of a theory of needs (the equivalent of which in political economy was the theory of demand).

This option was not open in the same way to seventeenth-century theorists. Instead of sidestepping rights theory they were compelled to argue within the constraints of their theory of rights, the hallmark of their own conceptual world. The need to phrase their arguments about community in terms of a rights theory made their idiom highly technical and perhaps even cumbersome. Nonetheless, the presence of rights theory foundations in their thought makes their ideas more interesting to us. Couching their notion of community in terms of a rights theory made it commensurable with descriptions of the modern commercial world of private

---

[6] Marx, *Paris Manuscripts*, p. 346. ('Private Property and Communism'); *MECW* 3. p. 295.

property owners, the world they lived in, and the world we live in today. This commensurability, however, did not mean that they were obliged to depict early communities in modern rights terms. Such reverse projection was precisely what the seventeenth-century natural law school of Grotius, Pufendorf and Locke sought to avoid.

They were at pains to show that the primeval community of mankind did not exhibit a system of property in the sense of modern exclusive property rights, whether individual or communal. If the early system was indeed different from the modern, then they were obliged to show how from a stage of no-property mankind could move to a stage where property came into existence. The first step involved the construction of the theory of negative community, which then led to a conjectural history of stages of property, expressed in terms of the institutional regulation of mankind's changing mode of subsistence.

The distinction between these two analytical steps was sometimes quite blurred. For some seventeenth-century theorists both the idea of 'negative community' and the idea of incorporating historical change into the content of natural law was paradoxical and unacceptable. They subscribed to the fundamental assumption that natural law was immutable. God had created it once and for all. For them, the idea of change in the laws of nature, such as might be needed for a concept of property rights, was a contradiction in terms. For theorists like Robert Filmer the solution to the dilemma posed by the time-honoured tradition of early communality and the later legality of private property lay in a simple declaration that private *dominion* had been present in mankind's history from the first moment and had, in its foundations, remained unchanged ever since.[7] The first private property was Adam's and the later system was built up by the multiplication of his providentially legitimate heirs. The Adamite theory, of which Filmer was by no means the sole or even the chief representative, was, despite its intended and apparent traditionalism, an innovation in terms of the natural law tradition and a radical departure from its mainstream understanding.

For traditionally the starting point of the older natural lawyers in the Christian tradition was the precise opposite to Filmer's Adamite theory of property. Their starting axiom was the one which was enshrined in the biblical Book of Genesis: God gave the Earth to mankind to use in common. The starting point of property was community. This could be interpreted rigidly and dogmatically, forming a counterpoint to Filmer, and many seventeenth-century radical property theorists did precisely

---

[7] Robert Filmer, *Patriarcha and Other Political Works*, ed. Peter Laslett (Oxford: Blackwell, 1949).

this. If God's law was indeed immutable, they argued, then God's gift of the Earth to mankind in common had to remain in common use forever. But the modern natural law theorists, the school of Grotius, who worked out the 'negative community' theory and the conjectural histories of property, attempted to find a *via media* between Adamite theory and the radical proponents of immutable community.

This project took the general shape of a radical simplification of older theories of justice, rights, property and community in order to close all the loopholes that allowed these controversies to persist. Aristotle's distributive justice was dropped from the newly defined domain of rights. This move excluded rights based on merit from the domain of justice along with many complicated issues of morality, such as the assessment of qualitative worth among the members of mankind from the point of view of talent, education and virtuous performance. Justice was restricted to strict or commutative justice, that is, to issues of equality rather than differential moral values.[8] This focus on equality was gained at the price of making the notion of justice relatively one-dimensional and poor in content. The notion of right was linked to the notion of self-preservation and to the definition of the self and its exclusive sovereign domain. A 'right', which could be attributed equally to every human being, was now understood as a principle for demarcating what could be defended as one's own; it belonged to the preconditions of one's existence, one's self. Right meant one's *suum*. A thing that belonged to a person's *suum*, to the sovereign domain of a person, had to belong to a person in its substance and in such a way that it could not belong to another person in the same way and to the same degree.

The qualification 'in substance' in this definition of a full and exclusive property right or *dominion* was crucially important. Owning something in substance meant to own the fruits of this substance too, that is, owning the substance in perpetuity. In the case of land, for example, private property gave a right to the harvest of its fruits, natural or cultivated. In the case of man, figuratively speaking, it meant not only the self-ownership of one's body but also a right to the products of one's labour. Full *dominion* also included *imperium*, the absolute right to dispose things within the constraints of God's natural law. The existence of such a full property right entailed an obligation by others, under natural law, to abstain from any interference with another's property.

---

[8] István Hont and Michael Ignatieff, 'Needs and Justice in the *Wealth of Nations*: An Introductory Essay', in István Hont and Michael Ignatieff (eds.), *Wealth and Virtue: The Shaping of Political Economy in the Scottish Enlightenment* (Cambridge: Cambridge University Press, 1983), pp. 1–44.

Despite this radical narrowing of the domain of rights and property, Grotius and his followers had accepted the tradition that God gave the Earth to mankind to use in common and in this sense continued the Scholastic tradition of natural law descending from Aquinas and the Spanish theorists of the 'Second Scholastics'. However, they also wished to legitimate the system of exclusive private property which existed in their own time, and which was in the process of being powerfully reinforced by the emerging commercial society. The theory of 'negative community' allowed them to reconcile these two theoretical objectives. It was an answer to both the dogmatic individualists and the dogmatic communitarians. Against Filmer and the like, its emphasis fell on community; against community theorists, its cutting edge was in the new understanding of primeval community as 'negative'.

Grotius, Pufendorf and Locke, then, affirmed the traditional starting point of natural law, the communality of God's gift. What they wished to deny was that this communality had been based on common property rights. They maintained that mankind in the earliest time had lived without the institution of property, as ancient sources suggested. They knew, to be sure, that the early stage talked about by the Greek and Roman poets was understood by many as a stage of common property. But, as Grotius famously argued in his *Mare liberum* (1609), his tract on the freedom of the high seas (the international ocean was seen by him as the best model for expounding the character of 'negative community'), this was a misrepresentation caused by the poverty of both technical and everyday language, neither of which possessed a set of appropriate terms to describe properly the communal arrangements of early societies. It was because of this linguistic equivocation that people could maintain the fiction of early positive communities of property. In his eyes the lack of a proper vocabulary to describe primeval society had led to a monstrous confusion, a confusion which, beside causing political problems, offended Grotius' sensibilities as the founder of modern natural law theory. 'Owing to the poverty of human speech', Grotius argued,

> it has become necessary to employ identical terms for concepts which are not identical. Consequently, because of a certain degree of similitude and by analogy, the (...) expressions descriptive of our modern customs are applied to another right, which existed in early times.[9]

The confusion was anchored in the indiscriminate use of the word 'property', making it near impossible to distinguish properly between

---

[9] Grotius, *Prædæ*, p. 227. (ch. 12: 'Wherein it is shown that even if the war were a private war, it would be just ...').

primeval community arrangements and the modern system of individual property rights. To Grotius' mind the difference between the underlying principles was pivotal.

[I]n the present age, the term 'ownership' (*dominium*) connotes possession of something peculiarly one's own, that is to say, something belonging to a given party in such a way that it cannot be similarly possessed by any other party; whereas the expression 'common property' is applied to that which has been assigned to several parties, to be possessed by them in partnership (so to speak) and in mutual concord, to the exclusion of other parties.[10]

In contradistinction to this conceptual framework, he maintained,

[I]t must be understood that, during the earliest epoch of man's history, ownership (*dominium*) and common possession (*communio*) were concepts whose significance differed from that now ascribed to them. (...) Thus with reference to that early age, the term 'common' is nothing more nor less than the simple antonym of 'private' (*proprium*); and the word 'ownership' denotes the power to make use rightfully of common (i.e. public) property.[11]

Grotius, as we have argued, did not wish to deny that early societies were communal. Rather, his concern was to point out the precise sense of community. In particular, he wished to show that their 'communal ownership' was a 'concept of fact but not of law'.[12] This distinction, so crucial later on to Friedrich Karl von Savigny's historical jurisprudence, which in turn informed Karl Marx's thoughts about the history of society and property, was highly relevant for natural jurisprudence.[13]

---

[10] Ibid.
[11] Grotius, *Prædæ*, pp. 226–227.
[12] Grotius, *Prædæ*, p. 227
[13] The Marx–Savigny relationship is discussed in Donald R. Kelley, 'The Metaphysics of Law: An Essay on the Very Young Marx', *American Historical Review* 83 (1978): 350–367. See also Hasso Jaeger, 'Marx et Savigny', *Archives de philosophie du droit* 12 (1967): 65–89. Marx was familiar with the work of Savigny, who was his professor in the winter semester of 1836/7 at the University of Berlin. In particular, he knew Savigny's famous work *Das Recht des Besitzes* (*The Right of Possession*), which discussed the possible interpretations of the distinction between possession and property in civil law and wrestled with the time-honoured issue 'first whether Possession is to be looked upon as a Right or as a Fact; secondly, if it is a Right, under what class of Rights should it be enumerated?', *Von Savigny's Treatise on Possession; or The Jus Possessionis of the Civil Law*, 6th edition, trans. E. Perry (London, 1848), p. 17. See the student Marx's legal theory enthusiasms in his letter to his father in *MEGA²* III/1, pp. 10–17. In the winter semester of 1836/7 and in the summer of 1838, Marx also went to the university lectures of Eduard Gans and thus became amply acquainted with the other side of the flaring controversy between Savigny and the Hegelians. Hegel, of course, also discussed the problems of possession and property in the *Rechtsphilosophie*, and Marx could follow the Hegelian opposition to Savigny as developed by Gans, the editor of the *Rechtsphilosophie* for Hegel's *Werke* in 1833 (the edition which Marx also possessed). Gans' attack on Savigny's thoughts on possession was published a year after

It was nonsense to use the words property and ownership in more than one sense in a legally precise discourse. Whatever the 'fact' of arrangements was in primeval communities, it was less than useful to describe it through modern legal concepts. As Grotius explained:

[A] certain form of ownership did exist, but it was ownership in a universal and indefinite sense. For God had given all things, not to this or that individual, but to the human race, and there was nothing to prevent a number of persons from being joint owners, in this fashion, of one and the same possession. But such a concept would be completely irrational if we were giving to them the term 'ownership' in its modern significance, involving private possession (*proprietas*), an attribute which did not reside in any person during that epoch. In fact, it has been most aptly observed that,
... All things belong to him
Who put them to his use...[14]

The implications of this distinction were not as easy to comprehend as it seems at first. What Grotius had outlined was a conceptual distinction without any obvious temporalised dimension. Such arrangements as described by the ancient poets were still possible in theory and perhaps in limited practice. But the modern world, as everybody knew, was no longer an unoccupied no man's land open for communal use. The system of individual private property had in fact been introduced gradually through history and was now firmly in place. To express this *de facto* development a conceptual scheme was required which was arranged in temporal, that is, historical, terms. Grotius recognised the need to put the theory of property into the form of conjectural stages. It was this mode of theorisation which could make the conceptual boundaries most clearly visible:

[T]he significance of these different terms will be very easily explained if, in imitation of the method employed by all the poets since the days of Hesiod as well as by the ancient philosophers and jurists, we draw a chronological distinction between things which are perhaps not differentiated from one another by any considerable interval of time, but which do indeed differ in certain underlying principles and by their very nature.[15]

This transformation of the conceptual differences between different regimes open to mankind for the appropriation of the environment and the satisfaction of needs into a stages theory of the history of property was

---

Marx had listened to the lectures under the title *Uber die Grundlage des Besitzes, Eine Duplik* (Berlin, 1839). For the general context of Gans' influence, see John Edward Toews, *Hegelianism: The Path toward Dialectical Humanism, 1805–1841* (Cambridge: Cambridge University Press, 1980).

[14] Grotius, *Prædæ*, p. 228.
[15] Grotius, *Prædæ*, p. 226.

a momentous move. But it was not yet the whole solution. The next task was to explain to those who live in a later stage, that is, the regime of private property, what the operational principles of the earlier stage were, without making use of categories which belonged exclusively to the later one.

This required a most pronounced historicisation of the term 'property'. The traditional view (deriving from ancient sources and supported by both the Scholastics and Christian canon law), that property was not a part of the early regimes of mankind, needed to be reiterated. Thus, Grotius clearly signalled his agreement with the notion that 'there was no private property under the primary law of nations, to which we also give the name "natural law"'. This was succinctly encapsulated, Grotius thought, in Horace's well-known dictum:

> Nor he, nor I, nor any man, is made
> By Nature private owner of the soil.[16]

In order to put in place an unequivocal set of definitions of what did and what did not count as a 'right' in the modern theory, and to radically simplify the technical language of natural rights theory, Grotius now contended that the stage before private property, although it had some notions of right, had to be described in terms of 'use', not property. This corresponded to the fact/right distinction. 'Use', Grotius explained, was 'a concept of fact but not of law'.[17]

To work out a full theory of the primeval regime of mankind in terms of patterns of use rather than rights was, of course, a difficult undertaking. The complete elimination of rights from the picture proved to be tricky; Grotius himself developed only certain parts of the new vocabulary for the correct description of mankind's early history. Telling the full story, at least up to Locke (who launched the most ambitious attempt to solve this problem), is not our task now. For the moment what we should realise is that once such a set of definitions was offered, primeval property, as it were, could be described negatively, as a regime of non-property. This move was not restricted to the contrast of individual 'use' and 'private property'. It could also be applied to communal property. The early history of community could also be redescribed, in this new language, 'negatively', as a system of communal use, and thus a non-community, in the sense of being a non-positive community, something radically different from joint ownership.

This explicit extension of the model was not the work of Grotius himself but primarily the work of Pufendorf and then, in a way, of Locke.

---

[16] Grotius, *Prædæ*, p. 227.
[17] Ibid.

The restricted definition of what counted as a right (i.e. a property) had two constitutive moments which helped Pufendorf's later construction of the theory of 'negative community'. First, according to the new definition no human practice could be subsumed under a 'right' if it did not contain a strict correlation between this right and the duty of all others to abstain from interfering with it. Every right had to imply a corresponding duty in others. Secondly, the name right was reserved only to fully formed (analytically complete) rights. Thus, a potential right such as a right of inclusion, which others had to honour only in some indefinite future when certain circumstances occurred, was not a property right. Only actual rights were rights. Furthermore, the requirement that dominion implies full ownership of the substance of a thing meant that individual appropriation of less than the substance was not 'property'. It was acknowledged that there were types of individuation and exclusive practices which were part of the process of forming full property rights at some later stage but which were not yet property rights as such. Again, only fully realised property was property. Mere use, temporary possession, imperfectly exclusive ownership or rights to less than the substance of a thing (such as land) were not 'property rights'. Those periods of history, or those institutions which were based on such arrangements, were not part of the 'age of property'.

Let us briefly consider each of these points separately, with particular reference to Pufendorf's development of the theory of 'negative community'. An important consequence of the correlation between rights and duties was to downgrade the language of rights.[18] If one could have a right only because others had a duty to respect it, if every proposition involving rights had to be directly translatable into a statement about duties, then the language of rights *de facto* ceased to be primary and in the end could be proven to be redundant. However, there was a more immediately important philosophical implication of the correlativity requirement. Only humans could have a sense of duty and perform the reciprocal observance of rights and obligations. Thus, the principle implied that rights were exclusively a quality of human interactions. Because rights required human agency and mediation, they were qualities of the relationships between man and man and not between man and things. Rights were the results of social existence. In other words, rights were strictly moral concepts, links between the principles guiding the actions of an individual in relation to objects of his need on the one hand and the principles guiding him in his co-operative or antagonistic

---

[18] Richard Tuck, *Natural Rights Theories: Their Origin and Development* (Cambridge: Cambridge University Press, 1979).

relationship with his fellows on the other. Rights represented a link between the productive code under which nature was appropriated, the moral code of natural sociability and the legal-political code of social institutions which regulated social existence in positive law.

This insight, or definition if you want, was used by Pufendorf to deconstruct those theories of the primeval age which maintained that it was a regime of rights. Initially he concentrated on Hobbes' theory, which held that primeval man lived in community in such a way that each and every member of the species had an individual right to everything. A relation between men and things, Pufendorf pointed out in his critique of Hobbes, could not give rise to a right, because inanimate things or animals were under no obligation to present themselves for human appropriation. Nor could a right arise from the mere simultaneity of human actions, if the reference fields to which these human activities were applied were only parallel in a random way, without previous coordination. Only interaction between self-conscious beings of the same nature could have specifically human effects, that is, rights. To quote Pufendorf:

[N]ot every faculty to do something is properly a right, but only that which concerns some moral effect, in the case of those who have the same nature as I. Thus, as in the fables, the horse had a natural faculty to graze in the meadow, and so had the stag as well, yet neither of them had a right to this because their respective faculties did not concern the other. In the same way, when a man takes inanimate objects or animals for his use, he exercises only a purely natural faculty, if it is considered simply with regard to objects and animals which he uses, without respect to other men. But this faculty takes on the nature of a real right, at the moment when this moral effect is produced in the rest of mankind, that other men may not hinder him, or compete with him, against his will, in using such objects or animals. Of course it is absurd to try to designate as a right that faculty which all other men have an equal right to prevent one from exercising.[19]

The implication of the correlativity principle was that property had to be man-made, an artificial liaison between men, a product of history. Property necessarily had to have a positive aspect; it had to be created by positive interaction between human beings. It was a result of binding human agreement, the archetype of which was a pact or a contract. This contract did not have to be positive in the sense of being explicit; the contract, the interaction, could be tacit, embodied in the practice of men customarily acting as though they had agreed upon a certain course of

---

[19] Pufendorf, *DJNG*, 3.5.3. On the correlativity principle in general, see David Lyons, 'The Correlativity of Rights and Duties', *Nous* 1 (1970): 45–55; and more closely to our context in Tuck, *Natural Rights Theories*, pp. 159–160.

action and observing certain boundaries. This was a positive relationship because it fell within the class of reflective human interaction. It was positive because it could have legal consequences. Under the new narrow definition, property always had to be 'positive'.

Positive community, accordingly, signifies a species of property, a situation when the property had not one owner but a group of individuals, all partners according to either a tacit or an express agreement. Dominion over their property in the substance of something, primarily land, required simultaneous positive determination of their intentions. This was an absolute requirement in relation to outsiders in their defence of the common property and had to be true at least to a minimum degree in their common conduct in using the property. In a 'negative' community, by contrast, these requirements did not obtain. The community had no need to relate to the environment as their 'property', certainly not in the precise and bounded sense of the concept which had been accepted as the only true meaning of this word.

Thus, by invoking the correlativity principle, Pufendorf could object to Hobbes' notion of primeval community. The community of Hobbes, preceding the war of all against all, was a notion of positive community because while it was pre-contractual and gave no boundaries to appropriation, it nonetheless expressed the consequences of God's gift of the Earth to mankind in common in rights terms, that is, in positive terms (everybody had a right to everything). Reinterpreting the community involved in receiving God's donation, Pufendorf could strongly assert that

> the grant of God, by which He allowed men the use of the products of the earth is not the immediate cause of dominion, as it has its effect in relation to other men (a proof of which is to be found in the fact that brute creatures use and consume things as if it were God's will, although no dominion is recognized among them).[20]

On the basis of correlativity, moreover, he could defeat the Adamite theory as well. These defenders of private property were as much opposed to the Hobbesian version of positive community as Pufendorf, but they also opposed the contractarian implications of correlativity. They regarded a contractarian foundation of private property as insecure and wished no compromise with the idea of primeval community of any sort, even if community was now to be regarded as 'negative'. Pufendorf's description of the historical shape of the evolving debate can give us an insight into the dialectics of the successive critical positions on community:

[20] Pufendorf, *DJNG*, 4.4.4.

Most recent writers differ entirely from us in the origin of dominion. Let us see what force there is in their argument. Now they acknowledge that community is taken in a double sense, either as that which, while undivided and proper to several, furnishes a common use to each person; or as that which acknowledges no proprietorship whatsoever, and serves the general use of all. But they deny things not only in the first kind of community at the beginning, as we also do, but also the second; and so they deny that at the beginning, when proprietorship was entirely lacking, all things lay open to common use, denying as well the consequence of this, namely, that individual dominions arose originally from division and occupation.[21]

Pufendorf shrewdly uncovered the mistake in this position. In order to protect the foundations of their absolutist political position, Filmer, Caspar Ziegler and others tried to undermine the consent theory of the origins of private property through historical argument, by pointing to the lack of historical evidence for any original contract.[22] But they missed the real point. Consent theory was not historically inspired; it was a theorem explicating the analytical consequences of the conceptualisation of rights as man-to-man relationships. Because of that, the Adamite ploy could be proven to be a dead-end analytically. The Adamite theory was based on an apparently astute move. It exploited a loophole in the scriptural story of the beginning of the use of earthly resources by mankind as a community. The Adamites simply argued that while the community of mankind was a true theoretical characterisation of the entity which was recipient of God's donation, it was also true that in the beginning there was only one man, Adam. Mankind, taken as a plurality, was the community of his descendants. Hence the original community, receiving the donation, was in fact one individual, and his right to everything on Earth was an individual property right.

But Pufendorf could dispose of this by invoking the correlativity of rights and duties. Even if it were true that one man had been the seed of the community of mankind and had the Earth open for his sole use, such use could not be the basis of a right precisely for the reason that he was no more than a single individual:

---

[21] Pufendorf, *DJNG*, 4.4.10.
[22] See Filmer's attack in 'Observations Concerning the Originall of Government, Upon Mr Hobs "Leviathan", Mr Milton against "Salmasius", H. Grotius "De Jure Belli"', in Robert Filmer, *Patriarcha, and Other Political Works*, ed. Peter Laslett (Oxford: Blackwell, 1949), pp. 273–274; for an interpretative context, see John Dunn, *The Political Thought of John Locke: An Historical Account of the Argument of the Two Treatises of Government* (Cambridge: Cambridge University Press, 1969), ch. 6. For certain similarities in the political outlook of Sir Robert Filmer and Caspar Ziegler, see the latter's *Circa Regicidum Anglorum Exercitationes* (Leiden, 1653).

The right of Adam to things was different from that dominion, which is now established among men; one may call it indefinite dominion not formally established, but only conceded, not actually, but potentially so. It has the same effect as dominion now has, that, namely, of using things at one's own pleasure; but it was not, properly speaking, dominion, because no other man was then on earth to whom it could oppose its effect; although, upon the increase of men it could pass into dominion. Therefore, so long as Adam was the only man, things to him were neither common nor proper. For community implies a sharer in possession, and proprietorship connotes the exclusion of another's right to the same thing, and so neither is intelligible before more than one man has come into being.[23]

Having in this way reinforced the Grotian separation of 'right' and 'use', denying that property rights, either communal or private, could issue from the biblical story of the beginning, Pufendorf had to defend the historicisation of the origin of property rights which was implied. Grotius referred to the tradition of the ancients in this respect, invoking Hesiod's ages of gold, silver and bronze. But how could this be squared with the Christian story based on the Bible? Clearly, the idea of historical change had to be accommodated within the established tradition of Christian natural law. To defend the 'negative community' theory, Pufendorf turned to the formidable conceptual arsenal of Scholastic natural law. Those who regarded natural law as immutable had taken either private or communal property as its true and immutable content. If property was lawful now, they contended, then it had to follow that 'proprietorship and dominion belong to natural law taken in its strict sense, and as it is engraved upon the minds of men'.[24] This, Pufendorf pointed out, ignored the tradition of the Fathers, and was nothing but a play on the word 'natural' in the phrase 'natural law'. 'Here it should be observed', Pufendorf wrote,

that the expression, 'this or that belongs to natural law', has a different meaning, according as it is applied either to some command, in the strict sense of the word, or to some institution introduced into human life. In the former sense it means that the law of nature commands that this be or not be done; in the latter, that some reason, upon a consideration of the general state of social life, advises that this be set up and established among men. For whatever institutions have been introduced,[25]

---

[23] Pufendorf, *DJNG*, 4.4.3.
[24] Pufendorf, *DJNG*, 4.4.14.
[25] This was indeed in accord with the Scholastic position. According to Suarez, for example, there was a sense of natural law, according to which 'a thing is said to pertain to the natural law merely in a permissive, negative, or concessive sense (...) Under this classification many things fall which, from the standpoint simply of natural law, are permissible, or conceded, to men – such things as the holding of goods in common, human liberty, and the like. With respect to these things, the natural law lays down no precept enjoining that they shall remain in that state; rather does it leave the matter to the management of men, such management to be in accord with the demand of reason.' Suarez, *De Legibus*, 2.4.16.

because of their special advantage to this or that state, are said to belong to civil or positive law. Therefore, when the question is raised, whether dominion traces its origin to natural law, the latter and not the former sense of the word is to be taken. That is, since the foundation of natural law is a social life, and the nature of man's mind shows clearly enough that among a great number of men, who are undertaking to advance life, by various arts, a quiet and decorous society cannot exist without distinct dominion of things, therefore, such were introduced in accordance with the proper requirements of human affairs, and with the aim of natural law. After this was done, the same law enjoins the observance of whatever things work to the end of the dominion instituted. But it was needless for all things, immediately upon the creation of mankind, and wherever located, to come under proprietorship by some definite precept of natural law; proprietorship, on the other hand, has been introduced as the peace of men seemed to require it. But the precept of natural law about abstaining from what is another's first exerted its force when men defined by convention what each should hold to be another's, and what his own. Till that time it lay dormant, so far as its strength was concerned, in that general precept about its preservation of pacts and about not impairing another's right. Nor does it involve an absurdity to say that the obligation to observe the law by abstaining from what is another's is coeval with mankind, and yet the institution of 'one's own and another's' was introduced later.[26]

The concept of 'negative community' was a direct derivative of this intellectual heritage, of Grotius' insistence upon establishing an unequivocal vocabulary for the basic concepts of rights under the aegis of an historicised natural law. Using the Scholastic distinction between concepts understood positively and negatively, Pufendorf could now assert that the beginnings of mankind, God's donation of the earth to mankind in common, could be understood properly if one paid more attention to the 'negative' and 'positive' definitions of community. One could avoid being confused by Grotius' assertion that the term common was nothing else than an antonym to private if one accepted that

the term community is taken either *negatively* or *positively*. In the former case things are said to be common, according as they are considered before the interposition of any human act, as a result of which they are held to belong in a special way to this man rather than to that. In the same sense such things are said to be

---

[26] Pufendorf, *DJNG*, 4.4.14. About the idea expressed in the last sentence of Pufendorf, Suarez said the following: 'In this connexion (…) one may fittingly apply the familiar illustration drawn from Augustine, namely, that just as the science of medicine lays down certain precepts for the sick, others for the well, certain precepts for the strong and others for the weak, although the rules of medicine do not therefore undergo essential change but merely become manifold, so that some serve on one occasion, and others, on another occasion; even so, the natural law, while it remains in itself the same, lays down one precept for one occasion and another, for another occasion; and is binding in one of its rules at one time, though not binding previously or subsequently, and this without undergoing any change in itself but merely because of a change in the subject matter.' Suarez, *De Legibus*, 2.4.12.

nobody's, more in a negative than a positive sense; that is, that they are not yet assigned to a particular person, not that they cannot be assigned to a particular person. They are, furthermore, called 'things that lie open to any and every person'. But common things, by the second and positive meaning, differ from things owned, only in the respect that the latter belong to one person while the former belong to several in the same manner.[27]

How then did the natural jurists restate the early community of mankind without invoking positive property rights, individual or communal? The two features of the new rights theory that we have discussed, the requirement for a correlativity between rights and duties and the denial of potential claims for inclusion as rights, were sufficient to define a community in 'negative' terms. In the formula 'God gave the Earth to mankind in common', mankind appeared as a communality, but only as an aggregate of the species, not as a morally – and even less as a politically – organised community. Mankind as a community was defined only to demarcate man from other species. The internal structure of the 'community of mankind' was undefined. God did not give a definite right to any particular individual in preference to others, which would have enhanced individuality, nor did he grant the use-right of the Earth to men only under the condition that they should cooperate, which would have diminished individuality.

What then is the appropriate characterisation of man–thing relationships outside the system of social mediation signified by the presence of 'rights'? If one were to theorise both the predecessor stage of 'before property' and the successor stage of 'after property' in a language that avoided abusing the word 'right', it was necessary to find concepts which were not subject to the restriction imposed by the principle of correlativity between rights and duties. Such a language was available if one was willing to utilise the concept of need, *chreia* in Aristotle's Greek, *indigentia* in the Latin of the natural jurists, *Bedürfnis* for Hegel and Marx.[28]

---

[27] Pufendorf, *DJNG*, 4.4.2.

[28] *Indigentia* was not the only word which could stand for need, and not the only one used by Pufendorf either. Nonetheless, when he cited Aristotle's *Nicomachean Ethics*, 1133b, he specifically translated *chreia*, the bonding agent which holds everything together, or more precisely creates *societas* (*koinonia*), as *indigentia*. In the same context, when referring to Plato's *Republic* or Aristotle's other works, the same translation was consistently maintained. While Pufendorf accepted, when discussing commerce and prices, that need bonded society, he specifically went out his way to criticise the Platonic notion that *indigentia* was the cause of the civitas (*Republic*, 369b–c). In late seventeenth- and early eighteenth-century Pufendorf translations, these terms appeared as follows: *chreia-indigentia* as *besoin* (Barbeyrac), *Notdürfftigkeit*, *Bedürffnis*, *Nothdurff* (in the 1711 German translation by Immanuel Weber and Daniel Schneider), *necessity, wants, indulgence* (Kennett); *civitas-polis* as *societez civiles*, *bürgerlichen Gesellschaften* or *Commonwealths*. While the French and German translations, by providing a consistent

Needs describe a direct relationship between man and the objects of his need, want or desire. The relationship is not only direct; it is also ultimately and irrevocably individual. Need could operate as the principle of individuation from the common because the need for consuming the most important means of survival was both necessarily individual and at the same time predetermined by man's biological, or God-given, constitution. Need was, thus, the distributional principle of negative primeval community. Christian Wolff, who gave perhaps the most detailed account of it, made this very clear:

> In primitive community, insofar as it is necessary, the use of necessary things lies open to each individual, according to his need (...) therefore nature allows him who needs more the use of more things than to him who is less needy. Nature does not distribute things for use equally, because not everybody is equally needy.[29]

The consumption of objects not made by man could be well described by a simple theory of needs. A man who picked up an acorn lying under an oak tree could rightfully, as it were, consume it, without paying attention to the needs of other men, because he needed no more than the permission of its 'maker' and that he already possessed by virtue of being a member of the human species, since God gave the Earth for mankind in common. Accordingly, the acts of first individuating and then

---

translation, preserved the unity of the underlying 'needs' discourse, Kennett's English (by substituting want, necessity, indulgence and, occasionally, need) fragmented it. This particular weakness, as it were, of the English language remained a semi-permanent fixture. While in modern German and French theoretical discourse it is possible to talk ontologically using *besoin* or *Bedürfnis* as a single dimension of the human condition, in English this immediately defaults to the duality of needs and wants. This implicit *kulturkritisch* dimension of modern English-American usage is ignored in the context of this paper and 'need' is used in the German or French sense.

[29] '*In communione primæva* usus rerum necessarius unicuique patet in quantum necessarius, seu prout cuique opus est. (...) qui pluribus indiget, ei etiam natura plurium concessit, quam qui paucioribus indiget. Natura res utendas non distribuit aequaliter, quia non omnes indigent aequaliter' (§ 28.), *Jus Naturae Methodo Scientifica Pertractatum* (Halle, 1742), 'Pars Secunda, in Qua Agitur De Dominio..., Caput I. De primæva rerum Communione', § 27–28, pp. 17–19. Wolff's German term for primeval community was 'der Gemeinschaft der ersten Zeit'. See his discussion of it in the *Grundsätze des Natur-und Völckerrechts worinn alle Verbindlichkeiten und alle Rechte aus der Natur des Menschen in einem beständigen Zusammenhange hergeleitet werden* (Halle, 1754). His opening sentence was: 'Man nennt den notwendigen Gebrauch der Sachen denjenigen, der dazu erfordert wird, das wie unserer natürlichen Verbindlichkeit ein Genügen leisten. (...) so haben überhaupt alle Menschen ein Recht zum notwendigen Gebrauch aller Sachen, es mögen seyn, was vor welche es wollen, nämlich sowohl zu der notwendigen, als auch der nützlichen und vergnügenden; folglich ist derselbe erlaubt', II. 1. §183, p. 116. [In English: The necessary use of things is that which is required to satisfy our natural obligation. (...) Thus, all people have a right to the necessary use of all things, whatever they may be, namely both for the necessary and for the useful and pleasurable; consequently, it is allowed.]

appropriating the acorn could take place without creating a right. In consuming the acorn, the gatherer merely satisfied his need without entering into any particular relationship with other members of his species. No correlation with others was required or indeed had taken place unless, that is, the particular acorn he consumed was the object of simultaneous need of more than one man. Such a situation would have called for a settling of rights, but it was extraneous to the description of a simple act of need satisfaction. The assumption of competition was a foreshadowing of the time the satisfaction of needs would take place within the matrix of human interactions required for sustaining similar acts of need satisfaction in the future. Rights would enter the immediate process of satisfying needs only when the object of need satisfaction and individual consumption was socially produced, in which case it was necessary to apportion the right share of each contributor who participated in the production process and even more the portion of those who were not a party to the social production themselves.

It was indeed in these terms that Pufendorf came to redescribe God's donation of the Earth to mankind in common. The key terms of the 'negative community' theory, in contradistinction to rights, were 'use' and 'needs'. These were the basic data of human existence, not rights:

That donation of God, described in the Sacred Scriptures, sets forth not a definite form of dominion, but only an indefinite right to apply things to uses which are reasonable and necessary.

'Therefore', he added,

it is incorrect to infer that man received a right from the donation of God: (...) For the donation of God only made man secure, on the assumption that God wished him to consume upon his necessities the things which He had created.[30]

Once this had been laid down with conceptual precision and certainty, Pufendorf could continue the Grotian initiative to project this onto a historical canvas in which property evolved by stages. Having defined the beginning negatively, he had to explain how community could turn to its positive opposite, private property. Conceptually there was no difficulty, since Pufendorf's post-Scholastic interpretation of natural law could easily allow him to say that

it is further understood, that the law of nature approves all conventions which have been introduced about things by men, provided they involve no contradiction or do not overturn society.[31]

---

[30] Pufendorf, *DJNG*, 4.4.10.
[31] Pufendorf, *DJNG*, 4.4.4.

It is important to note here that the two conditions set by this sentence were quite distinct. The first required only that the evolving arrangements of mankind should be free of internal contradiction. In Pufendorf's words, God gave to man an 'indefinite right to apply things to uses which were reasonable and necessary'. The requirements of reasonableness and the limitation to necessary use, which so powerfully exercised the mind of Locke somewhat later, were only 'side constraints' (to use Robert Nozick's expression) laid down by God's natural law. Within these constraints it was up to mankind collectively to decide upon the best use of the natural environment. 'It is true', says Pufendorf

that God allowed man to turn the earth, its products and its creatures, to his own use and convenience, that is, He gave men an indefinite right to them, yet the manner, intensity, and extent of this power were left to the judgment and disposition of men; whether, in other words, they would confine it within certain limits, or within none at all, and whether they wanted every man to have a right to everything, or only to a certain and fixed part of things, or to be assigned his definite portion with which he should rest content and claim a right to anything else.[32]

However, while it is true that Pufendorf relied on a historical scheme which left history potentially open-ended and was anything but deterministic in its basic shape, the conjectural history of property which developed from it was by no means an ideologically neutral instrument. His history of property was a history of private property. To arrive at private property from 'negative' beginnings he needed a definite explanation as to how it came about. Such a history was now an absolute necessity. To understand how his initially underdetermined scheme was turned into a history of progress, culminating in private property, we have to pay more attention to the requirement that no regime for using God's donation may lead to the overturning of society. The best regime at any given stage was the regime which could provide effective use of the resources while maintaining social peace.[33]

The choice as to whether God's donation was to be used communally or individually was left open. Any decision had to be man's and not God's. The only certainties about the Creation were, first, that God made man a particularly needy animal, burdened with insatiable and mentally generated desires, and, second, that at the same time his creation was

---

[32] Pufendorf, *DJNG*, 4.4.4.
[33] For an explanation of this idiom see my 'The Language of Sociability and Commerce: Samuel Pufendorf and the Theoretical Foundations of the "Four Stages Theory"' in Anthony Pagden (ed.), *The Languages of Political Theory in Early-Modern Europe* (Cambridge: Cambridge University Press, 1987), pp. 253–276.

an imbecile one,[34] quite incapable of satisfying his basic needs on his own, and hence in need of cooperation and division of labour in satisfying his desires. Man was a sociable animal, incapable of surviving outside society. The simple theory of needs and sociability underpinning Pufendorf's interpretation of primeval community required the real or imagined condition of relative abundance. Once scarcity became a factor, rights were also called into existence. Any theory that sought to theorise a stage 'before' or 'after' property had to articulate itself in terms of needs, abundance and scarcity. That is why these natural law theories of primeval community strike the modern reader as 'economistic' (in fact the relationship is the reverse, economics should strike the reader as 'natural-law-like'), and that is why there can be a direct link between the primeval community theories of natural jurisprudence and political economy, and of course *a fortiori* to Marxism too.

In negative community, in John Locke's memorable phrase, the world was like a 'great common', open to any taker.[35] In the absolute beginning, before the interposition of any human act, there could not be any property. At that time the Earth was literally a no man's land, a *res nullius*. This was the stage of absolutely negative community, mankind and property only existing as a potentiality. Once mankind was actually generated, every human being born was automatically included in the species and possessed the same potential aptitudes and capacities. They could all labour, for example, in order to transform nature into a shape more amenable for the satisfaction of human needs. As long as a relative abundance of natural fruits and natural shelter sustained and each individual could practise his aptitudes without conflict, mankind could exist without its members developing a system of either group or individual property rights. They had a need rather than a right to practise their capacities. Since there was room for everybody to satisfy their needs, there was no need either for rights or correlative duties to protect these activities. The 'negativity' of the absolute beginning could persist as long as this abundance, or relative abundance, could be sustained.

---

[34] The *imbecillitas* of man was described by Pufendorf as follows: 'A man left in the open, away from the assistance of his fellows, would be a miserable animal (...) a dumb and ignoble creature, with no power other than to dig up plants and roots, to slake his thirst at any spring, river or pool, he may happen upon, to crawl into caves so as to avoid the inclemency of the weather, to cover his body with moss and grass, to pass his time in tolerable inactivity, to tremble at every sound or at the passing of another animal, and finally to perish of hunger and cold or to be torn to pieces by some wild beast.' Pufendorf, *DJNG*, 2.1.5.
[35] John Locke, *Two Treatises on Government*, ed. Peter Laslett (Cambridge: Cambridge University Press, 1960), p. 334. (*Second Treatise*, ch. 5. §35.)

Two important facts need to be emphasised here. The first relates to the duration of negative community. If, according to the new strict theory of rights, only full rights in the substance of a thing counted as 'property rights', then a weak but nonetheless negative community could remain up to the point where a system of such rights became dominant. More precisely, mankind lived in negative community until full and exclusive private ownership of land was established. The substance of God's gift to mankind in common was the most important productive asset of the Earth – land itself. Mankind lived in negative community for a long period, for several historical epochs, until fertile lands became scarce for an overwhelming part of the human species. Hunting and gathering, pasturage and the early land-use systems, they all fell within the scope of negative community based on use rather than ownership. Mankind proceeded along the principles of first occupation. Occupation signified a needs claim but under conditions of relative abundance it did not necessarily lead to the creation of property rights. Families, extended families, tribes and nations of hunters and gatherers, or nomadic shepherds, could occupy the surface of the globe promiscuously, without contesting the very same bits of territory endlessly. The land itself was no man's land. It was still *res nullius*, held in negative community.

Second, the fact is that the history of mankind from negative community to private property, from abundance to moderate scarcity, was a gradual development. It was a process in real historical time and the natural jurists, when constructing their conjectural histories, utilised all the available historical and anthropological sources available to them, from Greek and Roman poetic materials and Roman histories of barbaric times to travellers' reports of contemporary rude nations still living in 'negative community'. The conjectural histories of the natural lawyers were not mythical constructs depicting emergence from a fictional state of nature, already individualistic, to the organised systems of individualism sanctioned by contracts. Such views, common in the secondary literature from Pufendorf's own time to today, are misunderstandings of their methodology. These histories did not start from individualistic anarchy but from unarticulated community. Then again, contrary to the usual view, from unarticulated coexistence they did not proceed directly to modern states based on individual rights. Rather, they depicted the development of mankind as a gradual process of creating actual local communities, now in the sense of positive community. They depicted the formation of nations as the separation of communities out of the negative. The very fact of separating out tribal territory for a collectivity made the tribe or nation a positive community vis-à-vis mankind. Furthermore, they understood that the early history of nations was a history of communitarian experiments in a stricter sense too. At first positive communities could organise themselves, on the inside, negatively, treating their 'common' promiscuously as in primeval times. But on the whole, and increasingly, elaborate local positive communities were formed with complicated, reciprocating and distributive rules. When the natural jurists came to characterise the final emergence of individualistic systems of full property rights, they explained it in terms of the difficulties and failures that positively communitarian systems experienced. Hobbes' *De cive* (1642) was only the most obvious example of deriving anarchy from the failures of communism. In terms of community theory, the conjectural histories of natural jurisprudence were thus quite complex. They proceeded from negative community to positive community and only then to the conscious, contractual reorganisation of the national positive community into a system of individual property rights underpinned by a full system of the correlativity of rights and duties.

The underlying discourse of this conjectural history remained a theory of need. The Aristotelian formula, that it was *chreia* – need – which acted as the bonding agent of society, was the starting point. The satisfaction of need called for intense co-operation. At the same time, it also gave scope for the growth of the pathological variants of need – covetousness and greed – which were seen as the ever-present, divisive factors in human history. While covetousness and greed functioned as incentives for labour, for the ever better and intensive utilisation of the resources of the Earth, their work also turned the initial abundance into scarcity, but a scarcity which was relatively less severe than might be naturally expected. Scarcity was not entirely or mainly the work of the covetous. It had arisen naturally, it was well understood, simply because of the growth of human population. This discourse revolved around the categories of population growth, need, labour and scarcity. To satisfy the need of growing populations from the limited resources available required constant innovation and intensification of labour. Communal government appeared at some stage as a protective and redistributive agency controlling the transition from negative to positive community. Finally, the development of private property was accomplished according to the basic requirement of natural law: that no regime of needs satisfaction was legitimate which brought with it the danger of overturning society.[36] Pufendorf emphatically asserted that the regime of 'mine and thine' was not the source of internecine war but a remedy for it.[37] Positive communities, by failing to assure an equitable redistribution according to the actual labour input of

[36] Pufendorf, *DJNG*, 8.1.3; 8.3.14.
[37] Pufendorf, *DJNG*, 4.4.7.

their members and by not keeping the internal boundaries clear, became sources of tension and possible social breakdown. Hence property rights were introduced to regulate and ensure the social peace of mankind.

The formation of the modern state was part and parcel of this solution to the problems of disintegrating community, completing the transition into a system of individual property rights. The state embodied the transition from 'use' to 'right', from fact to legality. In this context, the state appeared as a 'historical category', as the Marxist would have it (and potentially it could wither away once the need for it, as it were, would disappear). The conjectural histories of natural jurisprudence in the eighteenth century, particularly in the Scottish Enlightenment, became histories of the successive modes of subsistence for growing populations, of the division of labour as well as of the forms of government appropriate to each stage. These histories of stages in social development became incorporated into the core of political economy. A tradition was created, whose natural culmination was Marxian historical materialism, the quintessentially political-economic view of history.

[In conclusion, I should like to return to the question of traditions. If I am right in arguing that the core of Marxism, its theory of historical stages, is crucially indebted to some of the core arguments in the early modern theory of rights, then our usual dualistic view of the present stage of competing liberal and Marxist idioms of political theory can no longer be maintained. Both modern democratic rights theory and historical materialism appear instead as natural extensions of the same original corpus of early modern theories of rights. Instead of the familiar choice between two competing languages of political theory we find ourselves facing a single core problem: are the inherited categories of Western political thought – the discourse of rights and needs – adequate for understanding the relationship between economy and polity in the twentieth century?][38]

III

The difference between the natural-law-cum-political-economy history of property and its Marxian version lies, of course, in Marx's projection of a stage of renewed (in the sense of *Aufhebung*) negative community in mankind's future. Theoretically, this projection was entirely consistent with the earlier theory. What the 'negative community' theory posited was an open-ended history in which any agreement which was not self-contradictory or dangerous to the survival of human society was

[38] [The 1984 conclusion to this paper, which Hont removed when he added Part III.]

acceptable under natural law. If mankind could ever progress from the condition of moderate scarcity into a stage of relative, or even absolute, abundance, then there was no need for retaining property rights or their guardian, the state.

David Hume, for one, clearly spelled out this theoretical possibility, explaining that strict justice and rights were not immutable entities but artificial virtues produced by history. In conditions of abundance men could revert from a system of rights to a system of use, or use-values (such political economy terms were already used by Locke, who contrasted the primeval reliance of use-values to the regime of artificial or exchange values after the general introduction of money). Marx did not do much more than reassert the content of the original theory. In a system of use (and use-values) there was no need for keeping the correlativity principle. The new system could be an administration of things, not of men. Communism, in this theoretical perspective, was thus nothing but the idea of 'negative community' for our time, or more precisely, for our future.

Marx was faithful to the other facet of the natural law theory of legitimate historical change as well, to the requirement of maintaining the benign working of sociability under all circumstances. The regime of private property, it had been argued by the natural jurists, came into existence to keep the peace of mankind, to prevent the 'overturn of society'. Marx had never accepted their view. He rather contended that the dynamism of the established private property regime (a system in which property owners and the excluded, mere labourers, coexisted) led to a situation where society (that is, the regime of sociability underlying the political order) ran the danger of being 'overturned'. After a certain point in the growth of the system, Marx thought, the coexistence of owners and excluded could not remain manageable. The system of exclusive private domains would increasingly prevent needs, *chreia*, from acting as a bonding agent between haves and have-nots. Hence, the primary law of nature, the law of sociability and peace, might itself require the abolition of private property. This was a legitimate argument within the natural law tradition. Communism, 'negative community', Marx could now posit, was required to reincorporate the excluded into the progressive and socialising operations (*Verkehr*) of mutual needs.

Marx shared a commitment with the 'socialist' natural jurists, as Pufendorf and his school was called in the eighteenth century,[39] and also

---

[39] The term was used, and is most likely to have been invented, by Gottlieb Hufeland (1760–1817): 'Der wahre Vater des Naturrechts ist Samuel von Pufendorf. Er und viele seiner Nachfolger gründen das Naturrecht auf Geselligkeit und können Socialisten genannt werden', Gottlieb Hufeland, *Lehrsätze des Naturrechts und der damit verbundenen Wissenschaften* (Jena, 1790), p. 16 (§39). Thomasius was then

with the political economists, not only explaining mankind's beginnings as a 'negative community' but also in his passionate opposition to 'positive community'. The conjectural history of property developed by these theorists was a history of civilisation, not only a history of mankind's fight against scarcity but a history of progress, of developing higher needs and their satisfaction by ever more complex patterns of cooperation. As Pufendorf explained, private property was a result of men's desire to have a 'quiet and decorous society' in which life could be constantly advanced by 'various arts'. The needs theory underlying this theory of history itself rested on a constantly reiterated contrast, which one finds in Marx as well, between animal society and human society, between animal needs and human needs. This contrast had not only informed the theory of early communal structures but also highlighted the ability of the human species to transcend animal needs through *cultura*. Civilisation was regarded as the antithesis of animal-like barbarity. Men were capable of inventing new needs and also the means of their satisfaction through cooperation and society. These new needs were seen as the very sign of human superiority over brutes, a true sign of successful 'humanisation'. Private property was seen not only as the guardian of social peace but also as the guarantee of the development of human beings that were richer in needs and more cultured, more sociable. Continuing this idiom, instead of inventing it, Marx argued that any further development of men richer in needs now required not private property but its abolition. But such abolition of property had to proceed from the very foundations already established in the history of property described by the natural lawyers. Communism was not to be a regression from the levels achieved under the private property regime but its final fruition.

Since Marx's theory of communism makes sense only as an extension of 'socialist' natural jurisprudence (i.e. that of the Pufendorfian school), it is to be expected that he would have agreed with Pufendorf's criticism of modern 'positive community'. Pufendorf would not have approved of Marx's vision of the future. He thought that any idea of re-establishing the abundance of primeval times was a utopia, a reverse projection of the myth of the Golden Age. But the more dangerous idea, he recognised, was to establish communities in place of private property here and now. Such communities had to be positive; they had to be the result of group decisions to leave the world of private property and to manage their own affairs by joint decision, by positive agreement. In itself this was not

---

described as having been 'ein Freund der Socialisten' and then 'ihr erster wichtiger Gegner', p. 17 (§40). This book of Hufeland's was widely read in Germany on its appearance and was praised by Kant.

illegitimate. What was disingenuous, Grotius and Pufendorf maintained, was to legitimate such attempts as a return to the primeval communism of mankind. This early community, as we have seen, they regarded as negative not positive. Furthermore, they regarded the initial relative abundance as the result of natural simplicity. The point of establishing communities in the modern age was to opt out of the dynamism of history and cut oneself off from the development of needs and the ensuing necessity of regulating human interaction through property rights. The aim was to live in simplicity, but in an age when this could not but be artificial.

Grotius and Pufendorf acknowledged the right of positive communities to re-establish localised relative abundance and hence peaceful communality by consciously repressing their own needs. This idea was not new. Grotius claimed that the archetype of positive communism could be found in the community of the Essenes.[40] Community in modern times had to be like theirs, a community based on asceticism, not on an acceptance of modern culture and civilisation but on its critique. Such communities had to be small to be workable. They had to be communities of like-minded people who could go on regulating their affairs by joint decisions. Any extension of it to people who did not share their moral convictions regarding civilisation, on the other hand, was necessarily tyrannical.[41] Establishing it as a large system was also unmanageable. How could a large number of people participate in the joint deliberation regarding the best use of their common property on an ongoing basis? And finally, how could such a system cope with the ever-present tensions caused by population growth? That is, how could a large system of positive community avoid a relapse into poverty and barbarism when established under the conditions of advancing civilisation (normally underpinned by a system of private property)?

---

[40] Grotius contrasted the positive community of genuinely simple people to communities of artificial simplicity. The first, 'exemplified in the community of property arising from extreme simplicity, may be seen among certain tribes in America, which have lived for many generations in such a condition without inconvenience. The second (...) exemplified in the community of property arising from affection, was formerly realized among the Essenes, afterward among the first Christians at Jerusalem; at the present time, also, by a goodly number who live an ascetic life.' *DJBP*, 2.2.2.1.

[41] See Pufendorf's comment on Grotius' example of the Essenes and early Christians: 'For such a community can be instituted and maintained only by a small group, which is also endowed with singular humility of mind. When men are scattered to distant places it would a labour of folly to gather products into one place, and then distribute them from a common store; while among a large number of men many must necessarily be found who from a defective sense of justice and from greediness would be unwilling to maintain due equality either in labour or in consumption of food. And Plato, in *Laws*, Bk. V, suggests this very thing in assigning to the gods and their offspring this same state where there is a community of all things.' Pufendorf, *DJNG*, 4.4.7.

The natural jurists and their successors, the political economists, were unremittingly hostile to projections of positive community beyond the boundaries of small voluntary groups of self-conscious ascetics. But nobody was as scathing about positive community theory as Karl Marx. Let us reiterate his idea from the 'Paris Manuscripts' mentioned earlier in this paper. 'This type of communism' – he wrote,

> since it negates the *personality* of man in every sphere – is but a logical expression of private property, which is its negation. (...) Crude communism is only the culmination of this envy and of this levelling-down proceeding from the *preconceived* minimum. It has a *definite, limited* standard. How little this annulment [*Aufhebung*] of private property is really an appropriation is in fact proved by the abstract negation of the entire world of culture [*Bildung*] and civilisation, the regression to the *unnatural* simplicity of the *poor* and crude man who has few needs [*bedürfnisslosen Menschen*] and who has not only failed to go beyond private property, but has not yet even reached it. (...) The first positive annulment of private property – *crude* communism – is thus merely a *manifestation* of the vileness of private property, which wants to set itself up as the *positive community system*.[42]

I would suggest that it was not an accident that Marx used the term 'positive community' in this context, and I believe that he actually understood it as the opposite of 'negative community'. This cannot be proven with absolute certainty. But there is more to this suggestion than circumstantial validation through the sort of interpretation which has been attempted in this paper. The young Marx was a formidable thinker, but like everybody else he had his sources and used the ideas of others in his own writing. We have mentioned already that through his reading of Savigny and Hegel he was familiar with the distinction between possession and property and the debates about this distinction. However, neither Savigny nor Hegel were particularly interested in a polemic against 'positive community', certainly not with the intensity revealed in the 'Paris Manuscripts'. But there were other critics of communism on the left, besides Marx. Writing to his friend Arnold Ruge (1802–1880) in 1843, Marx had already expressed his strong opposition to the communism of Cabet, Dezamy, Weitling and others, arguing the same point which he expressed in his manuscript a year later.[43] Their communism, he wrote to Ruge, was 'only a particular manifestation of the humanistic principle' because it was 'infected by its opposite, private property'. 'The abolition of private property' was by no means 'identical with

---

[42] Marx, *MECW* 3, p. 295. *Paris Manuscripts*, p. 347. ('Private Property and Communism').
[43] [Étienne Cabet (1788–1856); Alexandre Théodore Dézamy (1808–1850); Wilhelm Christian Weitling (1808–1871)].

communism', he continued his criticism, it was 'only a particular, one-sided realization of the principle of socialism'. Distancing himself from the communists, Marx reminded Ruge that certain socialists – Charles Fourier and Pierre-Joseph Proudhon – had already lined themselves up against the communists and developed a powerful critique of their dogmatism.[44]

From the two socialists mentioned, one, Proudhon, made a really thorough study of the question of property. Marx was, at this time, an admirer of this work. In *The Holy Family*, written in the same year as the 'Paris Manuscripts', Marx praised *What Is Property?* as

the first resolute, ruthless, and at the same time scientific investigation – of the basis of political economy, *private property*. This is the great scientific advance he made, an advance which revolutionizes political economy and for the first time makes a real science of political economy possible.[45]

Marx came to regret this specific praise in due time. Nonetheless, it seems that when formulating his critique of positive community in 1844 he freely availed himself of Proudhon's idiom, and to this criticism as the foundation of the critique of political economy he more or less adhered throughout his life.

---

[44] Marx to Arnold Ruge, September 1843, 'Letters from the Franco-German Yearbooks' [1844], published in *Karl Marx: Early Writings*, trans. Rodney Livingstone and Gregor Brenton (London: Penguin Books with New Left Review, 1975), p. 207; *MECW* 3, p. 143.
[45] Marx, *The Holy Family* [1845], *MECW* 4, p. 32. Marx asserted that Proudhon's *Qu'est-ce que la propriété?* had done to political economy what Sieyès' *Qu'est-ce que le tiers état?* had done to politics. In this he expressed the very same idea with which his friend Moses Hess started his review essay of Proudhon's book in 1843 (remained in manuscript), see Moses Hess, *Philosophische und Sozialistische Schriften, 1837–1850*, ed. W. Monke, 2nd. ed. (Berlin, 1980), p. 255. Nonetheless, he already signalled that he wanted to go further than Proudhon: 'As the first criticism of any science is necessarily influenced by the premises of the science it is fighting against, so Proudhon's treatise (...) is the criticism of *political economy* from the standpoint of political economy. (...) [It] will therefore be scientifically superseded by a criticism of *political economy*, including Proudhon's criticism. This work became possible only owing to the work of Proudhon himself, just as Proudhon's criticism has as its premise the criticism of the mercantile system by the physiocrats, Ricardo's criticism of Adam Smith, and the works of Fourier and Saint-Simon. (...) He (...) consistently depicts as the falsifier of economic relations not this or that particular kind of private property, as other economists do, but private property as such and in its entirety. He has done all that criticism of political economy from the standpoint of political economy can do' (*MECW* 4, pp. 31–33). Marx's interpretation was verified by Proudhon's letter to him in 1846, where he explained that his principle was 'tourner l'Économie politique, la théorie de la propriété, contre la propriété', *MEGA*² III/2, p. 206. *The Holy Family* already contained a quite detailed dissection of Proudhon's ideas, by the way of a contrasting of Proudhon's original text to Edgar Bauer's anonymously published and confused rendering of it in No. 5 (April 1844) of the review journal *Allgemeine Literatur-Zeitung*, edited by Bruno Bauer.

Proudhon, a self-educated thinker and an avid, if indiscriminate, reader, used a great many modern French treatises on property, a fashionable topic in post-Revolutionary France.[46] He also picked up the topic of possession as a distinct category from private property. In this context he wrote a critical and not altogether inaccurate *précis* of Grotius' theory of primeval community in *Mare liberum*. Proudhon understood the key point that the earliest period of mankind, which the poets described as the age of gold, was the 'state of negative communism' or more properly 'negative community'.[47] He not only picked up the term; he made good use of it. It was the idea of 'negative community' which allowed him to break out of the vicious circle of previous theories. In these, he complained, 'property and community have been considered always the only possible forms of society'.[48] If property and community were the only alternatives, then it was no wonder, Proudhon explained,[49] that the private property theorists always triumphed:

The disadvantages of community are so obvious that its critics never have needed to employ much eloquence to thoroughly disgust men with it. The irreparability of the injustice which it causes, the violence which it does to attractions and repulsions, the yoke of iron which it fastens upon the will, the moral torture to

---

[46] [As Michael Sonenscher has pointed out, one of these French sources was Robert Joseph Pothier's *Traité du droit de domaine de propriété*, 2 vols. [1762] (Paris, 1772). In Sonenscher's translation, the central passage that caught Proudhon's attention goes as follows: 'The first of mankind had in common all those things which God had given to the human race. This community was not a positive community of interest, like that which exists between several persons who have the ownership of a thing in which each has his particular portion. It was a community which those who have written on the subject have called a negative community, which resulted from the fact that those things which were common to all belonged no more to one than to the others, and hence no one could prevent another from taking of these common things that portion which he judged necessary in order to subserve his wants.' Robert Joseph Pothier's *Traité du droit de domaine de propriété*, vol. 1, § 21, pp. 23–24. Quoted from Michael Sonenscher, *Capitalism: The Story behind the Word* (Princeton, NJ: Princeton University Press, 2022), pp. 80–81.]

[47] Pierre-Joseph Proudhon, *What Is Property? An Inquiry into the Principle of Right and Government*, trans. by B. J. Tucker (New York, 1970), p. 269. (V.2.2.). Tucker's nineteenth-century translation is imprecise and follows the fashion of the age. Community, 'commonaute', is translated as communism, see the original usage in *Qu'est-ce que la proprete?* (Paris, 1840). In the following citations all misuses of the word 'communism' are substituted with the correct rendering, 'community'. For a further check, see the letter of Proudhon to Marx, 17 May 1846, in which Proudhon noted that while certain 'socialistes allemands appelez *commonaute*', he was rather appealing to 'Liberté-égalité', *MEGA²* III/2, p. 206.

[48] Proudhon, *What Is Property?*, p. 259. (V.2.2.).

[49] As Proudhon put it sharply and bitterly, there was no need for 'another shipwreck on this rock'. The wrecks already there included Plato's communistic republic, Lycurgus' Sparta, the communities of the early church, the Jesuit experiment in Paraguay, Rousseau, Babeuf and the St Simonians. (*What Is Property?*, pp. 259–260 (V.2.2.).).

which it subjects the conscience, the debilitating effect which it has upon society; and to sum it all up, the pious and stupid uniformity which it enforces upon the free, active, reasoning, unsubmissive personality of man, have shocked common sense, and condemned community by irrevocable decree.[50]

But this was, Proudhon hastened to add, the problem of positive, or 'systematic community'. This misbegotten system was 'the deliberate negation of property – conceived under the direct influence of the proprietary prejudice'. If one had no other notion of community, then it had to be acknowledged that 'property is the basis of all communistic theories':

> The members of the community, it is true, have no private property; but the community is proprietor, and proprietor not only of the goods, but of the persons and wills. In consequence of this principle of absolute property, labor, which should be only a condition imposed upon man by Nature, becomes in all communities a human commandment, and therefore odious. (...) Community is oppression and slavery. (...) Community is essentially opposed to the free exercise of our faculties, to our noblest desires, to our deepest feelings. (...) Thus, community violates the sovereignty of the conscience, and equality: the first, by restricting spontaneity of mind and heart, and freedom of thought and action; the second, by placing labor and laziness, skill and stupidity, and even vice and virtue on an equality in point of comfort. For the rest, if property is impossible on account of the desire to accumulate, community would soon become so through the desire to shirk.[51]

Proudhon could break with the false dualism of private property and positive community,[52] because he could construe the primeval community of mankind, the true original condition of man, as negative community. This was no mirror of property; it was a state without property altogether, neither communal nor individual. The idea could also be expressed in quasi-historical terms. 'Property', Proudhon pointed out, was 'subsequent to community', to negative community that is:

---

[50] *What Is Property?*, p. 259. (V.2.2.).
[51] *What Is Property?*, pp. 258–262. (V.2.2.).
[52] The joint transcendence of private property and positive community in Proudhon puzzled his interpreters at the time. Moses Hess in his 1843 critique of Lorenz von Stein's *Der Socialismus und Communismus des heutigen Frankreichs* in the periodical journal *Einundzwanzig Bogen der Schweiz* has already pointed out von Stein's difficulty in positioning Proudhon in the radical intellectual spectrum of the time: 'Ein Communist ist ihm Proudhon nicht, obgleich er das persönliche oder Privateigenthum in der schärfsten Weise kritisirt und negiert. Nach dem Bilde freilich, welches *er*, Stein, sich von Communismus gemacht hat, kann Proudhon kein Communist sein, denn Proudhon is *wissenschaftlich*! Er kann aber auch kein Sozialist in dem Sinne Steins sein [for Stein real socialism covered chiefly St. Simon and Fourier], denn er negirt ja das Privateigenthum.' 'Socialismus und Communismus', in Moses Hess, *Philosophische und Sozialistische Schriften, 1837–1850: Eine Auswahl*, ed. August Cornu and Wolfgang Mönke (De Gruyner, 1961), pp. 204–205. Marx, of course, made the same ploy as von Stein. For him Proudhon also made a 'scientific' advance, a notion which later gave birth to the distinction between socialism, utopian and scientific.

Negative Community and Communism

Community – or association in a simple form – is the necessary object and original aspiration of the social nature, the spontaneous movement by which it manifests and establishes itself. It is the first phase of human civilization. In this state of society, – which the jurists have called *negative community*, – man draws near to man, and shares with him the fruits of the field and the milk and flesh of animals.[53]

Once men started to labour, the community lost its negativity. 'Little by little this community – negative as long as man does not produce – tends to become positive and organic through the development of labor and industry.'[54] The troubles of positive community, then, led to a new system, private property. Both systems, for Proudhon, were unacceptable. Positive 'community, mistaking uniformity for law, and levellism (*nivellement*) for equality, becomes tyrannical and unjust. Property, by its despotism and encroachments, soon proves itself oppressive and anti-social (*insociable*).'[55] Proudhon wanted something essentially different, a new stage of society (*forme sociale*), a kind of free association of men which could be the synthesis of community and property, preserving the best of both but eliminating their oppressive tendencies. Proudhon, a socialist, moved the concept of sociability to the centre.[56] The true future had to be, he believed, a restoration of man's original, spontaneous, natural sociability in civilised conditions. Such a consummation of civilisation, the true political economy, Proudhon wrote, will be the state of 'liberty'. But communism here, in the Hegelian formula of thesis-antithesis-synthesis, was 'negative community':

Community – the first expression of social nature – is the first term of social development, – the *thesis*; property, the reverse of community, is the second term, – the *antithesis*. When we have discovered the third term, the *synthesis*, we shall have the required solution. Now, this synthesis necessarily results from the correction of the thesis by the antithesis. Therefore it is necessary, by a final examination of their characteristics, to eliminate those features which are hostile to sociability. The union of the two remainders will give us the true form of association.[57]

There can be little doubt that when writing the criticism of crude communism, Marx had Proudhon's text nearby. Communism, Marx claimed, had to stand on the shoulders of the culture and civilisation

---

[53] *What Is Property?*, p. 258. (V.2.1.).
[54] Ibid.
[55] Levelling was a proximate English translation. Proudhon, just as Marx, used the word 'nivellement' and 'Nivellierung', respectively. *What Is Property?*, p. 280. (V.2.3.).
[56] This can also be argued, although less directly, in the case of some early English socialists, particularly Owen and the Scottish Owenites, see Gregory Claeys, *Citizens and Saints: Politics and Anti-politics in Early British Socialism* (Cambridge: Cambridge University Press, 1989), ch. 1 'Republicans, Puritans and Natural Jurisprudence'.
[57] *What Is Property?*, pp. 258–259. (V.2.1.).

achieved by private property. To be an advance on capitalism it had to be not a system of positive community, itself a species of property, but its negation, modern 'negative community', the negation of the negation, a system based on the direct use of the resources in our environment. Marx's synthesis for the future was richer and less crudely anarchistic than Proudhon. As he already told Ruge, the socialist criticism of dogmatic communism had to be rounded out with a criticism of man's theoretical activities, not only his *real* existence – with a criticism of modern science and religion. Nonetheless, the fundamental idea of his thought on the broadest, theoretical outlines of communism was set.

By pointing to certain crucial features of natural law theory and Marx's theory of negative community (via Proudhon), our aim is not to deny that in other aspects the two theories of 'negative community' also had features that were different. For Christian jurists the basic law of negative community was embodied in God's primary natural law, that is, in a number of simple but essential rules to guide sociability. Natural sociability, for Pufendorf, was not simply man's making; it was an expression of God's ways to men. Marx's (and Proudhon's) projection of a future negative community did not have a God to guide its associated producers to shape their social life. It was more thoroughly antinomian. But instead of further explicating the consequences of this crucial difference between Marx and natural law, I would like finally to underline the implications of their shared heritage. Marxism and old liberalism, whose core I take to be modern natural law, are both theories of civilisation with shared foundations in socialist (meaning primarily Pufendorf's 'sociability socialism' rather than Proudhon's) 'negative community' theory. This becomes visible once we recover Grotius' and Pufendorf's definition of the two notions of community. On the other hand, clinging to our impoverished modern vocabulary of community guarantees that we will miss this point.

In recent American political theory, the opposition between individualism and community is a much-discussed subject. By using an undifferentiated notion of 'community', however, this debate is in great danger of producing more confusion than enlightenment. It is crucial to understand whether a so-called communitarian has positive or negative community in mind or, in fact, no clear idea of community at all. Marxists and classical liberals can have grave differences about prospects for the future. Nonetheless, they can both accept community as a basic organisation of social and economic life only in its 'negative form'. Furthermore, they are both committed to civilisation. The dynamism of history for both commits them to defend, in some form of another, the achievements of the historical regime of private property against critics of civilisation. Hard line critics of civilisation traditionally used to accept the necessity that their critique had no bite without a reorganisation of man's socio-economic life. Christian sects and early socialists, and their followers today, were positive community theorists. The damages of modern civilisation, they maintain, have to be contained by the communal reorganisation of property as much as by creating moral communities. They understand that any communitarian theory of moral community collapses into positive community theory if realising its aims in fact requires tampering with those basic property structures which guarantee the dynamic character of the underlying needs structure of modern civilisation. Theories of custom-bound communities, taking their cue from the past, can hardly be compatible with the dynamism of communities of men 'rich in needs'. If such communities are restricted to small voluntary groups here and there, then they can exist quite peacefully, but in fact parasitically, within a larger sea of modern civilisation. To enlarge them, however, would require institutions of positive community with all the attendant problems pointed out by the defenders of civilisation.

Seeing this danger, many contemporary North American academic communitarians sidestep the suggestions of both the Marxian and classical liberal traditions regarding the crucial relevance of the modern economy to our societies. They wish no community of property in any form. Rather, they want only to reverse certain moral consequences of the system of private property. They want to reverse the radical moves in rights theory which Grotius and the school of modern natural law introduced when the modern theory of civilisation was established.[58] In particular, they would readmit Aristotelian distributive justice into the core of the modern system. Distributive justice, the justice recognising unequal moral worth, was sliced off the body of newly redefined 'strict' justice,[59] because it could not be made uncontentious and therefore compatible with the sustained peace of a society inhabited by the covetous and contentious as well as the morally virtuous. The rules of private property, it was believed, could be made strict and simple only on the

---

[58] See a longer discussion of the history and implication of this theoretical strategy in my (co-authored with Michael Ignatieff) 'Needs and Justice in the *Wealth of Nations*: an introductory essay', in *Wealth and Virtue*, pp. 1–44.

[59] 'Distributive justice', Grotius explained, was concerned with 'the rational allotment to each man, or to each social group, of those things which are properly theirs, in such a way as to give the preference now to him who is more wise over the less wise, now to a kinsman rather than to a stranger, now to a poor man rather than to a man of means, as the conduct of each or the nature of the thing suggests. Long ago the view came to be held by many, that this discriminating allotment is a part of law, properly and strictly so called; nevertheless law, properly defined, has a far different nature, because its essence lies in leaving to another that which belongs to him, or in fulfilling our obligations to him.' *DJBP*, 'Prolegomena', §10.

basis of formal equality. Distributive justice, by its very nature, was not a system of formal equality. Thus, it was excluded from strict justice, the core system, but not from the moral life of society. Private property owners, if they wished, were allowed to agree on secondary redistributive systems and honour imperfect rights.[60] Conceptually this would not involve community. Such good moral life had to be based on the moral consensus of private property owners remaining as jealous of their basic rights as ever. In modern natural law, distributive justice was specified as a voluntary system. Morally good societies could have it, others not. But if it encroached on the basic fabric of civilisation, then it was regarded as nothing else but a slippery slope to positive community.

Another variant of this critique of classical liberalism, usually equated with modern natural law, is embodied in the demand for the reinstatement of some very basic imperfect rights, more basic than those involved in Aristotelian distributive justice. This demand concerns the re-establishment of the community of mankind in the context of the potential inclusive right of each and every human being to the use of God's donation in circumstances when the system of private property proves itself incapable of fulfilling its promise of alleviating scarcity. This problem already exercised the mind of Grotius and Pufendorf quite intensely. They recognised a fundamental contradiction here. Such potential rights were incompatible with actual rights. Nonetheless, membership in the human species was meaningless if it did not imply at least a minimum entitlement to the means of survival. It was acknowledged that no clear-cut theoretical solution was possible in this case in strict rights terms. Hume, as usual, was the clearest about this. In great scarcity there was no place for hard and fast property rights at all, and the only distribution system possible under these circumstances was a communal one of total sharing. But instead of amending the regime of strict justice, it was concluded, the underlying problem had to be tackled. If scarcity could be eliminated or pushed to the very margins of society, then these potential inclusive rights were not in need of activation. If there was no famine, property systems did not face even temporary collapse. Scarcity then, in its turn, could be best alleviated by unleashing the full productive potentials of mankind; the reason, as Aquinas also understood, for which property rights were instituted. The inclusion of potential claim

---

[60] In the Grotian system, the domain of distributive justice, or attributive justice in his terminology, was the sphere of imperfect rights. Imperfect rights were embodiments of those virtues 'which have as their purpose to do good to others, as generosity, compassion and foresight in matters of government'. Imperfect or moral rights, as opposed to perfect ones, were 'honourable' but they did not 'impose an obligation, do not come under the term statute or law'. *DJBP*, 1.1.9.1.

rights into the modern system of private property, as a permanent feature, would diminish the efficiency of the system. Such a move, again, was yet another way of establishing positive community.

By reintroducing the distinction between positive and negative community and insisting on the relevance of socio-economic organisation for any theory of community, I do not wish to diminish the relevance of the issues debated by communitarian theorists. I wish only to clarify the real issues in these debates. By distinguishing between negative community and positive community we can assess more clearly the various criticisms levelled against modern civilisation. Furthermore, we can separate those who essentially demand positive community (a dwindling band of theorists) and those who aim at moral reconstruction within the boundaries of the system of modern civilisation.

Note on Chapter 4

This paper evolved gradually, and in several versions, out of Hont's work on the natural law foundations of political economy. The first version was presented to the Political Science Department at Columbia University on 9 March 1984. At this point, it was entitled 'The Concept of Negative Community and the Origins of Historical Materialism'. In July 1984, Hont presented a slightly different version of this text to the King's College Research Centre workshop 'The Identity of Political Economy: Between Utopia and the Critique of Civilisation', 1–3 July 1984. The title was retained but the text had now been included as 'Part 1' of a two-part paper entitled '"Negative Communities": Natural Jurisprudence and the Intellectual Origins of the Marxian Notion of Communism'. The second part of this conjoined paper was entitled 'The Antinomies of the Concept of Use-Value in Marx's *Capital*' (see Chapter 5 in this volume). In February of 1989, when Hont gave a series of lectures in Chicago, he separated the two texts again and presented a new stand-alone version of this text with the title 'Negative Community and Communism: The Natural Law Heritage from Pufendorf to Marx'. In addition to a few stylistic changes, this version is longer and includes new passages on the communitarianism versus liberalism debate, adaptations no doubt made for the benefit of the contemporary American audience. The text reproduced here is the full 1989 version, of which Parts I and II correspond to the original 1984 text, whereas Part III is almost entirely written for the new occasion.

5 The Antinomies of the Concept of 'Use-Value' in Marx's *Capital*
Economy and Polity after the Market

I

Marx himself frequently defined his original departures in political economy in terms of three main points:

1. What the capitalist buys on the labour market is not the worker's labour, but his 'labour power'.
2. That the categories of the tripartite theory of profit, interest, and rent can all be derived from one single concept, that is, 'surplus value'.
3. A fundamental reinterpretation of the significance of the category of 'use-value', in effect a discovery of its role in the historical determination of the market economy.[1]

It is the argument of the present paper that of these three 'discoveries' it was the third, the one relating to the concept of 'use-value', which plays the most important part in Marx's theory of socialism, even if the other two had their important role in the critique of capitalism and *a fortiori* in the working out of the idea that capitalism could be transcended. The category of 'use-value' was crucially important for Marx because it was independent of the market, but nonetheless it was still in some sense an 'economic' notion. As such it could potentially serve as the basis for a non-capitalist and post-capitalist economic theory whose theoretical object was socialism and communism. 'Use-value' was linguistically a convenient concept to be pushed in such a service. Its first half, 'use', could be detached from the second and suggest an immediate, unmediated relationship between the user and the object. At the same time, however, it was also a value, an economic category. Marx often exploited this possibility of playing on the double-sided nature of the concept of 'use-value' and frequently contrasted capitalist and post-capitalist society as two systems which centre on different forms of value, the first on

---

[1] [This tripart recapitulation of Marx's original contributions closely follows the argument of Ágnes Heller's *The Theory of Needs in Marx* (London: Allison & Busby, 1976).]

market value or 'exchange value', the second on 'use-value' or simply 'use' (meaning needs-satisfaction). The following quotation from volume one of *Capital* will suffice here to demonstrate Marx's idea:

> The law of capitalistic accumulation, metamorphosed by economists into a pretended law of Nature, in reality merely states that the very nature of accumulation excludes every diminution in the degree of exploitation of labour, and every rise in the price of labour, which could seriously imperil the continuous reproduction, on an ever-enlarging scale, of the capitalistic relation. It cannot be otherwise in a mode of production in which the labourer exists to satisfy the needs of self-expansion of existing values instead of, on the contrary, material wealth existing to satisfy the needs of development on the part of the labourer.[2]

The contrast employed here by Marx is certainly an important one. In one type of society, market capitalism, there is a core process consisting in the 'self-expansion of existing values', values which are that of a society characterised by inequality, while in the society which will come after it, in socialism, the wealth of society will directly, without an economic mediation, satisfy the needs of everyone, including those of the workers themselves. The important categorical point for the purposes of the present paper is the idea that in this society of the future, wealth will serve needs directly. Or in other words, instead of existing in the form of the values of capitalism (exchange value), it will entirely consist of use-values. If so, the coherence and plausibility of the hypothetical socialist society will depend in large degree on the explanatory power of the Marxian insistence on the centrality of use-value. If it turns out to be the case that there are problems with the concept of use-value, if the content of the concept reveals itself as contradictory, then we face a serious problem also in accepting the Marxian idea of socialism *tout court*.

Let's start the analysis of the content of the Marxian category of use-value with the text of *Capital* itself. Here the wealth of society is conceptualised as the aggregate total of all useful 'objects' available to a society, or to mankind. Some of these objects are not man-made but are the gifts of nature, such as virgin lands or as yet unmined ore deposits, which every economist would always count as part of the nation's stock. Other objects, in fact the majority of objects, are artificial, man-made. For Marx, at that level, these distinctions did not matter: 'The wealth of societies in which the capitalist mode of production prevails appears

---

[2] *MECW* 35, p. 616; *Capital I*, p. 772. [All quotations in this chapter are from Karl Marx. As in the previous chapter, the first-listed reference refers to the specific English translation used by Hont, whose choice of translation alternated from one quotation to the next, seemingly according to his estimation of its accuracy.]

as an "immense collection of commodities"; the individual commodity appears as its elementary form.'[3]

The *differentia specifica* of this capitalist 'collection of commodities', the cause of its homogeneity, however, is precisely in the fact that every single part of this collection can be substituted by another one through a clearing process in which they are exchanged for each other at a price level determined by their exchange value. Such a process of substitution would not change the economic value of the 'collection' one iota. Economically, only exchange values count. In capitalism the entire mass of national wealth is only a homogeneous, amorphous heap of values; the concrete shape, form, and quality of its constituent 'objects' are simply the material representations of exchange value, which in turn is said to be determined in the Marxian system by the abstract social labour time which was needed for their production or extraction. In this sense, exchange value was also reducible to the status of a 'representation' of something deeper, that is, of the ratio between the individual concrete labour spent on its production and the quantity of abstract labour that society in general would have spent on producing the same value. Although behind the concrete object there is the determination of the abstract exchange value, and behind the abstract exchange value again concrete labour, at the end concrete labour is socially determined by yet another abstract category, social labour. The actual act of market exchange traverses a space determined on many levels, stretching from a concrete exchange of material object to an equalisation of abstract social labour times. The concrete process is the one visible on the surface. Marx's definition of 'use-value' is related to this structure of layered determination. In *Capital* we are offered the following definition: 'The commodity is, first of all, an external object, a thing which through its qualities satisfies human needs of whatever kind.'[4] This definition has three moments, three constitutive arguments.

First, a use-value is a thing, an object, a commodity in its 'natural particularity', in its 'physical palpable existence'. Furthermore, it was

the usefulness of a thing which made it a use-value. But this usefulness does not dangle in mid-air. It is conditioned by the physical properties of the commodity, and has no existence apart from the latter. It is therefore the physical body of the commodity itself, for instance iron, corn, a diamond, which is the use-value or useful thing.[5]

---

[3] *Capital I*, p. 125; *MECW* 35, p. 45.
[4] *Capital I*, p. 125; *MECW* 35, p. 45.
[5] *Capital I*, p. 126; *MECW* 35, p. 46.

Since, however, most of the objects in the 'collection' are artificial products of man's purposeful activity, transforming mankind's natural endowment, the character of the concrete labour of the workman who 'created' them is preserved in these products and remains ever present in an 'objectified' form. Because most objects by now are products of human labour, the concept of wealth as an aggregate collection of use-values was essentially a historical one, since, as Marx argued, 'the discovery of the manifold uses of things is the work of history'.[6] However, in the ready-made product prepared for consumption the link to the quality of labour which was spent on its production appears only in a 'dead' manner, as irrelevances from the point of view of their capability of serving as utilities. We, as consumers, are only interested in the object itself, not in its history. In Marx's words:

> In considering bread as a use-value, we are concerned with its properties as an article of food and by no means with the labour of the farmer, miller, baker, etc. Even if the labour required were reduced by 95 per cent as a result of some invention, the usefulness of a loaf of bread would remain quite unaffected. It would lose not a single particle of its use-value even if it dropped ready-made from the sky.[7]

This is the reason why, from the point of view of use-values or utilities, it simply does not matter whether a useful object was nature's gift or man-made; there are a multitude of nature-given objects which satisfy human needs and assist in the survival of mankind. Obviously: 'A thing can be a use-value without being a value. This is the case whenever its utility to man is not mediated through labour. Air, virgin soil, natural meadows, unplanted forests, etc. fall into that category.'[8]

The second argument in Marx's theory of use-value is this. Of course, no thing or object is a use-value, or any value, without it being related to a human need, and from this point of view it simply does not matter whether the object was man-made or natural.

A use value has value only in use, and is realised only in the process of consumption.[9]

Riches which are identical with use-values are *properties of things* that are made use of by men and which express a relation to their wants.[10]

Thus, the 'collection' of use-values in any given society and epoch would be determined by the level of needs, by the 'particular need of the exchangers', themselves being products of history as well. For Marx

---

[6] *MECW* 35, p. 45; *Capital I*, p. 126.
[7] *CCPE*, p. 36; *MECW* 29, p. 277.
[8] *Capital I*, p. 131; *MECW* 35, p. 50.
[9] *CCPE*, p. 27; *MECW* 29, p. 269.
[10] *TSV III*, p. 129; *MECW* 32, p. 316.

human needs were historically constructed, they were social and not individual. Thus, he argued, since 'use-values serve social needs [they] therefore exist within the social framework'.[11]

Finally, the concept of use-value appears as the expression of the link between the two components already discussed, that is, use-values as objects and use-values as created by human needs. In this respect Marx had to qualify again what he said about the social determination of use-values. As he pointed out, 'the use-value of a thing [can be] realised without exchange, i.e. in the direct relation between the thing and man, while, inversely, its value is realised only in exchange, i.e. in a social process'.[12] Marx realised that the concept of 'use-value' reflected the direct, immediate relationship between a man and an object without the interference of other men. Because of this lack of human mediation, Marx had to revert to the description of use-value as a link to nature. 'Der Gebrauchswert drückt als solcher zunächst Beziehung des Individuums zur Natur aus', Marx wrote.[13] At another place, in the *Theories of Surplus Value*, he argued as follows: 'Use-value expresses the natural relationship between things and men, in fact the existence of things for men. Exchange value (...) is the *social existence* of things.'[14] What is more, he conceded that the measure of things as use-values had to also be natural (i.e. based on the natural properties of things): 'In so far as the product has a measure for Itself, it is its natural measure as natural object-, mass, weight, length, volume, etc.'[15] Thus, Marx declared that, at this high level of abstraction at any rate, the concept of use-value was outside the matrix of political economy. Use-values form the material content of social wealth. However, use-values *qua* use-values are simply indifferent to the form of society whose wealth consists in them:

Use-values are only realised in use or in consumption. They constitute the material content of wealth, whatever its social form may be.[16]

From the taste of wheat it is not possible to tell who produced it, a Russian serf, a French peasant or an English capitalist.[17]

---

[11] *CCPE*, p. 28; *MECW* 29, p. 270.
[12] *Capital I*, p. 177. *MECW* 35, p. 94.
[13] *MEGA*² II/2. 'Fragment des Urtextes von "Zur Kritik der politischen Ökonomie"' [1858], 4: 'Die edlen Metalle als Träger des Geldverhältnisses', p. 899. [In English: 'The first form of value is *use value*, the everyday aspect which expresses the relationship of the individual to nature' (*MECW* 28, p. 113).]
[14] *TSV III*, p. 296; *MECW* 32, p. 429.
[15] *Grundrisse*, p. 613; *MECW* 28, p. 532.
[16] *Capital I*, p. 126; *MECW* 35, p. 46.
[17] *CCPE*, p. 28; *MECW* 29, p. 271.

The concept of use-value describes for us how things exist for men in their 'direct', 'natural', 'real' and 'material' substances, as opposed to their 'social', 'fictional', 'formal' appearance in market societies, that is, as opposed to all those social attributes which are imputed to things by mankind's history and the specific socio-economic stages through which this history has passed. However, use-values are not totally divorced from historical existence. Use-values are the precondition of socio-historical existence; they are the carriers of fictional social relationships, rather than their embodiments. Quite clearly, in order to arrive at a specific high level of socio-economic organisation, at the stage of universalised commodity production, mankind already had to possess as a precondition a relatively sophisticated collection of objects as society's material wealth. Only use-values, objects related to human needs, could be transformed into exchange values in the emerging society of universal commodity production. 'To be a use value is evidently a necessary prerequisite of the commodity, but it is immaterial to the use value whether it is a commodity.'[18]

However, once use-values became carriers of a historically determined commodity form, this function transforms them into some sort of socio-economically determined objects. Marx here introduced the new concept of 'social use-value', which he contrasted with the ideas of the German economist Rodbertus:

> I have emphasised the characteristic form in which use-value – the product of labour – appears here, that is: 'A thing can be useful, and the product of human labour, without being a commodity. Whoever [directly] satisfies his needs with the produce of his own labour, creates, indeed, use-values but not commodities. In order to produce commodities, *he must not only produce use-values, but use-values for others, social use-values*' (This the root of Rodbertus' 'social use-value'.) Consequently use-value – as the use-value of a 'commodity' – itself possesses a specific historical character. In primitive communities in which, e.g., means of livelihood are produced communally and distributed amongst the members of the community, the common product directly satisfies the vital needs of each community member, of each producer; the social character of the product, of the use-value, here lies in its (common) communal character. (Mr. Rodbertus on the other hand transforms the 'social use-value' of the commodity into 'social use-value' pure and simple, and is hence talking nonsense.)[19]

Quite obviously, on the Marxian definition a man who only satisfied his own needs could not produce 'social use-value'. As a precondition, he had to be engaged in commodity production, he had to produce for

---

[18] *CCPE*, p. 28; *MECW* 29, p. 270.
[19] *MECW* 24, pp. 545–546. ('Marginal Notes on Adolph Wagner').

204 Political Economy from Pufendorf to Marx

others, for society. Thus, it was not entirely without effects on the use-value that its carrier was now a commodity, rather than a simple object. Nonetheless, in general we have to observe that in the Marxian analysis of use-value, the other side of the coin dominated. What was more important for him was to emphasise that the commodity form should be characterised by a wholly external linkage between the form of the commodity – value in exchange – and its concrete material embodiment, its use-value. Despite its Hegelian language, the following sentence conveys his meaning quite graphically: '[In the commodity] the aspects still immediately coincide and just as immediately they separate.'[20] In any case, it was one thing to argue that the concept of use-value – as developed within a model of barter – did not belong to political economy proper, and it was quite another to maintain that specific types and kinds of use-values could not play an important role in historically existing societies and socio-economic systems, amongst others, in capitalism. On the contrary, Marx considered it as his own special historical achievement that he had introduced the concept of use-value into 'real' economic analysis. He even regarded it as the hallmark of his own brand of 'critical' political economy as opposed to the bourgeois variety developed by Adam Smith and David Ricardo. He regularly criticised Ricardo for dropping the concept of use-value from his central analysis. By doing this Ricardo blocked the theoretical possibility of theorising anything else but a capitalist market economy within the framework of political economy:

> Is not value to be conceived as the unity of use value and exchange value? In and for itself, is value as such the general form, in opposition to use value and exchange value as *particular* forms of it? Does this have a significance in economics? Use value presupposed even in simple exchange and barter. But here, where exchange takes place only for the reciprocal use of the commodity, the use value, i.e. the content, the natural particularity of the commodity has as such no standing as an economic form. Its form, rather, is in exchange value. The content apart from this form is irrelevant; (...) But does this content as such not develop into a system of needs and production? Does not use value as such enter into the form itself, as a determinant of the form, e.g., in the relation of capital to labour? The different forms of labour? – agriculture, industry, etc – ground rent? – effect of the seasons on raw product prices? etc. If *only* exchange value as such plays a role in economics, then how could elements later enter which relate purely to use value, such as, right away, in the case of capital as raw material? How is it that the physical composition of the soil suddenly drops out of the sky in Ricardo?[21]

---

[20] *Grundrisse*, pp. 268–269; *MECW* 28, p. 199.
[21] *Grundrisse*, p. 267n; *MECW* 28, p. 197n.

Marx returned to this argument again and again in the *Grundrisse*, and claimed that

> Ricardo, e.g., who believes that the bourgeois economy deals only with exchange value, and is concerned with use value only exoterically, derives the most important determinations of exchange value precisely from use value, from the relation between the two of them: for instance, *ground rent, wage minimum, distinction between fixed capital and circulating capital.*[22]

Marx's insistence is more than understandable. He derived his other conceptual innovation in political economy precisely from the concept of use-value. As he emphasised, his own revolutionary concept of 'labour power' was inconceivable without the dialectics embodied in the category of use-value. In Marxian economics,

> *surplus value* itself is derived from a 'specific' *use value of labour power*, (...) hence use value with me plays an important role completely different than in previous political economy, but, *nota bene*, it only comes into the picture where such considerations spring from the analysis of given economic forms.[23]

It is this 'specific' but crucial instance of use-value, labour power, which we need to analyse in order to get to the bottom of the Marxian conceptual structure.

What makes the production of surplus value possible in Marxian economics? One simple fact, that the owners of capital and money could buy a specific product on the market which enabled them to produce more value out of that product than the equivalent they had given for it. The specificity of this commodity was in its use-value. Its use was to produce exchange value which was more than its own. This very specific exchange value producing use-value was nothing else than man's capability to work. The commodity in question was labour power. This sounds very easy, but in the light of our previous discussion we have to wait and see whether this new use-value conforms to the general definition of use-value or not. To include it in the collection of use-values may, at the end, overturn the whole theoretical construct of use-value altogether.

There are several difficulties in introducing the special use-value of labour power. First of all, up to now Marx derived all the categories of market exchange from a concept of wealth which only and exclusively included objects, that is, inanimate, non-human 'things'. But Marx defined labour power rather as the 'purely subjective existence of labour, stripped of all objectivity', the 'not objective itself', albeit in an

---

[22] *Grundrisse*, pp. 646–647; *MECW* 29, p. 34.
[23] *MECW* 24, p. 546. ('Marginal Notes on Adolph Wagner').

'objective form'.[24] Labour power was thus intimately and inseparably tied to the living subjective person of the labourer; it was his living ability and potential to produce. How could this *sui generis* non-objectivity be squared with the general definition of use-value?

Marx was aware of some aspects of the problem. He could clearly see the difference between slavery and 'wage-slavery'. In the first case it was not the labour potential of the producer which became a commodity, but his person:

> He and the owner of money meet in the market, and enter into relations with each other on a footing of equality as owners of commodities, with the sole difference that one is a buyer, the other a seller; both are therefore equal in the eyes of the law. For this relation to continue, the proprietor of labour-power must always sell it for a limited period only, for if he were to sell it in a lump, once and for all, he would be selling himself, converting himself from free man into slave, from an owner of a commodity into a commodity. He must constantly treat his labour power as his own property, his own commodity.[25]

On the basis of this analysis, and relying on the previous account of the definition of use-value (all commodities are use-values, the difference between one commodity and another flows only from them being different use-values), we could draw a logical and 'Marxian' conclusion that we are facing here two different use-values. One use-value is the living personality of the worker – this would be the use-value of the slave commodity – and the other would be the worker's labour power, his very own labour potential. What would divide the two is the quality of social relationships in which the worker was embedded. In practice we can distinguish between the two use-values by observing the length of the labour contract, whether it was forever or only for a definite period of time. This whole line of argument, however, would contradict the very notion that the category of use-value is a representation of the direct 'man-thing' relationship, that this relationship should be 'natural' and independent of any exchange transaction. In the original Marxian definition the nexus captured by the concept of use-value was supposed to be independent of the social relations of production.

We can reformulate the difficulty in the language of needs as well, more directly and at the same time on a higher level of abstraction. On Marx's previous definition, a 'thing' was a use-value if it was proven useful in satisfying a specific and historically determined human need. But can this definition be applied to the special use-value of labour power? At that level of abstraction, it is nonsensical even to ask the question

---

[24] *Grundrisse*, pp. 295–296; *MECW* 28, p. 222.
[25] *Capital I*, p. 271; *MECW* 35, p. 178.

whether somebody else's physical ability was 'useful' for another man or not. This utility can only be defined in the context of the historical and socio-economic stage in which these men live. In general, and also in Marx's own theory of society, man–man relationships cannot ever be of the kind of natural immediacy and unmediatedness presupposed in Marx's general concept of use-value. In capitalism, for example, only that labour can be counted as productive which creates capital in a direct fashion, that is, only labour which creates surplus value, quite independently of the actual object and product of this labour and irrespective of whether the product could satisfy a human need or not. Marx emphasised that, in the case of such type of labour, 'the material characteristics are in no way linked with its nature which on the contrary is only an expression of a definite social relation of production. It is a definition of labour which is derived not from its content or its results, but from its particular social form.'[26]

And we should remember Marx's fundamental contrast between the future society of use-value and market societies, in which, Marx argued, the specific use-value of labour power was intimately related to the exchange values of the market:

It cannot be otherwise in a mode of production in which the worker exists to satisfy the need of the existing values for valorisation, as opposed to the inverse situation, in which objective wealth is there to satisfy the worker's own need for development.[27]

This whole concept of 'the need of existing values for valorisation', as Marx well knew, did not really fit his previous effort to define human needs in their relationship to use-values. But this was precisely the specificity, the unique nature, of labour power. While the consumption and use of all other commodities took place outside the sphere of circulation, or the sphere of economics in general, while the using up of an average commodity was of

purely physical interest, expressing no more than the relation of the individual A in his natural quality to the object of individual need. (...) by contrast, the *use value which is exchanged for money appears as a particular economic relation*.[28]

The consumption of the use value itself here falls within the economic process, because the use value here is itself determined by exchange value.[29]

---

[26] *TSV I*, p. 158; *MECW* 31, p. 14.
[27] *Capital I*, p. 772; *MECW* 35, p. 616.
[28] *Grundrisse*, p. 274; *MECW* 28, p. 205.
[29] *Grundrisse*, p. 311; *MECW* 28, p. 237.

To sum up. In this very particular case, quite in opposition to the general rule we have discussed above, it is not a use-value which becomes the carrier of an exchange value, but rather the reverse case is true: an exchange value and the presence of very special, generalised commodity relations become the precondition of the existence of a use-value. Thus, what we find is that in the most important case of the Marxian analysis of use-value, the modified concept of use-value exhibited features quite incompatible with the first general definition. What is more, this 'upside down' definition comes to the fore in every single relevant case in which Marx was able to attribute a specific and true economic function to any variety of use-value. It would be superfluous to cite all these cases. One example will hopefully suffice. It is an example which actually precedes the introduction of special use-values into the unfolding Marxian system in *Capital*:

> The money commodity acquires a dual use-value. Alongside its special use-value as a commodity (gold, for instance, serves to fill hollow teeth, it forms the raw material for luxury articles, etc.) it acquires a formal use-value, arising out of its specific social function.[30]

The tension between the general definition and the specific special cases would be clearer, and it would be easier to understand its source if some attention was paid to the specific situations in which they enter Marx's theoretical discussion. This is what he writes in the *Contribution to the Critique of Political Economy*:

> Whatever its social form may be, wealth always consists of use-values, which in the first instance are not affected by this form. (...) Use value as such, since it is independent of the determinate economic form, lies outside the sphere of investigation of political economy. It belongs in this sphere only when it is itself a determinate form.[31]

Hence, use-values that are relevant for political economy are all use-values 'modified by the modern relations of production', or in turn, they intervene to 'modify these very relations'.[32] The utility of these use-values is connected with the fact that they are useful precisely for building these new relations of production, and thus they must all be exceptions to the general rule, according to which use-values are indifferent to the forms of economic activities. It becomes clear now that there is no mistake in the Marxian account, that we deal here with two very different situations. Superficially, it appears as the source of the difficulty that Marx used the

---

[30] *Capital I*, p. 184; *MECW* 35, p. 100.
[31] *CCPE*, pp. 28–29; *MECW* 29, p. 270.
[32] *Grundrisse*, p. 881; *MECW* 29, p. 252.

same word to describe two different phenomena or two different social relations. However, this was not all. Further analysis will show us that on the next level these contradictions re-establish themselves and would appear as far more serious than a terminological confusion.

II

Up to now we have dealt with the concept of use-value only in its qualitative abstraction. However, Marx knew very well that 'every producer of a commodity is obliged to produce a use-value, that is, he must satisfy a particular social need (though the extent of these needs differs quantitatively, and there exists an inner bond which attaches the different levels of need to a system which has grown up spontaneously)'.[33]

The abstract method in defining use-value was part and parcel of the abstract method applied in the first volume of *Capital*, where Marx supposed, as an idealisation, that all goods were sold on the market precisely at their proper exchange value. The supposition was that supply precisely met demand and that the structure of production, in quality and quantity, was largely in correspondence with the shape of effective demand. A lack of harmony between social production and the system of economically determined needs prevailing in the same society could occur in Marx's theory only after this initial idealisation of a market equilibrium has been abandoned. The discussion of the quantitative determination of needs became a subject of analysis only in some manuscripts of Marx, which Engels later edited as the so-called third volume of *Capital*. What we can read there is this:

> To say that a commodity has a use value is merely to say that it satisfies some social need. So long as we dealt with individual commodities only, we could assume that there was a need for a particular commodity – its quality already implied by its price without inquiring further into the quantity required to satisfy this need. This quantity is, however, of essential importance, as soon as the product of an entire branch of production is placed on one side, and the social need for it on the other. It then becomes necessary to consider the extent, i.e. the amount of this social need.[34]

The change of gear in Marx's discourse introduced a number of new insights into his discussion. First of all, Marx – in the same manuscripts serving as the basis of the third volume of *Capital* – redefines the notion of 'socially necessary labour'. Looked at from the level of aggregate social demand, or the aggregate actual need of society, use-values appear as

---

[33] *Capital I*, p. 476; *MECW* 35, p. 361.
[34] *MECW* 38, pp. 183–184; *Capital III*, p. 286.

being quantitatively determined at any chosen point of the social production process. At any moment there is only a definite amount of need to be satisfied. As Marx explains in *Grundrisse*:

> Use value in itself does not have the boundlessness of value as such. Given objects can be consumed as objects of needs only up to a certain level. For example: no more than a certain amount of grain is consumed etc. Hence, as *use value*, the product contains a barrier – precisely the barrier consisting of the need for it – which, however, is measured not by the need of the producers but by the total need of all those engaged in exchange. Where the need for a certain value ceases, it ceases to be a use value. It is measured as a use value by the need for it. But as soon as it ceases to be a use value, it ceases to be an object of circulation (in so far as it is not money).[35]

To follow up this line of argument, Marx also redefined volume one's notion of the relationship between use-value and value (i.e. exchange value). It is not the case anymore that use-value is regarded as the indifferent and neutral precondition of the realisation of the value of a commodity, or the definition of its value. Since Marx earlier argued that if use-value had a measure for itself, it is its 'natural measure as natural object', he now had to concede that on a real, as opposed to an idealised, market, use-value appears as the external limit governing the possibility of realising exchange values. This limiting function is external, because it is wholly indifferent to the substance of 'value', that is, the reified social labour which has created it. Marx demonstrated the phenomenon through the following example:

> The supply of use value and the supply of value to be realised are by no means identical, since quite different quantities of use value can represent the sarnie quantity of exchange value. The same value – £3 – can be represented by one, three or ten tons of iron. The quantity of iron (use value) which I supply and the quantity of value I supply, are by no means proportionate to each other, since the latter quantity can remain unchanged no matter how the former changes. No matter how large or small the quantity of iron supply may be, it is assumed that I always want to realise the value of the iron, which is *independent* of the actual quantity of iron and in general its existence as a use value. The value supplied but not yet realised) and the quantity of iron which is realised, do not correspond to each other. No grounds exist therefore for assuming that the possibility of selling a commodity at its value corresponds in any way to the quantity of the commodity I bring to market. For the buyer, my commodity exists, above all, as use value. He buys it as such. But what he needs is a definite quantity of iron. His need for iron is just as little determined by the quantity produced by me as the value of my iron is commensurate with this quantity (...). Insofar as he wants to buy my commodity, he may want either a smaller quantity than I supply, or the

[35] *Grundrisse*, p. 405; *MECW*, 28, p. 332.

entire quantity, but *below* its value. His demand does not have to correspond to my supply any more than the quantity I supply and the value at which I supply it are identical. Thus the demand for the quantity of use value I supply is measured not by the value I wish to realise, but by the quantity which the buyer requires at a definite price.[36]

When Marx presented his theory of market exchange as an idealised abstraction, he only emphasised that there were two different qualities which characterise a commodity, use-value and exchange value. Now, however, when he argues at the level of aggregates, and is obliged to follow the act of market clearance step by step, these qualities of the commodity appear not only as different but as contradictory. Now the argument is that the commodity has a double determination. As a use-value it has its own mundane natural limits. As a value it is determined purely socially and has no real measure which would determine its value limits. This contradiction, as we all know, is the seed of Marx's theory of economic crises.

These two levels of definitions clearly coexist in the third volume of *Capital* and not without friction. Nonetheless, Marx never tires of emphasising that the new aggregate definition of use-value did not invalidate the original definition derived from the model of simple exchange. For him the second step is only an evolution, a concretisation, an enrichment of the first. He sees it as the more perfect expression of the first idea. Let us follow him now to one of the critical passages of volume three, where he made his position on this issue very clear:

[I]f the use value of individual commodities depends on whether they satisfy a particular need, then the use value of the mass of the social product depends on whether it satisfies the quantitatively definite social need for each particular kind of product in an adequate manner, and whether the labour is therefore proportionately distributed among the different spheres in keeping with social needs, which are quantitatively circumscribed. (...) The social need, that is, the use value on a social scale, appears here as a determining factor for the amount of total social labour time which is expended in various specific spheres of production. But it is merely the same law which is already applied in the case of single commodities, namely, that the use value of a commodity is the basis of exchange value and thus of its value. (...) This quantitative limit to the quota of social labour-time available for the various particular spheres of production is but a more developed expression of the law of value in general, although the necessary labour-time assumes a different meaning here. Only just so much of it is required for the satisfaction of social needs. The limitation occurring here is due to the use value.[37]

---

[36] *TSV III*, pp. 101–102.
[37] *MECW* 37, pp. 629–630; *Capital III*, p. 774.

If we read the passage carefully, we would discover immediately that the argument is less than convincing. It looks coherent, but this coherence is due only to a linguistic sleight of hand. Marx, without noticing it, or at least without calling attention to it, endowed the term 'need' with two different meanings, and *a fortiori* uses two different meanings of use-value as well. In the first lines of the passage, when he refers the reader back to the discussion of volume one of *Capital*, he talks about the use-value of an individual commodity. Use-value here simply means that both the object and the individual using it are historically formed. Nonetheless, use-value refers to the naturally determined capacity of the object to be useful for humans. The link is direct and 'natural'. Similarly, 'need' simply means the desire and intention of a person to use the object in a purposeful fashion. However, and this is a crucial point, the concept of 'social need' is not a simple aggregate of these individual needs at the level of society. It is not simply a concretisation of the original abstraction in the context of society but rather something quite different. It is nothing else but what the political economists defined as 'effective demand', aggregate market demand. When Marx discussed earlier the quantitative limits of use-value in a real market situation, he already made it quite clear that 'effective demand' was not the same as the aggregate of 'genuine social demands' existing in society:

> It would seem, then, that there is on the one side of demand a certain magnitude of definite social needs which require for their satisfaction a definite quantity of a commodity on the market. But quantitatively, the definite social needs are very elastic and changing. Their fixedness is only apparent. If the means of subsistence were cheaper, or money wages higher, the workers would buy more of them, and a greater 'social need' would arise for them. (...) The limits within which the need for commodities in the *market*, the demand, differs quantitatively from the *actual social need*, naturally vary considerably for different commodities; what I mean is the difference between the demanded quantity of commodities and the quantity which would have been in demand at other money-prices or other money and living conditions of the buyers.[38]

Once we recognise the hidden shift of terms in Marx's discourse of use-value and social need as related to market phenomena, we can recognise instantly that the two levels of definitions are by no means simply different expressions of the same idea. Thus, Marx seems to be ignoring the characteristically 'Marxian' point that the level and pattern of demand – social use-value – is a function of the distribution of property and income and not therefore an aggregation of potential human needs. [The notion of 'social use-value', *de facto* equated with 'effective

---

[38] *MECW* 37, pp. 187–188; *Capital III*, pp. 289–290.

The Antinomies of the Concept of 'Use-Value' 213

demand', is genuinely in contradiction with the general a-social concept of use-value as a natural link between man and thing independently of the prevailing socio-economic conditions.][39] This is, of course, not simply our interpretation. Marx himself says it quite clearly in the following argument:

> It should be here noted in passing that the 'social demand', i.e. the factor which regulates the principle of demand, is essentially subject to the mutual relationship of the different classes and their respective economic position, notably therefore to, firstly, the ratio of total surplus value to wages, and, secondly, to the relation of the various parts into which surplus value is split up (profit, interest, ground-rent, taxes, etc.).[40]

If this is the real definition of 'social need', if the notion of use-value can be defined only relative to this understanding of need, then we cannot simply talk about the natural determination of use-value and the social determination of exchange value or value, as Marx made us to believe in volume one of *Capital*. It is obvious now that man's relationship with objects as use-values, at least in a commodity producing society, is inherently social, determined by the man–man relationships prevailing in the given society. The inherently static qualities of Marx's first level definitions of use-value and need, on which he still insists, now become quite inadequate. The same idea is expressed here again:

> Should the market value fall, this would entail a rise in the average social demand (this always taken to mean effective demand), which could, within certain limits, absorb larger masses of commodities. Should the market value rise, this would entail a drop in social demand, and a smaller mass of commodities would be absorbed.[41]

In general, we can say that the 'natural limits' of use-value could only apply if we regard prices and incomes as fixed. In a dynamic system, however, it is precisely the general level of prices which determine how useful use-values can be for individuals of this society. It is true, of course, that there is an absolute natural limit of use for the consumption of each and every commodity. Even if milk were free, nobody could consume more of it than what his or her natural constitution allows. But it is fair to point out that mankind has not arrived yet to such a level of general abundance that average individuals should meet the natural limits of consumption in relation to most of the things and objects which they need or desire. More importantly, even when a society approaches the natural limits of

---

[39] [This passage was removed from latest version of the manuscript.]
[40] *MECW* 37, p. 180; *Capital III*, p. 282.
[41] *MECW* 37, pp. 179–180; *Capital III*, p. 282.

consumption in relation to any need which they already have and satisfy, new needs will appear, awaiting satisfaction, both on the social and the individual level. Marx always claimed to be a 'historical' political economist. In historical terms the 'natural limit' of needs-satisfaction was irrelevant.

III

It should be obvious by now that in a society of universal commodity production the use-value of any commodity can be realised only if its value is realised in market exchange. The only way a man can use the use-value is if he buys it on the market. Marx's theory also stipulates that, while the market-realisation limit of needs-satisfaction is always present in such a society in a palpable way, in the long run this limit is pushed further and further as the capitalist economy progresses. In such a society, everything, in fact, becomes a use-value which can be sold on the market, quite independently of the 'rationality' of the transaction. If the object found a buyer, it did not matter whether it could be put to any rational use by the person who had decided that it was a use-value. Where was the 'direct and natural' link here between object and desire? Marx, of course, realised the relevance of the 'paradox of value' for the explanation of market societies, and admitted that 'the use value of the commodity in which the labour of the productive worker is embodied may be of the most futile kind. The material characteristics are in no way linked with its nature which on the contrary is only the expression of a definite social relation of production.'[42]

Thus, instead of use-value being the precondition of exchange value, in a society of universal commodity production it is exchange value which is the precondition of the rational and 'natural' use of objects. What is more, in the case of luxury consumption the exchange value property of the object could be a sufficient condition for the establishment of the man–thing relationship. In this latter case, use-value is historically and socially determined not only in a 'genetic' sense of being the result of previous labour activities, but even the actual synchronic functioning of the use-value is determined and mediated by socio-economic processes of a historically specific kind. It seems that a fundamental pillar of the logical foundations of *Capital* volume one – the 'naturalistic' definition of use-value and the man–thing relationship of need – is in real contradiction to Marx's own theory of how a market economy operates.

[42] *TSV I*, p. 158; *MECW* 31, p. 14.

It is somewhat strange that Marx resorted to such a naturalistic concept formation in the first place. In his own earlier theory of history, he established as an axiom of anthropology that men create their own history by constantly transforming both nature and their own human nature in that process. The productive effort of mankind had its *telos* not only in the adaptation of the earth's resources to pre-given needs, but mankind was the only species which also created new needs for itself and then generated new potentialities in order to satisfy these needs and so on. Marx repeated in the manuscripts of *Capital* his early starting point for the theory of the 'Paris Manuscripts': 'Man is distinguished from all other animals by the limitless and flexible nature of his needs.'[43] On that premise the status of use-value should be quite obvious. If 'needs' are historically determined, then the use involved in the satisfaction process should also be historical. Needs are historical; hence use-values must be historical as well. There can be no unmediated, natural relationship between man and object.

It is true that Marx constantly emphasised the point that in capitalism almost all needs are socially mediated. But his argument worked through a contrast between 'natural' and 'social' need. 'Natural' needs were those needs which were not created by society. The relevance of this term in Marx was blurred by the introduction of a different category in the discourse, that is, that of 'necessary needs'. It is worthwhile to follow his arguments in order to show that the first 'naturalised' concept of need had not disappeared from his thinking even in his most sophisticated passages. The *locus classicus* of these arguments is the mass of manuscripts which is now published under the title *Grundrisse*. Here Marx writes the following:

> Capital's ceaseless striving towards the general form of wealth drives labour beyond the limits of its natural paltriness, and thus creates the material elements for the development of the rich individuality which is as all-rounded in its production as in its consumption and whose labour also therefore appears no longer as labour but as the full development of activity itself in which natural necessity in its direct form has disappeared; because a historically created need has taken the place of the natural one.[44]

He also preserved the distinction between natural and socially determined need in the next passage, where the term 'necessary needs' also appears. It is interesting to note how little distance there is here between Marx's language and the discourse of eighteenth-century political economy:

---

[43] *Capital I*, 'Appendix – Results of the Immediate Process of Production', p. 1068.
[44] *Grundrisse*, p. 325; *MECW* 28, p. 251.

Luxury is the opposite of the *naturally* necessary. Necessary needs are those of the individual himself reduced to a natural subject. The development of industry suspends this natural necessity as well as this former luxury – in bourgeois society, it is true, it does so only in *antithetical form*, in that it itself only posits another specific social standard as necessary, opposite luxury.[45]

In the definition of the value of labour power it is the notion of 'necessary needs' which plays a key role: 'The value of labour-power is determined by the value of the necessaries of life habitually required by the average labourer.'[46] The level of necessary needs which a labourer had in any society for Marx were naturally social, and he well understood that the frontier of necessary needs could not be a fixed one: 'This realm of physical necessity expands as a result of his needs.'[47] But it seems that the way he modelled this change was to presuppose an initial set of genuinely natural needs and then to posit an inclusion process whereby more and more needs became regarded as belonging to the basic natural minimum for the given level of progress:

His natural needs, such as food, clothing, fuel, and housing, vary according to the climatic and other physical conditions of his country. On the other hand, the number and extent of his so-called necessary needs, as also the modes of satisfying them, are themselves the products of historical development, and depend therefore to a great extent on the degree of civilisation of a country, more particularly on the conditions under which, and consequently on the habits and degree of comfort in which, the class of free labourers has been formed. In contradistinction therefore to the case of other commodities, there enters into the determination of the value of labour-power a historical and moral element.[48]

What does not seem to be properly acknowledged here is that the utility of objects and products of other people's labour is not pre-given in a direct and 'natural' way. The procedures of using a use-value, even of recognising it, have to be learnt through a social process; it is not possible for a man to follow his biological instincts only. And even if the need as such is pre-given biologically, it is by no means obvious which objects would be able to satisfy this need and, if they do, how precisely they can be used for this purpose. If man is indeed a sociable being, unable to exist outside the bounds of society, then it is only 'natural' to suppose that his needs were shaped by his interaction with other members of the species. Both his needs and the way he would go about satisfying them would be firmly enmeshed in his social relations which would form the

---

[45] *Grundrisse*, p. 528; *MECW* 28, p. 452.
[46] *MECW* 35, p. 519; *Capital I*, p. 655.
[47] *MECW* 37, p. 807; *Capital III*, p. 959.
[48] *Capital I*, p. 275; *MECW* 35, p. 181.

boundaries of the 'possible' for him. Looking at the 'object side' of the equation, it seems to be similarly the case that the utility of things cannot be described as a bundle of socially neutral, natural properties; an object which is the result of previous labour activities is not only an 'artificial', rather than a 'natural' object, but it is also, according to Marx's early social theory, a piece of 'reified' labour, an end product of the process of 'reification'. The fact that the thing appears as useful to satisfy human needs in a 'rational' fashion is possible only because it embodies, in a reified form, socially determined human needs and potencies. In order to survive at the given level of civilisation prevailing in their societies, individuals have to learn the procedures of using socially constructed objects and then have to keep their knowledge alive in the process of continuous social reproduction. Marx's naturalistic interpretation of the notion of use-value in *Capital* volume one thus creates very serious problems for his philosophy of history. More importantly, it also runs counter to his characterisation of the stages of historical development, surely a central part of his 'critical' political economy. The naturalistic definition of use-value simply does not square with his basic insights into the typology of past socio-economic systems. The social mediation of the man–thing relationship entails the existence of social norms of use, and in a society possessing an articulated inner structure the norms of various groups and strata have to cohere into a system in order to enable this society to reproduce itself in time in an orderly fashion. The coordination of group and class norms of 'use' is the function, in every society, of institutions which can secure the smooth running of 'social use'.

Under capitalistic conditions, the harmonisation of the different spheres of production and the consumption of the various classes, Marx argued, was performed by a new, specifically economic institution, the market. However, he argued further, the institution of the 'generalised commodity market' was a result of long historical processes of formation. Markets existed in pre-capitalist societies but not as the central integrating nerve-centres of the whole society. However, there were other, non-market, social institutions which regulated the production and consumption of goods. Marx's theory of pre-capitalist modes of production, essentially an inquiry into the history of these 'use norm' defining and regulating institutions, is an interesting one and, in any case, it belongs to the very core of his overall system. What interests us here is an important feature of his typology of pre-capitalist societies, that is, that it does not make much sense if it is understood to be predicated on a 'natural' definition of use-value. What we find in these typologies is that they are based on a historicist and sociological interpretation of the notion of use-value and need. We cannot do more here than to sketch out those salient features of Marx's theory of pre-capitalist modes of production which help us to identify the place of use-value in his overall historical thinking, including his idea of a future, post-capitalist society.

In essence, Marx tried to prove that before the rise of capitalism, that is, the generalised market as an institutional process, the harmonisation of resources and needs was effected by institutions other than the market in these early societies. The norms and customs of everyday life, institutions of a political or religious character, all took part in the regulation of the balance of society. In most cases these institutions could also be the terrains of the production process itself. Production and political-religious life were one and the same; their 'institutions' were intimately intertwined. The purpose of productive organisation was not simply production itself; these institutions were not early anticipations of the capitalist factory. The institution which helped to regulate and organise production was the general unit for the organisation of all other aspects of life as well. Property relationships were also embedded in the very same institution. In Marx's words, all the pre-capitalist modes of production relied on 'the original unity between the worker and the conditions of production'.[49] The seedbed of this unity was the 'naturally arisen spontaneous community' inherited from primeval times. In such communities, he argued, 'each individual conducts himself only as a link, as a member of this community, as *proprietor* or *possessor*. The *real appropriation* through the labour process happens under these *presuppositions*, which are not themselves the *product* of labour, but appear as its natural or *divine* presuppositions.'[50]

Thus, in these societies the traditional and custom-guided social mechanism of community life secured a harmonisation of production and needs (at least in normal times), because both production and consumption were traditional and because both the means of production, the property forms which articulated them, and also needs appeared as 'natural or divine presuppositions'. The division of labour was natural; production techniques were natural (because they were traditional), and the purposes of production appeared also as natural. Under these conditions it is meaningful to say that production was the direct production of 'use-values'; there was a directness and immediacy in the way production served the purpose of a well-defined and traditional, 'natural' level of consumption. Since 'economic' relationships were firmly embedded in the process governing all aspects of social life, it was impossible to separate out the 'artificial' (i.e. economic) and the natural (i.e. social)

---

[49] *TSV III*, p. 422.
[50] *Grundrisse*, p. 472; *MECW* 28, p. 400.

determinations in the reproduction of the community. The system, in a very meaningful sense, was a closed one. There was no progress outside teleology. The ideal type that Marx had in mind was the village community:

> Those small and extremely ancient Indian communities, for example, some of which continue to exist to this day, are based on the possession of the land in common, on the blending of agriculture and handicrafts and on an unalterable division of labour, which serves as a fixed plan and basis for action whenever a new community is started. The communities occupy areas of from 100 up to several thousand acres, and each forms a compact whole producing all it requires.[51]

This last sentence was perhaps a crucial one. In Marx's model, pre-capitalist societies were supposed to be organised into local and natural units, each 'producing all it requires'. The terrain of needs was a circle. Of course, this natural determination of needs and production was not really natural. The social structure did change, but it changed extremely slowly, sometimes imperceptibly. Any great innovation shook the system in its foundation, changed the organisation of production dramatically, only to return to the slow flow of everyday existence within new 'natural' limits. Changes at one point of the larger society did not necessarily affect the other parts. The boundaries of communities were so constructed as to limit the effects of change by blocking the free flow of men and ideas between the natural units. The network of self-sufficient communities did not favour a quick chain reaction of change triggered off by the appearance of new needs and new techniques of satisfaction in specific communities. In Marx's view, pre-capitalist societies were simply lacking those transfer mechanisms which could have spread the innovations into the various packets of natural existence. Moreover, it was in the very nature of these early social organisations that they lacked such transfer mechanisms.

> The Asiatic form necessarily survives longest and most stubbornly. This is due to the fundamental principle on which it is based, that is, that the individual does not become independent of the community; that the circle of production is self-sustaining (...) In all these forms the basis of evolution is the reproduction of relations between individual and community assumed as given – they may be more or less primitive, more or less the result of history, but fixed into tradition – and a definite, predetermined objective existence, both as regards the relation to the conditions of labour and the relation between one man and his fellows, etc. Such evolution is therefore from the outset *limited*, but once the limits are transcended, decay and disintegration ensue.[52]

---

[51] *Capital I*, pp. 477–478; *MECW* 35, p. 362.
[52] *Foundations*, p. 82; *Grundrisse*, pp. 486–487; *MECW* 28, p. 410.

Marx's explanation was clear. If needs were not kept at their predetermined and 'natural' level, decay and disintegration was inevitable. That was precisely what had happened to the ancient Greek *polis*, an institution which Marx saw as one uniting the features of closed and open communities:

> where each individual is supposed to possess so many acres of land, the mere increase in population constitutes an obstacle (...) Suppose, for instance, that productivity could be increased without increase in territory, by means of a development of the forces of production. This would imply new methods and combinations of labour, the high proportion of the day which would then have to be devoted to agriculture, etc., and once again the old economic conditions of the community would cease to operate. The act of reproduction itself changes not only the objective conditions – e.g., transforming village into town, the wilderness into agricultural clearings, etc. – but the producers change with it, by the emergence of new qualities, by transforming and developing themselves in production, forming new powers and new conceptions, new modes of intercourse, new speech, new needs.[53]

Pre-capitalist societies for Marx were the epitomes of a static order. He described even ancient Greece as the childhood form of society, quite incapable to serve as a vehicle for developing all of man's potentials. When he had to compare capitalism to the ancient world, he blamed the political economists for painting a far too negative picture of social relations in the system of generalised commodity production.

> In bourgeois political economy (...) this complete elaboration of what lies within man, appears as the total alienation, and the destruction of all fixed, one-sided purposes as the sacrifice of the end in itself to a wholly external compulsion. Hence in one way the childlike world of the ancients appears to be superior; and this is so, in so far as we seek for a closed shape, form and established limitation.[54]

Capitalism was the first socio-economic formation which broke out from the straitjacket of regulation provided by integrated socio-political institutions of the whole of productive life. It was only in this new system that the 'economic' became separate from the other spheres of life, breaking the non-economic constraints foisted upon the productive sub-systems of all previous societies. The great innovation was the reduction of the many criteria of production and 'good life' existing in pre-capitalist societies to a single one. The single criteria, the economic one, then enabled the harmonisation of the various spheres of production and consumption into a single interconnected system, appearing as the national and international market. On the capitalist market all

---

[53] *Foundations*, pp. 92–93; *Grundrisse*, p. 494; *MECW* 28, p. 418.
[54] *Foundations*, p. 85; *Grundrisse*, p. 488; *MECW* 28, p. 412.

previous use-values appeared as potential values, and market agents, first and foremost the capitalists, choose between them only as better or worse vehicles of profit-making. The goal of production in capitalism is not anymore related to a pre-given traditional set of needs, which through habit could appear to both sellers and buyers as 'natural'. Since the new goal of production and market activity was to constantly expand the opportunities of valorisation and profit-making, the interest of capital was to push for a continuous expansion of the system of needs. As Marx emphasised,

in accord with this tendency, capital drives beyond national barriers and prejudices as such and beyond nature worship, as well as all traditional, confined, complacent, encrusted satisfaction of present needs, and reproductions of old ways of life. It is destructive towards all of this, and constantly revolutionizes it, tearing down all the barriers which hem in the development of the forces of production, the expansion of needs, the all-rounded development of production, and the exploitation and exchange of natural and intellectual forces.[55]

Marx was well aware of the ambiguity of his language. As we have seen, he complained that even the political economists seemed to have recoiled from the 'new barbarism' involved in any truthful description of the expansionary tendencies of capitalism. Thus, he was determined to make his positive point as forceful as possible. In comparison to old systems of direct production of use-values the new generalised system of commodity production, he claimed, was the dawn of a new civilisation, superior to all previous forms of social life and the harbinger of an even brighter future.

The ancient conception, in which man always (in however narrowly national, religious or political a definition) as the aim of production, seems very much more exalted than the modern world, in which production is the aim of man and wealth the aim of production. In fact, however, when the narrow bourgeois form has been peeled away, what is wealth, if not the universality of needs, capacities, enjoyments, productive powers, etc., of individuals, produced in universal exchange? What, if not the full development of human control over the forces of nature – those of his own nature as well as those of so-called 'nature'? What, if not the absolute elaboration of his creative dispositions, without any preconditions other than antecedent historical evolution which makes the totality of this evolution – i.e. the evolution of all human powers as such, unmeasured by any *previously established* yardstick – an end in itself? What is this, if not a situation where man does not reproduce himself in any determined form, but produces his totality? Where he does not seek to remain something formed by the past, but is in the absolute movement of becoming?[56]

---

[55] *Grundrisse*, p. 410; *MECW* 28, p. 337.
[56] *Foundations*, pp. 84–85; *Grundrisse*, pp. 487–488; *MECW* 28, pp. 411–412.

It is impossible not to notice that Marx here develops a dualistic theory of history. On one side of the divide there are all the societies which existed before capitalism, on the other there is the present and the future, as a seamless, continuous unfolding of a positive dynamics. It is perhaps needless here to reiterate Marx's well-known criticism of the consequences of such a revolutionary economic dynamic under capitalist social relations. In general and systemic terms, the price which society had to pay for enjoying the need-satisfaction provided by the new economy was that the interlinkages of the economy, the key economic institutions which ensured its continuous reproduction, slipped out from the net of socio-political control. The economy suddenly appeared as a new Leviathan facing society itself, following its own will and caprice. The economy was still manned by conscious human actors and their purposive organisations, but each productive and marketing unit had to operate in isolation. Both production and need-satisfaction became atomised. The single units were pushed to trust their very own self-interests and hope that their activities would he valorised by the anarchic market. The single units could not afford to keep the social harmonisation of production and needs in their sight. Had they tried to do so, their effort would have been futile in any case. It was the very essence of the system of generalised commodity production that the only institution which could connect the single units of production and consumption was the market. It was precisely this feature of the system which ensured that the traditionally regulated needs could break out from their previously enforced limitations. The market had a cardinally important epistemic quality. It defied the model of teleological human action. The market harmonises production and need only *post festum*, only after the production cycle had been completed by the isolated productive units who could not have reliable knowledge of the aggregate balance of market futures. However, the market is able to correct imbalances retrospectively. This correction may be extremely brutal, but, as Marx himself believed, it worked. The correction was brutal, because it smoothed out the trendline only through a successive series of imbalances. Every crisis claimed the 'life' of numberless productive units whose purposive activity was based on a miscalculation of the guidelines provided by *ex ante* markets. There can be no doubt whatsoever regarding the fact that for Marx socialism or communism was a social system which preserved the essentially dynamic character of capitalism. The new society also had to be a system of total need-satisfaction. Socialism for Marx would have been quite unacceptable if it was not to continue the heritage of the productive 'civilisation' of capitalism. An essential criterion of socialism was, therefore, that it retained the 'historical rationality' of market systems, that it had an 'economy' which could satisfy the needs of the free all-rounded human personality without the fetters of social systems, which had to be limited, because they did not have an 'economy'. In every other respect, however, socialism had to be the opposite of the 'actual rationality' of the market, which from the point of view of the model of 'human individual rationality' was irrational, or at least non-rational. The epistemic basis of the capitalist market, that is, that correction happens only after production had already taken place, had to be got rid of.

Social production and social need in socialism is harmonised by an openly goal-rational 'plan', performing all the positive functions of the commodity market without its epistemic drags. Marx well understood the Aristotelian point that the market was an instrument of sociability, that it was a bonding rather than an isolating agent. Thus, he posited socialism as the real apex of the inbuilt tendencies of sociability. Socialism was to be a society of associated producers, bonded into a society – but not local society – directly. There was, however, one essential difference between capitalist and socialist sociability. Capitalism brought out the tendency for generalised sociability inherent in human nature by disregarding the qualitative differences between men. The market could bring together all men and break down the limits posited by previous socio-political systems by making them absolutely equal in their reduced capacity as market agents. In socialism the qualitative differences were to be re-established. Everybody will once again be connected with everybody as true individualities, just as it was in the Greek polis, but on a totally generalised basis. If that happened, social reason – the 'wisdom of society' – would come into its own; production and needs would be brought into correspondence by production directly answering the need which called it forth in the first place.

We can return here to the opening quote in this paper. As we have seen, Marx's argument for socialism was the following. The problem of market sociability was that in it 'the labourer exists to satisfy the needs of self-expansion of existing values, instead of, on the contrary, material wealth existing to satisfy the needs of development on the part of the labourer'.[57] In capitalism, Marx argued, 'the process of production has the mastery over man, instead of being controlled by him'.[58] The production process as such has an irreducible essence, which socialism can retain from the system of generalised commodity production:

---

[57] *MECW* 35, p. 616; *Capital I*, p. 772.
[58] *MECW* 35, p. 92; *Capital I*, p. 175.

Economy of time, to this all economy ultimately reduces itself. Society likewise has to distribute its time in a purposeful way, in order to achieve a production adequate to its overall needs; thus, economy of time, along with the planned distribution of labour time among the various branches of production, remains the first economic law on the basis of communal production.[59]

But in other respects, socialism as a system could not be a slave of the production of 'values' but an 'economy' geared to the direct satisfaction of 'use-values'. In this respect socialism was like the pre-capitalist modes of production. Remember Marx's characterisation of the ancient *polis* economy: 'The ancient conception, in which man always appears (...) as the aim of production, seems very much more exalted than the modern world, in which production is the aim of man and wealth the aim of production.'[60]

The question is then the following. Socialism will have to have an 'economy'. All past systems which took 'man' as the 'aim of production' had a polity which regulated the harmonisation of productive possibilities and social needs. Capitalism, in the Marxian idealisation, was the almost complete domination of the market over the polity. If we do away with the market, what sort of social structure will emerge? An extrapolation of the Marxian logic, admittedly a crude extrapolation, would suggest that socialism would be a purely social 'economy', an 'economy' without polity and institutions which should bring it into harmony with needs. Needs and the pure socialist 'economy' would relate to each other directly, immediately and 'naturally'. The socialist economy should be able to perform in this fashion, because it would produce 'use-values' rather than values, and as we have seen, according to Marx, the use-value of a thing can be 'realised without exchange, i.e. in the direct relation between the thing and man'.[61]

However, in his analysis of previous societies of use-value, Marx gave the following epistemic analysis of the way the social norms embedded in the socio-political institutions of a closed community could match production to needs: 'each individual conducts himself only as a link, as a member of this community, as proprietor and possessor'. The real appropriation through the labour process happens under these presuppositions, which are not in themselves the product of labour but appear as its 'natural and divine presuppositions'. In other words, in pre-capitalist societies the 'natural' link between man and thing as a use-value could exist only on the presupposition that there was also a 'natural' determination of

---

[59] *Grundrisse*, p. 173; *MECW* 28, p. 109.
[60] *Foundations*, p. 84; *Grundrisse*, pp. 487–488; *MECW* 28, p. 411.
[61] *Capital I*, p. 177; *MECW* 35, p. 94.

what counted as a need. A more sophisticated analysis, such as that provided by Marx himself, would rephrase this proposition in social terms. What appeared as the 'natural' determination of need was the 'political' determination of need through time-honoured custom, epistemically as the accumulation of previous knowledge of what was possible for the society to satisfy without self-destruction.

IV

In our analysis of the concept of 'use-value' in *Capital* we have shown that the first level of the Marxian analysis, which presupposed a natural determination of use-values and needs, or at least the possibility of their ultimate 'natural' determination, led to contradictions in his analysis of societies which had an 'economy'. If we were right in this analysis, we have to accept the conclusion that the Marxian projection of a dynamic socialist society which is engaged in direct 'natural' production of use-values must inherently suffer from the same antinomies. If use-values are not 'naturally' linked to man's needs, then the socialism of the future cannot be a pure 'natural' (meaning teleological in an Aristotelian fashion) economy, unless, that is, there is also a polity, a network of socio-political institutions which make this 'natural' link a social and political one. What is more, these political institutions of socialism must be of a new epistemic quality. If they behave like the market, that is, if they realise the emergence of new needs and innovations in production only after they have happened, *post festum*, then they cannot be but constraints on the pure socialist 'economy'. This is an antinomy which can only be clarified, if not solved, by a fundamental rethinking of the meaning of politics in the classical liberal tradition and, to the extent that it does have a 'politics', in Marxism. Fundamentally, both traditions developed the notion that society moved forward by 'human action' resulting in unintended consequences rather than by 'human design'. How can a future socialist polity overcome the difficulties kept in store by this idea? Political theory facing the future must concern itself with this question.

Note on Chapter 5

This paper originated during the 'Political Economy and Society, 1750–1850' project at King's College Cambridge and was first given the very long title 'What Is Political Economy? II. Theories of Need and Conjectural Histories of Progress. The Antinomies of the Concept of Use-Value in Marx's *Capital*: Economy and Polity after the Market'. Subsequently, the text was intended to become (part of) the introduction to the ultimately unpublished volume of papers entitled *After Adam Smith: Political Economy and Theories of Commercial Society*. For this purpose, it was given the new title 'Alternative Political Economies? One Political Economy and Many Political Positions'. In July 1984, however, for the workshop on 'The Identity of Political Economy', the paper was combined with 'The Concept of Negative Community and the Origins of Historical Materialism' (i.e. the earlier version of Chapter 4 in this volume) to form '"Negative Communities": Natural Jurisprudence and the Intellectual Origins of the Marxian Notion of Communism'. When this happened, the first half of its original title was lost and the remaining title, the one chosen here, became its section subtitle. No major changes were made to the text itself, which has remained virtually the same through all its various incarnations. The text (and title) reproduced here is based on the July 1984 version, that is, the version that was united with its natural twin for the workshop 'The Identity of Political Economy'. At that event, Hont explained that, although the two parts had been written as separate papers and for separate occasions, 'read in sequence, they add up to a coherent and interrelated argument'. He further clarified that:

Both the first and second parts turn on the issue whether we can understand property and economic relationships as 'man–thing' relationships mediated by the concept of need, or whether we have to take into account that in modern societies as they really exist all such relationships must be understood as socially mediated 'man–man' relationships. As it is argued in both parts of the paper, the coherence (or otherwise) of the Marxian notion of communism depends on one's views on the above-mentioned theoretical problem. The second part of the paper, which discusses the contradictions of the Marxian notion of communism through an analysis of Marx's *Capital*, is heavily indebted to my reading of an influential Hungarian monograph typescript written by G. Bence – J. Kis – G. Markus under the title 'Is Critical Economics Possible at All?' which was submitted for publication in 1971 but subsequently was only circulated in 'samizdat'.[62]

---

[62] Hont, '"Negative Communities": Natural Jurisprudence and the Intellectual Origins of the Marxian Notion of Communism', Unpublished manuscript [1984], SC, The Papers of István Hont.

6 Socialist Natural Law, Commercial Society and Political Economy
A Contribution to the Understanding of the Idea of Social Science

The foundational myth of social science is that it is an expression of the progress of mankind. The thesis of 'the great transition' suggests discontinuity between earlier and modern thoughts on society. Those who dislike the genre of mythology tend to demur. A sceptic would insist on a critical perspective and investigate the merits of presupposing continuity and perhaps, at least as an initial hypothesis, would question whether 'improvement' is the right word to associate with the apparently entirely unidirectional process of 'transition'. In any case, the notion of transition presupposes that one understands what it is which transits and from where to where. My interest in this paper is to inquire whether the rise of the modern disciplinary social sciences (embedded in the idea of the modern research university and lately of democratic mass higher education) might be more fruitfully seen as a particular stage in a longer dialectic of concept formation, controversy and moral debate. Much of what goes on in the social sciences is disguised political and moral controversy and I believe that the pattern of controversy is repetitive, and that the basic line-up of the opposing parties has remained surprisingly (and perhaps distressingly) stable over the last 300 years or more. If so, then it is a necessary precondition of our understanding of the origins of the social science to recognise these recurrent patterns of debate, to map them and to provide as good and precise a historical analysis of their dynamics as possible.

The first task is to get the subject matter of social science more sharply in focus. Which of its two constitutive terms one should wish to explain, the 'social' or the 'science'? Should one first investigate the time-honoured tradition according to which social science started with the conceptual innovation of developing a self-contained notion of society, separated from politics (as well as from law and theology)? Or should one rather assume that the crucial move in the alleged 'great transition' was to adopt a scientific language and mode of thought for the discussion of human (as opposed to natural) phenomena? If both, what is the relationship between the two, both in theory and in history? Can the concept of society, as it were, be made more scientific? Or the concept of science more social? Is it the politics of social science which really matters? Or the institutional support which its practitioners can rely on?

My interest in this paper is in the uncovering of the meaning of the term 'social' in social science. I shall argue that social science has been, generally speaking, a continuation of the modern natural jurisprudence of the seventeenth and eighteenth centuries. More specifically, I wish to suggest that it originates from that specific variety of modern natural jurisprudence which from the middle of the eighteenth century onwards had been described as 'socialist' natural law, socialist because it strived to derive both moral normativity and the political principles of modern civilisation from a foundational notion of a specifically human sociability.

I would also like to show that the modern natural law idiom, whose chief characteristic lay in the attempt to derive moral normativity and the principles of social organisation from a strong notion of man as *zoon politikon* or *animal sociale*, contained two camps of thinkers who fundamentally disagreed about the sources of the social nature of man. One group took human sociability to be an intrinsic feature of being human and built its theory around the normative requirements of human fellowship and moral solidarity, expressed in love, charity and cooperation. Their opponents posited the origins of society in the usefulness of forming human groups in order to ensure the survival of both the individual and the species. Both groups claimed that their notion was that of a 'natural sociability' and both were named, at one point or another, as socialists. Most eighteenth-century Christians and nineteenth- and twentieth-century socialists belonged to the first camp, but in the late eighteenth century the epithet 'socialist' was more often attached to the latter. The kind of socialist natural law which sought to find the foundations of normativity and ground the institutions of justice in the utility of human cooperation, I will argue, became the theoretical basis of political economy. Constantly under attack by the partisans of 'true' natural sociability and 'true' morality, the twin discourses of utilitarian-socialist natural law and political economy came to dominate the late eighteenth century. The central and uniting concept of these twin discourses was that of a 'commercial society'. The political, moral and economic inquiry focusing on commercial society then came to be called, in one phrase, *la science sociale*.

I wish to argue that it is the notion of 'commercial society' which has been the relevant notion of 'society' for the study of modern Western (and increasingly world) developments and that it is the true cornerstone of modern social science. The current names for this notion of 'society' are well known, and a mere mention of them is enough to show why it has been, from the beginning, so controversial. 'Commercial society' is the underlying notion behind theories of bourgeois society, civil society, liberal society, economic society, exchange society or capitalist society. I am afraid that this family of concepts is not, on the whole, much better understood today than in the pre-disciplinary age of social understanding (before the 'great transition'). In many ways, its basic features are less clearly in focus today than in the past, mainly because of its continuing, explosive, political controversiality. By now each of these names carries such a heavy political baggage that a detached analysis is really difficult. Today (meaning the very recent past), the adherents of commercial society dominate the political scene, and the idea of a modern 'social' society (the socialists) seems to have been defeated. Why this is so, and why this may turn out to be a dangerous illusion, might be better understood if one locates the origin of social science in a long-term Western controversy over these foundational issues. The reinstatement of this long-term perspective, I shall argue, requires a reconstruction of the link between modern natural law and its successor, social science.

Natural Law and *la science sociale*

One (if not *the*) crucial move in demonstrating continuity between the prehistory and history of modern social science is to call attention to the link between natural law and social science as successive idioms covering largely overlapping and coextensive domains of knowledge. By natural law, in this context, I do not refer to the traditional and narrower concept of natural law (with its ancient lineage) but more the discourse or discipline of modern natural law (which started with Hugo Grotius) as a recognised mode of organising social-political-theological knowledge and to its teaching which flourished in Europe from the late seventeenth to the end of the eighteenth century (and in some instances beyond).

In this period, it is important to realise, natural law was a 'discipline' in a fairly modern and institutionalised sense. One could go to virtually any university in Europe and take a lecture class in the subject. Bookshops had textbooks for it in great abundance. But it had no single legal or meta-legal discursive identity: it was not a single discipline. Despite the legal connotations of the words 'law' and 'jurisprudence', the line dividing discourses belonging to natural law from other legal, political, theological and moral discourses did not simply fall between the essentially juridical and the inherently non-juridical but rather between foundational and non-foundational areas of thought, between general and specific modes of study. Natural law became a hallmark of seventeenth- and eighteenth-century social thought precisely because it became the property not only of lawyers and law schools but of philosophers, politicians, historians and theologians (in many universities it was thought of as part of philosophy or theology). It was the umbrella for all the discourses relating to human *nature*, encompassing the appropriate 'natural' foundations of moral and political philosophy, jurisprudence, history and theology. Thus, natural jurisprudence in actual historical practice was much more than just the most general, most philosophical part of legal science. Natural law, *Naturrecht, droit naturel*, was seen as the foundation of all theoretical knowledge about society, the foundation of the moral and political sciences. The emphasis in 'natural law' should fall on the word 'natural', as the feature common to natural law, natural theology, natural history, the discourse of natural price or natural interest rates, and so on, denoting the 'natural' variety of the numerous possible enquiries into the various spheres of human and social existence. Furthermore, 'natural' in this context meant natural to humans, and as far as one supposed that man could not live or even be imagined to live outside society (as most natural lawyers indeed presupposed), 'natural' could mean 'social' in the most general sense.

If there was a first great transition in the European university world, then it was the appearance of chairs of natural jurisprudence at virtually all universities of the Western and colonial world. It was seen as the proof of the modernity of a university that it acquired such a chair, and all over Europe one can observe the fierce political controversy surrounding its establishment. A few chairs of political economy were also established but almost always strongly attached to natural law, expressed either in the name of the chair or in the teaching subjects attached to it. In the second half of the eighteenth century, however, and even more in the last quarter, the identity of this omnibus natural law discourse became questioned. This is a complicated story, but perhaps it can be summarised briefly as follows. As natural jurisprudence became a legitimate idiom for theological and legal thought, it became victim of the usual academic and controversial habits of these two professions. Those who regarded the discourse as a reservoir of foundational social and political theories became impatient with the endless tedium of denominational and confessional controversy on the one hand and the logic-chopping, systematising predilections of lawyers engaged in producing interpretative commentaries. There was a desire to cut off the lawyers and the theologians from the discipline. On the other hand, the word 'nature' and the 'naturalist' methodology (such as in the 'state of nature') became the subjects of intense controversy, exposing the logical and political failings of the very mode of argument which served as the backbone of the disciplinary identity of modern natural law. The original core of the enterprise did not lose its sense or purpose, but it had to be unburdened from increasingly intractable debates and counterproductive terminology in order to make it appear more openly as a general, foundational discourse of morals, politics and legislation. I would argue that this was the message and meaning of the new phrase which came into usage in France at the end of the eighteenth century: *la science sociale*.

Condorcet, Sieyès, Garat, Lacratelle, Destutt du Tracy, Cabanis and others developed a language of *la science de l'homme, la science humaine, science de la vie humaine, science de l'ordre social, économie sociale* or simply *la science sociale*.[1] This notion, which owed a great deal to their critique and critical acceptance of the Physiocratic attempt to use natural law as the foundational discourse for political and economic reform, was almost always used in the singular, not because it depicted some conception of narrow, empirical social science in the modern sense but because it pulled together under a single umbrella all the relevant discourses of society available at the time, and most certainly those three which were called the sciences of civilisation, the sciences of legislation, and moral and political economy. '*La science sociale*' was the science of the legislator, the general guide to public policy, constitutional and economic reform, and, for some, revolution. No reform or revolution was possible, it was argued, without a general understanding of the moral, social and political relations of men, without a knowledge of human nature, human rights and duties, human passions, or without understanding the principles of happiness, good government, constitutions and the productive system of modern political economy. It is not difficult to see, I would argue, how natural jurisprudence was followed by the science of the legislator, and then by 'social science', as a general covering notion for all the moral and political sciences. Behind the apparent discontinuity of sequentially developing names in fact lay a continuous domain of discourse, overlaid but not broken up by the changes in the political language.

Social Science and Socialism

The French origins of the term itself are interesting to contemplate (this is also the case with many terms used in political economy). For a while the English language did not have an equivalent phrase, and

---

[1] See Keith M. Baker, 'The Early History of the Term "Social Science"', *Annals of Science*, 20 (1964): 211–226; Brian W. Head, 'The Origins of "La Science Sociale" in France, 1770–1800', *Australian Journal of French Studies*, 19 (1982): 115–132; Robert Wokler, 'Saint-Simon and the Passage from Political to Social Science' in Anthony Pagden (ed.), *The Languages of Political Theory in Early-Modern Europe* (Cambridge: Cambridge University Press, 1987), pp. 325–338.

science sociale was translated as 'moral science'. It was in the form of the 'philosophy of the human mind' that Dugald Stewart referred to it in his attempt to explain that disciplines of social knowledge, such as political economy, needed an underlying foundational discipline of the human mind to inform them. The term (as distinct from the idea) crept into English usage not through the heirs of the Scottish Enlightenment but through the utilitarians and the early English socialists. Its first user in a relevant context, William Thompson (1775–1833), defined social science precisely in the foundational sense we have mentioned, as 'the science of morals, including legislation as one of its most important subdivisions', requiring 'not only the knowledge of what is technically called morals and political economy, but the outlines of all that is known, with a capacity for following up on any particular branch that may be, on particular occasions, conducive to the general end', that is, social happiness.[2]

It would be interesting to follow the increasing use of the term 'social science' in England through John Stuart Mill, who actually managed to apply the term to the idea of Dugald Stewart (i.e. to denote by 'social science' the 'whole science of the nature of individual mind'),[3] but we should rather turn to the issue of the related term 'socialism'. Some early English socialists sometimes used the term 'socialism' as coterminous to 'social science', claiming that socialism as a science includes others which are usually considered separate and distinct sciences, including political economy, the science of morals and others.[4] The more frequent definition of socialism, however, soon acquired a more specific meaning than that. It continued to signify a foundational understanding of society which was necessary to guide political economy, legislation and so on,

---

[2] William Thompson, *An Inquiry into the Principles of Distribution of Wealth Most Conducive to Human Happiness* (London, 1824), pp. ix–x. For an interpretation, see Gregory Claeys, '"Individualism", "Socialism", and "Social Science": Further Notes on a Process of Conceptual Formation', *Journal of the History of Ideas*, 47 (1986): 81–93; also Peter R. Senn, 'The Earliest Use of the Term 'Social Science', *Journal of the History of Ideas*, 19 (1958): 569–570; and J. H. Burns, 'J.S. Mill and the Term "Social Science"', *Journal of the History of Ideas*, 20 (1959): 431–432; and Georg G. Iggers, 'Further Remarks about the Early Uses of the Term "Social Science"', *Journal of the History of Ideas*, 20 (1959): 433–436.

[3] 'This branch of science, whether we prefer to call it social economy, speculative politics, or the natural history of society, presupposes the whole science of the nature of the individual mind; since all the laws of which the latter science takes cognizance are brought into play in a state of society, and the truths of the social science are but statements of the manner in which those simple laws take effect in complicated circumstances.' John Stuart Mill, 'On the Definition of Political Economy; and on the Method of Philosophical Investigation in That Science', originally published in *The London and Westminster Review* 4 (1836): 1–29.

[4] Claeys, '"Individualism", "Socialism", and "Social Science"', p. 88n.

but not anymore in a neutral and general sense. It now referred only to that kind of foundational social science which emphasised morally positive social bonding – through benevolence, cooperation and love – which could guide public policy towards a more humane and ethically warm society than the one that actually existed in the early nineteenth century. Accordingly, socialism was more and more understood as that system of social science which could be successfully pitted against political economy, or more precisely against the anchoring of political economy in the sort of science of society which now became renamed as 'individualism'. Socialism, or the 'social system', was the social science of benevolence and community-building, while individualism or the 'anti-social system' (these are the terms of Robert Owen) were based on notions of self-love and individual competition. This meaning of socialism contributed heavily to the popularising of social science (see Lorenz von Stein's account of these developments in France in the 1830s) and also spun even more radical alternatives in 'communional' systems and communism.[5]

Socialist Natural Law

After the first decades of the nineteenth century the continuity between natural law, social science and 'socialism' became blurred. The association of natural law and political economy with 'individualism' represented quite an extraordinary change, because the earlier usage of the words 'socialist' and 'socialism' were precisely designed to highlight that the foundations of modern natural jurisprudence were in a theory of society. These words were used to isolate, in the most general sense, modern natural law, the school of Grotius, from its various more expressly Christian competitors. More specifically and powerfully, however, it denoted one of the chief schools of Grotian natural jurisprudence, the Pufendorfian one, distinguishing it even from Grotius. Pufendorf followed Grotius in accepting that man's primary duty was to conserve society through maintaining a life which was sociable, that is, compatible with living with others in order and social bonding. But Pufendorf built his theory not only on Grotius but on the work of Grotius and Hobbes together, and he made a very specific concept of sociability, which he called *socialitas*, central to his system.

---

[5] The myriad of quaint terms used in the first half of the nineteenth century to describe this opposition to political economy and individualism (mostly French or Gallicisms in English) is catalogued by Arthur E. Bestor Jr., 'The Evolution of the Socialist Vocabulary', *Journal of the History of Ideas* 9 (1948): 259–302. Lorenz von Stein, *Der Sozialismus und Kommunismus des heutigen Frankreich* (Leipzig, 1842); *Die sozialistischen und kommunistischen Bewegungen seit der dritten französischen Revolution* (Stuttgart, 1848).

From the middle of the eighteenth century, it was his particular variety of modern jurisprudence, widely recognised as perhaps the most influential version of modern natural law, which was specifically called 'socialist' natural law.[6] This usage, which was quite widespread in Germany and Italy, survived in traces until the middle of the nineteenth century. As in many such instances of 'naming', the motivation behind describing Pufendorf and his followers as socialists was critical rather than celebratory. Apparently, this critique of jus-naturalist 'socialism' was initiated by representatives of Catholic natural law.[7] The complaint went beyond a critique of Pufendorf's attempt to over-systematise everything and derive too many diverse principles from a single notion of sociability instead of retaining Christian principles, such as the will of God, as the foundation. While Pufendorf's jurisprudence was thus seen by these critics as almost exclusively anchored in a concept of society as the effective ground of rights, duties, politics and religion, the more important kind of criticism was aimed at the particular kind of sociability which stood at the centre of Pufendorf's theory of society.

The complaint was the same which made the nineteenth-century, left-wing socialists (after the term 'socialist' had changed valorisation) call modern natural law 'individualism'. Instead of positing love, benevolence or any other directly and intentionally sociable trait (or sociable instinct) as the basis of man's ability to form society (like in Grotius), the *socialistae*, it was argued, constructed a theory of society based on self-regarding anti-social drives such as interests and utility. Pufendorf's socialist tradition was not only society centred; it had built its notion of society on what Kant later aptly termed 'unsocial sociability'.[8] Or to rephrase it in the language of the modern socialists (and of modern social science, I believe), Pufendorf's sociability, the foundational principle of socialist natural law, was built on the paradox of individualist sociability.

---

[6] See Gottlieb Hufeland, *Lehrsätze Naturrechts und der damit verbundenen Wissenschaften* (Jena, 1790), p. 16; and Ernst Ferdinand Klein, *Grundsätze der Natürlichen Rechtswissenschaft nebst eine Geschichte derselben* (Halle, 1797), p. 356.

[7] See Wolfgang Schieder, 'Sozialismus' in *Geschichtliche Grundbegriffe*, ed. by Otto Brunner, Werner Conze and Reinhart Koselleck, vol. 5 (Stuttgart, 1984), particularly §2: '"Socialistae", "socialisti" und "Socialisten" in der rechtphilosophischen Terminologie der frühen Neuzeit', pp. 924–934; Hans Müller, *Ursprung und Geschichte des Wortes „Sozialismus' und seiner Verwandten* (Hannover, 1967); L. H. A. Geck, *Über das Eindringen des Wortes 'sozial' in die Deutsche Sprache* (Gottingen, 1963); Rodolfo de Mattel, 'La prima apparizione in Italia di termini "socialismo" e "socialisti"', *Storia e Poiitica internazionaie* 20 (1941); Franco Venturi, 'Towards a Historical Dictionary: 'Socialism', in Venturi, *Italy and the Enlightenment: Studies in a Cosmopolitan Century*, ed. Stuart Woolf, trans. Susan Corsi (London, 1972), pp. 52–62.

[8] Immanuel Kant, *Idea for a Universal History from a Cosmopolitan Point of View*, in Kant, *On History*, p. 15.

Although these studies of vocabulary are useful to indicate earlier historical connections, which subsequent changes in political and academic language hide from our eyes, one would be unwise to claim too much on this basis alone. But tracing vocabularies back to their original use does indicate something quite important that have not been noticed in the historiography of social and political discourse, that is, that there was a direct link between the reform of political, moral and legal science inaugurated by the natural jurisprudence of Grotius, Hobbes and Pufendorf (the founding fathers) and the later discourse of human sciences centred on the key word 'social'. Following this route, we can gain a more intimate understanding of the meaning of the word 'social' in *la science sociale*. When I claim that the rise of *la science sociale* follows the tradition of natural jurisprudence, I mean that it follows socialist natural jurisprudence and not any other kind of natural jurisprudence, least of all the Christian jurisprudence of its anti-socialist critics. When one links this type of jurisprudence to the notion of commercial society, which is at the heart of both socialist natural law and social science, one needs to remind oneself that the kind of natural jurisprudence in question has been the grounding notion of the politics of modern liberty (of human rights) and hence also underlies the theory of modern representative republics, the predominant constitutional arrangement of the modern world. If this is right, then it should not be all that surprising that socialist natural law was quite unacceptable to the critics of these modern developments. Nonetheless, Orthodox Aristotelians, Catholics, fundamentalist Protestants, republicans, left-wing socialists and other kinds of communitarians and proponents of 'social sociability' (if one is allowed to turn Kant's phrase inside out) contributed significantly to the rise of the social sciences by exposing and developing this 'unsocial' concept of society in order to make their critique of it more devastating and appealing (Rousseau being the most famous of them).

Hegel's *bürgerliche Gesellschaft* as a Notion of Commercial Society

The notion of (commercial) society lying at the heart of socialist natural law is perhaps best-known today in the formulation Hegel gave to it as civil society or *bürgerliche Gesellschaft* (not in a 'Treatise of Social Science' but in his natural jurisprudence lectures entitled *Philosophy of Right*). This was for him a social system based on the abstract freedom and morality of the individual, where free individuals entered society via a system of reciprocities constituted by their effort of mutually satisfying human needs. Civil society was a commercial society because it was by its very nature transactional; the most important class of transaction in the social nexus was barter and exchange, commercial traffic in general. As a theory of society, this was the work of modern natural law, Hegel claimed, naming Pufendorf as its real modern starting point. The science whose task it was to work out how the myriads of commercial interactions in such a society actually operated was political economy. Society as a system of needs, Hegel also claimed, was the actual reality of modern history; it constituted the backbone of modern civilisation. In this sense, Hegel was a determined defender of civil society.

However, he was critical of the natural law theory of civil society as political theory. By reducing the role of the political to the defence of the underlying civilisatory framework of commercial society, that is, to the administration of justice and the sanctioning of morality, there was no space left in it for a higher kind of social ethics, *Sittlichkeit*, and it also excluded any chance of re-establishing the liberty of ancient republics. The mutual satisfaction of needs through commerce did indeed create a society, but not a 'political community' or 'state'. This latter point is worth emphasising. It is generally believed that the essence of the rise of the modern notion of society (i.e. commercial society) is dependent on a process of separation between theories of society and politics. This notion is usually supported by reference to Hegel's famous distinction between civil society and the state. But Hegel was not laying down a separation between civil society and the modern state *per se*. He was developing a critique of the minimalist political state most naturally complementary to civil society – to the politics of modern (abstract) liberty – from the point of view of Hegel's own ideal of politics, a politics of not only rights but of virtue. His critical search for such a politics of virtue in civil society – a search for a truly modern *polis* – is truly fascinating. But it should not hide from us the fact that in Hegel's view the theory of commercial society is part and parcel of the development of the modern natural law doctrine of politics, even if this liberal doctrine is denigrated by Hegel as not truly political. Civil society is not separated from politics as such, but rather it restricts the domain of the political to those practices which appear to be compatible with the modern world of civil (i.e. commercial) society. Although deeply dissatisfied with it, Hegel himself was prepared to defend the politics of 'unsocial sociability' from the various advocates of 'social sociability', whether they were Christians or lovers of ancient liberty. Hegel's distinction between civil society and the state was not identical to the later distinction between politics and society understood as voluntary associationism; it rather turned on the distinction between two notions of politics corresponding to two notions of sociability: a political and a utilitarian or economic one. His notion

Socialist Natural Law and Social Science 237

of the discourse most appropriate to civil society was nothing else but *la science sociale*, socialist natural law plus political economy.

Socialitas and Commercial Sociability

How did the concept of commercial or civil society, in the way it was captured by Hegel a century and a half later, enter Pufendorf's natural jurisprudence? 'Enter' is perhaps the wrong word here, implying some sort of spectacular intellectual innovation. The question is rather why and how it appeared to be more prominent in Pufendorf's influential rendering of the modern jus-naturalist tradition than in some others.[9] The rhetorical impact was unquestionably there. A reader who opens Pufendorf's book will meet very soon the statement that the basis of 'all natural law' is the 'social life of man' or *socialitas*, implying that there was no purpose or theoretical (or indeed theological) justification to be found anywhere for any theory concerning human beings which ignored the fact that humans invariably lived in society.[10] Pufendorf used *socialitas* as the cornerstone of the anti-relativist or anti-sceptical intellectual strategy which lay at the centre of the modern tradition which he claimed began with Grotius and was continued by Hobbes.[11] This strategy can be very briefly characterised by two crucial moves. The first involves an attack on late medieval, Scholastic Aristotelianism (particularly in its Catholic version) in the name of the pluralist, relativist and sceptical spirit of late humanist or post-Renaissance social and political thought. The second was an attempt to contain the dangerous impact of scepticism (particularly of moral and political scepticism) without giving up this modern, relativist idiom altogether. This was attempted by regrafting onto it the idea of a general set of universalist rules for mankind (natural law) but without invoking preconceived dogmatic and theological foundations. The aim was to look for the foundations of stability and peace for human societies, both internally and internationally, and this was

---

[9] See Hont, 'The Language of Sociability and Commerce: Samuel Pufendorf and the Theoretical Foundations of the "Four-Stages Theory"', in Pagden (ed.), *The Languages of Political Theory in Early-Modern Europe*, pp. 253–276; and Fiammetta Palladini, *Samuel Pufendorf Discepolo di Hobbes* (Bologna, 1990).
[10] Pufendorf, *DJNG*, 'Preface to the Second Edition', p. ix.
[11] For an analysis of the relationship between scepticism and the genesis of 'modern' natural law, see Richard Tuck, *Natural Rights Theories: Their Origins and Development* (Cambridge: Cambridge University Press, 1979); 'Grotius and Selden', in J. H. Burns and Mark Goldie (eds.), *The Cambridge History of Political Thought, 1450–1700* (Cambridge: Cambridge University Press, 1991), pp. 499–529; and *Philosophy and Government, 1572–1651* (Cambridge: Cambridge University Press, 1993).

thought to have required a search for minimalist and context- or culture-independent foundations on which everybody in principle could agree.

Grotius, and particularly Hobbes, found such a foundation in every human being's desire for self-preservation. Pufendorf followed them, but he rephrased Hobbes in such a way that the idea of self-preservation became overtly linked not simply to the idea of individual self-preservation but invariably, and from the beginning, to self-preservation in society. The general drift of this rephrasing did not depart from Hobbes in its ultimate direction. The purpose of natural law was to ensure peace in society, and *socialitas* was used by Pufendorf to establish a duty for the preservation of social peace for creatures whom he also saw as very much inclined to disturb peace.

Pufendorf's rhetorical highlighting of *socialitas* has often been misunderstood as an advocacy of natural sociability, which posits some innate or 'natural' drive or aptitude in human beings which compels them to seek human company, to be social. This, however, was not the case. Pufendorf shared with Hobbes the rather dark view of human nature as strongly anti-social, competitive, irritable, wicked and bent on malice and aggression. Pufendorf shared Hobbes' sceptical view of the human aptitude to live in peace 'naturally'. He also accepted Hobbes methodological innovation of trying to establish the core principles of society and politics through mental experiments by imagining how human beings could live in an imagined 'state of nature', that is, without institutions and civilisation. This anti-sceptical methodology required taking for granted only what could not be doubted, that is, nothing but what could be taken as the core characteristics of human nature, clearly observable in all or most individuals belonging to the human race.

Hobbes used this method to develop a new political science with a theory of sovereignty, political obligation and citizenship in a single, elegant and, as Hobbes hoped, incontrovertible theory. Hobbes contrasted a state of nature to the existence of a properly constructed civil or political society, the *civitas*, showing that in the first there was war, fear, instability and barbarism, while in the latter there was peace, order, culture and civilisation. Hobbes ridiculed the Aristotelian notion that man was a *zoon politikon*, a creature born for society, and demonstrated that the *civitas* was entirely constructed, artificial, adventitious. For a whole range of reasons, the Hobbesian contractualist doctrine of the state as directly emerging from the state of nature, conceived as a state of war, proved to be unacceptable to many of his contemporaries. Too much in this theory became a creation of the state, reducing the scope for theories of virtue and rights based on natural foundations directly linked to the experience of mankind. Pufendorf – in many ways the most Hobbesian of the non-Hobbists – developed a series of emendations to the Hobbesian doctrine in which the key move was to argue that humans could form society before they set up civil, that is, political societies, a society in which moral norms and laws, despite the general instability of human affairs, could operate and social bonding could happen. In such a way, the problems associated with creating a contractual civil society out of total anarchy and instability could be obviated, at least to a degree. Technically, Pufendorf initiated his move by bifurcating the model of a state of nature into the investigation of man without society and man without political society (i.e. man in society but without a state).[12] In the newly added model he had to ask the question: what would be the consequences of imagining human beings in isolation, without society, facing alone a life in the usual conditions of our natural environment?

Commercial Society as *koinonia*: The Platonic and Aristotelian Foundations

Inviting his readers to contemplate what would be the life of individuals in a state of nature as 'opposed to a life cultivated by the industry of men', Pufendorf (like Hobbes) took care not to assume the pre-existence of a natural sociability in man, deeming any historical knowledge of such things as fictitious and unverifiable. He thus had to build a theory of society for asocial and, indeed, unsocial individuals.[13] The model to which he turned to explain society, as many of his contemporaries did too, was commerce. Strangers can come together and exchange goods without forming closer community or exhibiting a desire for company or love, because they need the services or goods of each other.

Both man and animals, Pufendorf argued, desired self-preservation. The animal's abilities, its faculties, were matched to its needs and in this respect the animal was superior to man. But this close match also had its limitations. The needs of animals were finite and firmly bounded by natural abilities. If they lived or acted together in society they cooperated solely under the guidance of their appetites and instincts, which were

---

[12] The division Pufendorf devised was triadic, but the first model did not in fact correspond to the proper 'state of nature' abstraction procedure he described. It was rather restatement of the ancient *topos* according to which the life of human beings could be best understood by contrasting it to 'the Life of Brutes', Pufendorf, *De Officio*, 2.1.3; see also the new English translation, *On the Duty of Man and Citizen According to Natural Law*, ed. James Tully, trans. Michael Silverthorne (Cambridge: Cambridge University Press, 1991): 'Considered from the first point of view, the natural state of man is the condition in which he was placed by his Creator with the intention that he be an animal excelling other animals.'

[13] Pufendorf, *De Officio*, 2.1.4.

uniform in all members of the species. With the satisfaction of present need their cooperation ceased. Man's position in creation was truly paradoxical, since man was at the same time both inferior and superior to the animals. Although created with the same basic need for self-preservation, he lacked the corresponding ability. Man was a 'mute and ignoble Animal, Master of no Powers or Capacities', displaying nothing else but 'exceeding Weakness', a 'wonderful Impotency' and 'natural Indigence'.[14] But this condition of *imbecillitas* and necessitousness, *indigentia*, was not the end of the matter.

In contrast to animals, the structure of man's needs was radically different. Human needs were neither finite nor uniform across the species. The desires generated by the working of men's minds did not cease when the instinct of self-preservation was minimally satisfied. Even the most elementary needs were transformed by man's nature. Food had not only 'to satisfy his Belly, but tickle his Palate'. Similarly, despite the initial handicap with which he began his life, man was able to turn 'the Infirmity of his Nakedness into an Occasion of Vanity and Pride'. 'Besides', Pufendorf continued, 'do not Men float in a whole Tide of Affections and Desires, utterly unknown to Beasts?' The consequences of this plasticity and diversity of needs and desires could be read in two ways. On the one hand, Pufendorf argued, man was thus subject to 'prodigious Corruption and Degeneracy'; on the other, however, he was perfectible, 'more capable of fruitful Culture and of useful Improvement' than any other creature.[15]

Although the moral critique was undoubtedly present in this picture, the theory of commercial sociability was built on the possibility that man was an improving creature. While a human being was helpless alone, what men had discovered was that they could be of use to each other in escaping their indigence by joining their efforts. Once cooperation started, men could not only satisfy their basic needs but also perfect their life and then create new needs. They could set up a system of exchanges, a sort of commerce. In fact, in order to keep their mutual need for each other going on a sustained basis, that is, in order to preserve themselves as a 'society', they had to keep on with their commerce, creating a rising spiral of needs and their satisfaction. The theory of society presented here was a theory of needs, *Bedürfnisse*, leading to a theory of civilisation and to the idea of a fully developed commercial society.

Placing this theory of society as a 'system of needs' in this key position of natural jurisprudence was perhaps new, but the idea of specifying

[14] Pufendorf, *DJNG*^{K}, 2.1.8.
[15] Pufendorf, *DJNG*^{K}, 2.1.6.

need as the cause of society in itself was by no means innovative. Nor did Pufendorf pretend that it was. When discussing, in other chapters, the origins of commerce and the origins of the state, Pufendorf readily recalled this idiom of needs with reference to Plato and Aristotle. Pufendorf, who once contemplated a history of the Greek theories of the *polis*, knew that Plato had argued in the *Republic* that it was *indigentia* or need which was the sole or the principal cause of the rise of city.[16] He had pointed out that it was wrong to see this as the origin of the political state, but thereby he underlined only that it was something else, that is, 'society', which was created by need. When discussing commerce, Pufendorf, following Grotius, also cited the *locus classicus* from Aristotle's *Nicomachean Ethics*, stating that it was '*chreia* [need, *indigentia*] which holds everything together', everything meaning society, or *koinonia*, on all scales, including the general society of mankind.[17] This was no mere *obiter dicta* on Pufendorf's part. He discussed in detail whether *chreia* should be regarded – as the 'just price' tradition maintained – as the foundation of pricing but concluded that need in a direct sense was the underlying principle of exchange (*permutatio*), not its measure (*metron*). And again he repeated the fundamental Aristotelian notion underlying his model of sociability, pointing out that where there is 'continual traffick [*permutatio*] (...) there must be *societas* [*koinonia*]'.[18]

The Anthropology of Needs and Commercial Society in Adam Smith

The moral qualities and the anti- or at least a-political nature of this concept of society elaborated by Pufendorf gave rise to tremendous controversy in the seventeenth and eighteenth centuries. This makes it even more important to reiterate that the underlying theoretical idiom sustaining this theory of commercial society was one of the most enduring patterns of modern social thought. We have seen that, in itself, it was not a modern but an ancient concept. Plato's theory of the origins of the city, and particularly Aristotle's distinction between *koinonia* and *polis*, provided the source for the modern theory of society. The notion that society or *koinonia* was a 'system of needs' was immensely influential through the centuries. It appears in Cicero and Augustine and through them in several early modern streams of moral philosophy, including the Jansenists and the French moralists in Pufendorf's own time.

[16] Plato, *Republic*, 369b–c. Pufendorf's reference is 1.2.
[17] Aristotle, *Nicomachean Ethics*, 1133b.
[18] Ibid.; Pufendorf, *DJNG^K*, 5.1.12.

The very same characteristic arguments which Pufendorf had introduced to sustain his theory of civilisation – the contrast drawn between man and animal and society as held together by *chreia* – appear as much in Hegel's explanations of *bürgerliche Gesellschaft* as in Marx's 'Paris Manuscripts' (making him the only major modern author who was a socialist both in the old and the new sense).

Most noticeably, this very same idiom played a key part in Adam Smith's political economy. Famously, Smith announced that the foundation of the division of labour and commerce lay in the human 'propensity to truck, barter, and exchange one thing for another'.[19] But perhaps it is less well known that according to Smith all this was a consequence of the most paradoxical of contrasts which offers itself to the observer: animal and human nature. 'Man has received from the bounty of nature reason, ingenuity, art, contrivance, and capacity of improvement, far superior to that which she bestowed on any other animals', observed Smith, 'but is at the same time in a much more helpless and destitute condition with regard to the support and comfort of his life'.[20] Animals were fully equipped for self-preservation, men were not. But once they cooperated, Smith observed, they could easily surpass animals. A multiplicity of new needs could be satisfied, completely transforming their way of living. The higher standard of living was a result of the separation of occupations made possible by men bartering selfishly on their own behalf. It was not 'from the benevolence of the butcher, the brewer, or the baker, that we expect our dinner', Smith explained, 'but from their regard to their own interest'.[21]

This famous dictum was nothing else but an explanation of the difference between commercial and non-commercial sociability. The bonding agent of Christian sociability is love. In contrast, the sociability which holds together the society of those who do not love each other, who are neither benevolent nor charitable, nor comrades in faith, is exchange and mutual needs-satisfaction. Because of the obvious economic context of Smith's *Wealth of Nations*, his statement about modern society being a commercial society, where the majority are 'merchants', is usually read as a statement about the fast-increasing level of trade in modern times. The more we trade, the more commercial we become. While this is obviously true, Smith was not simply making an economic statement about the nature of trading societies. Commerce is not just trade.

---

[19] Smith, *WN*, I.ii.1; compare with *LJ*(A) vi.44; *LJ*(B), 219; *ED*, 2.12.
[20] Smith, *LJ*(A), vi.8; compare with *WN*, I.ii.2; *ED*, 2.12.
[21] Smith, *WN*, I.ii.2; compare with *LJ*(A) vi.46; *LJ*(B), 220; *ED*, 2.13.

It is worth recalling here Smith's account of Pufendorf's sociability theory. According to Smith, Pufendorf's aim was to defeat Hobbes' theory of virtue by showing that the 'state of nature was not a state of war but that society might subsist, tho' not in so harmonious a manner, without civil institutions'.[22] In his *Theory of Moral Sentiments*, Smith explained in a very similar fashion what would happen in a society where virtue, love and benevolence were not present. The preoccupation with personal interests and utility, he explained, did not necessarily cause such a society to collapse into internecine war. When men help each other from benevolence and charity, their society may be a happy place; but when they address themselves exclusively not to the 'humanity' of their fellows 'but to their self-love', Smith declared, 'the society, though less happy and agreeable, will not necessarily be dissolved'. For there was an alternative to both societies of 'social sociability' and war. 'Society', Smith concluded, 'may subsist among different men, as among different merchants, from a sense of its utility, without any mutual love or affection; and though no man in it should owe any obligation, or be bound in gratitude to any other, it may still be upheld by a mercenary exchange of good offices according to an agreed valuation'.[23] Political economy, he claimed, was the anatomy of such societies in operation.

Nicole and Commercial Society: The Legacy of St Augustine

It is often argued that Smith's moral theory of commercial society was as much indebted, or perhaps more, to the tradition of the French moralists and Mandeville than to Pufendorf and the other natural jurists. The overall view of this tradition is usually thought to be encapsulated by the Mandevillian slogan: private vices – public benefits. The essence of this tradition is seen as a rescue of selfishness – materialism, greed, the traditional vices – from moral odium in the name of a consequentialist utilitarianism of civilisation. It has recently been argued that Smith's theory of commercial society was a direct descendant of this tradition, and in particular of the moral thought of one of its most important French representatives, Pierre Nicole.[24]

---

[22] Smith, *LJ*(B), 3.
[23] Smith, *TMS*, II.ii.2. The whole section is entitled 'Of the Utility of this constitution of Nature'. What Smith meant by this 'constitution' was that 'man can only subsist in society' where all members 'stand in need of each other's assistance, and are likewise exposed to mutual injuries'.
[24] David Wootton, 'Introduction' to *Divine Right and Democracy: An Anthology of Political Writing in Stuart England* (Harmondsworth: Penguin Books, 1986), pp. 74–75.

A friend and collaborator of Pascal, Pierre Nicole (1625–1695) was a Jansenist and as such he was a follower of the social teaching and theology of Saint Augustine. He was interested in issues of grace and saintly virtue, and as an Augustinian he accepted the sharp moral and political contrast drawn between the City of God and the Earthly City. In their fight against the Jesuits and in their general moral criticism of the manners of the Earthly City the Jansenists and Nicole were drawing a sharp dividing line between the virtue of the elect and the moral universe of ordinary, fallen and sinful mankind. The picture of fallen man in Jansenist thought was very close to the dark view of human passions and social instability which informed the work of Hobbes, and in fact Nicole was very much influenced by Hobbes' political philosophy. Politically, Nicole accepted that the only institution which could tame the fear of others and control the boundlessness of human selfishness was the political state of absolute sovereignty.

Fallen mankind was void of charity, love and virtue. However, following Augustine, Nicole observed that men possessed by self-love could, and in fact did, simulate many of the practical effects of true sociability. On an intermediate level – between anarchy and state – even selfish men could form a society of mutual services. The model for this was commercial sociability. Why did people serve the tired traveller with food, accommodation and hospitality? Not out of love or virtue, Nicole answered, but rather out of a selfish desire which could be satisfied only through the traveller paying for these services. Lamentably, the kindness of the hotelier was not true love, but this was not as bad as it might sound, Nicole continued, since most of us would also settle just for the good service. Cupidity could lead to behaviour identical in practical consequences to the dictates of genuine sociability and fraternity. Civilisation, both in the sense of material provision through trade and through civility in manners, could thus soften the effect of man's sinful nature, without fundamentally changing it. With some difficulty and without true morality, the Earthly City could produce a kind of simulated, but nonetheless real, social peace.

In his essay 'Of the Means to Conserve Peace amongst Men', Nicole posited commercial society as the peaceful agency amongst strangers. Speaking from the position of a recipient of grace on pilgrimage in the Earthly City, Nicole gave a clear account of the theory of *koinonia*, as a society held together by need. 'The world then is our city' – he wrote (I quote John Locke's English translation) –

and, as inhabitants of it, we have intercourse with all mankind, and do receive from them advantages or inconveniences. The Hollanders have a trade with Japan, we with Holland; and so have commerce with those people at the furthest end of the world: because the profit the Hollanders draw from thence has an influence on us, since it furnishes them with the means of doing us more good than harm. The same may be said of all other nations. They are linked to us, on one side or other; and all enter into the chain, which ties the whole race of men together by their mutual wants.[25]

In a scathing moral criticism of modern manners, Nicole made it clear that true society or fellowship could exist only between the good and the charitable, who thus deserved the chance of receiving God's grace. The only society self-love could create among fallen men was commercial society. Such a society was not virtuous, but it was useful. In Nicole's rendering, peace in the *civitas terrena* could only be expected from commercial sociability. Those whom commerce and commercial sociability could not make civilised, on the other hand, had to be restrained by absolute government.

A German literary scholar, Hans-Jürgen Fuchs, has argued that there is a fundamental similarity between Pufendorf's and Nicole's theories.[26] If our account is right then this is indeed the case in a certain sense (although not quite in the sense Fuchs understood of it). Those orthodox Lutheran divines in Germany and Sweden who incessantly complained against Pufendorf saw this all too clearly.[27] Socialist jus-naturalism, they argued, made natural law out of the nature of man after the Fall. If this was indeed the case – and it was more obvious in Jansenist social theology than in Protestant natural law – then the consequences for the nature and origins of social science are indeed somewhat melancholy. The theory of 'society', as a theory of commercial society, was no more or less than a theory of society among men fallen from grace.

After Virtue: Commercial Sociability, the Politics of Fallen Man and the Science of Man

Far from making virtue out of self-love (that is what moral revalorisation would have required), these theories of commercial sociability suggested that virtuous sociability – virtue as a principle of society – was beyond the reach of the vast majority of human beings. If the theory of commercial sociability has initiated a divorce between 'society' and 'politics',

---

[25] Pierre Nicole, *Discourses Translated from Nicole's Essays by John Locke*, ed. Thomas Hancock (London, 1828). Discourse 3: 'Concerning the Way off Preserving Peace with Men', p. 99.
[26] Hans-Jürgen Fuchs, *Entfremdung und Narzismus: Semantische Untersuchungn zur Geschichte der 'Selbstbezogenheit' als Vorgeschichte von französisch 'amour propre'* (Stuttgart: J. B. Metzlersche Verlagsbuchhandlung, 1977).
[27] See this presented admirably by Fiammetta Palladini, *Discussioni Seicentesche su Samuel Pufendorf: Scritti Latini, 1663–1700* (Bologna: Il Mulino, 1978).

it has done so only in a very special (although not irrelevant) sense. It was indeed built on the strongest possible denial of any kind of politics requiring significant amounts of virtue. The suggestion that the *civitate Dei* could not be established in this world obviously followed from the Augustinian assumptions. More importantly, it also followed that if modern society was a mere *koinonia*, then the restoration of the ancient *polis* was impossible too. Love and virtue could unite small groups of men (the usual meaning of *societas*, i.e. a limited number of human beings associating for a certain purpose) but not whole societies. However, this was not a denial of a need for politics altogether. Since peace through love and virtue was deemed to be impossible, it was clear that fallen man needed political society, or the state, as the ultimate guarantor of social stability and peace.

Hobbes' insistence of the direct modelling of the origins of the state and political obligations from fear and sheer human competitiveness created a theory of politics irreducible to a theory of commercial society. For Hobbes there was no fallback position of a mere society; a political breakdown for him was the virtual certainty of social breakdown. In Pufendorf's idiom of natural law the need for the political state arose only when the growth of population and the pathological manifestations of human need – cupidity, greed, selfishness – destabilised society to such a degree that positive (i.e. political) regulation of society became necessary. In this eventual need for a strong state, Pufendorf, like most other theorists of the age (Locke, Hume and Smith definitely not excluded) concurred with Hobbes. But once Pufendorf argued that before the *civitas* there could be society with a tolerable amount of peace, others could continue arguing that under certain conditions this commercially constituted network of human social coexistence could in itself contain (confine, curb, control) the dynamics of those centrifugal and corrosive human passions whose free rein in society called for the introduction of state legislation. Nicole in particular, following Augustine's hints, had shown effectively how man's acquisitive and competitive drives could be trapped in a web of self-restraint if the manners of civility were allowed to masquerade freely.

'After virtue' one had to have one's trust in the human power of understanding society.[28] As Immanuel Kant famously argued at the end of the eighteenth century, anybody who wanted to become a Kepler or Newton of the science of humankind had to start with the recognition of how mankind, through the civilising process, could develop a 'law-governed

---

[28] [Hont is implicitly referring to Alasdair MacIntyre's influential book *After Virtue: A Study in Moral Theory* (Notre Dame: University of Notre Dame Press, 1981).]

social order' (*gesetzmäßigen Ordnung*) from the pathologically enforced social union based on the 'unsocial sociability' of men. Man – Kant reiterated the humanist-sceptical (or Augustinian) view – was a creature constantly craving for 'honour, power or property', that is, 'status among his fellows, whom he cannot *bear* yet cannot *bear to leave*'.[29] 'Without these asocial qualities (far from admirable in themselves) which cause the resistance inevitably encountered by each individual as he furthers his self-seeking pretensions', he wrote, 'men would live an Arcadian, pastoral existence of perfect concord, self-sufficiency and mutual love'. But such life in community, he claimed, would have denied to mankind its specifically human capacity of being able to develop culture and civilisation. Nature endowed man with physical abilities only in the most niggardly manner: 'nature gave him neither the bull's horns, the lion's claws, nor the dog's teeth, but only his hands'.[30] But his design has also included the germs of man's eventual superiority over animals, the possibility of a glorious liberation from nature's constraints. Social incompatibility, enviously competitive vanity and insatiable desires were the catalysts of this liberation. The science of man, Kant maintained, starts only when one recognises that the unsocial sociability of man does 'seem to indicate the design of a wise creator – not, as it might seem, the hand of a malicious spirit who had meddled in the creator's glorious work or spoiled it out of envy'.[31]

On this basis, the idea of a sub-political social order emerged, the idiom which Albert Hirschman described in his book on 'the passions and the interests' as the political argument for capitalism before its triumph.[32] Very few thinkers (Paine, Saint-Simon, Marx, etc.) came to invest so much confidence in society – commercially constituted society that is – that they could envisage a future without the need for a political state to control society at all, a pure administration of things, without a government of men. But many argued, increasingly, that in the presence of a political state enforcing the rules of justice (including the rules of

[29] Kant, 'Idea for a Universal History with a Cosmopolitan Purpose', *KPW*, p. 44.
[30] For Kant's thought on this *topos* of comparing man to animal, see also his 1771 review of Pietro Moscati's *Von dem körperlichen wesentlichen Unterschiede zwischen der Struktur der Tiere und Menschen. Eine akademische Rede, gehalten auf dem anatomischen Theater zu Pavia...* (Göttingen, 1771) [Kant's review was published anonymously in Königsbergische Gelehrte und Politische Zeitungen, no. 67. The review has been translated into English under the title 'Review of Moscati's Work of the Corporeal Essential Differences between the Structure of Animals and Humans' and published in Kant, *Anthropology, History, and Education*, ed. Robert B. Louden and Günter Zöller (Cambridge: Cambridge University Press, 2007), pp. 78–81.]
[31] Kant, 'Idea for a Universal History', *KPW*, p. 45.
[32] Albert O. Hirschman, *The Passions and the Interests: Political Arguments for Capitalism before Its Triumph* (Princeton, NJ: Princeton University Press, 1977).

private property) and providing the security which Hobbes called for, there was no further need for the political control of that substratum of political society which was pure commercial society itself. Both Adam Smith, and in a different way the French *économistes*, posited the possibility of 'natural liberty' within the system of modern politics. However, for this new politics of liberty really to work – the politics of commercial society – an ever more extensive, and eventually universal, commercial society had to be helped into existence.

In theory, the politics of commercial society seemed a much less demanding idea than the politics of virtue. After all it required no heroic effort from men beyond keeping up their desire for trying to satisfy their needs. While moralists (i.e. the adherents of 'social sociality') complained from the seventeenth century onwards that there was far too much commercial sociability already in existence, in practice the extension from the core to the peripheries, and the drawing of ever-larger parts of the population into the orbit of purely commercial social bonding within the more commercially developed nations, proved to be a task more difficult than ever imagined. It appeared that there was enough commercial sociability in modern society to make the politics of virtue impossible, but not enough to keep the peace. The comparative statics of pre- and postlapsarian man – or man in the state of nature versus in culture and civilisation – had to be replaced by modelling a long and difficult civilising process. The jus-naturalist methodology was replaced by theoretical histories of civilisation elaborating the contrast with barbarism and violence in a dynamic rather than static fashion. Both supporters and opponents of the great Enlightenment reform project of converting the Earthly City into a commercial civilisation soon discovered that the actual shape, ground structure and *modus operandi* of commercial sociability must be understood in detail in order to deal with the consequences of this process. Political economy and social science were the direct and explicit outcome of this recognition.

Natural jurisprudence became the favourite discourse of the Enlightenment, because by its very nature it was a discourse of reform. It was the antidote to the thoroughgoing political and moral relativism of the sceptics; what it offered was the possibility of criticising the politics and morals of actually existing individual states from the point of view of the standards of mankind. It pitted the general against the particular, the lawlike against the historically contingent. In this sense, it was by its very nature highly subversive. When natural jurisprudence as a coherent intellectual and political project ran into difficulties in the late eighteenth century and gave way to political economy and social science, its demise partly stemmed from this fact. It was a rather blunt tool for practical reform, since it relied on a direct contrast between the normative demands of the *ordre naturel*, the general model of human society and its laws, and the positive, man-made, and hence imperfect, systems prevailing in the various countries of Europe and their colonial dependencies. The French *économistes* were rather extreme proponents of the use of natural law in just this way – as the guide for comprehensive, radical and hence final reform. This generated much opposition, and most of the social science of the late eighteenth century benefited from the insights into the social order produced by the critical opposition to Physiocracy. However, it would be misleading to see the essence of the move from natural law to social science and political economy as an abandonment of the normative reform project.

What has failed was rather the idea of using the word 'natural' to describe the sources of moral, political and economic normativity. The classics of modern natural law were quite clear from the beginning that the word 'natural' was far too ambiguous a phrase to characterise their project. The discourse, certainly the socialist variety (in the more general, Grotian sense) was often called *jus naturae sociale*, but the adjective '*naturale*' became the dominant one as the signifier which demarcated the laws of society in general from the laws of any particular society. The problem was compounded by the introduction of Hobbes' new methodology: to demonstrate the general features of the social and political order by positing its counterpart in an imaginary 'state of nature'. The purpose of this kind of thought experiment originally was to make the demonstration of the nature of general social order more scientific and hence more effective as a discourse of legitimation. The sole aim of imagining a 'state of nature' was to understand its opposite better, the 'state of society' (civil society). But once the genie was out of the bottle, it gained a life of its own. Speculation about possible versions of the state of nature proliferated, and it became the natural terrain of desperately bitter debates about the origins of human sociability. The most characteristic strategic move in natural jurisprudence in the mid eighteenth century was the dropping of the hypothesis of a 'state of nature' from the armoury of critical social and legal thought. As Adam Smith pointed out in his natural jurisprudence lectures, it was paradoxical for Pufendorf to prove against Hobbes that society could exist in the state of nature, for on his own account a state of nature thus has never existed.[33] Rousseau, in his immensely influential prize essay on the sources of inequality among men, has shown that the state of nature, as it really existed in the scientific anthropological sense, had no relevance for the solution of modern

[33] Smith, *LJ*(B), 3.

social and political problems. Hume had no time for the state of nature either. And in *The Spirit of Laws*, Montesquieu showed that the best way of developing a critical legal science was to relate laws to the nature of the social and political system within which they functioned.

Dropping the state of nature hypothesis from the elaboration of natural law truly made it a normative and general system of the laws of man in society, *jus sociale*. To distinguish it from natural law, it became renamed as the science of the legislator, *l'art social, la science social* or *la science l'ordre social*. It was the consummation of Grotius' and Pufendorf's socialist jurisprudence. It was not an empirical science simply describing how societies had actually functioned in the past or in the present. It was essentially concerned with elaborating a normative framework for institutional reform. When Sieyès used the term *la science sociale* in his *Qu'est-ce-que le tiers-état?* – in a clarion call for the destruction of the aristocratic monarchical order of France – he claimed it was the tool of disinterested general reform, which would make France conformable to the general model of modern society. From his text, and most abundantly from his copious notes (which have recently been made available for modern scholarship), we know that his reform strategy was a socialist one in the Pufendorfian, jus-naturalist sense.[34] He posited as the model of society a general system of exchange based on the division of labour and claimed that, henceforth, labour was the only valid ticket to the membership of society. In all likelihood, he never wrote his planned treatise on socialism, but we understand that he made the pre-existence of commercial society the necessary condition of the success of the modern representative republic.[35] Few would dispute that this position, and this interpretation of *la science sociale*, is the cornerstone of our modern culture of politics and social science too. Where would, one might ask, a 'great transition' lead us from here?

Note on Chapter 6

This is a paper that Hont gave on several occasions, the first time seemingly at a conference in Uppsala at the Collegium for Advanced Study in the Social Sciences, 5–7 October 1990. The title of the paper at

---

[34] Emmanuel Sieyès, *Ecrits Politiques*, ed. Roberto Zapperi (Paris: Editions des Archives Contemporaine, 1985), pp. 45–91. [On Sieyès and socialism, see Hont, 'The Permanent Crisis of a Divided Mankind: "Contemporary Crisis of the Nation State" in Historical Perspective', *Political Studies* 42 (1994): 193n49; *Jealousy of Trade*, p. 476n43].

[35] [Among Sieyès' manuscripts there is a note suggesting that he at one point planned to write a *Traité du socialisme ou du but que se propose l'homme en société et des moyens qu'il y a d'y parvenir*. See Hont, 'The Permanent Crisis of a Divided Mankind', p. 193n49.]

that point was 'Commercial Society, Civilisation, Political Economy: A Contribution to the Understanding of the Idea of Social Science'. The text reproduced here is based on the latest version prepared for a conference in Uppsala in 1993 on 'The Great Transition: Discourses on Society and the Rise of the Social Sciences'. The paper revisits many of the key thinkers and themes of the *Culture, Needs and Property Rights* project, relating them to the question of the rise of social science in the eighteenth century.

7 Unsocial Sociability
Eighteenth-Century Perspectives

The paper for tonight is not a simple or traditional one. I wish to report on research in progress, both on the first results of a larger research project I am involved with and on my individual research project which is attached to it. In these research projects, on both levels, my collaborators and I experience difficulties and our thoughts are somewhat improvised at this stage. Opening up the issues which are involved would therefore help a great deal, and I hope that tonight some such help will be forthcoming.

On the more general level, instead of developing a single argument in detail my chief aim is to call attention to a discourse, a language, a matrix of conceptual idiom in eighteenth-century thought, because I and my partners in this international project wish to claim that without focusing on it more purposively, or indeed without focusing on it at all (as is often the case), we cannot advance in our understanding of the birth of modern political thought. The language or conceptual idiom in question is the language of society or sociability. It is needless to emphasise the relevance of the concept of society for modern discourse; social science and sociology (as the terms imply) would be inconceivable without it. What interests us, and me personally, however, is not sociology but modern political discourse and the role of the concept of society in it (I don't care much about the current disciplinary divide between sociology, politics and history; I wish to keep them together). Today the concept of civil society is in the forefront of political discussion, both in practice and in theory and one wonders whether we have a clear and agreed understanding of what it means. It is pretty clear, actually, that we don't. In actual fact the reintroduction of the concept of civil society into current discussion is the result of a borrowing from the conceptual vocabulary of oppositional social and intellectual movements in Eastern Europe in the decaying phase of what once was sarcastically called 'really existing socialism'. As the reputation of Marxism waned in the West, this East European vocabulary (actually a misunderstood and bastardised Hegelo-Marxian language) has been imported Westwards. Since I am an East European myself, you will forgive me if I refuse to share the Western enthusiasm for this Eastern import. From an East European perspective this could only be seen as a cruel joke, perhaps the joke or cunning of history, if not of individuals. Civil society was intended to Westernise Eastern Europe, which at the time laboured under very sorry conditions. The very idea that the West could renovate itself with the help of tentative East European efforts of Westernisation seems to me fraught with unsolvable contradictions. However, there is a salutary lesson here. If I am right that civil society is the ideal-type of what Western society is, the West certainly does not need to import itself. But in terms of political thought, it may – indeed I am certain that it does – indicate that the West forgot what it is. This amnesia now produces an interesting spectacle. Karl Marx once prophesised that the intellectual and theoretical development of the Left will have to repeat the entire development of Western thought (and of society itself), exploring every *cul-de-sac* and blind alleyway which have been previously explored in grand political culture. Little he suspected that after the predictable demise of the vulgarised and bastardised version of his own avant-garde insights this very process will also be repeated in the reverse. Nowadays it is fashionable to praise the so-called utopian socialists over Marx and inevitably the concept of civil society is also a major vehicle in this retrograde journey. Retreating from Marxism, post-Marxism for some now means reading Tom Paine and the anti-federalists. Political theory at the end of the twentieth century, for a not at all insignificant group, is the rehash of the political thought of the eighteenth century. This is more generally true than just for those who now retreat from Marxism to republicanism and civil society, about whom I just spoke. The other tendencies, if I may call them like that, also travel under late eighteenth-century banners, Kant, Rousseau, Smith and Burke being the foremost among them. Each of these can be and is often called a theorist of civil society.

Historians of political thought tend to be dismissive of this categorisation. The term civil society did exist in the late eighteenth century, but it meant the *societas civilis*, the *res publica*, the commonwealth, the state, in the sense of the political (i.e. civil) state. The modern term civil society is a corruption of Hegel's term *bürgerliche Gesellschaft* (a German translation of the *civitas*) and is not applicable to late eighteenth-century thought (or not directly and unreflectively in any case). Hegel's notion was a critique of a certain conception of the state, not a subset of the state in some general sense, and specifically not in spatially specifiable terms. What would be a meaningful question to ask is not what the eighteenth-century meaning of *civil society* was but what the meaning of the term *society* was, including every kind of society and ultimately the true *civil society*, the state. More precisely, the question has to be directed towards the preconditions of the existence of society and state; towards the human ability to form, sustain and preserve society – in other words, towards sociability. The question in the eighteenth century was not so much to make a distinction between civil society and the state but to ask questions about the agency in each state-form and hence form of civil society, both morally and politically. State and society are determined by the quality of the community they give shape to, and it was understood that the various notions of states represented various conceptions of *sociability*, various modes of human agency and ability to create and sustain the forms of political societies in question. This is, of course, pretty obvious and in one or another form we all know this. Every theory of society and civil society, that is, the state, presupposes a theory of human nature, or to use the vocabulary developed by German idealist philosophy in the wake of Kant, a philosophical and political anthropology. That part of the theory of human nature or philosophical anthropology which directly deals with the foundations of society is, and was in the eighteenth century, called the theory of sociability. Any theory of society is (and logically must be) predicated on a theory of sociability. My *prima facie* criticism of contemporary theories of civil society and the movement to return to eighteenth-century (or earlier) political discourses is that they neglect or, worse, fudge the question of the underlying sociability.[1]

Talking about the eighteenth century or Enlightenment political thought as a unity with a theory of sociability attached to it makes no sense at all. What needs to be looked at is what happens in any place at any time, a debate (and not a single one but a series of debates) which defines the patterns within which thinkers line themselves up. I do not wish to ask what the eighteenth-century view of sociability was but what were the eighteenth-century views (in the plural) and what conception of society or politics was supported by each. I do not wish to labour this point because it seems to be such an obvious one. It is mainly in this sense that the history of political thought can be useful for modern political thinking. The very idea that we can or should return to a political idiom in the past implies that something which started in the past

---

[1] The only discourse which remembers its historical roots in this sense is the American inspired libertarian theory of civil society. And I don't talk here about the reverse movement of so-called post-modernism which denounces the entire eighteenth century as a foundationalist project precisely because it had a theory of sociability or human nature underlying it. The price which post-modernism pays for this is not to have a theory of society and politics at all, and it can be shown to be a descendent of arguments in the Enlightenment rather than simply against it.

continues up to today. But if that past idea had actually been noticed in its own time or subsequently, what makes sense is not just to return to the past idea which we favour but to return to the debate within which it was inscribed. Thereby we can know what the perceived weaknesses of that idea were, what the answers to it were and what happened to the dialectic of opposing positions. Otherwise we are just condemned to the repeating of cycles of debates without any, dare I say, progress effected. Some modern theorists of civil society have discovered that it does not work without a theory of popular sovereignty, but by proposing its revival they seem to have forgotten that debates about popular sovereignty were the very origin of that line of thought from which the idea of 'civil society' (in the modern, bastardised sense) emerged, precisely as a solution for avoiding the seemingly intractable difficulties of the concept of popular sovereignty. What I am proposing is the idea that these difficulties (not all of them, but some very important ones) can be correlated with various conceptions of human nature and specifically with various notions of the human ability to form society, for example, with various theories of sociability. Those who appeared in the great French revolutionary debates of the early 1790s clearly thought in these terms; Sieyès on the one hand, Robespierre and particularly Saint-Just on the other, were clearly devoted followers of diametrically opposed theories of sociability, and hence had very different perspectives on the nature of the newly emerging French republic.[2]

My professional interest of course is not simply to deploy the history of political thought against those who ignore it or practise it in a naïve fashion but rather to ask questions about sociability within the history of eighteenth-century political and social thought. Wearing my Cambridge hat rather than my Hungarian one, I can perhaps safely say that we haven't yet achieved sufficient clarity in understanding the political thought of the eighteenth century, and any summing it up, for example in the form of a *Cambridge History of 18th-Century Political Thought*, is distinctly premature.[3] The entire project of writing the history of political thought in Cambridge is driven by the desire of counteracting the sort of historical amnesia I talked about in relation to modern theories of civil society. There is also a distinct wish to get away both from the shapes of modern hegemonic discourses of political and moral theory and from

---

[2] [See Hont, 'The Permanent Crisis of a Divided Mankind: "Contemporary Crisis of the Nation State" in Historical Perspective', *Political Studies* 42 (1994): 192–217.]

[3] [A decade later, in 2006, a work with this title was published with a contribution by István Hont. See Hont, 'The Early Enlightenment Debate on Commerce and Luxury', in Mark Goldie and Robert Wokler, eds., *The Cambridge History of Eighteenth-Century Political Thought* (Cambridge: Cambridge University Press, 2006), pp. 377–418.]

hegemonic modes of earlier (chiefly German) attempts to write the history of political thought. But the new results, which as you can imagine I appreciate very highly indeed, are very partial; partly they still mirror the patterns of the hegemonic modern discourses which they were conceived as the critique of. We have ended up with two historical discourses for the seventeenth and eighteenth centuries, which we see as locked in debate: neo-classical republicanism and modern natural law. Recently, Christianity has been added to this, and this in itself tells us everything about the lowly starting point of this project of reconstruction (how could it happen that the most vulgar kind of Enlightenment propaganda became, even temporarily, a guide for serious historiography?). More recently, 'reason of state' has been added and linked to natural law (the obviousness of which did not escape earlier generations of scholars who saw natural law as a discourse on international law), but in many ways these discourses are still researched separately, each in its own tunnel (to use John Pocock's evocative self-description of his project). The task now is to see these discourses not simply as locked in debate with each other (this clearly happened) but penetrating and criss-crossing each other, as organised along various axes of specific debates. This is particularly relevant for the eighteenth century, for if we accept (at least temporarily, as a working hypothesis) that the seventeenth-century set up various, clearly delineated, post-humanist discourses, surely the eighteenth century was a more eclectic one, trying to grapple with the tensions set up within the previous theoretical constellation. As natural law, for example, became the dominant teaching discourse of the eighteenth century, it lifted most previous debates within its disciplinary boundaries, which made it very eclectic indeed and ultimately led to its demise as a far too broad and unwieldy container of so many incompatible views.

The starting point of my current enquiry, and the larger project I have mentioned, is an attempt to reconceive the history of natural jurisprudence as a multifarious discourse of rather disparate elements. Moreover, I am interested in its relation to the emergence of political economy, which in many ways became the successor discourse to modern natural jurisprudence, especially in its capacity as a theory of commercial society. Looking at the internal debates within natural law – a reservoir of moral, theological, legal, political and economic discourses – it is clearly insufficient to see it as a counterweight to republicanism, as a discourse of rights against a discourse of virtue. I am, moreover, looking for fissures within this reservoir discourse which separate out the different mainstreams of moral and political thought within it, privileging those which lead to the development of political economy, which I take to be a constitutive discourse of modern republicanism as against neo-classical or ancient ones. The proposition is that a key element in such an exercise of differentiation and reconstruction of intra-discursive – as opposed to inter-discursive – debate is precisely a theory of sociability, that is, the theory of the various kinds of societies which can be carriers of various political forms, moral life and legality. Discussions of sociability occur in current historiographical debates, but rarely explicitly. The project in which I am involved wishes to focus on this particular stream of debate and see whether it helps us to break out from our self-imposed, discursive straitjacket of republicanism, natural law and Christianity. What I want to do is to look at the notion of sociability in the political thought of Immanuel Kant, then show some of the lineages of his views (necessarily very cursorily, because it is an enormous topic) and to say something about its importance for a particular conundrum in the history of political though in which I am particularly interested, the so-called *Das Adam Smith Problem*.[4] The essence of the latter is that there is a deep incoherence in Adam Smith's theory of society, that his two major works express two different views of sociability, the *Wealth of Nations* a frigid and detached one, a true variety of capitalist civil society, the *Theory of Moral Sentiments* a more humane and hence sociable variety, centring on the notion of sympathy between human beings. In its crude version the thesis is obviously wrong, but the recent total debunking of it I take to be a sign of gross insensitivity towards the more sophisticated problem lying under it, without which Smith's theory of civil society, which I take to be the dominant one today, remains incomprehensible and incoherent. It opens the door to such crude statements as that of ex-Prime Minister Mrs Thatcher – an advocate of a vulgar-Smithian, libertarian version of civil society – that there is no such thing as 'society'.[5] The essence of my reading is that the *Theory of Moral Sentiments* can only be understood if it is seen as a theory of sociability. There is not so much a problem with what Smith did (whereby I don't mean that his work was perfect or even that it was successful within its own terms), but rather there was a problem which Smith tried to grapple with, and which we need to understand in these terms.

The title of my talk tonight is not simply 'Sociability: Eighteenth-Century Perspectives' but 'Unsocial Sociability', which refers to a famous phrase by Kant, the most widely known occurrence of which is in his philosophy of history, that is, in his theory of the development of

---

[4] [On the 'Adam Smith Problem', see Hont, *Politics in Commercial Society: Jean-Jacques Rousseau and Adam Smith*, ed. Béla Kapossy and Michael Sonenscher (Cambridge, MA: Harvard University Press, 2015), ch. 2, pp. 25–47.]

[5] [Margaret Thatcher in an interview with Douglas Keay from September 1987. The Margaret Thatcher Archive (THCR 5/2/262).]

the human species. I want to focus on his deliberate oxymoron, because it reveals a central facet of the eighteenth-century debate I am interested in, namely that the choice was not simply between sociability and a-sociality, but that there was a third term which had no name, at least not before Kant, and whose presence makes the restoration of the debate much more complicated in terms of political languages. Anybody who wanted to become a Kepler or Newton of the science of humankind must start with the recognition of how mankind, through the civilising process, could develop a 'law-governed social order' (*gesetzmäßigen Ordnung*) from the pathologically enforced social union based on the 'unsocial sociability' of men. Man – Kant reiterated the late humanist sceptical (or Augustinian) view – was a creature constantly craving for 'honour, power or property', that is, 'status among his fellows, whom he cannot *bear* yet cannot *bear to leave*'.[6] 'Without these unsocial qualities (far from admirable in themselves) which cause the resistance inevitably encountered by each individual as he furthers his self-seeking pretensions', he wrote, 'men would live an Arcadian, pastoral existence of perfect concord, self-sufficiency and mutual love'.[7] But such life in community, he claimed, would have denied to mankind its specifically human capacity of being able to develop culture and civilisation. Nature endowed man with physical abilities only in the most niggardly manner: 'nature gave him neither the bull's horns, the lion's claws, nor the dog's teeth, but only his hands' – Kant paraphrased the famous Urtext of this in Seneca's discourse on benevolence.[8] But his design has also included the germs of man's eventual superiority over animals, the possibility of a glorious liberation from nature's constraints. 'Social incompatibility', 'enviously competitive vanity' and insatiable desires were the catalysts of this liberation. The science of man, Kant maintained, starts only when one recognises that the unsocial sociability of man 'seem to indicate the design of a wise creator – not, as it might seem, the hand of a malicious spirit who had meddled in the creator's glorious work or spoiled it out of envy'.[9]

The Hobbesian overtones of Kant's notion (witness his account of the 'mania for domination' in his *Anthropology*) were both obvious and entirely deliberate.[10] The emphasis was on all the anti-social traits of

---

[6] Immanuel Kant, 'Idea for a Universal History with a Cosmopolitan Purpose', *KPW*, p. 44.
[7] Kant, 'Idea for a Universal History', *KPW*, p. 45.
[8] Kant, 'Idea for a Universal History', *KPW*, p. 43. [Seneca, *De beneficiis*, 2.29.1.]
[9] Kant, 'Idea for a Universal History', *KPW*, p. 44.
[10] Immanuel Kant, *Anthropology from a Pragmatic Point of View* [1798] (Carbondale: Southern Illinois University Press, 1978), part I, bk. III, §85.

man, but it was also made clear that there was no such thing as a man truly outside society, that none of these competitive or anti-social traits meant anything without other men constantly being present, that this was not how things ought to be, but nonetheless how things really were. His view was very dark, almost rivalling Pascal's *Pensées* (1670). It is not just that man is the victim of 'external nature', so that he is ravaged by 'destructive operations – plague, famine, flood, cold, attacks from animals great and small'.[11] What is still worse is that his own 'inner nature' – his psychology or (as Kant will have it) 'pathology' – 'betrays him into further misfortunes' such as 'the oppression of lordly power' and the 'barbarism of wars', so that the human race has 'ruin', not happiness, to look forward to. Indeed, Kant insists, the 'value of life for us, measured simply by what we enjoy (...) by happiness, is easy to decide. It is less than nothing.'[12] But at the same time this very darkness was the only basis of Kant's famed optimism. It was the basis of his famous theory of 'practical teleology'. In this respect, as in many others, Kant was a dualistic thinker. There was no possibility for 'unsocial sociability' to be part of his moral theory, or the basis of natural law as far as he had subscribed to such a notion. As we shall see later this dualism is crucial for the understanding of his system. Some resolution of this tension was attempted in his third *Critique*, the *Critique of Judgment* (1790), whose importance for the understanding of Kant's thought cannot be underestimated. But a full exposition of the third *Critique*'s theory of practical teleology cannot be our task here and, in any case, it is a difficult theory which requires an understanding of Kant's theology as well (I am not sure that I understand all its facets). On the other hand, it is crucial to notice that 'unsocial sociability' is a more permanent fixture of his thought than sometimes assumed. It occurs not only in the essay on *Universal History* (1784) but also in his anthropology lectures and various essays on anthropology; it figures in the third *Critique*, in the famous essay on *Perpetual Peace* (1795) and in the late masterpiece on the *Contest of the Faculties* (1798). One should take note of the fact that the unsocial sociability treated in *Idea for a Universal History* is not just a datum of 'social psychology' for Kant but has an end or *telos* or function: its purpose is to hasten the advent of a 'perfect civic constitution' and a cosmopolitan peace.[13] He wants to show that even something pathological such as unsocial sociability may (by an infinite path) lead towards ends that we 'ought to have' on moral grounds alone. For Kant,

---

[11] Kant, *Critique of Judgement*, §83.
[12] Ibid.
[13] Kant, 'Idea for a Universal History', *KPW*, p. 47.

a pathological motive may 'legally' advance moral ends that should have been pursued. Moral ends such as peace, though they ought to be pursued from good will alone, may be slowly approximated from the 'legal' wish to survive (eternal self-love): even an intelligent 'devil' – not just 'unsocial' but malevolent-bad-willing may, after long and devastating experience, embrace *Pax Perpetua*. The whole enterprise of civilisation, Kant says, amounts to 'splendid misery'.[14] But what redeems that misery is the fact that antagonistic social relations (e.g. unsocial sociability) provide the occasion for the springing up of a 'civil community', a community which will legally realise some moral ends even in the absence of good will. In his theory of history and practical politics, Kant uses the notion of 'unsocial sociability' to prove that antagonistic civilisation will accrue a profit to the human race without moral improvement.

> Violence will gradually become less on the part of those in power, and obedience toward the laws will increase. There will no doubt be more charity, less quarrels in legal action, more reliability in keeping one's word, and so on in the commonwealth, partly from a love of honour, and partly from a lively awareness of where one's own advantage lies, and this will ultimately extend to the external relations between the various peoples, until a cosmopolitan society is created. Such developments do not mean, however, that the basic moral capacity of mankind will increase in the slightest, for this would require a kind of new creation or supernatural influence.[15]

It is perhaps worth hammering the point just a little bit more, since one of the most fashionable new tendencies in contemporary civil society theory is to refer back to Kant's essay on *Perpetual Peace* and its notion of a cosmopolitan civil society. These modern variants (with their elaborate institutional designs) resemble, however, a rehashed version of the ideas of the Abbé St Pierre more than that of Kant. The notion of 'unsocial sociability' in that context means for Kant that the chief agency of peacemaking is war, the politics of passions being pitted against passions (a condition of right was possible, he wrote, even among devils, if the organisation of their state was crafty enough, opposing passion to passion), rather than a march of reason and universal goodwill, or sociability (obviously now in a sense of some sort of 'social sociability'). For Kant there were two paths towards an eternal peaceful equilibrium between 'Republican' governments of consenting citizens (who increasingly dissent from war and violence): the purely moral path of good will, which aims at an (automatically peaceful) Kingdom of Ends or 'ethical commonwealth' and the path of intelligent self-love, whose

[14] Kant, *Critique of Judgement*, §83; *KPW*, p. 49.
[15] Kant, 'The Conflict of the Faculties', *KPW*, p. 188.

near-fatal, unsocial collisions with other self-loving selves may inspire (perhaps reluctantly) an attachment to 'culture' and 'right'. To be sure, these paths are in no way equal. But Kant's optimism was invested in the second rather than the first path.

Wars, tense and unremitting military preparations, (...) are the means by which nature drives nations to make initially imperfect attempts, but finally, after many devastations, upheavals and even complete inner exhaustion of their powers, to take the step which reason could have suggested to them even without so many sad experiences – that of abandoning a lawless state of savagery and entering a federation of peoples.[16]

It was only the distress of actually experienced war, he argued, which would lead countries to the negotiating table. At first, states certainly try to subjugate each other in order to establish peace. It will be sheer exhaustion within any state which will lead to a constitutional reform that limits the ability of the sovereign to wage war or create public debt. Wars, Kant wrote, were just so many successive attempts to remodel inter-state relations. Only after the ability for sustained warfare was diminished, would legal international arrangements be automatically favoured for security reasons. Threats of war usually push states into a frenzy of negotiation, 'just as if (*als ob*) they had entered into a permanent league for this purpose; for by the very nature of things, large military alliances can only rarely be formed, and will even more rarely be successful.'[17]

If people did not wish to form a state out of duty or morality, they were forced to organise themselves to repel their aggressive neighbours. Political expediency required, Kant wrote, that the empirical conditions which permit the proposed end can be assumed to exist. For in the creation of cosmopolitan order much knowledge of nature (i.e. causation) is required, so that one can use its mechanisms to the intended end. Peace was obviously the answer to the primary condition of war. But war did not require motivation; it was ingrained in man's original nature. War, rather than peaceful desire, which was the source of a moral code, was associated with love of honour and selflessness. *Perpetual Peace* was an outcome of an analysis of the new perspectives which the creation of the French Republic brought about, but Kant refused to endorse just wars either for republicanism or for world peace. He resolutely followed the logic of his 'unsocial sociability' argument, that is, unintended consequences. In its capacity as an *animal* species, mankind's primary agency of development was war.

[16] Kant, 'Idea for a Universal History', *KPW*, p. 47.
[17] Kant, 'Perpetual Peace', *KPW*, p. 114.

I emphasise these aspects of Kant's brutal realism in order to use it as an emblem for making my point about the nature of sociability debates in the eighteenth century. First of all, I want to remind you that if there is a *Das Adam Smith Problem* in the perceived tension between the *Wealth of Nations* and the *Theory of Moral Sentiments*, then there must be a *Das Immanuel Kant Problem* of more gigantic proportions (as indeed there is, just nobody calls it that). It is simply parochial to discuss the Smithian problem in terms of the Scottish Enlightenment alone. Secondly, and equally if not more importantly, it is useful to establish the character of unsocial sociability as the third term of the sociability debate. For if Kant's theory still creates a revulsion in most of us (and it must in modern civil society theorists, I would conjecture), then we can safely assume that it created at least as much trouble in the eighteenth century. Furthermore, if we can see that this kind of theory belongs perhaps to the most conventional part of Kant's thought, and I don't think that this is a difficult argument to develop, then we can readily accept that the kind of debates about the foundation of society in which this kind of position was one of the foundational terms of controversy had to be just a long, ongoing, historical scandal. It definitely was, and in some sense this is the history of modern natural law. Grotius' foundational work in this tradition was a treatise on the laws of war and peace, and Hobbes' infamous notion of the natural state of mankind as being a state of war rather than peace can also readily be seen as predecessors of this part of Kant's argument. Hobbes in fact occupies a double position in this story, and it is worth spending a little time distinguishing the 'unsociable sociability' argument from his argument about the state of nature. In sociability debates the classic Hobbesian position is not the third term but clearly the term of pure natural unsociability. Unsocial sociability is an alternative to Hobbes' crisis model of the birth of civil society out of asocial anarchy. That notion of Hobbes was, on the one hand, the target of constant attack, because of its stark choice of civil society (or the state) or nothing, and because of the very strong notion of civil society he derived from it. On the other hand, however, it was less controversial than unsocial sociability, because it was well understood that it was not so much a developmental theory of society but an explanation of the immediate crisis circumstances which necessitated the birth of strong artificial or political sociability, and as a proximate explanation or justification of man-made sociability it was very widely accepted across the spectrum of political and religious thought. It was a solution for a breakdown of sociability. Unsocial sociability, in some sense, was a more dangerous idea. (We can see this today as well. Many can accept the state who would viciously oppose the idea that large-scale community is impossible.) The lack or breakdown of sociability could be opposed by a notion of positive sociability, either in an Aristotelian or in a Christian form, positing the possibility of society among humans out of other-regarding motivations or sentiments, out of love, benevolence and truly humane bonding. This was usually regarded as an opposite theory to natural sociability. Unsocial sociability undermined this position in the sense that it could also claim to be a theory of natural sociability (i.e. following from human nature directly) but showing that instead of being a system of direct and intentional sociability, society was only indirectly sociable, and instead of being specifically humane it was human only in the worst sense of the word. It was a more dangerous phenomenon than a mere breakdown cured by setting up the state. Benevolent, social sociability had to contend with it all the time; it was a contrary force both before and after the birth of the state, following its own dynamic and in the long run, as Kant and others have shown, neutralisable only by its own force. In more modern discourse, the idea of unsocial sociability came to dominate even the state, since it was shown that after the birth of the modern economy, so called, the state could survive only if it followed a trajectory parallel to, and based on, the dynamics of the antagonistic civilisation of society based on utility. The positive image of a society formed out of unsociable sociability is the market or commercial society. The term commerce here appears in its widest signification, as the model of reciprocal transaction based on common utility, with trading being just one example of it. In any case, commercial society is a description of a type of unsocial social bonding where the members relate to each other as if they were traders (the emphasis is not on the trade of goods but trading as the internal structure of the community). It is contrary to morality as Kant defined it, where every being had to be regarded as an end rather than as a means. Commercial society is where everybody is just a means for others, a utility, and not a value in themselves.

Such a conception of sociability lay at the heart of modern natural jurisprudence, or at least the mainstream of it, which can be hallmarked with the names of the founding triumvirate of Grotius, Hobbes and Pufendorf. The engine of this social imagination, just as Kant described it, lay not in a theory of rights in the first instance but in an underlying theory of human needs. This was driven by the time-honoured image of comparing man to animals and pointing out that humans were inferior to animals individually because of their lack of capacity to satisfy their own needs of survival, but in society, together in cooperation, they were superior to any other creature in the creation. This brutish view of the weakness of human nature, and the resulting notion that the birth of society is in necessity or utility, was recognised as a continuation of ancient

Epicureanism and was heavily indebted to the insights of late humanist, sceptical relativism. As a system of natural jurisprudence this particular tradition received the name of the 'socialist' tradition from the hands of its eighteenth-century historians (it crops up in the histories of natural law written by Gottlieb Hufeland, Ernst Klein and others, and in Italy by the critic of Cesare Beccaria, Appiano Buonafede, followed by a spate of Italian, French and German authors in the very late eighteenth and early nineteenth centuries). Socialism, or society-ism, which is mainly connected to the name of Pufendorf because of his coinage of the term *socialitas* to highlight it, argued that the origin and purpose of the law was to protect the existence and survival of society, that morality and legislation was guided by this singular overarching utility of human survival in the only way humans can survive, in society. Many recognised, Rousseau among them, that this was also Grotius' theory, not only Pufendorf's, and it was also widely understood that Hobbes was a major contributor to it and that Pufendorf, while modifying the emphasis of Hobbes' theory away from the state and towards highlighting unsocial sociability, was heavily indebted to Hobbes. Natural law in this Grotian idiom was social natural law, with the purpose of protecting society and peace.

Socialist natural law was from the beginning locked into a debate with Aristotelianism and orthodox Christianity, which were both heavily invested in the sociable nature of man and in the notion of human fellowship (it was originally Seneca, among others, who latinised Aristotle's *zoon politikon* as social animal).[18] Christian thinkers in fact both supported certain facets of the socialist tradition as well as opposed it. Neo-Augustinian theology, particularly in France, gave a strong helping hand to unsocial sociability because of its proximity to the Augustinian view of the *modus operandi* of fallen human nature. The Jansenists, and particularly the ex-Jansenist Pierre Nicole, developed these ideas very explicitly into a theory of commercial society. When Smith came to this discourse in the middle of the eighteenth century, he received it from both these sources, from modern natural law, and from the French moralists and theologians. In the first half of the eighteenth century, as I have already mentioned, modern natural law was the dominant teaching discourse, and the fight over sociability took place within it. Socialist natural law was opposed by a more strongly Christian version of a similarly jurisprudentially developed discourse. The two streams met in the work of Francis Hutcheson, Adam Smith's teacher at the University of Glasgow. Hutcheson was once seen as the father of the Scottish Enlightenment, whatever that is, but today it is quite clear that the Hume–Hutcheson

---

[18] Seneca, *De beneficiis*, 7.1.7.

relationship was not one of discipleship but one of sharp opposition and debate. Hume's theory of justice as an artificial virtue was pure 'society-ism', and Hume famously claimed that the essence of the moral and social theory of modern natural jurisprudence was disguised utilitarianism.[19] The same, however, is not true about Smith, for whom Hutcheson's inaugural discourse *On the Natural Sociability of Mankind* (1730) held a particular fascination.

Hutcheson's text is interesting not just because he highlighted the issue of sociability as a key issue for modern natural jurisprudence, the teaching of which was his new task, but also because the lecture represents a perfect meeting point between the various discourses which clashed on this issue. Prior to his appointment at Glasgow, Hutcheson spent his time on doggedly attacking Bernard Mandeville as the most disturbing representative of modern Epicureanism and Hobbism, identifying *The Fable of the Bees* (1714) as the beginning of the cycle of the eighteenth-century debate. He now aligned himself with Shaftesbury and made it clear that in embracing the ideas of Mandeville on sociability, one would have to concede that neither Christian morality, nor a good society, nor republicanism was viable. But he now transposed the debate into the terms of natural jurisprudence and put Hobbes and Pufendorf especially in the place of Mandeville. The programme which Hutcheson outlined, entirely in tune with other moderate, Protestant, patriotic thinkers throughout Europe, was to establish the foundations for a direct notion of sociability which could serve as a basis for the origins of morality and republicanism, for a celebration of virtue in both moral and political terms. Hutcheson attacked socialism; he did not deny that commercial society existed and that it was important, but he denied its primacy and its status as the source of morality and the law. Hume disagreed with this judgement and weighting, but Smith apparently took it to heart. He inherited Hutcheson's natural jurisprudence course in the 1750s, and it can be safely argued that his *Theory of Moral Sentiments* (1759) was his attempt to grapple with the issues raised by Hutcheson's inaugural lecture, which was republished just at the time when Smith wrote his book. Smith's book was much more sophisticated than Hutcheson, but it can be rightly said that it concentrated on attacking the heritage of Mandeville with all the weapons of modern moral theory – chiefly continental but partly also Humean – which had become available after the 1720s. The programme was announced clearly, to my mind, in Smith's review of continental moral philosophy in the first *Edinburgh Review*, in the essay which includes his famous encounter with the newly published

---

[19] See Hume, *Enquiry Concerning the Principles of Morals*, 'Appendix III'.

Second Discourse (1755) by Jean-Jacques Rousseau, the discourse on the origins of inequality and whether it was authorised by natural law. Without understanding the paradoxical role which Rousseau's *Second Discourse* played in the European debate on sociability, it is not possible to grasp Smith's achievement, or for that matter to see the ideas behind Kant's unsocial sociability clearly. This was the work by Rousseau which created the most ripples in European thought, not the *Contrat Social* (1762). Smith's response was not all that different from that of his continental fellow thinkers, who were taken aback by the double-edged nature of Rousseau's text. It was clear that Rousseau was a mortal enemy of the society of unsocial sociability, and his republican credentials were acknowledged by patriots everywhere, including Smith. But many of them – Isaak Iselin (1728–1782) was one in Switzerland, and particularly Smith – also noticed the trap which Rousseau set to the friends of sociability. Rousseau's essay was a most sophisticated, critical reconstruction of socialist natural law, and particularly the Hobbesian variety, historicising and deepening its foundations rather than simply or directly contradicting it. Because it was presented as a critique, and it was, a critique, it had credentials which Smith particularly resented, accusing Rousseau of giving this discourse the 'sublimity of the morals of Plato' while developing an argument which was essentially inimical to it.[20] Smith did not put Rousseau on the same moral plane as Mandeville; we do not know whether he knew Rousseau's *Preface to 'Narcissus'*, where Rousseau bitterly condemned Mandeville's influence. 'Mandeville and a thousand others have chosen to achieve distinction among us in the same manner' – Rousseau wrote – 'and their dangerous teaching has borne so much fruit that, although we still have some true Philosophers eager to recall to our hearts the laws of humanity and virtue, one is horrified to see how the maxims of our reasoning century have carried contempt for the duties of men and citizens.'[21]

Nonetheless, Smith thought that Rousseau in fact followed Mandeville's arguments against Shaftesbury in the second volume of *The Fable of the Bees* (1729) but making it even more radical. By stripping back human nature to its scientifically discernible origins, Rousseau stripped every possible moral attribute from it, save pity, just like Mandeville. Smith noticed that pity was differently constructed in Rousseau than in Mandeville, but it was the worse for it from a Hutchesonian–Smithian point of view. What the anti-socialist looked

---

[20] Smith, *ER*, 12.
[21] Jean-Jacques Rousseau, *Oeuvres complètes*, ed. Bernard Gagnebin and Marcel Raymond (Paris: Pléiade, 1959–1995), vol. II, p. 966.

for was a virtue which could help sociability in a civilisation of unsociality, but Rousseau denied this kind of countervailing effect, taking pity as a datum present in the entirety of human history, in both amoral and pre-moral agents. First and foremost, both Mandeville and Rousseau, but the latter much more conclusively, had shown that 'there was in man no powerful instinct which necessarily determines him to seek society for its own sake'.[22] The impact of Rousseau was clear. Any future anti-Mandevillian or pro-sociability argument, or more precisely any critique of the socialist theory of the origins of morals, had to accept some of Rousseau's premises, many of which were far too socialist for Smith's taste (for example the contractarianism, which was taken to be a major plank of the socialist view of man). Smith, in his subsequent work, doggedly pursued a number of Rousseau's key ideas, trying to refute them one by one.

The Rousseau–Smith relationship is quite different from the one presupposed in the uncritical literature. Rousseau is supposed to be on the warm, sociable side, while Smith is seen as the cold theorist of commercial society. These adjectives of warm and cold are misleading anyway. The point is rather that Rousseau used his political theory, his republicanism, to balance his theory of sociability, while Smith was adamant to squeeze out something from a combination of Epicurean and Stoic moral philosophy which could counteract the socialist theory of utilitarian sociability and morality. The *Theory of Moral Sentiments*, it seems to me, entered this debate decisively on the counter-utilitarian sociability side. 'How selfish soever man may be supposed, there are evidently some principles in his nature', Smith opened his book tellingly, 'which interest him in the fortune of others, and render their happiness necessary to him, though he derives nothing from it except the pleasure of seeing it'.[23] Smith pointed to the passion of pity or compassion as the moral sentiment exemplifying the existence of such a trait. But, countering both Mandeville and Rousseau, he immediately went on to develop the notion of pity further. Instead of restricting it to fellow-feeling with pain, misery and sorrow, he insisted that the model could be infinitely generalisable to 'our fellow feeling with any passion whatsoever'.[24] The development of this theory was the subject matter of his book, for it was this generalised fellow-feeling, generalised pity, which he insisted on calling 'sympathy' or 'moral sentiment'. This generalisation of pity is the foundation of his spectatorial theory, which usually dominates

---

[22] Smith, *ER*, 11.
[23] Smith, *TMS*, I.i.1.1.
[24] Smith, *TMS*, I.i.1.5.

discussions of Smith's moral theory. In order to support the first idea – that pity should be generalised – he developed a radical generalisation of the reciprocity mechanism underlying the model along which pity was supposed to work, the simple role-switching of agents. It was not simply role-switching, with potentially selfish and utilitarian implications, which shaped moral sentiments, Smith claimed. Our capacity for moral judgement owed its origins to a model of multiple reverse role-switchings, performed with the help of our imagination, iteratively producing a moral norm embedded in a sympathy-based mechanism of conscience.

What is relevant to our purposes is to see what lineage Smith provided to his own anti-utilitarian, anti-socialist theory of the foundations of ethics. While he praised virtuous Hutcheson and some others, the available alternatives to socialism in the British tradition he dismissed very briskly. The two alternatives to the sociability thesis which could be considered were to nominate either reason or some special human sentiments as the origin of normativity (despite his flirtation with Christian models, Smith had never seriously considered a proper theological solution to the problem). But Cudworth's notion of human reason as the origin of the distinction between right and wrong was cast aside by Smith nearly as radically as Francis Hutcheson's moral sense theory. Against 'reason' as the signifier of human dignity, Smith clearly opted for a theory of moral sentiments, just as Hutcheson, but he then dismissed the idea of a 'moral sense' and insisted that the source of moral sentiments must be found in the ordinary range of recognised human responses as catalogued in one's own experience and in the books of history. No special, extra-social solution for the countering of socialism was allowed. The system which Smith took most seriously appears in the book under the rubric of the moral system of self-love, whose chief exponents he claimed had been Hobbes and his followers, Pufendorf and Mandeville. Their theory, Smith explained, had been built on two steps. The first was the utilitarian theory of natural sociability, that is, the argument that man had been 'driven to take refuge in society, not by any natural love which he bears to his own kind, but because without the assistance of others he is incapable of subsisting with ease and safety'.[25] Their second step was to argue that judgements of vice and virtue were therefore dependent on whether one considered an action to be destructive or supportive of the stability of human society. Smith explained that Hobbes' politics was a natural consequence of this view, since it was appropriate then to identify virtue with obedience, and vice with disobedience, of those rules which according to the sovereign were deemed

[25] Smith, *TMS*, VII.iii.1.1.

to be conducive to the preservation of society. This Hobbesian politics Smith dismissed as odious, but he acknowledged that society as a source of moral judgement could function through the filtering device of our imagination connected to our love of the beauty of systems, as explained by Hume. But he dismissed the idea that the preservation of society could be a principle of direct moral motivation, since it required a far too refined, complicated and mediated reflection to fulfil such a role. Smith nevertheless recognised that 'how destructive soever this System may appear, it could never have imposed upon so great a number of persons, nor have occasioned so general an alarm, (...) had it not in some respects bordered on the truth'.[26] Hence, he focused the reader's attention on the actual, practical principle which the advocates of the selfish system touted as their solution for the foundation of morality, for example the Stoic idea of reciprocity operating through role-switching as the source of moral judgement. Smith argued that this was an incoherent version of his own theory of deriving moral judgement from sympathy, which, although it was connected to reciprocity in some way, could not properly be regarded as a selfish principle. If the socialist system of self-love was a corrupt, misunderstood or oversimplified version of the theory of sympathy (in Smith's sense of the word), then it had to be true that Smith's own moral theory was its refinement.

It is crucial to recognise that Smith developed a similar sort of dualistic view as Kant, although his own anti-socialist moral theory with its principle of infinitely generalisable pity corresponds to the drift of Kant's pre-critical understanding of morality only. On the one hand, Smith vehemently defended civilisation against Rousseau and the role of deceptive moral understanding in it. On the other hand, in every significant part of his moral and political theory he inserted anti-utility arguments. In the *Theory of Moral Sentiments*, he criticised Grotius for his socialist-utilitarian theory of punishment, which would have cancelled out his own theory of moral sentiment without utility. The interest of society did form an important part of the legitimate basis for punishment, but it could not be, Smith argued, its origin or its primary motivational force. Punishing on socialist principles could easily lead to the sacrifice of an individual to superior numbers. He could very grudgingly accept it in the case of military court martials and other special institutions, but otherwise he insisted that society must be seen and is always felt as an aggregate of individuals for whom socialised moral agents feel separately.

---

[26] Smith, *TMS*, VII.ii.4.14.

We are no more concerned for the destruction or loss of a single man, because this man is a member or part of society, than we are concerned for the loss of a single guinea, because this guinea is part of a thousand guineas, and because we should be concerned for the loss of the whole sum.[27]

And in one of the most tantalising passages of the whole work (a passage of which we fortunately have an original, pre-first-edition draft), Smith invoked the example of Christianity, the notion of atonement and the signal of Jesus Christ's sacrifice as proofs that we imagine, or believe in, other kinds of punishments than the absolute necessity of retributive punishment in this life, including the sacrifice of human life, 'merely on account of the order of society'.[28] A similar anti-utilitarian sentiment made Smith oppose Hume's theory of moral judgement based on the beauty of utility.[29] Such a sentiment, while it might fit to judge a well-contrived machine or a system, was wholly inapplicable for handling the relationship between genuine human agents. True sympathy was a conduit for entering into a consideration of an agent's motives for action and into the sources of a feeling of gratitude (if appropriate) on the part of the human recipients of this action. Smith many times insisted that the world was a web of unintended consequences, and it was a mistake to believe that important springs of human action, such as the ones concerning fellow-feeling or punishment, were left by Providence (or nature) to rely entirely, or even mainly, on such uncertain devices as the accurateness of our reflections on the consequences of individual actions for the entire society. In other parts of his work, he dismissed Locke's labour theory of the origins of property and insisted that property derives from not immediately utilitarian considerations via our sense of aesthetic order. He even rewrote the famous analogy between animal and human needs, arguing that the guiding principle in understanding the structure of human needs was taste and judgement rather than material satisfaction.[30] In politics he argued against contracts and against purely liberty-based systems of utility, claiming that a principle of authority must always be present as the second basis of any viable political system.[31]

To return now to the general argument which I presented at the beginning of the paper, I hope that I have managed to put the discussion of

---

[27] Smith, *TMS*, II.ii.3.10.
[28] Smith, *TMS*, II.ii.3.12.
[29] Smith, *TMS*, II.ii.3.6.
[30] Smith, *TMS*, II.ii.3.5.
[31] [Hont's most detailed interpretation of Smith's politics is found in Hont, 'Adam Smith's History of Law and Government as Political Theory', in Richard Bourke and Raymond Geuss (eds.), *Political Judgement: Essays for John Dunn* (Cambridge: Cambridge University Press, 2009), pp. 131–171.]

sociability in the eighteenth century on the map. I deliberately tried to produce unfamiliar images of two of the most important thinkers of the late eighteenth century – Kant and Smith – showing very strong contrary tendencies in their thought to the perceived modern image. I hope I have also managed to indicate that some of the received image of Rousseau needs emendation too.[32] I also hope the recovering of the old socialist tradition may make an impact and people will ponder on the meaning of such a term as 'socialist'. I hope that future discussions of the modern natural law tradition will include their hitherto neglected theories of sociability. By doing this I only scratched the surface of the eighteenth-century debate. There were many treatises and pamphlets written on the issue, and as the century came to a close, from the 1770s onwards, sociability became one of the most used terms in the political-moral vocabulary. But the issue is not simply the bulk and complexity of the material. I did not talk about the relationship between theories of sociability and political forms such as republicanism, which preoccupied not just thinkers like Rousseau but also, just to name two, Montesquieu and Gabriel de Mably. I haven't talked about the early nineteenth-century aftermath either, the contribution of Schiller, Fichte, Hegel and eventually Proudhon and Karl Marx. I haven't followed up the interesting change in the vocabulary in the nineteenth century, whereby the earlier socialists became re-described as the proponents of the 'anti-social system' or 'individualism', while socialism came to occupy the former structural position of the Christians, referring to that kind of foundational social understanding which emphasised morally positive social bonding – through benevolence, cooperation and love – which could guide public policy towards a more humane and ethically warm society than the one that actually existed in the early nineteenth century. Socialism – or the 'social system' – was the social science of benevolence and community-building, while individualism – or the 'anti-social system' (these are the terms of Robert Owen) – was based on notions of self-love and individual competition, exemplified by political economy and later economics. What Hegel and Marx had attempted was to reconcile the two meanings in their various ways – try to *aufheben* it into a new kind of sociability. Perhaps what I can say in conclusion is that the retreat from there will take more than to revive Christian communitarianism, rereading Tom Paine or reheating phrases like the 'nation' or 'civil society'. Let us ask in each case what theory of sociability you assume, and what is your position on 'unsocial sociability'?

---

[32] [The result of Hont's revision of the received image of Rousseau is published in Hont, *Politics in Commercial Society*.]

Note on Chapter 7

This paper was given on 4 January 1996 at the Political Thought Conference at New College, Oxford. From 1994 to 1995, Hont held a Visiting Fellowship in Hungary at the Budapest Institute for Advanced Study where he organised and participated in an international research workshop on 'Unsocial Sociability: Commercial Society, Natural Law and Moral Life in Early Modern Political Thought'. It is most likely to this 'larger research project' that Hont is referring in the opening paragraph of this paper. As to the 'individual research project' that Hont also mentions, the theme and content of this talk suggest that it was closely related to the concerns of the *Culture, Needs and Property Rights* project. Reflecting on the fall of communism in Russia and Eastern Europe, the paper serves as an appropriate coda to Hont's efforts to understand the conceptual origins of Marxism and the idea of civil society more generally.

Select Bibliography

Published Works

1983 *Wealth and Virtue: The Shaping of Political Economy in the Scottish Enlightenment*, co-edited with Michael Ignatieff (Cambridge: Cambridge University Press, 1983); Japanese edition, ed. Chuhei Sugiyama and Hiroshi Mizuta (Tokyo: Miraisha, 1991).
'The "Rich Country–Poor Country" Debate in Scottish Classical Political Economy', in *Wealth and Virtue*, pp. 271–316. Republished in *Jealousy of Trade*, pp. 267–322.
'Needs and Justice in the *Wealth of Nations*', co-authored with Michael Ignatieff, in *Wealth and Virtue*, pp. 1–44. Republished in *Jealousy of Trade*, pp. 389–443.
1986 'The Language of Sociability and Commerce: Samuel Pufendorf and the Theoretical Foundations of the "Four Stages Theory"', in Anthony Pagden (ed.), *Languages of Political Theory in Early Modern Europe* (Cambridge: Cambridge University Press, 1987), pp. 253–276. Republished in *Jealousy of Trade*, pp. 159–184.
1989 'The Political Economy of the "Unnatural and Retrograde" Order: Adam Smith and Natural Liberty', in *Französische Revolution und Politische Ökonomie*, Schriften aus dem Karl-Marx-Haus, vol. 41 (Trier: Friedrich-Ebert-Stiftung, 1989), pp. 122–149. Republished in *Jealousy of Trade* as 'Adam Smith and the Political Economy of the "Unnatural and Retrograde" Order', pp. 354–388.
1990 'Free Trade and the Economic Limits to National Politics: Neo-Machiavellian Political Economy Reconsidered', in John Dunn (ed.), *The Economic Limits to Politics* (Cambridge: Cambridge University Press, 1990), pp. 41–120. Republished in *Jealousy of Trade*, pp. 185–266.
1993 'The Rhapsody of Public Debt: David Hume and Voluntary State Bankruptcy', in Nicholas Phillipson and Quentin Skinner (eds.), *Political Discourse in Early Modern Britain* (Cambridge: Cambridge University Press, 1993), pp. 321–348. Republished in *Jealousy of Trade*, pp. 325–353.
1994 'Commercial Society and Political Theory in the Eighteenth Century: The Problem of Authority in David Hume and Adam Smith', in Wilhelm Melching and Wyger Velema (eds.), *Main Trends in Cultural History* (Amsterdam: Rodopi, 1994), pp. 54–94.
Review of Murray Milgate and Shannon C. Stimson, 'Ricardian Politics', in *Political Theory* 22/2 (1994): 339–343.

'The Permanent Crisis of a Divided Mankind: "Contemporary Crisis of the Nation State" in Historical Perspective', in John Dunn (ed.), *The Contemporary Crisis of the Nation State* (Oxford: Blackwell, 1994), pp. 166–231; *Political Studies* 42 (1994): 166–231; republished in a slightly abbreviated version in *Jealousy of Trade*, pp. 447–528.

1995 'Naturrecht, Politische Ökonomie und Geschichte der Menschheit: Der Diskurs über Politik und Gessellschaft in der Frühen Neuzeit', co-authored with Hans Erich Bödeker, in *Naturrecht – Spätaufklärung – Revolution*, ed. Otto Dann and Diethelm Klippel (Hamburg: Meiner, 1995), pp. 80–89.

2000 'Irishmen, Scots, Jews and the Interest of England's Commerce: The Politics of Minorities in a Modern Composite State', in *Il Roulo Economico delle Minoranze in Europa secc. XIII–XVIII*, ed. Simonetta Cavaciocchi (Florence: Le Monnier, 2000), pp. 81–112.

2005 *Jealousy of Trade: International Competition and the Nation-State in Historical Perspective* (Cambridge, MA: Harvard University Press, 2005).

'Jealousy of Trade: An Introduction', in *Jealousy of Trade*, pp. 1–156.

2006 'The Early Enlightenment Debate on Commerce and Luxury', in Mark Goldie and Robert Wokler (eds.), *The Cambridge History of Eighteenth-Century Political Thought* (Cambridge: Cambridge University Press, 2006), pp. 379–418.

2007 'Correcting Europe's Political Economy: The Virtuous Eclecticism of Georg Ludwig Schmid', Special Issue on Republican Political Economy, ed. Béla Kapossy, *History of European Ideas* 33/4 (2007): 390–410.

'The "Rich Country-Poor Country" Debate Revisited: The Irish Origins and French Reception of the Hume Paradox', in Margaret Schabas and Carl Wennerlind (eds.), *David Hume's Political Economy* (London: Routledge, 2007), pp. 243–321.

2009 'Adam Smith's History of Law and Government as Political Theory', in Richard Bourke and Raymond Geuss (eds.), *Political Judgement: Essays for John Dunn* (Cambridge: Cambridge University Press, 2009), pp. 131–171.

2015 *Politics in Commercial Society: Jean-Jacques Rousseau and Adam Smith*, ed. Béla Kapossy and Michael Sonenscher (Cambridge, MA: Harvard University Press, 2015).

Index

Adelung, Johann Christoph, 145
Aquinas, Thomas, 63–69, 75, 86, 88, 168, 196
Aristotle, 66–67, 108, 115–116, 167, 178
   Aristotelian, 38, 116, 184, 223, 225, 235, 263
   Aristotelianism, 237, 264
   distinction between *koinonia* and *polis*, 241
   distributive justice, 74, 78, 195–196
   theory of needs, 241
   zoon politikon, 38, 228, 238, 264
Augustine, 244, 246–247

Bacon, Francis, 149
Balázs, Éva, 13
Barbeyrac, Jean, 152
Barbon, Nicholas, 58
Basil, Saint, 65
Beccaria, Cesare, 264
Bence, György, 10, 12, 33, 226
Berlin, Isaiah, 38
Blair, Hugh, 6
Boecler, Joannes Heinrich, 101
Boswell, James, 131–132
Buonafede, Appiano, 264
Burke, Edmund, 253

Cabanis, Pierre Jean Georges, 231
Cabet, Étienne, 189
Cambridge school, 255–256
Campanella, Thomas, 108
Campbell, T. D., 18
Carneades, 51
Charron, Pierre, 51
christianity, 194, 233, 257, 263–264, 268, 271
   and Adam Smith, 270
   Christian jurisprudence, 176, 235
   Christian sociability, 242
   and historiography, 256

   neo-Augustinian theology, 264
   and positive community, 195
   and socialism, 271
Cicero, Marcus Tullius, 65, 70
civic humanism, 47, 56, 125, 128
civil society, 124, 134–137, 143, 157, 235–237, 249, 252–255, 257, 260, 262, 271
   and commercial society, 229
   and Hegel, 235–237
   and Pufendorf, 239
civilisation, 8, 49–50, 54–55, 114, 120, 124–125, 130–147, 153, 157, 186–189, 193–197, 216–217, 221–222, 228, 231, 236, 238, 240, 242–244, 247–248, 258, 260, 263, 269
Coleridge, Samuel Taylor, 138
commercial society, 46–48, 122, 133, 161, 168, 235, 241, 243–245, 264
   and Adam Smith, 49, 62, 242
   and civic humanism, 48
   and civil society, 235
   and civilisation, 49, 124, 131, 236, 240
   and Emmanuel Sieyès, 250
   and four stages theory, 44, 46
   and Hobbes, 246
   and Hutcheson, 265
   and Kant, 263
   and natural law, 236
   and neo-Augustinianism, 243
   the paradox of, 61
   and political economy, 46, 60, 256
   the politics of, 248
   Pufendorf's assessment of, 119
   relation to social science, 228
   and Rousseau, 267
   and unsocial sociability, 263
   and virtue, 130
communism, 50, 163, 165, 187, 194, 233
   critics of, 189
   Marx's concept of, 159

communism (cont.)
  and negative community, 159, 186
  and positive community, 163
  primeval/primitive, 53–54, 110, 188
commutative justice, 167
Condorcet, Marquis de, 63, 231
Cudworth, Ralph, 268
Cumberland, Richard, 149

Davie, George, 18
Descartes, René, 51
Destutt du Tracy, Antoine-Louis-Claude, 231
Devine, T. M., 18
Dezamy, Alexandre Théodore, 189
distributive justice, 61, 74–75, 78, 80, 93, 167, 195–196
Dunn, John, 7, 17

Edinburgh Review, 265
Elias, Norbert, 139, 142
Engels, Friedrich, 164
Enlightenment, 13, 39, 47, 132, 147, 232, 248, 254, 256, 262, 264
Epicureanism, 264–265, 267

Ferguson, Adam, 23, 43, 49
feudalism, 6, 46
Fichte, Johann Gottlieb, 271
Filmer, Robert, 52, 166–168, 175
Forbes, Duncan, 15–24
Fourier, Charles, 190
Fuchs, Hans-Jürgen, 245

Garat, Dominique Joseph, 231
Gassendi, Pierre, 51
Genovesi, Antonio, 46
German historical school, 52
Gibbon, Edward, 46
Grotius, Hugo, 50–53, 61, 63, 65, 68–77, 79–80, 84, 97–99, 102, 104, 106, 114, 143–144, 147, 157, 159, 166–172, 176–177, 188, 194, 229, 233–235, 237–238, 241, 262–263
  confusion of language, 71, 93, 168–169, 177
  distributive justice, 74, 78, 196
  negative community, 168
  positive community, 188
  primeval society, 168
  Pufendorf's account of, 76, 106–107
  and Rousseau, 264
  socialism, 250

Haakonssen, Knud, 37
Hegel, G. W. F., 39, 124, 134–137, 143, 161, 164, 178, 189, 193, 204, 271
  bürgerliche Gesellschaft, 135, 235–237, 242, 253
Heller, Ágnes, 10, 12, 33, 198
Hesiod, 170, 176
Hicks, John, 17
Hirschman, Albert, 247
Hobbes, Thomas, 38, 51, 81, 104, 153, 159, 173, 184, 233, 235, 237–238, 246, 258, 263–265
  and Adam Smith, 268
  influence on Pierre Nicole, 244
  influence on Pufendorf, 149
  natural unsociability, 262
  positive community, 174
  the state, 238
Hont, János, 9
Horace, 72, 108, 171
Hufeland, Gottlieb, 186, 264
Humboldt, Wilhelm von, 138
Hume, David, 13, 15, 41, 43, 45–46, 49, 57, 59, 246, 265, 270
  negative community, 186
  state of nature, 250
  theory of justice, 31, 196, 265
Hunter, Ian, 37
Hutcheson, Francis, 43, 59, 264, 268
  sociability, 265

Iselin, Isaak, 266

Jansenism, 64, 241, 244–245, 264
Jesuit, 64, 86, 244
Johnson, Samuel, 131
Jones, Gareth Stedman, 17, 36
Jones, Peter, 18

Kames, Lord, 43
Kant, Immanuel, 137–145, 246, 253, 263, 271
  anthropology, 254, 258
  Das Immanuel Kant Problem, 262
  perpetual peace, 260
  unsocial sociability, 257, 263, 266
  war as agent of peace, 260–262
Kelley, Donald, 126
Kemény, Klára, 9
Kennett, Basil, 150, 152, 156
Kepler, Johannes, 246, 258
King James I, 6
Kis, János, 10, 12, 33, 226
Klein, Ernst, 264

Index

Lacratelle, Jean Charles Dominique de, 231
Lauderdale, Lord, 43
Levine, Norman, 44
liberalism, 45, 50, 194–196, 225
libertarianism, 254, 257
Lieberman, David, 18
Linguet, Simon-Nicholas Henri, 46
Locke, John, 50, 53, 159, 166, 182, 186, 246
  labour theory of property, 270
  negative community, 168, 171
Lukács, György, 12
Lukes, Steven, 29, 161

Mably, Gabriel de, 271
Mackintosh, James, 63
Madarász, Aladár, 18
Mandeville, Bernard, 59, 243, 265–268
  and Adam Smith, 268
Márkus, György, 10, 12, 33, 226
Marx, Karl, 1, 15, 38, 63, 159–166, 169–170, 178, 185–191, 193–195, 198–225, 242, 247, 253, 271
  anthropology, 161
  antinomies of a socialist society, 225
  capitalism, 165, 217, 220–221, 223
  communism, 165, 186, 193
  communist theory, 159
  correlativity principle, 186
  critique of communal ownership, 162
  critique of Ricardo, 204
  crude communism, 163, 189, 193
  effective demand, 209, 212–213
  epistemic quality of the market, 222
  hidden shift of terms, 212
  negative community, 160, 165
  positive community, 163, 165, 189
  primeval community, 164
  and Proudhon, 190
  rights theories, 161
  socialism as a purely social economy, 224
  state of nature, fallacy, 162
  surplus value, 205
  theory of community, 161
  theory of history, 160, 169, 187
  theory of needs, 165
  village community, 219
Marxism, 15, 44–46, 48, 55, 160, 182, 185, 194, 225, 252
  and civilisation, 50
  in Hungary, 13
  and liberalism, 50
  post-Marxism, 253
  retreating from, 253

Meek, Ronald, 15, 44, 50
Meinecke, Friedrich, 41
Mersenne, Marin, 51
Mill, John Stuart, 138–139, 232
Millar, John, 6, 43
Mirabeau, Victor de Riqueti, Marquis de, 132
Mitchison, Rosalind, 18
Montesquieu, Charles Louis de Secondat, baron de, 49, 59, 250, 271
More, Thomas, 108, 149

Necker, Jacques, 64
negative community, 53–54, 80, 84, 86, 92, 98–103, 106–107, 109–116, 159–160, 162–163, 165–168, 171–172, 177, 180, 182–187, 189, 191–194, 197
  and communism, 186
Newton, Isaac, 246, 258
Nicole, Pierre, 243–246, 264
North, Dudley, 58
Nozick, Robert, 181

Ovid, 109
Owen, Robert, 233, 271

Paine, Thomas, 247, 253, 271
Palladini, Fiammetta, 37, 237, 245
Pascal, Blaise, 64, 244, 259
Pascal, Roy, 44
Phillipson, N. T., 17, 22–24
physiocracy, 231
  natural liberty, 248
  natural order, 249
Plato, 107, 241, 266
Pocock, J. G. A., 17–18, 21–24, 47, 125–130, 132, 139, 256
Porter, Roy, 15
positive community, 65, 67, 69, 78, 84, 100–103, 106, 108–110, 163, 165, 171, 174, 183–197
Postan, Michael M., 16, 18
Proudhon, Pierre-Joseph, 190–194, 271
  and communism, 193
  and Grotius, 191
  negative community, 191
Pufendorf, Samuel, 38, 50, 53–54, 56–57, 63, 76–80, 91–124, 159, 166, 187, 243, 245–246, 263
  and Adam Smith, 241, 249, 268
  commercial society, 237
  correlativity principle, 174–175, 184
  distributive justice, 61, 196
  and Hegel, 236

278 Index

Pufendorf, Samuel (cont.)
  and Marx, 187, 194
  negative community, 80–86, 146–157, 168, 171–174, 176
  and Pierre Nicole, 245
  positive community, 184
  primeval community, 173–174, 182
  and Rousseau, 144
  socialism, 233, 250
  socialitas, 147–148, 233, 237–238, 264
  theory of *cultura*, 146–157
  welfare, 61

Quintilianus, Marcus Fabius (Quintilian), 70

reason of state, 40, 256
Reid, Thomas, 43, 145
Ricardo, David, 58, 133, 204
Robertson, William, 43, 46
Robespierre, Maximilien, 255
Rodbertus, Johann Karl, 203
Roman law, 53, 55, 65, 95
Rousseau, Jean-Jacques, 6, 49, 140, 144–145, 235, 253, 264, 266–267, 269, 271
  Rousseau–Smith relationship, 267
  state of nature, 249
Ruge, Arnold, 189, 194
Rüsen, Jörn, 43

Saint-Just, Louis Antoine Léon de, 255
Saint-Pierre, Charles-Irénée Castel, abbé de, 260
Saint-Simon, Henri de, 247
Savigny, Friedrich Karl von, 169, 189
scepticism, 51, 54–55, 75, 143, 237
Schiller, Friedrich, 271
Schumpeter, Joseph, 56–57, 61, 63
Seneca, 101, 258, 264
Shaftesbury, Anthony Ashley Cooper, Earl of, 265–266
Sieyès, Emmanuel, 231, 250, 255
  socialism, 250
Skinner, Andrew S., 18
Skinner, Quentin, 37
Smith, Adam, 2, 6, 15, 20, 23, 41, 43, 45–46, 48–51, 56–63, 126, 132–134, 144–145, 204, 241–244, 246, 253, 257, 264–271
  account of Pufendorf's theory of sociability, 243
  critique of Grotius, 269
  critique of Locke, 270
  critique of Mandeville, 265
  critique of Pufendorf, 249
  Das Adam Smith Problem, 257, 262
  distributional welfare paradox, 61
  influence of Hutcheson, 265
  natural liberty, 248
  Rousseau–Smith relationship, 267
Smout, T. C., 18
Sombart, Werner, 15, 44
Sonenscher, Michael, 36, 191
state of nature, 36, 52, 59, 91, 103, 121, 135, 146, 157, 162, 164, 183, 230, 238–239, 243, 248–250, 262
Stein, Lorenz von, 233
Steuart, James, 15, 43, 57, 61
Stewart, Dugald, 43, 63, 232
stoicism, 75, 101, 106, 147, 267, 269
Suarez, Francisco, 86–90

Temple, William, 59
Thatcher, Margaret, 257
Thompson, William, 232
Treuer, Gottlieb, 152
Trevor-Roper, Hugh, 16
Tuck, Richard, 143
Turgot, Anne-Robert Jacques, 46, 50

unsocial sociability, 141–143, 234, 236, 247, 257–266, 271
  alternative to Hobbes, 262
use-value
  aggregate definition of, 211
  contradiction between definition and special cases, 208
  contrast with exchange value, 199
  definition of, 200–203, 217
  double-sided nature of, 198
  relation to exchange value, 208, 210
  relation to labour power, 205
  relation to 'social use-value', 203
  relation to surplus value, 205
usufruct, 53, 74, 78, 86, 92, 94–95
utilitarian, 39, 228, 236, 267–270
utilitarianism, 232, 243, 265

Verri, Pietro, 46

Weber, Immanuel, 152
Weitling, Wilhelm Christian, 189
Winch, Donald, 18, 23
Wokler, Robert, 37
Wolff, Christian, 179

Ziegler, Caspar, 102, 175

For EU product safety concerns, contact us at Calle de José Abascal, 56–1°,
28003 Madrid, Spain or eugpsr@cambridge.org.

www.ingramcontent.com/pod-product-compliance
Ingram Content Group UK Ltd.
Pitfield, Milton Keynes, MK11 3LW, UK
UKHW022131120326
468942UK00020B/1885